ESSAYS
IN THOMISM

Essays in
THOMISM

by

Robert E. Brennan, O.P.

EDITOR

Jacques Maritain	Charles J. O'Neil
Rudolf Allers	Mortimer J. Adler
Vernon J. Bourke	Yves R. Simon
John K. Ryan	Walter Farrell, O.P.
Hilary Carpenter, O.P.	John A. Ryan
John O. Riedl	Robert J. Slavin, O.P.
Anton C. Pegis	Immanuel Chapman

Herbert Thomas Schwartz, T.O.P.

The King's Library
Essay Index Reprint Series

BOOKS FOR LIBRARIES PRESS
FREEPORT, NEW YORK

First Published 1942
Reprinted 1972

NIHIL OBSTAT:

    CHARLES J. CALLAN, O.P., S.T.M.
    JOHN A. MC HUGH, O.P., S.T.M.

IMPRIMI POTEST:

    TERENCE S. MC DERMOTT, O.P., S.T.Lr., PROVINCIAL

NIHIL OBSTAT:

    JOHN H. FLANAGAN, S.T.D., PH.D., J.C.B., CENSOR LIBRORUM

IMPRIMATUR:

    ✠ FRANCIS PATRICK KEOUGH, D.D., BISHOP OF PROVIDENCE

Library of Congress Cataloging in Publication Data
Main entry under title:

Essays in Thomism.

    (Essay index reprint series)
    Reprint of the 1942 ed.
    Bibliography: p.
    1. Thomas Aquinas, Saint, 1225?-1274--Philosophy--
Addresses, essays, lectures. I. Brennan, Robert
Edward, 1897-   ed.
[B765.T54E75 1972]   189'.4   72-1149
ISBN 0-8369-2834-2

PRINTED IN THE UNITED STATES OF AMERICA

"Prius autem sal quam lux dicti, quia prius vita quam doctrina: vita enim ducit ad scientiam veritatis."

[HOMILIA S. THOMAE AQUINATIS SUPRA MATTHAEUM 5]

To the Memory of
DOM AUGUSTINE WALSH
and
DOM VIRGIL MICHEL
of the Order of St. Benedict

CONTENTS

FOREWORD

THESE ESSAYS I should call samplings in the Thomistic synthesis. They illustrate, not so much the extensiveness as the profundity of the Angelic Doctor's thought. The adventure here made into the realm of speculation has also been an adventure into the sphere of living. Communication with the authors of the essays reached the intimacy where the buying of homes and the building of families was discussed. Such is the moving character of Aquinas's philosophy that the love of truth which it instils also begets the love of friendship. To each essayist who has shared in the labors of this symposium, I wish to express my deepfelt thanks and gratitude. What these men have given of their wisdom and charity will, I feel sure, make all of us immeasurably richer in the knowledge and love of truth.

ROBERT EDWARD BRENNAN, O.P.

First Essay

TROUBADOUR OF TRUTH

by

Robert Edward Brennan, O.P.

Troubadour of Truth

I N PHYSICAL appearance, Aquinas is described by Tocco as large
of body and erect of stature, as befitted his magnanimous soul. His
complexion was the color of ripened wheat. He had an imposing
head, with organs that were well-disposed to serve the demands of a mind
which was relentlessly in pursuit of truth. Being endowed with an abundance
of physical strength, he put all his natural resources to the exercise of good
habits.[1] We can picture him, as one of his disciples caught his placid pose,
seated in the lecture hall and holding a book in his lap. The fingers, full of
fluent grace, are sweeping upward in a symbolic arc, as he explains some
point of doctrine. Like Plato, whom he loved affectionately above all the
Greeks, he is broadbrowed, though his face is neither wrinkled nor melan-
cholic. It is a sweet and calm face, with meditative eyes, well-chiselled lips,
and a full jaw which reposes graciously upon his ample chin. There is the
vigor of the old Roman in the carriage of his head, and the refinement and
delicacy of the Greek in the patterning of his fingers.

Such was the Thomas who championed the cause of Truth; who went
up and down Europe singing the song of Truth that was in his heart; whose
mise-en-scène was not the actor's hall but the classroom and the pulpit;
whose dress was not a Thespian cloak but the sombre robes of the Friar;
who wore neither sock nor buskin but the humble footgear of the mendicant;
whose head was covered, not with the gayly pointed hood of the minstrel,
but with the plain black cap of the doctor. This was the Troubadour of
Truth who gave his life and magnificent energies to his Mistress Verity, with
the assurance that she must prevail in the end over the minds and hearts of
men.[2]

I. PROLOGUE

The life of Aquinas corresponds fairly well with the rise, poise and decline
of the 13th century. In a sense, he is the greatest figure of his age—a figure
which stands for the best elements in the Middle Age culture. Like his cen-

[3]

tury, he is the outcome of all the intense activity of the centuries that preceded him. Yet, in some ways he rose head and shoulders above his contemporaries. He was in maturity far in advance of his time, indicating a future that, strangely enough, did not materialize—at least not in the fullness of promise which was given by the tremendous achievements of the Angelic Doctor himself.

When the *Cambridge Modern History* first began to appear at the turn of the present century, the editors made special note of the fact that great additions had been made to our knowledge of the past; with the result that "the long conspiracy against the revelation of truth has gradually given way."[3] This is very encouraging, and I should be the last to question the movement towards a greater enlightenment; yet, it is likely that the final work of readjusting the viewpoints inherited from a century-old historical conspiracy against the revelation of truth will take more than a short generation or two to accomplish. In his highly popular *Story of Philosophy*, Will Durant dismissed both the Christian Church and the philosophy of the schoolmen in a single paragraph. Durant's book went through a number of editions. Its outlook can now be recognized as a last flaring-up of the fires of a decadent bourgeois civilization which began with the *Renaissance* and became an increasing conflagration with the *Enlightenment* and the *Industrial Revolution*, but ended definitely by the first quarter of the present century. There was really no excuse for Durant since the current revival of studies on medieval history was in full swing when he wrote his book.

We find something symbolic in the experience of Victor Cousin, browsing in one of the bookshops along the Seine, and stumbling by sheer accident upon the works of "a certain Aquinas who," to Cousin's critical acumen, "did not lack originality and depth." The tide in favor of Thomism has begun to turn; yet I doubt if it is quite accurate to say, as one writer puts it, that "all are ready to acknowledge the claims of Aquinas to be a philosopher worthy of attention."[4] For the great conspiracy against truth is still in our midst and, like all conspiracies, it parades under the guise of innocence. Thus Franz Alexander, psychiatrist at the University of Chicago, calls the philosophy of the schoolmen "a sterile form of deductive thinking, developed as a harmless outlet for the reasoning powers of man in a period of intellectual servitude where man could not observe the world around himself lest an observation come in contradiction with prevailing dogmas. . . . Free observation of facts was forbidden; rigid acceptance of preconceived ideas was the highest requisite of these medieval centuries."[5] Nothing is farther from the truth! Yet, the habit of shutting one's eyes to the scientific knowledge which may be had today about the Middle Ages is not an isolated instance in Dr. Alexander's case. Worst of all is the sad realization that statements of this sort can be made in the name of up-to-date scholarship!

The fact is, of course, that the philosophy which has been ridiculed and cast out of academic circles for centuries is the philosophy of a decadent period—a philosophy which is much farther removed from the thirteenth century of Thomas Aquinas than from our own day. We are still inclined to take the castigations of Francis Bacon and Descartes and the satires of Molière regarding the scholasticism of their day as a genuine description of the grand synthesis of Aquinas! It is as though future scholars of the 26th century were to judge the pragmatism of the 20th century by what it may have turned into three centuries from now, if indeed it will survive that long!

Being in the throes of a new era of politics and culture, we are witnessing the conjunction of extremes in respect to the philosophy of the Middle Ages. On the one hand, there are those who apotheosize the schoolmen, especially the men of the 13th century, as intellectual supermen incapable of committing a mistake. On the other, there are those who despise all scholastics as downright imbeciles. As it turns out, we are repeating in our own lives something of the heated emotionalism that stirred the scholars of the 13th century in regard to the mooted problems of the day, including matters that were of personal interest to Aquinas. The Angelic Doctor himself, as his enemies reluctantly admitted, was able to keep himself free of the bias of passion. Not only was his head remarkably clear in debate, but his heart was divinely generous towards those who questioned his views. It is in imitation of his own angelic spirit, therefore, that a true judgment on his personality, thought and times must be sought. It would be far from this spirit, indeed, to discern nothing but truth in the writings of Thomas, and nothing but perfection in the Middle Ages. To be sure, we cannot gainsay its great achievements; yet the men of that day were human, too, and subject to the warring forces of passion, pride and ignorance in constant conflict with the supernatural efforts of grace. This was a period in which European culture was neither completely civilized nor completely Catholicized. It was, moreover, a prescientific age, limited in its outlook by an almost universal lack of knowledge of physical nature as we understand that area of reality today. Man's practical intellect had not as yet begun to transfigure matter, so that he was unable to develop the order of material events that would seem to be requisite for the full growth of humanity. More important still, it was an age that exhibited an imperfect general consciousness of the sublime content of Catholic belief. There was far too much coercion of conscience to satisfy the demands and the spirit of a true Christian freedom. It was an age wherein reason and revealed religion were at loggerheads with unreason and superstition, an age

[5]

in which magic and an irrational fear of nature were as yet unexpelled from the body of society.[6]

Aquinas exemplifies in the highest degree all the main characteristics of medieval thought. His passion for systematizing was insatiable. It was a trait of every great schoolman, as it has been of all philosophers of note, like Aristotle, Plato, Spinoza, Kant, Hegel, and the rest. The men of the Middle Ages were encyclopedic in their collections of facts and problems which embraced the whole world of known reality. They reconstructed the hierarchical order of being, ranging between the levels of God and the cosmos, spirit and matter, man and the elements. These things, for the schoolmen, were not the poles of an absolute dichotomy, but the differing scales of a continuum which represented the whole *eschelle d'être*: from the purely spiritual being of First Cause, through the orders of angelic substances, to man, who, as a microcosmos, was described as a meeting place and horizon between spirit and matter; and thence on down, by way of the besouled organisms of the animal and plant kingdoms, to the universe of nonliving being. Between the reaches of the purest forms, on the one hand, and the passive potentialities of matter, on the other, it was possible to fix the gradients of all created being. Both natural and supernatural knowledges were harmonized; and through the development of both species of truth ran the metaphysics of being, infinitely dynamic in God, and relatively dynamic in creatures by virtue of the realization of their potencies towards a more and more perfect actualization. The great scholars of the Middle Ages sought to think about reality in unbroken and whole-making schemes. Their goal was a *summa*: of the head, like the *Summa Theologica* of Aquinas; or of the heart, like the *Divina Commædia* of Dante; or of the hand, like the cathedral of Cologne. By making their inheritance their own, they produced the priceless treasures which it was their fortune to hand on.[7] Universal knowledge of this sort was in fact mentioned by Aquinas as one of the causes of philosophy whose ultimate function is to open the eyes of man's understanding to all reality, "so that the order of the whole universe and the parts thereof may be inscribed upon the tablet of his soul."[8]

While Albert the Great and Roger Bacon had a great appreciation of the natural sciences and of the value of exact experiment, their enthusiasm was not wholly shared by Aquinas. It was the experience of every man rather than the experiment of the investigator to which Aquinas most frequently appealed as the ultimate evidence for some fact, or as the inductive basis of his speculations. He shared the views of his contemporaries regarding the immutable nature of the heavenly bodies and their influence on human affairs; yet he would never allow mere opinion to run away with sound judgment. For example, he refers to the common belief that lightning strikes church towers more often than other exposed places because of the instrumentality of the devil. He acknowledges that such an explanation is not impossible, but adds that the phenomenon may be due to the heights of such towers; "for we are asking here not what God permits but what nature does."[9] His well-known caution about the astronomical theories of his day was later ignored by many of the schoolmen, to their shame: "While appearances are saved by such suppositions, it does not follow that these suppositions are true; for it is at least probable that some other account may be made of the facts in question."[10]

To the balancing of sense knowledge with rational speculation and of natural knowledge with supernatural revelation must be added the salutary influence of common sense upon scientific learning. The schoolmen were realists; and their universally-shared conviction as to the objective reality of the cosmos in which they lived at once supplied a basis for the general unity and agreement which they shared on fundamental problems. The position they refused to surrender was what Maritain calls "the common sense of natural understanding," which is far removed from the "common sense of primitive imagery" whose fanciful explanations are bound to give way with the growth and maturation of human knowledge.[11]

The realism of Aquinas was also a personalism. It is a concept fundamental to his ethical philosophy in general and to his social doctrines in particular. The human person was central in his thought, not merely as a speculative theory, but also and more importantly as a matter of practical consequences. Thus the aim of Thomas and his contemporaries was not so much to educate people to citizenship and affluence (in the sense in which modern pedagogy unblushingly proclaims these as final ends today) as to rear up honest and courageous, wise and energetic men for the service of the Church militant. The dignity of the individual man and his personal worth in the eyes of his spiritual and temporal rulers was carefully preserved and developed.

We said a moment ago that Aquinas was beyond doubt the outstanding figure of the 13th century learning. In him we find summed up the three characteristics attributed to medieval thought by DeWulf: first, the deeply religious motivation with which most of the serious reflective work on the problems of reality was undertaken; secondly, the desire for universal knowledge, as well as a sharp instinct for systematizing such knowledge; and thirdly, an absolute confidence in the ultimate triumph of truth which bore good fruit in the optimism and serenity with which the labors of mind were prosecuted.[12]

A judgment on the cultural position of Aquinas in the light of our present standards is hardly fair to one who lived in the Middle Ages. The writings

[7]

of the Angelic Doctor represented the most perfect forms of philosophic and theological speculation in his day. He was not beyond the linguistic attainments of his contemporaries; yet his command of source materials, even if secondhand at times, was something prodigious. He had the best knowledge of Aristotle of any living scholar, and was familiar with the works of Plato, Boethius, and most of the Neoplatonists. He cited copious excerpts from the works of the Fathers. He was well acquainted with the earlier schoolmen, the Scriptures, and the philosophers of his own age. He quoted generously from Church Councils, Roman and ecclesiastical jurists, and the classical Latin writers. In his control over these widely-differing sources, he displays a remarkable power of co-ordination and a ready facility for extracting the precise data that were pertinent to his discussion. He was never idle, it appears, and at times employed several scribes at once. Indeed, his tremendous energies seem to have remained with him till his last days were at hand. His collected works total up to more than thirty volumes in folio, and this despite the fact that his lifespan was comparatively short. Of him it is true as of no other man of his day that his learning was the culminating synthesis of all previous knowledge which had been slowly forming itself from the period of the encyclopedists of Charlemagne's reign at the very rise of the medieval schools.

The task of Aquinas, however, was by no means one of mere compilation. Through all his researches went the mark of the independent thinker who weighed things for himself, improved on arguments, redisposed subject matter, and exhibited originality to the extent of being described, by some of his contemporaries, as a bold and brash innovator. "In Albert and Thomas" says Grabmann, "the philosophy of Aristotle is transformed and adapted according to the doctrines of Christianity, thus forming a Christian Aristotelianism . . . Taken all in all, medieval Aristotelianism shows a high degree of intellectual vitality, one that has not yet been explored in detail, especially in the manner in which the metaphysical, psychological, ethical and political views of Aristotle were developed in harmony with Christian convictions and became operative as a living constituent of the medieval world-view."[13] This conjunction of the old with the new is rightly regarded as the great cultural achievement of the Angelic Doctor.

II. ACTION

Thomas was born at Roccasecca, in the ancestral castle of the counts of Aquin, about 1225. The family lived within sight of the great Benedictine abbey of Monte Cassino, and quite naturally viewed the community of monks who lived there with the eyes of a legitimate ambition. When the parents of Thomas offered their five-year-old son at the doors of the monastery, an uncle of the young oblate was head of the powerful institution. Tradition says that Thomas was handed over not without the pious hope of seeing him one day follow in the footsteps of his relative. At Monte Cassino the foundations of the later development of Aquinas were laid by the monastic successors of those who had christianized Europe after the barbarian invasions and had saved learning for subsequent generations. There can be little doubt that the sacred solitude to which the boy Thomas was now introduced permanently influenced his maturing faculties and fostered in him the seeds of learning, contemplation, and the inner life which blossomed so beautifully in his later years.

But the solitude of the budding scholar was disturbed by the quarrels between emperor and pope, in which the abbot of Monte Cassino and the count of Aquin were active participants. The school-life of Thomas was disrupted when Frederick II took violent possession of the abbey as the seat of the powerful ally of his papal enemy. Thomas was transferred to Naples in 1239 where he pursued his education in the liberal arts. Here he came in contact with the new Order of St. Dominic which was at the moment in the first fervor of its adolescent age. The spirit of the friars was spreading contagiously, and everywhere they were drawing into their ranks the most energetic, the most ardent and the most talented men of the period, both young and old.

In 1244 Thomas was clothed with the wool of St. Dominic and in the following year was commissioned by his superiors to repair to the University of Paris for further study. But the religious authorities had not reckoned with his family. While still on the road to the capital of France, the youthful friar was taken prisoner by his brothers and held at home in a mild captivity, with the hope that such sober treatment might cool his ardor for the newly-embraced life of beggary. This opposition was only a foretaste of the strife and opposition that seemed later on to dog the footsteps of the peace-loving Thomas. After a year of parental restraint the ban was lifted and he was allowed to proceed to Paris.

Arriving at the University, Aquinas was met by his teacher and fellow Dominican Albert the Great, who was destined to become one of the most influential factors in the life of the Angelic Doctor. Albert was a self-made man of enormous industry, a man who did his own thinking and often found himself off the beaten tracks of his time. He championed Aristotle with all the rugged vigor of his nature, even at the expense of the good opinion of his confreres.[14] During his teaching days at Paris he published a set of commentaries on Aristotle and thus helped to revolutionize the scholastic philosophy of his day. In natural science Albert was perhaps the most pre-eminent scholar of his period, and his wide range of knowledge has excited the admiration of many modern scientific investigators. To quote the words of Zoeckler, he was "the most learned of the natural philosophers of the Middle Ages, and in many ways the most direct predecessor of scientific investigation in the sense of that term which corresponds almost entirely with the modern conception of it and of its task."[15]

Thomas remained three years at the University under the constant tutelage of Albert. In 1248 the two travelled together to Cologne where Albert was to take charge of the studies of the Dominican studium which had been founded there not long before. Several stories are told by his biographers about this period of Thomas's life. There is the incident, for example, of his being called a "dumb ox" because of his habit of silence—and the reply of Albert: "The bellowing of this ox will be heard throughout the world." There is also the tale about Thomas's generous efforts to help his fellow students and their discovery of his notebook with its "addition of things that the teacher had not said." From these and similar happenings, it was not hard for Albert to predict the future greatness of his pupil.

Aquinas completed his theology at Cologne and, upon the advice of Albert, was sent back to Paris to begin his teaching career. He lectured on Holy Writ as a Bachelor of Scripture till 1254, and on the works of Peter Lombard as a Bachelor of the Sentences till 1256. At this particular time, the quarrels between the regulars and seculars at the University were so bitter that the pope had to interfere. It was only after written orders had come from Rome that students were allowed to attend the lectures of the regulars. In 1256 Thomas received his license to teach publicly. He was made a Master of Sacred Theology (the highest title his Order could confer) and given a free hand to devise his own courses as he saw fit.

In 1256 a treatise from the pen of William of St. Amour against the regulars was condemned by Alexander IV. The condemnation was largely the fruit of Thomas's efforts. In this as in all else that he set his hand to, he manifested a complete and endless patience along with an originality which was so vigorous that it startled the faith of some of his followers and most certainly made him suspect in the eyes of his opponents. Tocco says of him: "He introduced new articles into his lectures, founded a new and clear method of scientific investigation and synthesis, and developed new proofs in his argumentation."[16] That his novel treatment of philosophic and theological questions did not injure his popularity is attested by another old biographer who relates: "When Thomas had entered upon his duties as a professor and organized his disputations and lecture material, students flocked to his school in such numbers that the hall where he taught could scarcely accommodate the large numbers who were attracted and spurred on to progress in the pursuit of knowledge by the learning of such an eminent master."[17]

The practical solicitude of Thomas for his pupils may be seen from the fact that he wrote his most famous work, the *Summa Theologica*, especially for them. Its plan was to provide an easy introduction to sacred science, a text for beginners; and though the matters treated therein are of the utmost profundity and importance, yet the Angelic Doctor has truly succeeded in imposing upon its content a simplicity and clarity that every student must admire. For his monumental work has become, in the truest sense, the standard of reference for practically all theological discussion. The *Summa Theologica*, it should be said, was never delivered in lecture form. It was begun about 1266 and continued with intervals till 1273, when the Angelic Doctor suddenly threw away his pen and confided to his intimate friend, Reginald of Piperno, that he could not go on with the work. The actual completion of the *Summa Theologica* is from the hand of Reginald.[18]

To return to the story of Thomas's life: despite the controversies raging at Paris during the first term of teaching at the University, it was a most fruitful and productive period for the hard-working professor, now in the prime of his life. In 1259 he was called to the general chapter of the Dominicans held at Valenciennes where he helped to reconstruct the program of studies for the schools of the Order. With the closure of the chapter he went to Italy where in 1260 he began his most important apologetic work, the *Summa contra Gentiles*, written to aid his Dominican confreres in their missionary activities among the Spanish Moors.

From 1261 to 1264 Thomas resided at the court of Urban IV as papal theologian, first at Orvieto and then at Viterbo. He continued his work on the *Contra Gentiles* during this time, composed the office of the new feast of *Corpus Christi*, and made the acquaintance of William of Moerbeke whom he induced to translate Aristotle from the original Greek. This was the more readily accomplished since the crusades had made it easier for western scholars to consult the Aristotelian corpus in its primitive form. In 1261 the Latin empire at Constantinople fell and Thomas had to investigate the Greek cause. This resulted in the composition of his *Contra Errores Graecorum*. While at the court of Urban he also edited the *Catena Aurea* which explains the text of the four Gospels. With the aid of Moerbeke's translation he also began his *Commentaries on the Works of Aristotle*. All this scholarly achievement was nearly brought to an end when Clement IV, successor of Urban, offered Thomas the episcopal chair of Naples. But by dint of much begging and many tears the Angelic Doctor finally was able to escape the threat to his scholastic career. The years 1265-67 see him at Rome in the capacity of regent of studies for the Roman province of his order. By 1267 he was again at Viterbo, teaching under the patronage of Clement IV. These years of his early forties were signalized by a tremendous literary activity that never saw his pen still.

The autumn of 1269 again finds the Angelic Doctor at the University of Paris where he taught theology till 1272. He had now reached the peak of his literary output and was beginning to show the strain of constant writing, lecturing, and preaching, as well as of the numerous debates he had to sustain. A very delicate problem regarding the perfection of the religious life was at issue at the time. The Dominicans appointed Thomas once more as the champion of their cause and he came gallantly to the breach with his *Treatise on the Perfection of the Spiritual Life*. The work was directed mainly against the theories of Gerard of Abbeville since he was the chief antagonist of the religious orders. Gerard spoke of the mendicants as innovators and egotists who preached their own justice and not that of Christ. He called God and his conscience to witness that he did not intend his strictures against any individual community, much less any individual person. Thomas introduces his work on the spiritual life with the simple declaration that "since persons not acquainted with perfection have made bold to say many idle things about it, we have resolved to write a treatise on the subject of perfection." The whole argument of the Angelic Doctor Aquinas is cool and strictly impersonal.

Thomas was now at the height of his reputation; and even his severest opponents, like Roger Bacon and Siger of Brabant, rank him as the equal of Albert the Great—a remarkable tribute if we consider the difference in ages between the master and his pupil and the fact that Albert's encyclopedic knowledge was naturally more impressive and appealing than the deeper synthetic work of Aquinas. The battle of the mendicants with the seculars, to which we referred above, still raged with bitter vehemence. But the former, because of their greater unity of effort, began to get the upper hand in the controversy; so much so that Roger Bacon could say in retrospect (and with some exaggeration) that for forty years the seculars produced nothing except what they got out of the notebooks of the young mendicant professors.

Another matter that must have sorely tried the heart of Aquinas was the critical attitude of those who opposed the introduction of philosophic reasoning into the sacred precincts of theology. There was the older Franciscan school, for example, built on Augustine. It held for a double source of natural human knowledge: experience and God. Thus it made the claim that the information we have of necessary truths is impossible without contact between the human mind and the Creator, that is to say, without a special illumination from above. Aquinas was solidly set against such a position. Trouble arose with some of the younger Franciscan school also against whom Thomas declared for the primacy of intellect over will, the foundation of the natural law on God's essence rather than on His free will, and, last but not least, the unity of the formal principle in man. During these years of protracted controversy, the opposition was not always between Thomas and the Friars Minors. Some of his own brethren were at loggerheads with him in the issues for which he fought. One of these was Robert Kilwardby who became archbishop of Canterbury and openly preached against the Thomistic doctrine. In fact, three years after the death of Aquinas, Kilwardby actually condemned several of the propositions that were defended by the Angelic Doctor. In 1270 the bishop of Paris, Stephen Tempier, was on the point of laying a censure on two propositions of Aquinas which were to be included with the various theories of Averroes anathematized at the time. Though the condemnation did not fall, the two propositions of Thomas are mentioned as being almost universally objected to. In 1277 the bishop did finally put a ban on some of the Angelic Doctor's teaching.

Thus the difficulties that Thomas had to encounter during his last stay in Paris were really quite formidable and divided themselves eventually into the opposing tenets of the so-called Dominican and Franciscan schools. Speaking of the marked divergence between the two schools, John Peckham writes to the chancellor of the University of Paris: "Certain brothers of the Dominican order boast that the teaching of truth has a higher place of honor among them than in any other existing religious body." The academic debates were serious enough to provoke the glee and malice of the seculars who compared the twin orders to Jacob and Esau quarrelling in their mother's womb.

During his stay in Paris, Thomas had a third and final struggle to maintain which confirmed his reputation as the great defender of a christianized Aristotle against the Latin Averroism of the University. The discussion with the Averroists centered around such topics as the eternity of the world, the denial of divine providence and of man's freedom, the numerical oneness of the human intellect—matters that immediately touched certain fundamental dogmas of faith. Siger of Brabant was the chief figure in the Averroistic camp. Basing his views on what he declared to be the genuine doctrine of Aristotle, Siger openly accused Thomas of departing from the authentic teaching of the Stagirite. The controversy therefore settled down to one of Christian versus Averroistic Aristotelianism. The outcome was rather unfortunate for the cause of philosophy in general and of Aristotle's position in particular since it gave some of the "orthodox" professors a real handle on which to swing their allegations against all metaphysical discussion. The handle became more efficacious when the Averroists tried to defend themselves with the double-standard principle that what is true in philosophy can be false in theology and vice versa. It was during this famous controversy that Thomas wrote one of the most significant of all his philosophic treatises: *De Unitate Intellectus contra Averroistas Parisienses.* His victory was doubly assured when the Averroism of the Latins at Paris was condemned in the December of 1270 by Bishop Tempier. During all these disputes and amidst the welter of conflicting feelings, Thomas always remained humble and courteous even if firm and unyielding in his defense of truth. Perhaps the closest approach he ever made to a show of emotion under debate is found at the end of his masterful polemic against the Averroists of Paris: "If anyone, puffed up with a learning which is knowledge only in name, should have a mind to contradict what I have written, let him not talk about it on the street corners or to children who are too immature to pass judgment on such difficult matters; but let him take up his pen against what I have written, if he dare; and he will find not only me, who am indeed the least of men, but many other lovers of the truth who will resist his errors and give counsel to his ignorance."

After Easter of 1272 the general chapter of the Dominicans recalled Thomas from Paris. The change came as a surprise and a shock to the University authorities and the most earnest efforts were made to have their greatest light restored to his professor's chair. Aquinas himself seems to have taken these appeals rather indifferently. It is possible, surely, that as a result of all the disturbing conditions to which his peace-loving soul had been subjected, he was in a state of complete detachment as regards his teaching post at the University. He was now charged by his religious superiors with the task of reorganizing all the theological courses of the order and allowed to choose both the method which he would impose and the place where he would work. He elected to perform his new duties at Naples.

In 1274 he was called by Gregory X to the General Council of Lyons. But his days were numbered. Despite a growing weakness of body, he set out for Lyons. He got no farther than Fossanova where he was received by the Cistercian monks. He knew that his hour had struck and he calmly awaited the end. He died on March 7 of that year. The news of his passing moved the faculty of arts at Paris to send a letter to the general chapter of the Dominicans expressing sympathy, giving a glowing tribute to the genius and personality of the Angelic Doctor, and asking that his remains be brought to Paris for burial as no other place was so fitting for this distinction.

III. CURTAIN

Mention was made of the fact that Bishop Tempier of Paris as well as Archbishop Kilwardby of Canterbury condemned certain propositions taken

Troubadour of Truth

from the writings of Aquinas. Another Dominican, Durand of St. Pourcain, turned out to be one of the most virulent critics of the work of Aquinas. The opposition of the Franciscans continued after his death and crystallized itself around the scintillating writings of a keen-witted young man known as Duns Scotus who afterwards came to be called the Subtle Doctor and founded a philosophic school of his own. The differences between the Thomist and Scotist points of view were listed by William de la Mare, himself a Franciscan, in his *Correctorium Fratris Thomae*.

Against all this opposition, however, the faithful pupils and friends of Aquinas took up the defense. Quite naturally, the staunchest and most persistent advocates of Thomism were the confreres of the Angelic Doctor. They fought against the condemnations of the bishop of Paris and answered the work of William de la Mare with a *Correctorium Corruptorii Fratris Thomae*. The master-general and general chapters of the Order also entered the struggle with great warmth and seriousness. As early as 1278 two preachers were sent to England to set the *fratres Angliae* aright on the teaching of Aquinas. The popes themselves began to speak unreservedly about the sound and satisfying doctrine of the Angelic Doctor, and in 1323 his canonization took place. One year later Stephen of Porreto, then bishop of Paris, officially retracted the condemnations which had been laid upon some of Thomas's theses by his predecessor.

But this victory of the Thomist doctrine had its disadvantages as well as its good points. The overemphasized glorification of Thomas was surely not in the spirit of the Angelic Doctor himself. In fact his own words (as the ending sentences of the *De Unitate Intellectus* reveal) could be quoted most damningly against the manner and the degree in which he was extolled. At any rate, such devotion did not prevent a rapid decay of philosophic speculation—a state of affairs that was in large measure due to William of Ockham whose nominalistic teaching began to show a widespread influence.[19]

The seeds of corruption could be detected within the scholastic system almost so soon as Thomas had passed away. Thereafter the Dominicans and Franciscans, or more specifically the Thomists and the Scotists, were more concerned with their differences of opinion than with the great truths which they held in common and which formed the matrix of the living tradition of philosophy. Some engaged themselves exclusively with theological matters; others emphasized one particular aspect of the scholastic synthesis to the neglect and detriment of the tradition as a whole. As a sample of such a trend we may mention again the epistemological problem raised by the nominalists which apparently preoccupied the best minds to the exclusion of other problems that necessarily called for treatment. There are two fields, however, in which creative work continued in the 14th century; and these, peculiarly enough, were mysticism and scientific speculation. One can hardly conceive of wider poles for human theorizing than the subject matters of these two types of knowledge. With mystical theology the names of Meister Eckhardt, Tauler, and Suso are prominently associated. But loosed from its moorings in a sound metaphysics, mysticism soon veered into channels that led farther and farther away from truth and reality. The real advances of the time, strange as it may sound to modern ears, were in the fields of natural science. Pierre Duhem has proved conclusively that the work of Copernicus and Galileo in the 16th and 17th centuries was definitely anticipated by men like William of Ockham, John Buridan, Albert of Saxony and Nicholas of Oresme. These men, according to Duhem, can rightly be called the originators of modern astronomical physics and dynamics.[20] But here, again, speculation in one field was divorced from the background of a whole-making view of reality and did little or nothing to keep up the general creative tradition of philosophy which Thomas Aquinas represented in such an outstanding way.

It is this particularism among the later schoolmen, more than anything else, that scholars like Grabmann and Gilson emphasize as the cause of the scholastic decadence.[21] To it may be added the sterilizing influence of the nominalist philosophy, and the formalism of Thomas's followers who lost sight of the spirit of their master and swore by the letter of his text. Grabmann denies that the humanists, as such, were responsible for the decay of vital scholastic thinking, since their relations with the schoolmen were friendly, on the whole, throughout Italy and Spain.[22]

From the 14th to the 17th century we find a number of famous commentators on the writings of Aquinas, such as John Capreolus, Thomas Cajetan, Sylvester Ferrara, and John of St. Thomas. For the most part, however, the work of the disciples of Aquinas was expository rather than creative. Francis of Vittoria made some definite contributions to the field of international law; just as Francis Suarez and Robert Bellarmine became prominent in the field of political thought. The names of Suarez and Bellarmine are mentioned in the English literature of their day as champions of the "impious popish doctrine of democracy" against the principle of the divine right of kings. During this period, which brings us roughly to the end of the 16th century, theological speculation was rife but spent itself chiefly in controversies of one kind or another, especially between the Dominicans and the Jesuits.

Modern philosophy, so-called, which begins with the 17th century, can be characterized in almost every main viewpoint as a denial of some leading principle of the Thomistic synthesis. The Spinozan metaphysic, for example, blotted out the fundamental differences between the Creator and His creatures. Berkeley and his disciples made a figment of the universe of matter, while Hobbes went to the other extreme, gainsaying all reality to the world of spirit. The rationalists laughed at the idea of a supernatural life and the positivists refused to set any value whatever on philosophic thinking. The Cartesians rejected the substantial unity of man's nature by their absolute divorce of mind from matter; while the Hegelians impugned the sacrosanct character of the human person. The pragmatists disavowed the notion of any continuity in the historical ordering and development of truth. Most of these philosophical heresies are still in our midst; and when their history is completely told, it will be seen as the story of a futile negativism in which the basic truths of the Thomistic synthesis were called into court, one by one, pilloried on the rack of ignorance and irrationality, and exiled to oblivion!

With the passing of the ideas of Thomas went the broad daylight of common sense and the consciousness, shared by the brotherhood of men, of the reality of truth, life, and liberty. Gone was the ancient wisdom that could reconcile the highest feats of metaphysical speculation with the most ordinary matters of everyday experience! For, whatever we may say about the profundities of his learning, the fact remains that Aquinas was always on the side of simplicity, which means that he was always ready to support the ordinary man's insights into things. There was no limit to his reasonableness even if there was a limit to his reason. Some truths the human mind simply cannot discover for itself. To deny the supernatural in the name of absolute reason is to fall ultimately into a universal scepticism.

The dethronement of God and the apotheosis of human reason is really a denial of the whole order of reality. It is insanity. Was it a mere accident that the "enlightened minds" of the French revolution set an unclean woman on their altars to represent the freedom of human reason? In each of the three great spiritual crises of modern history, as Maritain observes, "in the humanist Renaissance, the Protestant Reformation, and the rationalist *Aufklaerung,* man achieved an historical revolution of absolutely unparalleled importance, at the end of which he conceived himself as the center of his universe and the ultimate end of his activity on earth."[23]

Reason, unleashed from rational bonds, gave rise to a categorical imperative, then to an absolute spirit creating its own consciousness, then to a reified unconsciousness, then to an insatiable will-to-power—at which point it ceased to be reason any longer. The supremacy of the irrational has brought us to the zero-value of manhood. Witness the doctrine of race suicide which is leaving the fabric of familial society weak and exposed to attack from within and without! Witness the totalitarian purges that are undermining the dignity and inalienable rights of the human person! Witness the collectivism of the racial spirit that is growing like a cancer on the nations of the earth!

Chaos in human thinking and human acting has become the order of the day.

But in the cyclic trends of man's history, chaos is sometimes the prelude to better things; and it is not impossible that hope should be born of the womb of despair. In the moment of humanity's deepest travail, the voice of a great Pontiff is heard echoing to the extremes of the earth: *Back to Thomas!* Back to the Angel of the Schools! Back to the Doctor who so wonderfully illuminated his Church by the profoundness of his learning! Back to the Saint who so abundantly fertilized the Church by the example of his holiness! Such is the message of Leo XIII's great encyclical on the revival of Thomism; and surely if the message of the *Aeterni Patris* was ever needed in the world's history, it is needed today!

IV. ENCORE

The plea of Leo XIII was not for a resurrection of the dead, but for a return of the modern world to the spirit of Aquinas; to his whole-making views of life and reality; to his reverence for religion and its ethical norms; to his philosophy of the social nature of man; to his ideals of education and politics; to his zeal for study and the higher pursuits of the human mind. This spirit is to be recaptured, not by consulting the decadent formalism of those who loved Thomas too well and not wisely; but by going back to the freshness and vitality of the original texts, by sifting out critically what is of lasting value in the thought of the master himself and then of his greatest disciples. In Leo's grand scheme of renascence, the modern Thomist movement is to be a continuance of the philosophic tradition of centuries, a creative amalgamation of what is true in the old with what is true in the new, to the advantage of learning, of the liberal arts, of the natural sciences, of ethics, politics, sociology and education. Indeed, if the human mind is to continue its development and if religion is to remain a living force in the world, then the work which Aquinas accomplished must be carried on and made significant for our own day. Our objectives, therefore, are clear: the combining of high speculative thought with profound spiritual convictions; the reconciliation of newly discovered truths with the wisdom of the perennial philosophy.[24]

Note, however, that the rebirth of Thomistic ideas does not mean a return to Thomas alone or to his age alone. It is something much larger than that, in the sense that the philosophy of Aquinas is much larger than Aquinas himself. Rather the return to Thomas is a return to the truth which he so ably represented. What is generally received as "the tradition" in philosophy is really not confined to Aquinas or Aristotle or any other individual thinker. The fact is that the seeds of truth have been scattered over the face of the earth. There is no race of people however primitive, no group of thinkers however immature, no single mind however deluded by false reasoning processes that has not exhibited some insight into the meaning of reality. Truth has taken root in divers ways and places and often has grown up in surroundings that were anything but encouraging to its development. Wherever the thoughts of men have shown an enduring character they will be found, on examination, to contain some germ of veraciousness. What we call the perennial philosophy—which is simply the truth about reality—began its existence with ancient peoples and in climes far removed from the Athens of Aristotle or the Paris of Aquinas. The Babylonians and Assyrians, the Chinese, Hindus and Egyptians, all sought to formulate their ideas about the cosmic world and its Author; about the human soul and its existence beyond the confines of time; about the moral life. Before philosophy moved into Greece where it grew so luxuriantly, it had already accumulated a tradition upon which the great Hellenic thinkers could look in retrospect. We speak of Aristotle today as an ancient and of ourselves as moderns. With equal correctness Aristotle could speak of his forebears in the profession of philosophy as ancients and of himself as a modern.

It is impossible, of course, to know in detail all the complex sources from which the Stagirite drew his inspiration. Like Aquinas, he explored every avenue of knowledge that was open to him in order to discern the truths that had already been discovered by the mind of man. He was a debtor to Plato and Socrates; to the sophists and the atomists; to the Eleatics and the Pythagoreans; even to the philosophers of Persia, India and other remote lands of the Orient. What he claimed for himself was the right to use anything that his predecessors had said truthfully. What he did in the cause of wisdom was to correct their errors, supply their defects, complete their beginnings, expand their surmises, and thus, gradually, by means of them as well as by his own superior powers of invention, to enlarge upon the range of truth and to refine the analysis of reality. This, I take it, is what all of us mean by "the tradition"; and so, when we say that Aquinas labored in the tradition of Aristotle, we mean no more and no less than that he labored in the interests of truth.

To go back to Thomas, therefore, is to return to the living stream of philosophic speculation of which he was the outstanding exponent in his day. The necessity of such a return implies that a great deal of the truth of the Thomistic synthesis has been lost to the modern world. Not only is this actually the case, as we have already pointed out, but what has been lost must be restored before we can begin to march forward. It cannot be denied that the tradition of which we speak had suffered badly since the 16th century. If it has been alive at all, it is an underground current which

[19]

must be brought to the surface again before it can fertilize the fields of our confused human thinking. And when it does reappear it must not be narrowly philosophical but must embrace within its sweeping reaches the whole of humanity's life and learning. Thus, the larger renascence which is envisioned should be supernatural as well as natural, scientific as well as philosophical, literary as well as historical. For this, we may be quite sure, was what Leo XIII had in mind when he promulgated the *Aeterni Patris*.

The first books that came out in response to the pope's appeal faithfully repeated the thought of Aquinas. They were, in fact, too literal a transcription of his work to serve any really progressive purpose. Even the objections cited were often the objections of the 13th century, brought forward in the Thomistic texts and adequately disposed of by Aquinas himself. Then came the period which witnessed the revival of Kant and the doctrines of associationism. All the old idealistic and atomic errors were restored to life and refuted with a wealth of distinctions that savored too often of academic aloofness and unreality. It is a rather curious thing to note, too, that the general arrangement of philosophic subject matters and their order of exposition followed the rationalistic Christian von Wolff rather than the genuine tradition of Aristotle and Aquinas. Today, of course, we have passed this stage which may be looked back upon as the adolescent period of the Thomistic renascence. Its plenitude is upon us and the task which it imposes is twofold.

First, we must have careful and intelligent expositions of the thought of the Angelic Doctor. This has already been accomplished in several manuals of Thomistic philosophy by men like Mercier, Gilson, Maritain, Olgiati, Sertillanges and Manser. Such studies are of value precisely because they have grasped the vital meaning of the Thomist synthesis and have clearly and convincingly expounded its life and essence. They represent a challenging presentation of the mind of the Angelic Doctor; and our only complaint in this direction is that so little work of the sort has been contributed by our English-speaking scholars.

The second task is really the more important of the two and follows from the first. It is nothing less than a complete modernization of the thought of Aquinas. By this I mean that if we are to be true Thomists we must think and speak and write in terms of the problems of our age. We must consider seriously the intellectual needs of the times, the confusion and chaos with which our generation has been afflicted. We have the tools to do constructive work, because we have the principles on which all straight thinking is grounded. This discussion of contemporary problems must be wrought with the same spirit and balanced temper that distinguished Aquinas in his dealings with his own age. It must be accomplished by men who, on the one hand, are thoroughly sympathetic with the *Zeitgeist* and its peculiarities, and who, on the other, are keen enough in philosophic insight to discern its fundamental errors, and strong enough in philosophic virtue to apply the remedial measures. Only those thinkers who, like Aquinas, are vibrating with the lifepulse of their age, can lead profitable discussion at the round-table, from the lecture platform, in the literary circle. For these are the marks of a vital and personalistic philosophy: when it becomes the food and very sustenance of the mind; when it presents reasonable answers to our difficulties; when it fortifies us against the mistakes of the past; when it gives us an earnest of peace and harmonious living for the future. With a wisdom such as this we shall be protected against our own selfish inversions which would shut us off from communication with our own fellowmen. We shall realize, too, that neither the body of our philosophy, which is temporal and changing, nor its soul, which is eternal and immutable, can be neglected if we would have a complete vision of its truth.

To be in the genuine Thomistic tradition, our work must exhibit the same basic characteristics that distinguished the work of Aquinas. These are, in the main, two: a constructive critical quality, and originality.[25] A work is *critical*, first, when it searchingly analyzes its own constructions for the flaws and weaknesses that are inevitable to human thinking; second, when it examines and sets a correct value on everything that comes under its reflective consideration. It is not critical, therefore, simply because it destroys what someone else has built up with careful labor.

A work is *original* when it is the achievement of real personal effort, when it is independent and creative in thought and expression, when it can show new solutions to old problems or old solutions to new problems, when it can arouse in others genuine efforts to come to grips with reality. It is not original, therefore, simply because it is pleasantly diverting, or because it falls in with the latest fashions or even because it starts revolutions. In terms of the dual burden which I set on the shoulders of the Thomist a moment ago, I should say that the critical spirit is most proper to his first task, which is the exposition of Aquinas; and that the spirit of originality is most proper to his second office, which is the modernization of Aquinas.

A vigorous Thomistic philosophy must meet the requirements of present-day modes of expression as well as presentday ways of thinking. The demands here are not for the abolition of all technical language (which would be quite impossible under the circumstances), but rather for a studied effort to clothe the principles of our Thomistic heritage in symbols that are familiar and appealing to our reading public as a whole. Frequently we hear it said that what our English-speaking Thomists lack today, more than anything else, is the literary genius of a William James or a George Santayana or an Aldous Huxley! Matter and content they have in abundance, but good literary form is almost an unknown quantity. This is all the more a pity since truth is so precious a thing and deserves the richest habiliment in which we can clothe her. But when we say that every Thomist should be able to express himself in the best modes of the vernacular, we do not mean that there should be any sacrifice of the clarity of our philosophic symbols to vague mannerisms of speech or to modernistic forms of wit and fancy! What we do mean is that our philosophers should learn to cultivate a clearer and more sympathetic medium of expression, a more fluent and abounding style. Too often the manner in which books on philosophic subjects are written is defective, either because of a stodgy academic tone that narrows down their influence to a small public; or because of their exaggerated use of dry aprioristic types of reasoning which make them seem out of touch with real experience; or because they overlook or underestimate the contributions of the moderns.

We must be cautious, too, against the mistake of thinking that the work of making Aquinas understandable is completed by the verbal transcription of Thomistic thought into the idiom of the day. There is the correlative duty of trying to grasp what the moderns mean by their own special use of words. This is a difficult feat but it is vitally necessary since identical symbols often have widely different meanings for the Thomist and the non-Thomist. Accordingly, we must be on our guard against the assumption that we are understood simply because our readers or listeners are familiar with the terms that we are employing. But, all in all, the matter of language is of secondary importance. If our thinking is vital and responsive to the needs of the times, if it is penetrating and developed from the wells of knowledge within us, it is hardly too much to expect that our diction will largely take care of itself. In any event, the thing of capital import is the precious deposit of truth which we possess and which, to be effective, must be critically expounded and developed with insight and originality.

The methods of general education today are not calculated to produce rugged thinkers and genuine lovers of wisdom like Aquinas. Fundamentally, the reason for this state of affairs may be traced to false concepts that have grown up around the nature of man. It too often happens that those who are primarily interested in pedagogical matters do not know the truth about the human mind and its active potentialities for learning. Aristotle said that the mind of man is *pos panta*: everything, as it were. Aquinas develops the principle into a whole psychology of cognition. The soul of man stretches out toward infinity in its quest after knowledge. Its goal is the universe of visible and invisible being. It is all these to the extent that it can know them, since knowing is becoming what one knows. The capacious bosom of intellect is like a reservoir without boundaries, a maw that can be satisfied only by the vision of Divinity itself. This being the case, is it any wonder that scholars have discerned a theocentric ideal behind the whole Thomistic synthesis? It could not be otherwise. Reality, for Aquinas, can have no meaning if it is not ultimately grounded on a personal self-subsisting Deity Who is the last end to which all the potentialities of being, life and mind are ordained. Such a stupendous world-view is diametrically opposed to the false anthropomorphism of our day which would estimate everything in terms of human nature as a starting point, and refer everything to human progress and human well-being as a final end.

It is easy to discern the advantages which the Thomistic outlook has over the modern ideologies: its stability of principles; the clearness, depth, and expanse of its statement of problems; the confidence it manifests in its ability to reach solutions; the sublimity of its mission, which serves to keep alive the faculties of comprehension and to turn to account the speculative truths that lie at the roots of all obligation. The positivistic creed, the most vicious of all the modern heresies, has laid its trust in the mechanical methods of science to free the world of the incubus of philosophic thinking. But the fruits of mechanism can be only temporarily fascinating to men who, after they have made themselves comfortable, are likely to discover that they have minds. The science we have to repudiate and the machinery we must fear is the kind that would make a closed experiment out of human thinking or a smooth-running clock out of the human mind. In an age of relativism such as ours, with its fluid epistemology, its changing standards of religion, ethics, and philosophic inquiry, its virulent passion for contingency, it is hard to see how there can be any critical labor or any original work, in the best sense of these terms, since a hierarchy of tentative values must inevitably produce an environment that is destructive of the critic and the originator. Under such circumstances, the best efforts of our thinkers are reduced to a bucolic exercise wherein "one man milks a he-goat while another holds under a sieve."

People today, whether they are conscious of it or not, are looking for more solid moorings to which they can tie up their views on things, more permanent foundations on which they can build their ethical behavior. From a very human subject that is beginning to despair of its self-glorification, they are turning again to the only *Object* that is capable of lending a steady support to the tottering ego of humanity.[26] It is to souls such as these that we must make our treasures accessible. Then the outlooks of the ancient and the modern wisdoms may be compared. Then men can be described once more, not as children of the *Renaissance* or the *Enlightenment* or the *Industrial Revolution*, not as children of Erasmus or Voltaire or Karl Marx, but as children of the *True Living God*.

[23]

For the knowledge of Truth and Life is the knowledge that reaches from end to end mightily, stretching its vision from the cellars of the cosmos to the empyrean and beyond. This is the wisdom of wisdoms that disposes all things sweetly and sets the world of its ideas in heavenly order. This is the Ultimate Wisdom whose strength and sweetness and majestic grandeur utterly possessed the soul of Aquinas.[27]

Second Essay

REFLECTIONS ON NECESSITY
AND CONTINGENCY*

by
Jacques Maritain

Reflections on Necessity and Contingency

WHEN a certain bee visits a certain rose at a certain instant of time, we say that the event is contingent. Still, neither the rose nor the bee is a *free* agent; everything which befalls them is *determined* by the meeting or the interaction of properties of the nature of each and of the actions occasioned by the environment. As a result, to a divine intellect which would know absolutely all the ingredients of which the world is made, all the factors involved in the world and the entire history of all the successions of causes which have been evolved in the world since its beginning, the visit of that bee to that rose at that particular instant would appear as an infallibly or necessarily determined event.

How, then, can we call this event contingent?

In reply to this question it is indispensable, in the first place, that we distinguish two kinds of necessity: the first *de jure*, which is a necessity *by essence* or *by right* (*de droit*); and the second *de facto*, which is a necessity in actual fact. And, moreover, we must recognize that the *simple contingency* of an event (I do not say its *freedom*, which is a special form of contingency[1]) is inconsistent with the first type of necessity, but compatible with the second. An event can be *determined* or *necessitated in actual fact* by its antecedents and still be contingent from the moment that its *antecedents* themselves could have been other than what they were. It is important to understand this point clearly if one wishes to form a correct idea of contingency in the physical order. But first it is advisable to indicate precisely the meaning of the words "necessary" and "contingent."

That is said to be *necessary* which cannot *not be*, and that which can *not be* is said to be *contingent*; in other words a thing is necessary when it *cannot* be prevented, contingent when it *can* be prevented.

A thing is *absolutely necessary* when nothing can prevent it from being. Thus the properties of the sphere are absolutely necessary. A thing is

---

* Translated from the French by Professor Lionel J. Landry, member of the Thomistic Institute of Providence College.

hypothetically necessary when nothing can prevent it from being, *on the supposition* of certain conditions: that all the radii of this metal sphere be equal is necessary *on the condition* that this sphere of metal exist.

I now say that *necessity by right* (*de droit*) is a necessity which derives from the very essence of a thing or from some *essential structure* demanding, by its very nature, that a thing be so and so. Thus the essence of the sphere requires that all its radii be equal. It is in this sense that Saint Thomas, following Aristotle, understands the word "necessary" when he defines it as "that which *by its nature* is determined solely to being";[2] in other words, that which, in virtue of some essential requirement, cannot not be.

Whenever the *sufficient* reason for the positing of an effect is the exigency of an essence, whenever such a necessity suffices for the positing of an effect, whether absolutely (as in the case of the properties of the geometrical sphere) or hypothetically (as in the case if the properties of the metal sphere), we will say that the effect itself is *necessary by right*. It is enough for the placing of the effect that there be a certain nature or essential structure of which it is a property.

But it may so happen that a necessity by right *does not suffice* for the placing of the effect. Thus heavy bodies tend naturally towards the earth, but that is not sufficient if the fruit is to fall to the surface of the earth, since it must also be detached from the tree. In a case such as this, to the extent that the placing of the effect depends upon a simple necessity of fact with a necessity by right combined with it, the latter is, so to speak, clothed with contingency.

Whenever the *sufficient* reason for the placing of an effect is not a necessity by right (whether a necessity of fact be combined with the necessity by right, as in the preceding example; or whether there be pure necessity of fact and no necessity by right at all, as in the case of fortuitous events; or whether there be neither necessity by right nor necessity of fact, as in the case of free acts), we then say that the effect itself is *contingent*; for the existence or the positing of such and such elements of determination, by virtue of which the effect is brought into being, is itself only a fact and could have been different from what it was.

With these notions clearly in mind, let us now consider *the singular events that take place in the universe.*

That the sphere of metal which ornaments this balcony really has—from the moment that it exists—all its radii approximately equal; that this green plant is really endowed—from the moment that it exists—with the power of manufacturing and assimilating by means of its chlorophyll; that this black powder in the making of which a student amuses himself and which is called nitrogen iodide is really—from the moment that it exists—a detonating substance: such properties and the events which they imply cannot not exist. They will always be brought about necessarily and with an infallible regularity from the moment that the things themselves of which they are properties exist. They are brought to pass formally *ut semper*. Hypothetically necessary (and for that very reason contingent in a certain respect), they are necessary *by right*.

On the contrary, that this blossoming hazel tree bears fruit is an event towards which vegetative nature undoubtedly tends—and so we call it an *event of nature*,[3] but an event of which vegetative nature cannot be the sole cause. Thus, on the supposition that it exists, the hazel tree will necessarily tend to the production of fruit; but in order that a number of its blossoms become nuts, we must further suppose that neither hail nor frost nor insects nor any other element of destruction attack these blossoms—and such an ensemble of conditions is not derived from any essential structure or cause in the world as a property thereof or as an effect towards which such an essential structure or cause tends by itself. The event in question depends upon an exigency of nature (that is to say, upon a *de jure* hypothetical necessity, which is insufficient) and upon a whole constellation of placements of facts.

This bird's falling from its nest today is an event towards which no nature tended of itself. It is a purely fortuitous or chance event[4] and is due simply to the interference of a number of independent sets of causes. And interference such as this, produced by several causal series, is not derived from any essential structure or cause in the world as a property thereof or as an effect towards which such an essential structure or cause tends by itself. The event in question depends solely upon an assemblage of factual events or upon a purely factual necessity.

These singular events, whether they belong to the category of events of nature or to that of events of pure chance, are determined by their antecedents (which antecedents are similarly determined) according to combinations of indefinitely complicated sets of historical events that inter-cross in the course of time. But these combinations of series—which in fact did not prove to be different from what they were—*could* have been different: there was nothing to prevent their being different either through the intervention of some free agent[5] or because of a difference at the beginning of things, in the initial placements of all the historical series here involved (initial placements, let it be noted, by virtue of which the "constellation" occurred in a certain way; but no essential structure of these initial placements, and, for that matter, no cause in the universe *necessitated* the "constellation's" being the way it was). The fall of the bird and the appearance of the fruit, which actually took place, could therefore not have taken place; they could have been prevented from coming to pass. These events, *on the supposition of all their antecedents,* were necessitated by them; but the antecedents themselves, not having derived from a cause or an essential structure which by itself required them, could have been different from what they actually were; consequently, they remain contingent; they are never anything but facts.

In short these events were infallibly predetermined in the constellation and the history of all the factors that were posited in the beginning. But there is nothing in the occurrence of these events except a *necessity of fact,* which may or may not be conjoined to some *necessity by right (de droit).* For not only is it possible for the original group of factors here involved to have been quite different; but it is also possible for the innumerable meetings which have occurred among the various causal series in the course of the evolution of the world down to the time of the events under discussion *not to have taken place.* And this would not have violated any rational necessity discoverable in the demands of a nature or of any determined essential structure. Although necessary by *necessity of fact,* such events as these are really contingent.

We have been emphasizing the contingency of two clearly distinct kinds of events: *events of chance* and *events of nature.* We now observe that the latter kind of events (events of nature) gives rise to a subdivision. The examples brought forward to illustrate this sort of contingency were examples of events which (like the production of the fruit following upon the blossoming of the tree), considered in their totality, actually occur *in fact* most of the time, but which are also sometimes prevented *in fact* from becoming (events occurring *ut in pluribus,* to which we may refer as *imperfectly assured* contingent events, that is, imperfectly assured in the special causes that were preordained to bring them about). They are, indeed, precisely those cases of non-occurrence in fact which made us note that events of nature, depending not only on tendencies or ordinations of essential structures but on a whole group of placements of fact as well, are contingent events, although necessary from a certain point of view. We will say that they are expressly or manifestly contingent, and necessary in fact in the second degree.

Let us now suppose that certain events which are dependent, like those which we have just considered, not only on an exigency of nature, but on a group of placements of fact, actually happen always and with infallible regularity. In such a case they would have the appearance of events that are essentially necessary and would resemble essential *property-events.* In reality, however, they would be simply events of nature, and *contingent* in structure (but of a somewhat disguised contingency); for even though they

Reflections on Necessity and Contingency

always occur and are never prevented, it still remains true that they *could have been* prevented from occurring in fact and they could, by right, still be prevented from occurring without violence to any essential constitution. This is the case, for example, with astronomical events. That the sun should rise tomorrow and that Neptune should complete its revolution around the sun in 165 years are events that result not only from the nature of matter, but also from an immense multitude of placements of fact which happened in the past when the world of stars was in the course of formation, and which a disturbing cause intervening unexpectedly in the solar system (but whose occurrence is of the greatest improbability in fact) could now prevent from coming to pass.

The system that conditions them being once constituted, they depend on a necessity by right (*de droit*) which is hypothetic and which is *sufficient in fact* since the causes capable of hindering it do not exist, this non-existence of preventive factors being a placement of fact. They belong to that category of contingent events which in fact always occur; and which take on the appearance of events that are necessary by essential structure (*de droit*). An event of this kind· may be called *contingens de facto ut in omnibus*,[6] that is, a contingent event well assured in fact, in the peculiar cause preordained to it. We may refer to phenomena of this sort as distantly or occultly contingent events, and necessary in fact in the first degree. Such contingents are quasi-necessary by right (*de droit*). For this reason the ancients attributed a *divine* and *eternal* structure to the celestial spheres, and we are sometimes tempted to regard the universe as a machine whose whole plan of construction has the value of an essential structure, and which gives to all of its events the same necessity that a geometric essence gives to its properties (like the Spinozan concept of nature). Actually, of course, it is something quite different: the world of stars and in particular the solar system is the effect of a long evolution called for by the nature of matter and at the same time by a tremendous sequence of placements of fact.

Finally, when a man makes up his mind to profit by an opportunity of revenge, or, conversely, decides to let the occasion go by, we are dealing with a purely spiritual event, an act of will which is a free event[7] and which, not being determined by its antecedents, is not even necessary by a necessity of fact (pure and simple as in events of chance, or combined with a necessity by right—not sufficient—as in events of nature). Such an act has for its cause a faculty which, in its dominating indetermination towards every particular motive, is itself the determining agent that brings the volitional event into existence.[8] Such an event is not only *contingent*, but *free*.

The following diagram will help to summarize the points that we have discussed:

[31]

CONTINGENCY

occult — with regard solely to the existence of the subject

necessity by right — with regard to the event itself

manifest — with regard to the event

EVENT

Necessary by right

- *absolutely*: *Essential property:* the perpendicular of an isosceles triangle bisects the base into two equal parts

- *hypothetically*: *Property-events:* all the radii of this metal sphere are equal; this capsule of nitrogen iodide is a detonating body (*contingens ut semper*)

} sufficient for the event

Contingent

- *necessary in fact*
  - *in the first degree,* or in relation to the proper cause that is preordained to produce it. *Event of nature, well assured* in fact, or quasi-necessary by right: the sun will rise tomorrow; (*contingens ut in omnibus de facto*)
  - *in the second degree;* or in relation to the entire ensemble of causes from which it results
    - *Event of nature imperfectly assured* in the proper cause that is preordained to produce it: this blossoming hazel tree will bear fruit. (*Contingens ut in pluribus*)
    - *Event of chance* (or without proper cause that is preordained to produce it): this bird falls from the nest. (*Contingens ut in paucioribus*), dependent solely on a necessity of fact.

  } not sufficient for the event

- *in no way necessary*: free event: Peter will or will not deny his Master. (*Contingens ad utrumlibet*)

In God alone *existence* is necessary by essence or by right (*de droit*). He is Being itself subsisting through itself.

II. COMPLEMENTARY OBSERVATIONS

1. Let us note that, except for the two extremes of absolute necessity by right on the one hand and freedom on the other, contingency and necessity are always to be found combined to varying degrees. An "event of nature," taking place *ut in pluribus* is, as a singular event, contingent in regard to the proximate cause which gives rise to it. For instance, it is possible to conceive of this hazel tree's not bearing fruit. But from another point of view this event of nature is necessary, insofar as it corresponds to a demand on the part of a certain nature; as a result, taken in general, it takes place in most cases. Hence it is quite proper to say that *the hazel tree* produces nuts, without specifying as to this or that hazel tree. Moreover, it is necessitated in fact, as a singular event, by the totality of proximate and remote causes that have contributed to its production. And so we have what may be called a necessity of fact in the second degree. If, then, we take into consideration all the activities of all the agents of the universe and their complete history,[9] in regard to this multitude which cannot be exhausted by any created mind, it is a necessary result that this blossom of this hazel tree should or should not produce a nut.

A "property-event" occurring *ut semper* is necessary by right but by hypothetical necessity, and therefore it is contingent in a certain respect, since it is necessary only *if* the subject of this property is itself existing.

An event of nature occurring *de facto ut in omnibus* and *resembling* the property-event has, like the latter, only a hypothetical necessity. Moreover there is still the *possibility* by right that such an event may be prevented from occurring, even on the supposition that the subject has existence. Hence the reason why this event, though necessary in fact in the first degree, and though involving a very strong necessity by right besides its necessity of fact, is itself contingent.

2. It will be further observed that it was not without reason that Aristotle and Saint Thomas defined the contingency of a thing by reference to its *proximate* cause,[10] or, more exactly, to *the proper cause preordained in itself to that particular thing* (cause or *raison d'être* which cannot be prevented from producing its effect in property-events; which can be prevented in events of nature; which does not exist in events of chance; which is itself master of its own determination in events of freedom).

Aristotle and Saint Thomas, who laid down the principles of the philosophy of contingency and necessity, elaborated their teaching as a fundamental part of their theory of knowledge. They clearly perceived not only that necessity by right alone *causes knowledge*, but also that, once we have gone beyond the proximate cause of the event concerned, or beyond the cause preordained thereto in itself, in order to give an account of all the more or less remote elements that contribute to the necessity in fact (compatible with contingency) of that event, we have to deal with multitudes of placements of fact, which, if not properly infinite, as Leibniz said, are at least beyond the reckoning of any created mind, angelic or human, and consequently neither of utility nor of interest for knowledge.

3. Regarding the prevision of future events, four points are to be noted:

First: "Future contingents" (manifestly contingent, that is to say, future events that belong either to the category of events of nature imperfectly assured in their proximate cause—occurring *in plüribus*—or to the category of events of chance, or, in a wholly special manner, to the category of events of freedom) are *not capable in themselves of being foreseen with certitude.* This is so either because the proper cause that is preordained to produce them is preordained to them only in an insufficient or variable[11] or indeterminate manner, or because such a cause does not exist for them,[12] or because they depend on a cause which, being exceedingly rich in causality, is master of its own determination.

Now to *foresee* or foreknow is to see or recognize a thing *in its cause,* before it actually happens. Therefore, when the cause is of such a kind that it fails to make known with certitude the thing to which it is preordained, such a thing is not in itself capable of being foreseen with certitude.

This, however, does not prevent future contingent events (events of nature imperfectly assured in their causes, or again events of chance), which are to be produced in the course of time, from appearing necessitated in fact with regard to the transfinite multitude of factors that we would have under our eyes, were we able to take into consideration, as we said above, all the placements of causes of all the agents of the universe and their complete history (excluding, by hypothesis, the intervention of free agents).[13] But, on the one hand, this multitude of factors is beyond the comprehension of any created mind, so that with regard to a finite intelligence the future contingents of which we are speaking are not in themselves previsible with certitude.[14] And on the other hand—and especially—to perceive in detail (if that were possible) the course of all the historical events that will intercross in time would not be to foresee or to foreknow a thing; rather it would be to live in spirit through the entire sequence of effects that antedate the thing, to exhaust the multitudinous array of events that led up to it, that is to say, to experience the very history of the universe until the production of this thing; but it would not be to know the thing in the more simple light or the more intelligible abridgement which is the cause or reason of the thing's being. In this sense it must be said in a *universal way* that the future contingents which we are discussing—although necessitated in fact with regard to the almost infinite number of actual factors in the universe since the first moment of the existence of the universe—are not capable by themselves of being foreseen with certitude.[15]

Secondly: A future contingent, whether it be an event of nature occurring *ut in pluribus*, or an effect of chance, *can be foreseen with certitude by accident*. Thus it may so happen, in certain relatively simple cases, that the mind embraces in the unity of its knowledge the plurality of independent causal series from which the occurrence of such a future contingent results. The meeting of two balls rolling down an incline is an event of chance (dependent upon an irreducible pluralism in causality); and their meeting can be calculated with certitude if the conditions of the problem are sufficiently determined.

It happens that, as a result of considerations of human interest slipping into our theoretical judgments without our noticing it, we find that the explosion of a meteor at a certain place on the surface of the earth appears to us at first as an event of chance; yet we are unwilling to admit that the same thing may be true in the case of an eclipse. The former event will undoubtedly never be repeated, it is not capable of being foreseen by our scientific study and investigation and presents itself as something quite out of the ordinary so far as our daily lives are concerned; whereas the latter event is regular and calculable beforehand, capable of being foreseen by scientific analysis and investigation, and, although it always excites the interest incidental to rarity, it has ceased to appear as something extraordinary in our daily lives because of common knowledge and the information supplied by the almanac. However, looking at things more closely, should we not say that an eclipse is a simply accidental event, like events of chance? The earth pursues its course in accordance with the special laws of its movement; and so does the moon. For these two independent series of gravitational events to intervene at a given moment in such a way that the cone of shadow cast by the earth veils the brightness of the moon, or for the moon to be interposed between the sun and the earth is, in either case, a simple result in fact, a simple *meeting* which does not depend upon a cause preordained for it. Yet this simply accidental event is rigorously calculable, and capable of being foreseen with entire certitude, because the transit of the moon around the earth and the transit of the earth around the sun are wholly regular, and, by reason of a connection with a proper cause that determines them without being subject to hindrances, each gives rise, on its own account, to a series of events which are necessary in fact in the first degree, or quasi-necessary by right. Are we not face to face here with events of quite a singular character, simply accidental events, not to say disguised events of chance, in which the meeting of two independent causal series is found to be regular by accident, in consequence of the regular return of the same conditions or of the same circumstances in the two independent series on which it depends?[16]

Suppose a crossroad of which one branch leads to village A and the other to village B. Mass is said every morning at seven o'clock in village A, the market opens every Thursday in B at eight o'clock. Peter goes every day to assist at Mass in the church at A. Paul goes every Thursday to sell his products in the market at B. They live on farms some distance from each other and the roads they take are such that in order for Peter to reach A at seven o'clock and for Paul to reach B at eight o'clock the two men must meet at the crossroad in question at half-past six. Every Thursday at half after six they pass each other regularly at the quadrant of the roads; yet their meeting is chance, too, since it results from a simple conjunction of two independent series of causes (each one depending not on activities of nature, but on human wills ordering themselves to an end, to describe which the ancients used the word *fortuna* rather than *casus*). But the regularity of their chance meeting is due, not to chance by any means, but to the constancy of certain structures and to the uniform character of certain conditions which are *presupposed*.

Thirdly: In regard to free events, it is for the best of reasons that they are incapable of being foreseen. Neither in themselves nor by accident can they be known beforehand in themselves with certitude, their nature being such that they are *absolutely* inamenable to certain foreknowledge, since they depend on no necessity, neither necessity by right nor necessity of fact. For this reason God, though possessing a fully comprehensive knowledge of created wills, nevertheless does not know free decisions in their created causes, that is to say, in the previous disposition of these wills themselves, nor in any other created cause, He knows free human decisions in their state of always being *present* to His divine Vision. And so He knows them with certitude.

They can, however, be foreseen in a way that is more or less *probable*, to the extent that one knows the motives that influence free acts or the dispositions, passions, and inclinations of the subject. In this way it is even possible to foresee with a probability approaching certitude the average conduct of a given human·multitude in given circumstances. The free act, thus foreseen, will take place *ut in pluribus*. But this probability is much smaller in regard to the conduct of such-and-such an individual. "If we suppose the existence of a town whose inhabitants are all splenetic in character," states Thomas Aquinas, "then it is safe to say that in such a town riots will not be readily avoided. Yet such a statement would be more easily caught in fault in the case of an individual, whose reason may be superior to his passions."[17]

But in any case, it is in itself impossible to foreknow absolutely and with a *certitude* which is objectively founded the choice that will be made in the intimate exercise of free will.

Fourthly and finally: If we reflect upon all the considerations set forth in this and the foregoing paragraphs, it is obvious that we are presupposing a concept of the world from which we have been lured by the pernicious habit of purely mechanistic imagery. According to this concept, the collection of causes with regard to which an event of nature is necessitated in fact, while always remaining a contingent event, constitutes a family or republic of natures, not a machine where all would be bound together by necessary connections. The reflections that we have set forth also presuppose a certain determined idea of that which is a cause—an idea that we must describe as *ontological* or *philosophical*, in contradistinction to the empiriological idea of causality.

The Thomistic teaching on necessity, contingency and chance can be understood only in the perspective of an ontological or properly philosophical conceptualization, in which the *efficient* cause appears as a *nature* preordained in itself to a certain end—the *final* cause as the reason for the action of such a nature—the *formal* and *material* causes as the intrinsic principles of the ontological structure of this nature.

Third Essay

INTELLECTUAL COGNITION

by
Rudolf Allers

Intellectual Cognition

QUINAS left us no special treatise on psychology in the modern sense of the term. Like many of his predecessors and successors he had no predilection for psychological facts as such. To him, these facts were important only insofar as they were relevant either to the metaphysics of human nature or to the ethics of human behavior. But as a true disciple of the Philosopher, he was perfectly aware of the need that philosophy, both speculative and practical, has for empirical facts as a foundation and a means of illustration. Accordingly, we find many references to problems of psychology in the writings of St. Thomas. Some passages deal *ex professo* with such problems, others refer to them only incidentally. If all the texts pertaining to matters of psychology are integrated, they present a consistent and quite complete story of human nature. Out of the many questions discussed by Aquinas, the problems pertaining to the psychology of intellectual cognition are chosen here, because nowhere else, perhaps, do the methodological principles of Thomistic psychology become so evident, and because the rational faculties hold a central place in St. Thomas's gnoseological and anthropological speculations.[1]

The Thomistic psychology of cognition in general and of intellectual cognition in particular rests on several principles which had best be stated before an attempt is made at a more detailed report.

Sense impressions are the only primary source of knowledge. *Nihil est in intellectu nisi prius fuerit in sensu.*[2] There are no "inborn ideas"; nor are there any notions, within the natural range of experience, infused into the mind by a Divine influence. Before the intellect has received the impressions of sense, it is *tabula rasa*, a tablet—the comparison is taken from tablets covered with wax for making notes—without any sign engraved on it.[3] Stimulation of the senses by some object existing outside of the organism is the necessary condition for the start of mental life. If a sense is lacking, no corresponding ideas can be formed by the mind.[4]

Sense-experience is achieved through objects acting on the sense organs by means of material agents. The object acts either immediately on the sense-organ, as in the case of touch, or mediately, its influence being transmitted to the organ through a medium, as in the case of vision or audition. The effect of this action on the part of the object is a passive immutation of the sense organ. That such an immutation takes place was remarked by Aristotle. St. Augustine too comments on the fact and uses the after-image as a demonstration of the immutation in vision.

The alteration of the sense organ is, ontologically speaking, an information of the sense-organ by the (accidental) form originating in the sense object. This is only a particular application of a general principle, according to which all change demands an agent from which the power of change emanates, and is to be explained by an accessory form being added to the thing affected.

Sense cognition is due, therefore, to the reception of a form by the sense-organ first, then by the other sensitive faculties, as we shall see presently. There must be some affinity or similarity between the organ and the affecting agent, otherwise such an affection is not possible. This similarity is defined as a similarity of nature. *Similia similibus cognoscuntur.* Though subservient to the mind, the senses are material instruments of the body; hence they can be affected only by material agents. Further, the end-result of this affection must be primarily a material change. Sense cognition, therefore, refers only to material objects. Yet, because it is part of the psychophysical organism, the sense in act also brings about a psychical immutation.[5]

The information by an accidental form results in a new being, the nature of which depends on both the informing agent and the informed subject. Receptivity of forms is limited not only by the generic nature of the receiving subject (thus material organs are capable of being informed only by material agents, and immaterial faculties only by immaterial forms), but also by the particular nature and the momentary state of the receiving subject. An axiom of Scholastic philosophy reads: *Omnia recipiuntur secundum modum recipientis.* The *modus* determining the manner of interaction between the informing agent and the informed subject refers, e.g., in the case of sensitive cognition, to the generic nature of sense organs, their particular nature, viz., the capacity of being stimulated by a definite kind of physical agent, and their momentary state, as for instance, adaptation in the eye or in the sense of temperature, fatigue, or any abnormal condition.

The alteration produced by the physical agent in the sense organ is called a *species sensibilis.* Concomitant with the alteration of the organ, there is a psychical immutation, so that the *species sensibilis* is a psycho-physical process or the result of such a process. The *species sensibilis* is described as an image or a *similitudo* of the perceived object. This terminology has caused some misunderstanding of the Scholastic theory of cognition. The words "image" and "*similitudo*," are used both in a narrow and literal sense and with a broad and metaphorical meaning. A portrait is an image and a *similitudo* at the same time. But the *species sensibilis* is called a *similitudo* only in a metaphorical sense. "*Similitudo*" is, in fact, the term by which Aquinas—or William of Moerbecke—translates the Greek term for "symbol."[6] Thus words are *similitudines* of concepts, the written word is a "similitude" of the spoken word, the percept is an "image" of the object, and so forth. One must not conclude from this that the schoolmen believed in the existence of real images, copies or reduplications, as it were, of the objects; their teaching has nothing in common with the *eidola* of Democritus and the other materialistic philosophers.[7] The terms "image" and "*similitudo*" have to be taken rather in the sense in which we call a curve an image of a chemical process. These terms refer essentially to a strict correlation between things of a different nature, scil., that the one thing may stand meaningfully in some context for another. There need not be a one-to-one correlation, since we cannot speak of such a correlation as existing, for instance, between the word and the concept which it signifies.[8]

Cognition is essentially adequate, although limited and incomplete. Reality is intelligible, and the nature of things as well as the laws governing their behavior can be grasped in an adequate manner by human reason. Since the operations of reason depend, as will be shown presently, on the material supplied by the senses, the idea of an intelligible reality implies the assumption of the reliability of sensory awareness. Aquinas, in fact, asserts that the sense as such cannot err; all errors are on the part of reason which eventually mishandles the evidence supplied by the senses. The same position had also been held by the predecessors of St. Thomas; it is expressed clearly, for instance, by St. Anselm of Canterbury.[9]

Mistaken judgments on sensory data arise, e.g., by relying on the evidence of one sense only in cases where this evidence ought to be checked by the evidence supplied by other senses. Thus the rod which appears to be broken when half immersed in water is shown to be straight by the sense of touch. Emotional states, or passions, as Aquinas calls them, may exercise a disturbing influence and thereby falsify our impressions; so may an overactivity of imagination.[10] These facts are too well known to make any illustration necessary. Reason, however, should be aware of this eventually falsifying influence of emotions and imaginations, and should take account of these facts when forming its judgments. This is not always possible, given the limitations of human nature. Reason may be blinded and overcome by passion; and the spontaneous activity of imagination may present to reason images which are not true "*similitudines*" of reality.

It is hardly necessary here to expatiate on the ontological principles of Thomistic philosophy insofar as they concern cognition. A brief summary will be sufficient.

Every particular or singular thing, which is the proper object of sense cognition, owes its being to individualizing first matter and a specific form. Whatever is material exists as a particular, and all particulars are necessarily material. In the particular resides, so to speak, the specific and universal form which is common to all particulars of one species, but which has no real existence outside of the individual particulars. Anything whose existence depends on matter is a particular, and can be known only by an equally material faculty. Particulars, therefore, can be known only by the senses. Furthermore, anything acting is capable of action insofar as it is in act. Mere potentiality has no efficacy and cannot cause a form to exist in another being. The objects of sensitive cognition, accordingly, affect the sense insofar as they are actual. The senses, on the other hand, have to be receptive of the influence exercised by their objects; the senses are in potency in regard to their objects. The sense is actualized by the agency of the object impinging upon it. Hence: *sensibile in actu est sensus in actu.*

The ideas of Aquinas regarding the special operations of the external senses are not relevant in a study of his psychology of intellectual cognition. The basic Thomistic doctrine of ideogenesis as well as the Angelic Doctor's notions on the relations between the sensitive and intellectual processes need not be altered in spite of the great differences between modern conceptions and those of Thomism. It makes no difference, in fact, whether there are five external senses, as Aquinas taught, or more than five. True, our knowledge of the anatomy and physiology of sense organs forces us to assume the existence of at least three, perhaps four, senses located in the skin, the senses namely of touch or pressure, of temperature with its division into warm and cool receptors, and the sense of pain. It does not matter either that kinesthesia, the type of experience which is conditioned by changes in muscles and other parts of the body, was unknown to Aquinas; or that the still doubtful vibratory sense was not listed by him. His theory of sensitive cognition and its bearing on intellectual operations is in no way dependent on the number of the external senses or the particular notions he had about the manner in which these senses function. The external senses supply, according to Thomistic psychology only the raw material or "stuff" of perception. Perception itself, the awareness of particular objects and their properties, is effected by the internal senses operating on the material supplied by the sense organs.[11]

The notion of "internal sense" sounds somewhat strange to our modern ears, because we have become accustomed to applying the term "sense" only to the organs described by anatomy and physiology. The preponderance of viewpoints characteristic of these disciplines has become so great that we even speak of the vestibular part of the inner ear as a sense organ. This organ is doubtless sensitive in nature, as we may infer from its anatomical build, its relations to the central nervous system, and its physiological reactions. It is not so much of a sense, however, when studied from the viewpoint of psychology. The other senses inform us either of things outside and their properties, or of changes in the state of the body. The latter is the case with the stimuli arising within the body in painful affections of the inner organs, in fatigue, hunger and other conditions of a similar nature. But the stimulation of the vestibular organ does not condition any awareness of the one or the other kind. With the single exception of the awareness of positive or negative acceleration, there is no conscious datum referring to any object or state of the body caused by stimulation of this organ.

All this, however, has no bearing on the main problems of Thomistic psychology. The habit of giving the name "sense" to an organ which does not contribute to our knowledge either of the outer world or of the states of the body, may be used as an illustration and, in a way, as a justification of the different meanings attached by medieval and modern psychologists to the term "sense."

For St. Thomas, sense means a material organ, serving mainly our cognition of outer reality. Because material, its proper object is the corporeal particular. But we know such particulars not only when they are actually present and, therefore, perceived, but also when they are not actually present. These things may be re-presented to consciousness. Such a representation is called an image. It is important to notice that here, too, the term "image" must not be taken to mean strictly a "copy." There are, of course, memory images which practically amount to copies, by their richness of details and their close resemblance to things actually present. But there are many images which are very far from being really like the thing they represent or of which they are images. Although when he speaks of images Aquinas is referring mostly to visual imagery—as do, in fact, most of the modern psychologists— he is perfectly conscious of the fact that there are other images also and that an image need not be an exact likeness.[12] This becomes clear when we read that the image of a word may be a substitute for the image of the thing. When I think of Peter, who surely is a singular, I need not have any particular picture of Peter in mind—neither a complete one amounting to a portrait, nor an incomplete one containing only a few of his characteristics; it is enough to have his name in my consciousness and to know that it refers to my acquaintance Peter.

Reproducing some kind of image, however, is the adequate performance

[45]

of the internal senses, and especially of the sense called "imagination." To be reproduced after an interval of time, the image has to be conserved from the moment of perceptive awareness until the moment when it is called back. This capacity of retention and eventual recall is called "memory" in modern psychology. St. Thomas, however, credits what he calls imagination with both retention and reproduction.[13] Memory, to him, is also one of the internal senses; but its function is limited to adding the formality of pastness to the image, that is, to endowing the image with a peculiar character by which it is recognized as reproduction. This different use of the two terms "imagination" and "memory" has caused some misunderstandings between modern empirical and Thomistic psychologists, and should be carefully noted.

While the notions of memory and imagination have been retained by modern psychology (though with somewhat altered meanings), the case is quite different with the other two internal senses which play important rôles in Thomism. One of these is known as the *sensus communis*, the other as the *vis aestimativa* (in animals) or *vis cogitativa* (in man). The Thomistic idea of intellectual cognition remains unintelligible unless the performances of these two internal senses be made clear.

The *sensus communis* has been renamed the "synthetic sense" by Thomas V. Moore.[14] Dr. Moore's term covers more, in fact, than what Aquinas meant by *sensus communis*. But it gives a good idea of the function and place of this internal sense in the total organization of the mind. It is the task of this internal sense to synthesize the data supplied by the external senses into the perception of one object. The data of several senses may refer to the same object. We see and touch a thing; we hear it eventually, for instance, by tapping on it with the knuckles. But the external senses, as such, are unrelated. Vision supplies only an awareness of color, size and shape, location in space. Hearing makes us conscious of auditory phenomena, but cannot coordinate the sounds with the visual impression; and so forth. A special power is needed, therefore, to bring the different impressions together and to form the perception of one object so that we can attribute to it the various properties apprehended by the senses.[15]

As Dr. Moore has shown, there is good evidence, especially in the field of brain pathology, for the existence of such a function as a distinct and well characterized part of sensory organization. To the facts mentioned by this author, which cannot be reported here, one may add the observations by A. Galli on apparent movements conditioned by stimulation of two different senses. The phenomena of apparent movement are well known in vision. Two lines of different direction, e.g., one horizontal and one vertical, appearing shortly in succession, give the observer the definite impression of movement. If the vertical line appears first and then the horizontal, we "see" the first line turning on its basis and falling, so to speak, into the other position. This is the *phi*-phenomenon, first studied thoroughly by Max Wertheimer. V. Benussi had shown that similar phenomena also exist in the field of tactual awareness. Galli was able to prove, by an ingenious experimental arrangement, that successive stimulation of disparate senses also may condition the phenomenon of apparent movement.[16] To give a simple illustration: if we see a bell at a certain point and then immediately afterwards (the room having been darkened) hear a bell sounding from another direction, we get the definite impression that the bell which we saw has moved from the first to the second place. For a satisfactory explanation, this phenomenon demands that there be an instance in consciousness—or in the brain, if one prefers—which unifies impressions coming from different sense organs and different central nervous mechanisms. Since the *sensus communis* is credited by Aquinas with just such a synthetic capacity, we may consider the experimental evidence as a proof for the view of St. Thomas. Moreover, he does not hesitate to ascribe a definite place in the brain to the *sensus communis*. As a material function, this sense must have an organ, just as memory and imagination are supposed, by Aquinas, to be "localized" in definite parts of the brain.[17] This idea, incidentally, is not peculiar to Aquinas; it is quite explicit in some of his predecessors. Also, it may be well to remember that certain contemporaries of St. Thomas, teaching at the medical school of Salerno, had developed a fairly wide knowledge of nervous functions. They knew, for example, of the "crossed relation" between the hemispheres of the brain and the body. Hugh of St. Victor speaks of imagination residing in a particular "cell" of the brain. And there are other such instances.

Synthesis, however, is not the only function of the *sensus communis*. The sense of vision is aware only of visual impressions; the sense of hearing of nothing but sounds. Sensitive consciousness, however, distinguishes the impressions arising from the different external senses. Accordingly, there has to be a special function or instance which simultaneously gets hold of these heterogeneous impressions, because to be aware of their differences, the power here involved has to compare them, and to do this it must have all of them present together.[18]

The *sensus communis* could thus be called the organ of perception, were it not that perception implies more than the gathering together of elementary sense data about an object. This simple synthetic performance can be conceived as existing only in the yet undeveloped mentality of the infant. We may imagine that the first perceptions formed in the child's consciousness are brought about by the *sensus communis* alone. But already the perceptions of a somewhat older child depend on more than this simple synthesis. Child psychology has convincing observations to prove that memory is functioning within the first few weeks of life. And memory, in the modern sense, means also the co-operation of imagination, as understood by Thomistic psychology. Self observation as well as experimental analysis shows that in the mature mind perception is never simply a synthesis of sense data; it is always due to the co-operation of the two internal senses of imagination and of memory.

But it is, of course, true that the material entrusted to imagination has to be prepared by the *sensus communis*. This sense is, so to speak, the first station where all the pathways connecting the mind with the outer world converge.[19]

The fourth of the internal senses offers particular difficulties to interpretation especially in relation to the systems of modern psychology.

When introducing the notion of the *vis aestimativa*, St. Thomas refers to the phenomena known to-day as instinctive behavior. The sheep runs away from the wolf; the bird gathers material suitable for building its nest. But nothing in the mere appearance of the wolf bespeaks dangerousness, nothing in the mere sense data tells of the usefulness of straw or wool. There must be a special power, St. Thomas argues, enabling the animal to recognize certain things as good or evil, as useful or harmful. This special power entails an appreciation or estimation of such properties and is, therefore, rightly called a *"vis aestimativa."* The impressions arising from this power release certain activities on the part of the animal; these impressions urge the animal towards an appropriate behavior and therefore are called *instinctus*. The term "instinct," in Thomistic psychology, refers to the sensory data that release activity, being employed in a narrower sense than "instinct" in modern psychology where it is used to indicate both awareness and response.[20]

The *vis aestimativa* thus corresponds to the "afferent branch" in the mechanism of instincts. Psychologists to-day do not worry about explaining how the animal becomes aware of the data that release instinctive activity. For them it is enough to observe the fact. They are content with assuming a certain selectivity as an inborn capacity, by which the animal is made to react to certain stimulus situations. Usually, such reactions are not made to simple stimuli. The new-born infant responds, by sucking movements, to every tactual stimulation of the lips; but soon a differentiation sets in and the stimulus situation becomes more specified and accordingly less simple. Simple stimuli release only simple responses. The complex behavior of instincts corresponds also to complex "configurations" of the environmental situation. Such a way of looking at these things would not appear satisfactory to the traditional psychologist. He would want to know what it is, in the organism.

Intellectual Cognition

that conditions the well adapted response. St. Thomas answers by crediting the animal with a special power to perform precisely this sort of task. He himself does not inquire any further into the manner by which an awareness of such properties as usefulness or dangerousness is brought about. Later schoolmen spoke of *species insensatae*, species which are not sensed, although founded upon the data supplied by the senses and included, as it were, in the *species sensibiles*. One has to admit, however, that not much is gained by the introduction of this new terminology. It only restates, on another level, the notion of Aquinas without contributing to a better understanding.

The powers of sensitive cognition are essentially the same in man and the brutes. There are, of course, differences among animals—the higher organisms possessing either more or better developed senses. Many of the facts brought to light by recent researches in comparative psychology would have appeared to Aquinas as perfect confirmations of his views. The instinctive performances of termites or wasps, the capacity of "learning" observable even in lowest animals, and suchlike findings, would have been interpreted as welcome empirical proofs of the Angelic Doctor's teaching which credits animal organization with the four internal and most of the external senses.

The differences of perfection existing among animals were not ignored by Aristotle or Aquinas; neither were they ignorant of the profound differences that separate man from the highest animals. Notwithstanding their similarities to the cognitions of the brute, the sensitive functions of man acquire a deeper significance and a loftier dignity, as it were, because of the fact that they spring from an infinitely higher form, which is the rational soul. As St. Thomas repeatedly remarks, man's lower powers are "ennobled" by their closeness to his intellectual faculties. By becoming subservient to a so much higher principle of operation, they are raised to a new dignity themselves, just as a squire entering the service of a great lord participates somewhat in the latter's dignity.

The differences that arise from its being rooted in the rational soul is emphasized particularly, by Aquinas, in regard to the *vis aestimativa* which in man is always called *cogitativa*. Its performances are said to "come close" to those of reason. It is credited with a "quasi-syllogistic" capacity. It forms something like judgments.[21] Such operations, to be sure, are not true judgments or true syllogisms, but only *like* these rational procedures. The reason why the *vis cogitativa* is supposed to be capable of such high achievements is intimately linked with the Thomistic notion of man's intellectual acts and can be properly discussed, therefore, only in connection with the theory of ideogenesis.

"*Cogitatio*" is a word which is used by the older schoolmen, and occasionally by Aquinas himself, as synonymous with reasoning. Usually, however, St. Thomas is careful to reserve the term for the performances of the *vis cogitativa*. One may ask what led Aquinas to choose a name which might lead to some misunderstanding. Thus, if he found it possible to use the words "memory" and "imagination" of animal life, why did he not retain the name "*vis aestimativa*" when talking of man's estimative faculty? No definite answer can be given. It may be pointed out, however, that Abelard's use of the term "*aestimatio*" aroused the wrath of St. Bernard who reproached the famous logician for dragging down the highest truths of faith to the level of mere estimation. Thus, it may have been considered unsuitable to speak of *aestimatio* in regard to man's most perfect sensitive acts— the more since such operations, as we shall presently see, play an important rôle in his truly human accomplishments of intellect.[22]

In speaking of the ideogenetic process, St. Thomas usually assigns to imagination the office of presenting the phantasms to the intellect. But he also says that the phantasm is in the *vis cogitativa*. To understand this, one has first to consider that the phantasm is elaborated by the *sensus communis*, but that the other internal senses may co-operate. The phantasm is not simply a reproduction of the sense impression; it is something less and, at the same time, something more. It is less, in the average case, because it does not contain all the details revealed in perception; e.g., the phantasm of visual impressions is usually less colored, less clear, not so definitely related to space, as the original experience. True, there are types of images called eidetic which reach the clarity of perception in regard to details and color. But such images are not common with most people. Again, only particularly gifted persons have auditory phantasms of the same clarity and distinctness as auditory perceptions. The task of the phantasm is, in fact, not to reproduce the perception, in the literal sense, but to represent the once perceived object. The object is "meant" or "intended" by means of the phantasm. On the other hand, the phantasm is or can be more than the datum of perception because the activities of the other internal senses also enter into its formation. This contribution may so enrich the phantasm that it becomes more than the percept, but the additional features may also bring about a certain falsification. It is a common experience that our memory images often prove to be wrong in important details when confronted with the object which they represent. Features which are missing in the phantasm but which are felt to be necessary are supplied by memory and imagination; and there is no absolute criterion by which we can distinguish "imaginary" additions from those which correspond to reality.

In many cases the phantasm presented to the intellect for further operation refers to an absent object and thus is truly and solely an image. But there are also instances in which the intellect operates on phantasms of things which at the same time are actually present. This is the case, for example, when the scientist studies certain phenomena with the idea of determining their exact nature. It would seem that under these such conditions no phantasm, as a conscious product of imagination, is necessary. The percept itself apparently may serve as material for further elaboration. Thomistic psychology, however, maintains that the intellect always and exclusively operates on a phantasm presented by imagination. That this opinion is right may be gathered from the facts referred to above. The phantasm, even when of an object still present to the external senses, is more than the mere percept; it contains all the contributions made by imagination and also by the *vis cogitativa*. These contributions cannot mingle with the percept; they are added to it after the percept has been worked out by the *sensus communis*, although in ordinary cases we may not be aware of these various steps culminating in the production of the phantasm.

The rôle of the *vis cogitativa* in the building up of the phantasm seems to be of two kinds: (a) either it transmits to the phantasm of imagination the data of which it itself has become aware, namely, the axiological aspect of particulars—in which case the result of the activity of the cogitative sense is incorporated in the phantasm and reproduced together with the imaginal features; (b) or the *vis cogitativa* works on the phantasm. We know that we can, up to a certain point, deal with a memory image as if it were an object existing outside of the mind. In returning to some perceptual experience in memory, we may discover features which were overlooked at the time of perception. We say, for instance: "Now that I think of it, I feel sure that this or that was the case, that he really meant this" and so forth, whereas we had a different opinion at the time of the actual occurrence or did not notice some peculiar note which becomes manifest in remembering the whole incident. In the same manner we may also remember values adhering to objects and events to which we paid no attention at the time of the actual occurrence. Since it is the *vis cogitativa* by which we become aware of values[23] and since the phantasm is a material particular, it may easily become an object for the *vis cogitativa* to work upon.

Whenever the value-aspect of a thing is emphasized it is the *vis cogitativa* which is operative. To act upon something, the psychological power must have got hold of this value-content; and such is evidently the meaning of Aquinas when he speaks, in certain cases, of the phantasm being in the *vis cogitativa*. That this is indeed what St. Thomas has in mind is proven by the fact that he frequently refers to the *vis cogitativa* as a *ratio particularis* and assigns it the task of co-operating with the rational faculties in the formation of judgments pertaining to action. Action by its very nature is destined to realize some value, and accordingly presupposes an awareness of the value as well as a capacity of referring the will to the particular good in question.

Thus far we have considered the working of the sensitive powers as preliminary to and preparatory for the operation of the intellect. But however close their relationship, the sensitive and rational faculties of man are separated by an unbridgeable gulf. The sensitive faculties are material, operating by means of corporeal organs; their proper objects are material particulars. The intellect, on the other hand, is immaterial and its proper objects are universal and immaterial forms.

The statement just made about the materiality of the sensitive faculties and their products must not be taken to mean that the matter of things perceived and imagined actually enters into cognitive powers. A certain dematerialization takes place in sense perception and in all other operations accomplished by the sensitive faculties.[24] It is a material agent which actualizes the senses, and the senses themselves are material. They supply, so to speak, a matter of their own which becomes informed by the form transmitted by the material agent. The *species sensibilis* is no more matter of the matter of the object than it is an image or shell detached from the object. To interpret the Thomistic doctrine in this way is to completely misinterpret it. Only insofar as the matter underlying the individual percept or image is matter informed by the rational soul, is it correct to speak of a dematerialization taking place. Only insofar as it does not enter the mind in its gross materiality, but has its "intentional inexistence" as an accident of the mind, is it permissible to speak of a spiritualization of the material object.[25]

From the time of Plato who put the teaching of his master Socrates into words and enriched it by his own ideas, it had been the conviction of most philosophers that the concept, as the mental awareness of a universal nature, is essentially different from the percept and the image as sensible representants of individual things. Although Aristotle did not follow Plato in giving ideas an existence in a "supercelestial sphere" and denied to them all kind of existence outside of the particular, he still recognized that the universal is of a nature essentially different from the particular and that the mental operation by which the intellect becomes aware of the universal is essentially different from the process which brings about cognition of the particular. Furthermore, since he denied real existence to the universal, he had to explain how universal notions are formed out of sense experience. The latter, according to the *sensus-intellectus* axiom quoted before, is the only source of the material for mental operations. The senses perceive only particulars, since nothing else is to be discovered in cosmic reality. The universal nature common to many particulars of one species has, therefore, to be disengaged from the individual percept. The process by which this is accomplished is the process of abstraction.

Until the revival of Aristotelianism in the 13th century, the mediev·il world was divided into two camps on the interpretation of universals. The extreme realists, *qui legebant in re,* asserted the reality of universals in the Platonic sense. The *Timaeus,* in translation, together with the commentary of Chalcidius and certain neo-Platonic texts, were the main sources. On the other hand the nominalists, *qui legebant in voce,* held that the universal is nothing more than a mere word, designed to indicate the similarity of many particulars. Extreme nominalism fell into disrepute in the 11th century when Roscellinus of Compiègne, severely criticized by St. Anselm and condemned by the ecclesiastical authorities, had to retract the teaching which had led him into a tritheistic heresy. But nominalism was far from dead. Although John of Salisbury reports that this doctrine had been abandoned, it is evident that Abelard was in truth a nominalist. He won a famous victory over old William of Champeaux and forced the latter to admit that extreme realism was untenable. Abelard, too, incurred the censure of the authorities. Famous though he was, succeeding philosophers hardly mention his name; still their indebtedness to this great logician can be discovered in many places. The extremes of realism and nominalism having been shattered, the time was now ripe for a middle solution. The formula for this solution was found in Avicenna whose writings were well known and confirmed by the Aristotelian texts which were available, partly in translations from the Arab commentators (especially Averroës), and partly in translations made from Greek texts. After Aquinas had secured the services of the Dominican William of Moerbecke to translate the whole *corpus Aristotelicum,* the renaissance of Aristotelianism was an accomplished fact.

Aquinas took over the formula coined by Avicenna, because this formula proved to be in the genuine Aristotelian spirit and in perfect accord with the principles of Thomistic philosophy. The universal is said to have a threefold manner of being: (a) it is real in the creative mind of God, the exemplar of all things created, and thus *ante rem*; (b) as the nature common to all beings of one species it exists in the particular or *in re*; (c) it is in the human mind which "abstracts" it from the particulars known by means of sense cognition and so has existence *post rem.*

The ontological aspect of this theory is beyond the scope of our essay; but the process of abstraction and the other features of the Thomistic ideogenesis have to be exposed at some length. Moreover, it may be useful to point out the relations between the Thomistic conceptions and the findings of modern empirical psychology.

In the treatises of Aristotle, Aquinas found a whole array of satisfactory doctrines regarding the human intellect. It has to be admitted that the Aristotelian texts are not always perfectly clear and that there are certain contradictions between them. Through the efforts of W. Jaeger and other great Greek scholars, we are able today to explain some of these contradictions as the result of a gradual development in the ideas of Aristotle, so that notions he held previously were either corrected or abandoned in his later life. But there are also other ideas on which the Philosopher himself apparently did not reach full clarity of vision or a definitive solution. Among these latter notions, some refer to the intellect and its operations.[26]

Aristotle distinguished two powers of intellect. One of these, νοῦς παθητικός is translated as "passive intellect" or, more commonly, as "possible intellect." For the second Aristotle had no special designation. The name νοῦς ποιητικός or "active intellect" occurs first in the writings of a later commentator, Alexander of Aphrodisias, although the idea is plainly stated by Aristotle. This interpretation of intellectual operations Aquinas made his own.

The universal nature is enclosed, as it were, in the particular. The intellect has this universal nature as its proper object, but cannot reach it until it is disengaged from the material aspects with which it is bound up in the particular. In other words, the universal nature must be stripped of all its material appendages. This cannot be accomplished by any material power, since immateriality can be realized only by an immaterial agent. Such a notion is·a necessary corollary of the general principles of Thomistic philosophy. The cause is of a higher dignity than the effect; an agent cannot communicate to another being something that it does not possess. Immateriality, therefore, cannot be conferred by a material agent. Hence the dematerialization through which the universal nature becomes disengaged from matter has to be the work of the intellect, and the intellect has to be immaterial.[27]

The freeing of the universal nature is achieved by the process of abstraction in which the "active intellect" operates on the phantasm presented to it by the sensory powers. It is to be noted that abstraction is not the same as generalization; neither is it the discovery of a likeness or similarity in things.[28] In modern experimental psychology, as well as in certain types of philosophical writing, the term "abstraction" is used in a sense very different from the one given to it in Thomistic philosophy. Thus a psychologist may talk about the "abstraction of likeness" in a study in which figures are exposed a brief space of time and the observers are asked to discover likeness. This may be called "abstraction" in a literal sense, since the feature of likeness is abstracted, that is, raised to particular importance, while other features are disregarded. But this is not abstraction in the Thomistic sense.

The "abstraction of likeness" is a performance which remains throughout on the level sensitive consciousness. No universal concept is formed. It is not the universal notion of likeness which is produced, but the sensible relation of "being alike" which is observed. The use of the same term in such different contexts has caused many misunderstandings, both on the part of the scholastic philosophers when they criticize the statements of the experimentalists, and on the part of the investigators when they object to certain propositions of scholastic psychology.

The universal nature disengaged from the phantasm and thus made intelligible is called the *species intelligibilis impressa* and becomes, after informing the possible intellect, the *species intelligibilis expressa* or what St. Thomas calls the *verbum mentis*. This *verbum* must not be taken as a true term of "inner language." It is rather an element of "preverbal thought." It is destined to become the meaning of a spoken (or imagined) word; but it is not itself a word like the words of a spoken language. The *verbum mentis* is the concept and the spoken word is the symbol of this concept. Spoken words are *notae earum quae sunt in anima passionum*. They signify the concepts and indirectly the class of beings of which they are the concepts. This distinction is clearly stated by Aristotle. It is also stated in an unmistakable manner by St. Augustine when he says that a spoken proposition is preceded by a mental one which does not belong to any language (*nullius linguae*).[29] This statement of the Bishop of Hippo is quoted by practically every author dealing with the problem of *verbum*, a problem which arose in medieval treatises in connection with Christological discussions. None of the medieval writers would have agreed with the notion that thinking is nothing more than "implicit verbal behavior" or that thought is always and exclusively a "covert form" of the particular motor behavior underlying verbal utterance.[30]

It cannot be gainsaid that the theory of abstraction—not the factual observations on which it rests—presents several difficulties. It is not easy to form an adequate and satisfactory idea of the manner in which the active intellect deals with phantasms. The expression "illumination" is not very helpful and is not much clarified by the subtle remarks of Cajetan on the point. Neither is it easy to get a satisfactory perspective of the co-operation between the sensitive and intellectual powers in general.[31]

This co-operation is not limited to the presentation of the phantasms for sake of abstraction. The intellect has as its proper object the universal nature which, because universal, is also immaterial. This assertion can be understood only in the light of the principle of individuation, as conceived by Aquinas. He holds that individuation is due to matter and matter alone. Individuals or particulars exist only as material things. The intellect as such is, therefore, incapable of getting hold of the material and the particular. On the other hand, there must be some connection between the intellect and the particular, because we form judgments about particulars when we relate a particular subject with a universal predicate. For example, Socrates is a man. Man here is a universal, whereas Socrates is an individual particular.

The performances of the intellect are not restricted to the formation of concepts. Thus, concepts are further elaborated by the possible intellect in the process of judging and reasoning. A judgment is produced by the combining or dividing activity of the intellect, the former leading to assertion, the latter to negation. Judgments are further combined in syllogisms. Thus, the intellect proceeds from single concepts to an awareness of relation between them and to a further awareness of relation between propositions. This is discursive reasoning. Reasoning and judging, however, may refer also to relations obtaining between universals and particulars. Since reasoning is an intellectual performance, it follows that the intellect must be able to get hold of the particular. But the particular, because material, is beyond the reach of the intellect, and so we are brought face to face with a serious dilemma.

St. Thomas proposes a solution, but his answer appears to be incomplete. One gets the impression that he himself was not perfectly satisfied with the way he resolved the problem—as if his proposal were tentative rather than definitive. His reply hinges upon the peculiar power of the intellect to reflect on itself, a power that must be explained before we can properly discuss the intellectual cognition of particulars.

The terms *reflexio* or *reditio* have to be taken in their literal sense. The intellect is able to bend back on itself or to go back to itself.[32] Its own operations may become objects of intellectual cognition. Reason is aware not only of its objects but also of itself and its acts in regard to its objects. This reflection must be distinguished from the mere repetition of acts that it has already performed. In the process of reflection the intellect does not turn back to the object but to its own performance. Nor is this reflective procedure necessarily subsequent to the intellectual performance, e.g., of abstraction or reasoning. It may also accompany such a performance, and usually does go along with it, since the intellect knows itself as being active in this or that manner.[33]

In reflecting on its operation, says St. Thomas, the intellect knows the concept that it possesses and so discovers the *species intelligibilis impressa* by means of which the concept was realized in the possible intellect. It goes still farther back to the performance of the active intellect abstracting the concept and thus finally arrives at the phantasm from which the concept was abstracted. The phantasm, however, is itself a material particular and represents, very often, a material particular thing. It is all a very ingenious explanation but does not, unfortunately, eliminate the difficulty. It still remains a problem how the immaterial intellect can combine a term referring to an individual (Socrates) with a universal (man).

It is at this point that Aquinas introduces the *vis cogitativa* as the intermediary between the intellect and the particular as grasped by the sensitive powers.[34] By enabling the mind to become aware of individual values, the *vis cogitativa* becomes the link between the rational will and the particular action which necessarily aims at a particular and therefore a material end. Because it is capable of forming quasi-judgments, the *vis cogitativa* supplies to the intellect the particular propositions. The syllogism: "All men are mortal, Caius is a man, Caius is mortal," entails two particular propositions; but it is, because a syllogism, performed by the intellect, although not by the intellect alone. Still the difficulty is not removed because the *vis cogitativa*, howsoever "ennobled" by its closeness to reason, is nevertheless one of the internal senses and therefore material. The "continuity" between the sensitive power and the intellect is no more intelligible here than it is in the other cases mentioned before.

We must admit, then, that there is an unsolved problem in Thomistic psychology. Perhaps it is not only unsolved but unsolvable since it points to ultimate facts of the mind, facts which escape further analysis. That there are such facts is indubitable. Thus, we cannot "explain" why the color purple appears to be placed between red and blue. We cannot explain why the syllogistic forms compel the mind to think in accordance with their laws. We cannot explain why there are so many kinds of mental states. Abstraction, too, is simply a fact. We may describe its characteristic features, so as to distinguish it from mere generalization or from the formation of a general image, but we cannot explain it any further. This way out of the difficulty is, however, hardly practicable. As it stands, the thesis of the essential distinction between materiality and immateriality or between the particular and the universal, must be made to harmonize with the general system of Thomism, on one hand, and with the imposing array of empirical facts, on the other.

Since the intellect depends on the phantasm for the elaboration of the concept,[35] the operations of the sensitive faculties acquire a decisive influence. If imagination, crudely speaking, presents the intellect with a falsified phantasm, the intellect has no means of discovering this circumstance and is inevitably led to the formation of a wrong concept, and further on of a wrong judgment. The intellect is indeed immaterial in its nature and operations; yet it needs the material supplied by the senses. The intellectual activity starts when the first phantasm is presented by the sensitive powers. At once the active intellect—which is always in act and does not need any actualization—gets hold of the phantasm, abstracts the universal, and transmits it to the possible intellect which is in potency and becomes actualized by the *species intelligibilis impressa*. Here, too, a rule reigns, parallel to the one reported in regard to senses: *intelligibile in actu est intellectus in actu.* The intelligible being, the universal, does not exist before it has become real as a *verbum mentis* in the possible intellect, and possible intellect is not actualized before the concept is formed.

Simultaneously with the first actualization of a concept, however, a second actualization occurs. The first principles of intellect are not inborn ideas, existing in reason antecedently to and independently of any concept. Rather they are the modes according to which the intellect, by its proper nature, operates. Since reflection accompanies the intellectual operations, we have already said, the intellect becomes aware of the rules governing its operation. Thus, no experience or induction is needed for the genesis and application of a knowledge of the principle of contradiction. For example, the initial awareness of a relation of part and whole actualizes immediately the general principle stating that the whole is greater than any of its parts; and so forth.

The most universal concepts are those which are formed first. *Conceptus qui primo cadit in mentem est ens.* The *primo* here refers not only to the logical place of the notion of being, but also, to a primacy in the temporal sense. From both these angles, the statement is in accord with the observations of the child psychologists.[36]

It may be pointed out, at this juncture, that there is a definite analogy between sensitive and intellectual cognition.[37] If we see a man approaching from a great distance, says Aquinas, the first fact that we apprehend is that there is a thing; then we distinguish something of its shape; next we become aware that it is a human shape, and afterwards that it is a man; finally we are aware that it is Peter. Similarly, intellectual knowledge proceeds from very general concepts to more specialized ones. But this is not the only analogy between the two modes of cognition. St. Thomas never tires of emphasizing the unity of human nature. It is not the faculty of will which wills, or the faculty of reason which reasons, or the sensitive faculties which apprehend particulars; it is man, the whole human being, who by means of these faculties accomplishes these various tasks. There is little of the much feared "reification" in the Thomistic theory of faculties. The scornful criticisms of the moderns are really justified only in regard to later forms of the "faculty psychology," not in the case of the Angelic Doctor's position. Thus, the teachings of Christian von Wolff have been responsible for many misunderstandings, although these teachings deserve more consideration than the ultra-modern, progressive, and scientific psychologists are willing to accord them, probably because they have only a secondhand knowledge regarding von Wolff's philosophy.

Many other features of the Thomistic psychology of intellect could be profitably discussed; yet we must forego further analysis and ask whether or not modern psychology can accept the Thomistic notions, whether these notions are confirmed or disproved by experimental research, and whether the general spirit of Thomistic psychology is compatible with the "scientific" psychology of our own day.

We need not repeat that the ideas of Aquinas on the special functioning of the sense organs are not any longer acceptable, based as they are on a primitive and very incomplete knowledge of physiology. Yet, in many instances, only a slight modification is necessary to make the statements of St. Thomas fit into the conceptions of modern biological research. Take, for example, the following passage in the *De Ente et Essentia*, chapter 2, where Aquinas is discussing the relation of essence and form. He points out that things are named by the principle of being which includes all other principles; and he goes on to say: "This is easily seen in tastes, in which the sweet is produced as an effect of warmth which decomposes the humid; although warmth is thus the cause of sweetness, a body is not called sweet because of warmth but because of its taste which includes warm and humid." One may translate this statement—which at first sounds rather abstruse to modern ears—in the following manner: "the sweet taste is brought about by a definite chemical composition of the sapid substance and by its impinging, when in a state of solution, on the gustatory cells; but we do not call a body sweet because it has a definite chemical composition, but because of the gustatory impression which results in the manner described." Similar translations into the terminology and conceptual system of modern physiology are feasible in many instances.

On the other hand, St. Thomas's strictly psychological statements, which do not imply any definite notions of physiological processes, may be much more readily accepted. The general principle that intellectual operations depend for their material on the activities of the senses is of course in basic accord with modern ideas. But many psychologists deny the existence of intellectual operations as mental facts *sui generis*; they claim that there is no distinction to be made between sense awareness and intellectual cognition. Some, e.g., the behaviorists, deny the existence of any truly mental facts; all mental facts, they contend, are reducible to physiological, especially motor, processes. One cannot help admiring the daring spirit of these authors who, by a stroke of the pen, eliminate what mankind for thousands of years has considered as a most convincing and impressive reality. From the time St. Augustine and Descartes proposed their *scio me scire* and *cogito ergo sum* as the starting points of their speculations until the behavioristic principle was "discovered," nobody doubted the existence of mental facts; indeed, there is no reality about which we can be more sure. This is not the place to discuss the foundations of behaviorism. We can dispense with such a discussion all the more, since the behavioristic school has made some rather remarkable concessions in recent years and is evidently on the decline. It was very "modern" a short time ago. But "modern" means *modo hodierno*, according to to-day's fashion, and the fate of behaviorism and some of its allied schools of psychology is a striking illustration of the point.

Nor shall we attempt here a justification of the much decried "faculty psychology." This name has become little more than a catchword; it frightens psychologists so much that they become restless whenever they hear something reminding them, however faintly, of the idea of faculties. They do not seem to be conscious of the fact that they are referring to much the same thing when they speak of "functions." Even the word "factor" has unpleasant associations for many of the modern psychologists, obviously because of its definite implications of the old and outmoded "doctrine of faculties."[38]

It is noteworthy that those experimental studies which are concerned with intellectual operations, and especially with abstraction, have failed to produce any evidence invalidating the Aristotelian-Thomistic views. Among these studies, one by Alexander Willwoll deserves mention. The author reaches the conclusion that the actual process of forming concepts is quite what Thomistic psychology asserts it to be.[39]

The independent studies on "thinking," initiated by K. Bühler and R. S. Woodworth in 1907, have made clear the existence of intellectual states well distinguished from images and their combinations.[40] This is exactly what one would expect on the supposition that the Thomistic teaching is correct. Although the concept is derived from an image or phantasm, it is essentially different from the latter datum. The concept is a new entity, a mental fact belonging in a class of its own, not to be confused with any other. Previously, psychology had been too much under the influence of sensistic philosophies. The *sensus-intellectus* axiom was distorted into the thesis that there is nothing in the mind which is not a sense impression or some trace of it. The ideas of Hume dominated the fields of research more perhaps than many psychologists knew. The experimental evidence furnished by the studies of Bühler and others reinstated intellectual phenomena as a separate class of data. The "new" discovery won approval only gradually with the rest of the psychologists. Many were so thoroughly convinced that nothing could be in the mind except "sensations" that one of them went so far as to protest, in the "name of orthodoxy," against the assertion of "imageless thought."

Intellectual Cognition

Neo-scholastics, too, felt obliged to oppose the notion of "imageless thought" as contradicting a fundamental principle of Thomistic psychology. In doing so, however, they were led astray by a misunderstanding of the statements made by the experimentalists. Aquinas does indeed declare that the intellect not only needs the phantasm for abstracting the concept, but also returns to the phantasm every time it re-inspects its ideas. But he does not say that this return has to be to the very same phantasm from which the abstraction was originally made. Rather, he implies that any phantasm having some relation to the concept may function satisfactorily; and so the original image may be replaced by the word-image or by any other symbol. And he expressly asserts that the proposition has no corresponding phantasm. The notion of "imageless thought" refers mainly to the thinking of propositions, as a look at the reports on Bühler's studies will show. To this extent, then, there is no contradiction between the modern views and those of Aquinas. Nor can such a contradiction be alleged in regard to those experiments which prove that the meaning of words or symbols can be grasped before an adequate image appears in consciousness. Since a completely adequate image is not necessary and any image will do, and since words or symbols are sensory data supplying the mind with phantasms, the conditions laid down by Aquinas are perfectly fulfilled.

The existence of the active intellect can hardly be demonstrated by experiments. We are indeed conscious of a definite activity when trying to form a new concept, especially under the somewhat difficult conditions that Willwoll used in his researches. But this consciousness of activity is not equivalent to an introspective awareness of the active intellect. The reason why Aquinas, following Aristotelian tradition, deems it necessary to credit man with two distinct performances, the abstraction of the concept by the active intellect and the final formation of it by the possible intellect, is not within the province of empirical evidence to determine. This reason is of a philosophical or speculative character. The universal nature is in the phantasm as potentially intelligible. For it to be made actually intelligible an agent, itself actual, is indispensable. This agent has to be of the intellectual immaterial order, otherwise it cannot actualize the universal which is intelligible and immaterial. The intellect, therefore, has to possess the capacity of actualizing the universal nature: hence the saying of Averroës, quoted with approval by Aquinas: *Intellectus agit universalia.*[41]

The question whether the notion of the active intellect has to be retained or abandoned cannot be answered within the field of psychology alone, not even of rational psychology. It is closely linked up with the fundamentals of Thomistic philosophy. Already in the 13th century there were several scholars who thought that the active intellect was a superfluous element;

[61]

Durandus a S. Porciano is among the more prominent of this group. But all of them had to introduce so many profound alterations into the basic structure of the system that their philosophy, however Aristotelian in appearance, differed essentially from the Thomistic interpretation. To keep intact the fundamentals of Thomistic philosophy, it is absolutely vital that one retain the notion of the active intellect. Empirical psychology can have no objection to this notion since it is not of an empirical nature, but belongs to the philosophy of the mind alone.

The rational faculties are conceived as being immaterial, that is, of not needing a material organ for performing their proper acts. On the other hand, they depend on material faculties, the senses, for the material on which to operate. The intellect must be regarded as such an immaterial faculty so long as the principles referred to before are maintained. The universal is not material, because not individualized; and individuation, as has been said before, is brought about exclusively by matter. The knowledge of the universal therefore demands a cognitive power of no lesser dignity than the object known. Also the capacity of reflection is an achievement which cannot be attributed to any material being since such a being is incapable of "bending back" on itself in the manner characteristic of the intellect.

The notion of reflexion, it may be noted incidentally, implies a difficulty similar to the one mentioned in regard to the intellectual cognition of particulars. Thus, reflexion is not only on the intellect itself and its performances, but on consciousness in general, i.e., on the whole array of cognitive functions. Reason knows not only itself, but also its dependence on the senses. If it had not this knowledge, it could never arrive at the statement that the phantasm is a necessary condition of intellectual cognition. But the senses are material, and the mode of their being known intellectually is rather mysterious.

The intellect is credited by Aquinas with a memory of its own.[42] Intellectual memory is not a distinct power but a peculiar performance of one and the same intellect. It is clear that such an intellectual memory has to be assumed. The intellect not only knows that it has performed certain operations before—formation of concept, syllogistic reasoning, and so forth—but also remembers what concepts it has formed. Fortunately, we do not have to go over the whole chain of operations again when we want to make use of a concept already possessed. It would be quite interesting to trace the similarities between the Thomistic notion of a sensitive and intellectual memory and the two memories as distinguished by Bergson.[43] There are also relations between the Thomistic doctrines and the ideas underlying the many studies on rote memory as contrasted with insight or understanding. To discuss these problems, however, is impossible within the space allotted to this study.

Fourth Essay

THE PROBLEM OF TRUTH

by
John K. Ryan

The Problem of Truth

PILATE was not jesting, as Bacon thought, when he asked his question. He did not stay for an answer because his words were themselves an answer rather than a question. For the skeptic too has his theory of truth. In fear of the truth, hostile to it, or in despair of reaching it, the skeptic holds that truth is non-existent, or that if it does exist the human mind is incapable of attaining it. Subjectivistic as the skeptical attitude and its accompanying dogmas are, they yet contain some recognition of truth as an objective value. If truth did exist, it would be something independent of our minds. If truth does exist, it is something transcendent and beyond our ability to know.

In contrast to this skeptical position, and yet with points of contact with it, stand the truth theories that are the characteristic product of the modern mind. Idealistic monism has given rise to the coherence theory of truth. In accordance with the general character of absolutism, it is held that truth is equated with conceivability. Conceivability means systematic coherence and consistency; to be conceivable means to be a "significant whole," one "such that all its constituent elements reciprocally involve one another."[1] So also the modern temper, partly in reaction against absolutism and partly in fulfillment of it, has produced another theory of truth. In the various forms of pragmatism emphasis is placed upon the partial, the particular, the local and the temporal. The true, says the most authoritative and candid of pragmatists, "is only the expedient in the way of our thinking, just as 'the right' is only the expedient in the way of our behaving."[2]

There is an older doctrine of truth than that of the skeptic, the absolutist or the pragmatist. It is the doctrine of the natural man, who does not hesitate to say that truth is real, and that it is his discovery rather than his creation. It is the doctrine as well that has been given expression in part or in whole by the greatest figures in the long history of the Platonic and Aristotelian philosophy. Plato, Aristotle, Augustine and Anselm are names that appear in an account of this doctrine. This, too, is the theory of truth

[65]

accepted and developed by Thomas Aquinas, and illustrated by the whole method and content of his thought.

Aquinas's point of departure in his discussion of the nature and kinds of truth is his agreement with Aristotle's dictum that truth and falsity reside not in things but in the intellect. Why this is the case St. Thomas shows.[3] The term "good" denotes that towards which the appetite tends, and the term "truth" denotes that for which the intellect strives. A man possesses knowledge in so far as the thing known is in the mind of the knower. On the other hand, appetite exists in so far as the desirer reaches out for what is desired. Hence the term of the appetite, that is, the good, exists in the object found desirable, whereas the term of the intellect, that is, truth, exists in the intellect itself. Good exists in the thing because the thing in question has a certain relation to the appetite. The appetite in turn is called good if its object is good. Likewise in the case of truth. Truth is in the intellect in so far as it is conformed to the thing intellected. Hence the idea of truth passes from the intellect to the thing known. The thing is said to be true in so far as it has a certain relation to the intellect.

Truth, therefore, resides primarily in the intellect. It is, says St. Thomas accepting the definition attributed to Isaac ben Salomon Israeli, the equation of thought and thing. Yet it may be objected that truth is found in our senses, and also that there is more than one way in which it can be found in the intellect. In answer to these objections Aquinas makes the nature of truth still clearer. Everything is true, he points out, in so far as it has its own proper form. So too the intellect, in so far as it knows, is true. It possesses the likeness of the thing known, and this is its form, as knowing. To know this conformity of intellect and thing, which constitutes truth, is to know the truth. This the senses cannot do. Sight, for instance, has the likeness of the object seen, yet it cannot itself know the conformity existing between the thing seen and that which sight apprehends concerning it. Sight does not see itself. On the contrary, the intellect can know its own conformity with the intelligible thing.

Not only can we perceive objects with our senses, but our intellect can and does grasp the essential nature of things. Yet here too we do not find the complete and formal nature of truth. This obtains only when the intellect passes judgment. When the intellect judges that a thing really corresponds to the form that it apprehends of that thing, then it knows and affirms the truth. The act of judgment is either an affirmation or a denial. In every judgment the intellect either applies some form signified by the predicate to the subject, or removes it from the subject. Such affirmation or denial is absent both from sense-perception and from the intellect's simple apprehension of a thing's nature. Sense is true in its operation and the intellect is true in its apprehension of essences, but in neither case is there the knowledge and apprehension of the truth. Hence although truth may exist in sensations and simple apprehensions, as in whatever is true, yet it does not exist there as the thing known in the mind of the knower. This latter is what is formally and primarily connoted by the word "truth." The perfection of the intellect is the truth as known. Therefore, logical truth, or truth in the strict and proper sense, resides in the intellect affirming and denying, that is, in the judgments of the intellect.

In addition to logical truth, there are two further kinds of truth. These are ontological truth and moral truth, or the truth of discourse. "Truth" and "being" are convertible terms. Everything, in so far as it possesses being, can be known. All things are therefore true in that they are conformable to the intellect. So also, the realer a thing is, the more of being that it possesses, the more intelligible it is and the truer it is. All things are truly what they are and can be truly known for what they are. "Stones hidden in the bosom of the earth" are true stones. One being is a true horse; another a true man, and so on. Even things that appear to be other than what they are must yet be said to be true. The metal that we hastily take for gold is not true gold, but yet it is true brass. Not in the thing but in us is the falsity. The paste jewels are true imitations. The hypocrite, the villain and the deceiver are truly what they are. Even the lie, if it is such, is a "true lie," is truly a lie.

All things are truly what they are and are truly known for what they are by the perfect and omniscient mind of God. So too, by Thomistic definition, is God truth itself: "Truth is found in the intellect in so far as it apprehends a thing as it is, and in the thing in so far as it has its being conformable to the intellect. This is found most of all in God. For His being is not only in conformity with His intellect, but also it is itself His own understanding. His own act of understanding is the measure and cause of all other things and of all other intellects. He is His own existence and understanding. Hence it follows that not only is truth in Him but He is truth itself, the highest and the first truth."[4] God's intellect, St. Thomas emphasizes, is the measure of all created things. The divine intellect is the measure of all created things, but is not itself measured by them. The things of nature, from which our intellect draws its knowledge, are the measure of our intellect. It is our task to discover the truth, to bring our minds into conformity with the real nature of things. Therefore, while natural things are both measures and measured, our intellect is measured, but is not itself a measure of truth, except with regard to its own productions.[5]

Finally, there is moral truth, or the truth of discourse. Our speech is true when it is in agreement with our mind. It is false when we speak against our real state of mind. It is false when we say what we know to be false. It is false when we say what we think to be false, even though our words may be in harmony with what is actually the case. It is false when we utter, as true, statements with regard to something concerning which we have no genuine knowledge. To speak truly, we must establish a conformity between our discourse and our mind; we must make actual in our words what is already actual within our thought.[6]

The Thomistic doctrine is the natural and realistic answer to the problem of truth. In the last analysis it is difficult to the point of impossibility to conceive truth in any other way than that of agreement and conformity. Positively, we recognize that we possess the truth only when our judgments are in agreement with the thing judged. The reality that is the object of our concern must inform us, and our minds must be conformed to it, if we are to say that we truly know that reality as it is. Negatively, we recognize that we do not possess the truth, that our judgments are erroneous, only when there is a discrepancy between the mind and its object, when there is an absence of the agreement and conformity that constitute truth. "Washington was the first president of the United States" is a true judgment because it conforms to the real order. "Lincoln was the second president of the United States" is a false judgment because it does not conform to the real order. "Washington, John Adams, Thomas Jefferson . . ." that real order of succession among the presidents must be preserved and actualized again in the realm of thought if I am to possess the truth in their regard.

So too the normal and ordinary conduct and procedure of men in the familiar tasks of life give illustration to the clearness of vision and sureness of statement that produced the Thomistic doctrine. When we try to "discover the truth," or "to get at the facts," we do precisely this: we attempt to get our minds into conformity with what is actually the case. Thus in our reconstructions of the past, in our solution of difficulties, in our philosophical reflections and scientific researches, what do our efforts to build up working hypotheses, successful theories, and practical systems amount to except to attempts to get our minds into actual and complete harmony with the objective order? The perfect history, perfect because completely true, what is this but one in which men and things move in the minds of the historian and of his readers just as they once moved in fact? The complete solution of things obscure and hidden, can this be other than a mental actualization of the things that gave rise to our wonder, to the end that ignorance and doubt be displaced by truth and certainty?

The theories of truth that have been put forth as rivals of this traditional doctrine are at best only partial and inadequate answers to the problem of truth. The coherence doctrine, advanced as the idealist's solution of the problem, is vague and unrealistic, remote from the exigencies of the commonplace. Like all monistic doctrines, it does not come to terms with reality as we experience and know it. Its fault is that of Emerson, who could say, "I love Man, but not men." Disdainful of and unconcerned with the real men existing in this real world, Emerson could seemingly delude himself and content himself with devotion to an abstraction. So also the idealistic monist is concerned with Truth in the abstract, with some vague, vast, all-inclusive Truth, rather than with the more immediate and practical problem of truth in the concrete and particular.

Like all extremist doctrines, the coherence theory takes a part and makes it the whole. What the absolutist rightly insists on is that truth, or better, a system of truths, must be self-consistent and coherent. If there are gaps in our knowledge, we obviously possess only part of the truth. If there are contradictions in our knowledge, or rather in what is claimed to be knowledge, then we have error as well as ignorance. Hence completeness and systematic coherence are a mark and sign of truth and a consequence of it. *Omne verum vero consonat.* If we reflect upon the symmetry, the coherence, and the consistency of the Catholic dogmatic system, we see that this is the case. Each particular doctrine of the Church's teaching is of the most complete consistency with all the others. They all unite and cohere to form a perfect whole. So complete and perfect is this coherence that we cannot pick and choose among the Church's teachings: if we reject one we must reject the entire system. This holds for the individual: loss of membership is visited upon the man who decides what he will accept and what he will reject among the articles of faith. It holds also in a larger way for whole nations and over long periods of time. It has been thought that some few things that the Church asserts as true could be denied and all the rest retained. Yet the logic of the initial rejection inexorably demands that all else in the Catholic dogmatic system be likewise rejected. It may well be that centuries are needed for the fulfillment of this process of rejection and negation, but the complete paganism that was once only implicit and unseen finally becomes explicit and evident.

Actually, consistency has always been taken as a sign and consequence of truth. But we must recognize clearly that this is what consistency is. It is an effect of truth, not its cause and essence. One doctrine coheres with another because they are both true; they are not true because they cohere. Again, how do we know that propositions and doctrines are consistent or inconsistent with one another? Only by getting our minds into correspondence with these doctrines considered in an objective way. Basic to the idealistic theory of truth is the doctrine that truth is found only in the conformity of mind and thing. Still further, it may be objected that the terms "coherence" and "consistency" are themselves only failing attempts to provide a substitue for the older and more satisfactory terms "conformity" and "agreement."

As in the case of the coherence doctrine, so also of pragmatism may it be said that it offers a criterion and a test of truth rather than a sound theory of the nature of truth itself. Men have always recognized that truth is practical. If a doctrine is true, it will turn out well in practice; it will display its truth by the way in which it works. Conversely, if sufficiently rigorous practical tests are made, a false theory will show itself to be false by the way that it breaks down and fails. This pragmatic test has always been known and used. "If you be the children of Abraham, do the works of Abraham." "By their fruits you shall know them." "You shall know the truth, and the truth shall make you free." These and countless other recognitions of practical results as a manifestation of truth may be instanced. The scholastic philosopher had his *argumentum ex consectariis* in which he applied the pragmatic test to a doctrine by considering the way in which it worked. If a doctrine turned out well, it was judged to be true; if it turned out ill, it was judged to be false in some part or way. But what modern pragmatism has done is to take a consequence, an effect, a sign and manifestation of truth, viz., utility, and exaggerate it into the essence and cause of truth. Usefulness, the effect and consequence of a doctrine's initial and essential truth, is here claimed to be the very stuff of truth. Effect is here confused with cause; appearance with substance.

Put in its very lowest terms, the pragmatic account of truth claims that a doctrine is true because it works, and that it is true only if, when and as it works. In contradiction to this, a sound account of truth holds that doctrines work because they are in accord with the real order of things. Theories and systems work because and in so far as they are true; they break down and fail because and in so far as they are false. Certainly this last is the logical order of analysis, just as it is the chronological order as well. If success and utility are the essence and cause of truth, as the pragmatist holds, why do they not come early instead of late, first instead of last, in the order of time? In some manner the cause always precedes the effect. Yet in the pragmatist's doctrine, the asserted cause, utility, is the last thing arrived at and established. We can never be sure of the truth until we are sure that the doctrine in question is completely and finally successful. To hold this is really to repudiate all hope of truth and certainty.

It is evident that the pragmatic account of truth is a form of relativism and skepticism. For it there is no such thing as absolute, final and unchangeable truth. Truth is merely a matter of time, place and persons. Even so the pragmatist suffers doubts and misgivings. Unable to rid himself completely of his metaphysical past, he still seeks the absolute and is ready to admit the

The Problem of Truth

existence of the absolutely false even as he denies the existence of the absolutely true.[7] Yet to hold that there is "absolute falsity" is to admit at least by implication that there is also an absolute truth.

More objections can be brought against the shallow and extremist doctrine that is pragmatism in its several statements as experimentalism, instrumentalism, humanism and the rest. How are we to know that a doctrine works well and is therefore true, or works ill and is therefore false? How are we to apply this pragmatic theory of truth? Obviously, we must know what success and failure are in any given instance before we can judge whether the doctrine works well or badly. Obviously, we must recognize success and failure in fact before we can say that the doctrine is true or false. Hence we must get our minds into conformity with the real order before we can pass our pragmatic judgments. In other words, the pragmatic theory of truth is not a basic and adequate explanation. It presupposes the only genuinely basic and satisfactory explanation of the nature of truth, the doctrine that truth resides in the conformity of our judgments with the reality judged.

No doctrine can be completely at fault, and no Thomist could fall into James's crude error of condemning as "absolutely false" doctrines that he dislikes. Systematic coherence, conceivability and utility do have their necessary relation to truth, and the Thomist assigns their place to them in his account of truth and error. The doctrine of truth as conformity is in fact a higher synthesis, including all that is of value in the other doctrines and avoiding their extremes and extravagances. It is evident that any doctrine that includes whatever is sound in the opposing accounts together with its own positive and constructive elements is the stronger doctrine. The constructive is to be preferred to the destructive; the creative to the merely critical; the synthetic to the merely analytic; the complete to the partial. This is found to be the case when a comparison is instituted between the correspondence doctrine and the coherence and pragmatic theories.

The Thomistic account insists that truth is practical, useful, satisfactory of human needs. It grants and maintains that truth is not static but dynamic, that it can and must expand and grow. It points out the extent to which truth depends upon human experience: all our knowledge begins with sense-experience. It holds that the will plays its part in the production of truth: we can make things work, make things come true. Because men and things come and go, it holds that certain doctrines that are true and good at certain times and under certain conditions may no longer stand up under changed circumstances. All this has been held by the Thomistic doctrine for long centuries before William James and his fellow pragmatists appeared. Our doctrine has always included these elements. At the same time, it

[71]

points out that truth itself yet remains to be explained. We not only make our plans turn out well and our hopes come true, but we discover the truth. Truth is not merely experimental and utilitarian, not merely a matter of human will and effort. Truth is the conformity of the mind with the thing known.

So also with regard to the coherence theory. The Thomist's doctrine has always held that consistency is a test and sign of truth. It holds that the law of contradiction is the basic law of thought: a thing cannot be and not be at the same time, in the same place, and under the same conditions. What is self-contradictory is inconceivable, impossible and false. But it must further be held that consistency is a product of truth, not its cause and essence. The Thomist cannot fall victim to the inconsistencies of the consistency doctrine any more than he can fall victim to the impracticalities of the pragmatic doctrine. Yet he can and does hold fast to what is good in both. Finally, in the ancient doctrine that every being is one, good and true, that is, in the doctrine of ontological unity, goodness and truth, the Thomist's doctrine again anticipates and surpasses the coherence theory. Every being is what it is; every being is truly what it is; every being is true. Every being is known for what it truly is by the omniscient mind of God. Not only is all being conceivable, but it is actually conceived. God knows all truth; being infinitely real and infinitely wise, He is truth itself.

Thus the Thomistic account of truth not only includes all that is good in the other theories, but it has its own positive solution to offer. It is only upon the basis of this contribution, namely, that truth is essentially a conformity of mind and thing, that the problem of truth can be solved. Likewise, only on this basis can the concomitant problem of error be solved. Certainly the problem of error can never be solved by the essentially skeptical doctrines that are pragmatism and the coherence theory.

While utility and consistency cannot be held to be the essence of truth, they may be taken as signs of its presence and nature. Yet even in their character as criteria of truth, coherence and practical consequences cannot be ultimate. No pragmatist would betray his own doctrine by holding that men cannot be mistaken as to what is really useful. Nor would the advocate of conceivability as the stuff of which truth is made deny that a fictitious coherence often obtains in men's thoughts. Must they not, therefore, have recourse to some norm by which to test the presence and genuineness of utility and consistency? Must they not admit the need for a further criterion to test their norm, and so on and on? Such a regress is to be escaped only by the admission of what obtains in the order of experience as well as in the order of thought. Ultimately, it must be admitted that the consequences of a doctrine are advantageous or the reverse because they give evidence that they are such. Ultimately, the presence or absence of coherence among our thoughts and doctrines must be admitted because of the evidence at hand. We must hold that certain judgments are inescapable because it is evident that they are true.

Certain things and certain principles must be accepted as true because they are self-evident to us. Must evidence therefore be advanced as the ultimate and universal criterion of truth? To do so involves difficulties arising both from the nature of evidence and from the nature of a criterion. It seems preferable to accept evidence as the ultimate motive of assent and of certitude, to reject as uncalled-for the modern search for an ultimate criterion, and to advance particular criteria or tests for the presence or absence of truth such as will serve under particular conditions. These will include the pragmatic test and the test of consistency. Connected with both of them is the test found in the "logical consequences" of a doctrine. If a doctrine directly and necessarily involves consequences untenable in the order of thought, that may be taken as an indication of its falsity. However, this test is subject to certain disabilities and must be used with reserve. Doctrines do not always involve the dire consequences or lead to the enormities of thought and conduct with which critics sometimes charge them.[8]

Conceivability and inconceivability too are to be taken as criteria of truth, but it is preferable that they be used in the precise and restricted way of St. Thomas. In his theory and practice, reduction to first principles is the nearest that we can come to an ultimate test for argument. In the last analysis, any chain of reasoning must rest upon a basis of first principles, which are themselves evident and therefore not susceptible of proof.[9]

Authority must also be taken as a standard of truth. Particularly in these latter days when so many voices claim to speak with authority and when their words are heard and read by so many millions, is it important to recall what St. Thomas has said of the weight that is to be granted to authority: ". . . for although the argument from authority based on human reason is the weakest, yet the argument from authority based on divine revelation is the most efficacious."[10] Because the modern mind tends to interpret all reality mathematically, or in terms of the category of quantity, a new variation of the argument from authority has appeared. Statistics are gathered and polls are taken. It is found, for instance, that 80 per cent of the people hold to one opinion or practice in contrast to 20 per cent who hold the alternative. To the opinion of the majority "greater weight" is attached; it is thought to be true, or at least "truer" than the other. Yet truth is not a quantitative affair, and a false doctrine does not become true because of general acceptance, any more than an evil deed becomes good because of general practice. Especially when it may well be a matter of the opinion of the unthinking many that is accepted as authoritative, must we remember that "the argument from authority based on human reason is weakest."

What is truth? What are its kinds and its criteria? These questions concern truth as a problem of speculation, of intellectual abstraction and analysis. There is another problem of truth that is moral and practical. How is truth to be attained? In its completeness truth shows itself to be a problem confronting the will as well as the intellect. Truth is something to be discovered by us: *intellectus noster est mensuratus, non mensurans*. It is objective and not a mere creation of thought and volition. Yet we do not attain to truth by intellect alone. The actual possession of the truth, especially in matters of the highest and most lasting importance, can come only as a result of will and effort. We must have a will to truth, if we are to attain it. Pascal's demand made before opening discussion with atheists sums up the whole problem. Were the atheists willing to accept God if His existence were demonstrated to them? Without this declaration of sincerity of mind, Pascal refused to begin his discussion. Without this will to truth, it was evident that the whole debate would be to no purpose, or even to an evil one.

In manifold ways our world shows lack of this will to truth. We still hear of a "healthy skepticism," of the attitude of doubt with which every problem, every principle, and every pronouncement, in no matter what field and by no matter whom proposed, should be approached. Yet only a little reflection is enough to see that there cannot be a healthy skepticism. Skepticism is essentially abnormal and unnatural; it is a disease of the mind. Health is by definition something natural and normal, and the health of the mind, its perfection, as St. Thomas calls it, is the mind's sure knowledge that it possesses the truth. Doubt and uncertainty, on the other hand, are so painful and distressing in themselves that they cannot naturally and normally be sought as something good and permanent. What the investigator can and must have is something very different from the morbidity of doubt for doubt's sake, or doubt adopted as a sort of masochistic self-indulgence. The philosophic and scientific spirit means an open mind and a suspended judgment in matters upon which we are competent to judge but where we still see the need for further evidence. This philosophic and scientific spirit means also a good will. This includes both recognition of limitations upon our personal competence—that there are authorities higher than the individual—and the determination to come to a decision and to accept the truth and its consequences when the needed evidence has appeared. The honest man must have the will "to follow the argument where it leads." The true lover of wisdom, the true philosopher and scientist, must possess above all the virtue of veracity, and this virtue excludes self-deception as well as the deception of others.

Being essentially morbid, this wide-spread acceptance of skepticism as a superior intellectual value has had its necessary effects. These are found in the uncertainty and confusion of the individual, his lack of stability and self-confidence, and in the weakening of his moral and intellectual fibre. They are reflected in the communal and social mind, in its uncertainties, confusions and contradictions. The method of doubt results in intellectual disintegration, or rather is itself a process of disintegration. Unable to cast off its natural need for certainty and rest, the individual mind instinctively seeks for some security and for something to affirm. Hand in hand with a formal refusal to accept the highest truths, no matter how great their evidence may be, goes the real acceptance of contradictory doctrines that are devoid of all evidence. Hand in hand with a formal rejection of authority possessing the highest credentials goes an acceptance of authority with no credentials. *Extrema se tangunt.* The uncritical criticism and the unreasonable rationalism that have made a cult of skepticism have produced a mind that is without strength and unity. It is a soft and plastic mind, ready to be molded by the dogmas of the theorist of state absolutism, by the demands of its practitioners, and by the arts of the propagandist. The modern Caesars and their apologists, who take *Mundus vult decipi* as a motto and in contempt of the people cause them to feed upon lies, are of course most culpable. But the people themselves are at fault because they suffer from a disease of the intellect and will, an atrophy of moral powers that shows itself in an indifference to the truth, even in a hatred of it.

In the production of this modern situation the part that idealistic monism and utilitarianism with their accompanying logics have played may be seen. The transition from the Hegelian doctrine to the Marxist theory and practice is as notorious as it is easy and inevitable. The totalitarian state with its assertion that it alone is the source of all human rights and duties is the frank expression of the absolutist philosophy. In it the reality of the individual gives way before the concept of man in the mass, and the mass-man, having neither freedom nor right, has no right to the truth that would make him free. For the new Caesars, in whom the absolute state is personalized, there is no superior law imposing duties. For them there is no duty to tell the truth. Expediency alone decides whether the truth shall be made known and whether promises shall be kept, for " 'the true' is only the expedient in the way of our thinking, just as 'the right' is only the expedient in the way of our behaving." So the lie is exalted by Lenin and Hitler, is practised by countless underlings, and is used by the state as a matter of policy and system. In the reign of absolutism and pragmatism, moral truth is no longer a supreme virtue. With the attempt to destroy the individual, logical truth is denied as something vain and illusory. With the rejection of God, ontological truth too must go, together with all values that transcend the new Leviathan.

In the face of these errors of thought and evils of practice that mark our world, the Thomistic doctrine of truth stands as an epitome of what must be thought and done if something better is to prevail. If our difficulties are the result in no small measure of the application of skepticism, absolutism and pragmatism to the affairs of men, it is not too much to say that to know and to profess the *sana doctrina* as to the nature and kinds of truth is a first condition for the construction of a better world.

We are only too able to perceive that the ordeal of the modern world is resulting in a *dehonestamentum humani generis.* In this perception we see to some extent what man is and what he ought to be. *Know thyself* now becomes more than ever an absolute command that each man must obey. At this period of crisis man must turn his mind's eye inward and reflect anew upon what he sees there. To know truly what man is proves now as always to be the precondition of the second injunction, *Be thyself.* For man's troubles have resulted from a lack of truth—he has ceased to know himself for what he truly is—and from a consequence of that lack of truth—he has acted against his true nature. This is "the true lie" of which Plato tells, the lie "hated of gods and men." By it modern men are too often "deceived or uninformed about the highest realities in the highest part of themselves, which is the soul." And, as Plato has Socrates explain, "this ignorance in the soul of him who is deceived may be called the true lie; for the lie in words is only a kind of imitation and shadowy image of a previous affection of the soul, not pure and unadulterated falsehood."[11]

What then is that true nature of man that we must know if we are to expel the true lie from the mind and heart of the modern world? It is that we are not brutes or machines, but creatures made a little less than the angels. Made of spirit as well as of matter, ours is a unitary nature, one that needs lower things and moves among them, and yet needs higher things as well.

> *What is a man*
> *If his chief good and market of his time*
> *Be but to sleep and feed? a beast, no more:*
> *Sure, He that made us with such large discourse,*
> *Looking before and after, gave us not*
> *That capability and god-like reason*
> *To fust in us unused.*[12]

The Problem of Truth

If we rightly use that god-like reason, it will lead us from the truth of the things within us and about us to the affirmation of God. "Among things there are some more and some less good, true, noble and the like. But 'more' and 'less' are affirmed of different things in so far as they approach in their several ways something that exists in the very highest degree . . . so that there is something that is truest, something best, something noblest, and consequently, something that is uttermost being; for the truer things are, the more truly they exist, as is said in the second book of the *Metaphysics*. What is complete in any genus is the cause of all in that genus . . . Therefore, there must be also something that is to all things the cause of their being, goodness, and every other perfection. And this we call God."[13]

By consideration of what we are and of what all other finite things are, and by reflection upon the scale of perfection found among things, we arrive at the knowledge of a being who is seen to exist most truly, God, who is truth itself. "Man is obviously made to think," says Pascal. "It is his whole dignity and his whole merit; and his whole duty is to think as he ought. Now the order of thought is to begin with self, and with its Author and its end."[14]

Reason and human science alone are not enough. There is a further and higher knowledge than that of reason. This higher knowledge must be had if we are to know ourselves for what we truly are and if we are to know what deeds we must do for our own true good. "It was necessary for man's salvation that beyond the physical sciences, which are sought out by human reason, there be some doctrine revealed by God Himself. First, because man is ordained to God as to an end that exceeds the comprehension of his reason: 'The eye hath not seen besides Thee, O God, what things Thou hast prepared for them that wait for Thee.' (Isaias 64:4) It needs must be that the end be foreknown to the men who are to order their minds and their deeds to that end. Hence for man's salvation it was necessary that certain things that exceed human reason be made known to him by divine revelation. Even in the case of those truths about God that human reason can search out, it was necessary for man to be instructed by divine revelation, for the truth about God searched out by human reason could be attained only by a few men, after a long time, and with an admixture of many errors, whereas man's whole salvation depends upon a knowledge of that truth which is in God. Hence that salvation might come to men more fitly and securely, it was necessary that they be taught by divine revelation. Therefore, beyond the philosophical sciences, which are investigated by human reason, it was necessary that sacred science be known through divine revelation."[15] To know ourselves, therefore, in this highest and most important way, we must know and accept the affirmations of faith: *I believe*

[77]

*in God, the Father Almighty, and in Jesus Christ, His only Son, Our
Lord; Who was conceived by the Holy Ghost, born of the Virgin
Mary* . . .

Knowing what we are, whence we come, by Whom and for Whom we
are made, by Whom we have been redeemed and at what cost, can we be
content with anything less than the truth in our relations with one another?
If we know ourselves as made to the image and likeness of God, Who is
truth itself, and if we strive to be ourselves, the lie will be driven from
human affairs. No longer will there be toleration among men of the cynical
pragmatist or of the ruthless absolutist in the places of control. Among
private individuals, the true man, perceiving his own nature and its dig-
nities, and recognizing the right of his fellowmen to the truth, will see that
the lie, even in its most trivial form, is something against and beneath his
character as a man. "Little lie, innocent lie—does such a thing exist?" once
asked Victor Hugo. "To lie is the absolute form of evil. To lie a little is
not possible: he who lies, lies the whole lie. To lie is the very face of the
demon. Satan has two names; he is called Satan and Lying." To banish the
lie that is not little and not innocent from national and international life,
this is a necessary condition of the peace and justice for which men of good
will hope. The highest ideal of truth and the strictest adherence to it must
be found among men, not for some Utopian dream, but for any real and
enduring society of men who know and respect themselves.

Beyond the truth of discourse that should obtain between individual men
when they speak to one another, there is a more inclusive veracity that must
be found in a good society. There are more means of expression than the
words that we speak directly to our fellows in the affairs of daily life. We
express ourselves in what we do: in our social and political institutions, in
our literature, our architecture, our sculpture and painting and music. In
all of these must there be truth. Each book that is written, each picture
painted, each song and symphony composed must be the veracious expression of what we are and of what we strive to be. Each tool and machine,
each house and shop must be known for what it is and for what it should do,
and must be made into conformity with our knowledge and expressive of it.

Particularly must veracity mark the outward expression of what is deepest and loftiest within us. We give utterance to our faith by the churches
that we build, the music that we make, the vessels and vestments that we
fashion, and all the rest. Here especially must we see these things for what
they are and do, and ourselves for what we are. If this logical truth is
present and if it is followed by the highest kind of moral truth, then we
may expect to see a true new order of the ages arise. The past will not be
broken with, but fulfilled. The borrowed idiom of other ages and places

will be replaced by our own authentic way of speech. Then will the imitation and the pretence of the present scene disappear. Informed by true religion and giving assent to its doctrines with their complete being, men will give outward expression by everything that they say and do to their real acceptance of the truth. Then again will successful social and political institutions be built. A unified and healthy society will tell of what it is and for what it strives in a glorious art and literature.

In contrast to what should be and one day will be is the sombre spectacle of the world today. The tragedy of our time, its rejection of unity, truth and goodness, is apparent upon every side. Modern history and modern thought increasingly show themselves to be a process of disintegration, of destruction, and of annihilation. Hate and greed and fear have usurped the places of love and generosity and trust. Reliance on force has displaced reason. The unity of our race is denied. Men and nations no longer recognize themselves as brothers who are to live in peace and amity under one God and Father of all. The negations of atheism have been preferred before the affirmations of Christian faith.

It is this denial of God that has brought on the denial of man, for when man ceases to know God he likewise ceases to know himself for what he truly is. Ceasing to know God and himself, modern man has brought on this night of ignorance and error and evil, how long to endure no one can tell. Far distant or not, the dawn ending our night will come. In that dawn the light will be that of the Christian revelation, of the Catholic Church, its doctrines and its deeds, its theology and philosophy, its arts and institutions. Therein will be found the truth in its fullness and purity, the truth of intellect, of being, and of word, the truth that makes men free.

Fifth Essay

THE ONTOLOGICAL ROOTS
OF THOMISM

by

Hilary Carpenter, O.P.

The Ontological Roots of Thomism

THE chief difficulty in attempting any exposition of the science of ontology arises from the almost universal blanketing of all truly metaphysical concepts by the nominalistic heresies resulting from three centuries of scientific materialism and empiricism. During that period, indeed, there has poured forth an unending spate of pseudo-metaphysic, outcome of an innate intellectualism that cannot in all cases be content with a mere progressive empiricism, yet is so warped by the latter as to seek its satisfaction in imaginative speculation entirely divorced from the reality of things. It is significant that the word "theorize," denoting in its original Greek form the most incisive effort of the human intellect to penetrate into the basic truths of all objective reality, is now used almost exclusively in the totally opposite sense of moving away from reality in the direction of pure fantasy. So that for the many the only reality is the tangible and material; while a few, wrongly styled "philosophers," give full rein to the fantastic subjectivism inevitable in a mind that is no longer anchored to a common-sense investigation of what "is." Materialist and subjectivist alike have fallen victims to a perennial nominalism; and the fundamental concept of all reality and truth, namely *"being,"* is for them no more than a name.

The science of metaphysics, or *ontology* as it is now more commonly called, is the ordered investigation into "being" in its most absolute significa-tion, that is to say, into the essential content of that actuality which is predi-cated of all things that exist in any way. From its earliest history mankind, at any rate in its more thoughtful element, has sought to penetrate into the mystery of "being" and, as M. Jacques Maritain has so well observed, "even before philosophy took shape as an independent discipline, most of the great philosophic errors had already been formulated."[1] The tide of human thought-fashions shows a recurring tendency to ebb away towards sheer materialism and a phenomenalistic interpretation of reality; or to flood over the shores of common sense, like a tidal movement that gathers force from some hidden matrix of energy in the bosom of the sea, as it sweeps along in a mounting wave of idealism and subjectivism. But throughout the history of philosophic thought there has stood, more or less well defined in different eras, the indestructible coastline of a balanced intellectual appreciation of reality. This appears definitely in the embryonic philosophical thought of the Old Testament, remarkably clearly in the common-sense philosophy of Aristotle, and perfected with compelling force in the comprehensive synthesis of St. Thomas Aquinas. The subsequent "flight from reason" led by Descartes has only in recent years begun to be effectively checked by the general recrudescence of interest in Thomism, the *philosophia perennis* preserved within the inviolable sanctuary of all truth, the Church.

In view of the prevailing misconception of fundamental (as distinct from phenomenal) reality and in the face of the engaging futilities of subjectivism, it seems highly desirable that this present essay in ontology should take the form of a positive re-statement of some of the fundamental metaphysical concepts expounded in the Aristotelic moderate realism of St. Thomas and its derivative metaphysic. This is all the more urgent because of the essential dependence of all philosophic inquiry upon "first philosophy," as Aristotle calls ontology; for this science is architectonic, not merely from its supreme place in the hierarchic order of the sciences, but still more because of the absolute and eternal verity of its immutable principles and unassailable conclusions. "Metaphysics," writes M. Maritain, "brings order—not the so-called law and order of the policeman, but the order which springs from eternity—into the speculative and practical intelligence. It gives his equilibrium and his motion back to man, which are, as we know, to gravitate towards the stars with his head while hooked on to the earth by his two legs. It reveals to him the hierarchy of authentic values through all the extent of being. It gives a center to his ethics. It maintains justice in the universe of knowledge, making clear the natural limits, the harmony and subordination of various sciences; and this is far more important for human beings than the most luxuriant proliferation of the mathematics of phenomena. For what is the use of gaining the world and losing right reason?"[2]

The immediate objects of human knowledge, and therefore the only avenues of natural knowledge, are the material, mutable things of everyday contacts. But because, as Aristotle observed, "we are said to know a thing only when we know its principles or causes," the aim of the human mind is to penetrate the outward shell of these things and to uncover or abstract the underlying reality, that which makes them to be what they are, and ultimately that which makes them to "be" at all—their "beingness," if the awkward coining be allowed. The most elementary form of this uncovering or abstraction of the "being" of things is concerned with material "being" precisely under its aspect of materiality whereby it contacts with the sense. The second and deeper degree of abstraction concerns itself with the quantitative aspect of material "being," and results in the philosophy of mathematics. The third and profoundest degree of abstraction penetrates to the "beingness" of all things, to that element which justifies the universal common predication made when we say that a thing exists. This notion of "beingness" is the adequate object of the human mind and opens the way to a scientific apprehension of the nature of "being" in itself, of "being" apart from the limited and diversified forms of "being" which are actualized in all the material things of our acquaintance. "Being" in the third degree of abstraction, then, is the proper object with which the science of ontology or metaphysics is concerned.

Obviously so universal a notion as "being" cannot be defined, for it is outside and above all genera and species and differences, being the ultimate terminus in the analysis of every objective concept and itself entirely simple. Yet, in the infinitely varied manifestations of reality wherein "being" is recognized by the mind to be actualized, there is seen to be a multiplicity in "being" comprehending every individual thing that exists. This very multiplicity makes it possible for the human mind, which must needs progress by the method of analysis and synthesis, to grasp the content of that primary common and undefined notion of "being." And in making the initial advance, any further concepts of underlying reality must begin from some addition, not itself extrinsic to "being," but an expression of elemental modes of "being" implicit in the general concept. It consists either in the analysis of those properties which attach to all "being" as such, or in an examination of the special modes of "being" presented by the categories. In both cases the general concept of "being" becomes particularized; the notion of actual existence is introduced. St. Thomas and the scholastics generally were equally alive to the importance of both lines of thought and added materially to the science of "being" by their doctrine of its transcendental attributes, as well as by their development of the Aristotelian doctrine of the categories.

The "transcendentals," as they are called, are six in number: *ens, res, unum, aliquid, bonum* and *verum*. (Strictly speaking, perhaps, *pulchrum* should also be included.) It is to be understood that we have already departed from the simple notion of common "being," and *ens*, which is the first of the transcendentals, is the first concretion of that notion. We are now concerned, as Aristotle was, with individual actualities which go to make the sum of reality. Of such or any of these it can be said that it is a *being,* a *thing, one,* and so on. These attributes precede the categorical divisions of being; they are outside and above all divisions[3] and are applicable to all the modes of being which may result from the latter. The doctrine of the transcendentals is of prime importance from a Thomist standpoint, not only in the exposé of the actual constitution of the real, but also with respect to the completeness of creation, the conservation of being and divine providence.

The first addition to the concrete notion of "being" results from a consideration in any being of *that which* is rather than of the fact of its existence. Thus we attain the notion of *res* which differs from that of *ens* inasmuch as the latter notion is taken from the act of existence, whereas the former expresses the quiddity or essence, of which actual existence is the principle of complete realization. Proceeding now by way of negation we can arrive at a further modification of "being" inasmuch as every being is individual in itself, having an intrinsic unity. And if this negation be made with respect to other beings, the notion of the separateness of each being from all others emerges, a notion expressed, according to St. Thomas, in the word *aliquid* (*quasi aliud quid*). These three, *res, unum* and *aliquid,* are intimately interconnected, being in fact complementary in establishing the complete idea of transcendental unity.

On the difficulty and importance of a correct doctrine of "unity" and "being" in their relation to reality, Aristotle has expressed himself very decidedly, calling it "the hardest inquiry of all" and "most necessary for a knowledge of truth." But he had made a discovery which enabled him at any rate to put his finger on the fallacy in the conclusions of Pythagoras and Plato with regard to the "One." They had perceived the close relation between "being" and "unity," but they had failed to distinguish between the *unity* which "being" connotes and the *unit* which is the principle of number, with the result that they made mathematical numbers the substance of things. For Aristotle, on the other hand, "to be one" means "to be indivisible (being essentially a 'this' and capable of existing apart) either in place or in form or thought"; or "to be whole and indivisible." To be one is just to be a particular thing. "Being" and "unity" are convertible terms whether in their universal or in their particular application, but the "one" in question is not the numerical unit; it is always one "something" and not just unity.

This, however, is not the whole of his thought. "To be one" means especially "to be a first measure of a kind" and above all of quantity; for it is from this that it has been extended to the other categories. It is only by thus obtaining a unit of measure in any class that knowledge can be acquired.

While appreciating the advance in thought made by Aristotle in this connection, it is necessary to insist, with St. Thomas, upon a clear distinction between unity as connoting indivisibility and unity as the "first measure of a kind." "One" signifies nothing else than "undivided being" and to this extent "one" and "being" are convertible terms. It is not as the "first measure" that "one" coincides with "being," but precisely as expressive of intrinsic indivision. In so far as a thing is a being, so far is it a unity; the destruction of the one is the destruction of the other. In the scale of "being," the degree of unity, i.e., indivisibility and therefore indissolubility, of each thing, is determined by its degree of participation in "being," perfect unity being found only in the perfect Being, God. "Being," in the strictest sense, connotes actual existence and thus unity is to be found only in what can most truly be said to "be," viz.: the *suppositum*, a substance actually existing. And vice versa, each thing *is* in so far as it is *one*, and what is not really one is not really a being.

The recurring application of this doctrine in the Thomistic system is well exemplified in the treatise on the Incarnation. Though positing, in accordance with Christian belief, two distinct natures, human and divine, in the one divine person of the Son of God, St. Thomas can defend on philosophical grounds the unity of the God-man. The question of unity leads not merely to the nature but ultimately to the *suppositum*, or subsisting individual. Though the human nature, conjoined with the divine in Christ, is individual, it does not constitute a human *suppositum* or person, for only an individual substance *actually existing of itself* constitutes a *suppositum*. Existence in Christ is one, that, namely, of the divine Person. Thus human nature has no separate existence of its own, but partakes of the higher existence, just as the head or hand of Socrates has no separate existence of its own while forming part of the body. The unity of the God-man is defended, therefore, as the unity of an individual actually existing.

But the doctrine of transcendental unity is important, too, in the general question of "the one and the many," from its relation to transcendental multiplicity.

The concept of "being" in general, in the Thomistic system, carries with it, as we have already had occasion to note, an essential implication of multiplicity. "Being" in general can be said to be divisible in so far as it is realized variously in the different essences, though this division is based upon analogy. The different essences, or kinds of being, can therefore be said to constitute a plurality, but not a plurality based upon the relation between the things measured and the measure, for there is no homogeneity in the things which constitute the plurality in question; nor yet a plurality based upon the potential divisibility of a common substratum such as matter, for the multiplicity which derives from matter does not result in new kinds of "being." Further, none of the essences which divide "being" includes the notion either of unity or multiplicity in the absolute sense; this is to be found only in their individual realizations, though at the same time, the unity of the individual is based upon the indivisibility of the essence. This indivisibility, or formal unity, of the essence remains intact even in a plurality of particularizations. But if there is no basis in an essence for such a plurality, in other words, if there is no matter, the formal unity of the essence will coincide with the absolute unity of the particular in such a fashion that the multiplication of the particular will necessarily mean the multiplication of formal unities, that is to say, of specifically distinct essences. In such a case the "one" is not the measure of a class except in so far as each particular of itself constitutes a distinct class, and the multiplicity which results is not that of "one and ones" or "white thing and white things" but an abstract multiplicity based upon analogy, as if one added together the white and the good and the true. A concrete example of this doctrine is to be found in the famous Thomistic thesis of the *specific* (as opposed to numerical) distinction and multiplicity of the angels.

. . . .

Aristotle did not consider that "being" as truth enters into the discussion of "being" as such, for truth and falsity are not in things but in the mind. That which *is* in the sense of being true depends on a combination in thought and is an affection of thought. Truth is, however, a relation or adequation between the intellect and the objective reality, so that while truth is an effect of intelligence it is rooted in the object. "It is not because we think truly you are white that you *are* white, but because you are, we who say this have the truth," as Aristotle has it. The measure of "being" is the measure of truth in anything. In so far as he considers truth to be the adequation of the thing and our intelligence, Aristotle is justified in rejecting it from the immediate examination of "being" as such. But he himself recognizes, in his criticism of Democritus and Empedocles, that the stability which truth connotes does not depend upon sensible appearances nor yet upon the intellect which is capable of attaining truth by knowledge. It depends rather upon some objective stability in the thing known, resident in its very being, the more unchangeable in proportion as its being is unchangeable.

Let us consider the matter still further. The architect, building a house, does not attain his knowledge of the house from the finished work but rather the house comes into being as the result of his knowledge. The adequation of the thing and the intellect in this case results from the form pre-existing in the mind of the architect. This is the standpoint from which

The Ontological Roots of Thomism

St. Thomas views the question. Granting that truth is in the intellect according as it conforms with the thing known, he points out that the latter too may be called true in so far as it has a certain order to intelligence. This order can be twofold: *either* essential, with respect to that intelligence whence the thing known depends in its very being; *or* accidental, with respect to that intelligence whereby the thing known is knowable. A judgment about a thing is most properly made from its essential and not from its accidental properties; therefore a thing is judged to be true strictly speaking only with respect to that relation which it has to the intellect whence its "being" depends. Thus natural things are said to be true precisely in their correspondence with the idea in the mind of their Creator. St. Thomas concludes, therefore, that truth is principally in the intellect, secondarily in things as comparable with the intellect which caused them. In his examination of the whole question in the *Summa Theologica* and at greater length in the *De Veritate*, the different aspects of truth, resulting from the *creating* intellect on the one hand and the *created* intellect on the other, is continually insisted on. It is his solution of the difficulties pointed to by Aristotle, in *Metaphysics*, book I, as resulting from making our intellect the norm of truth in things.

Hence in the Thomistic notion of transcendental truth which consists primarily in the perfect conformity of every natural thing in the completeness of its being with the idea in the mind that created it, the need of an exemplar in the mind of the maker of anything is an accepted fact. The First Cause, therefore, intelligent *par excellence*, must have the ideas of all those effects produced by it.

The main significance, however, in St. Thomas's doctrine on ontological truth lies in the real identity of "being" and "truth," the two being distinguishable only by reason. It is the basis of Thomistic intellectualism—an intellectualism not of the abstract but of the real as existing in concrete being. Truth, which is the object of all philosophy and the attaining of which is the ultimate end of man, is to be found in objective "being," in the real, as related to intelligence. The real and the intelligible become convertible terms, and both are to be referred in their principle to God, the Supreme Reality and the Supreme Intelligible. It is of importance, moreover, to remark that genus and species, the logical classifications which are combined to form the definition, are not to be confused with the *idea* of a thing properly so-called, as it is in the mind of the creator. They have their basis in objective reality, it is true, but objective reality means particular individual things. The ideas of things, therefore, in the divine mind must be individual, completely expressive of each thing *qua* individual, with all its qualifications, actual or potential. This is the basis of the Thomistic metaphysic of the individual exemplified in the doctrine of creation, of contingency, of providence, and of "physical premotion," so-called.

The absence of that stability which truth implies, is not to be ascribed to objective reality, but rather to the feebleness of our intellects. But philosophy, and above all "first philosophy" or ontology, is the science of truth and can only be found in that which is the cause of truth, i.e., in "being." In the ultimate analysis it is immutable and eternal truth that is sought and this can be found only in immutable and eternal "being." The reason for this is that those things which are not permanent in their mode of "being" are not permanent in their truth. And those things which have a cause of their "being" have also a cause of their truth, because the "being" of a thing is the cause of a true conception of the thing in our minds. By his own doctrine of ontological truth which grows out of this, of truth which is not merely an *a posteriori* adequation between things and the created mind, but an *a priori* adequation of things to the mind that created them, he has pushed the inquiry to its furthest limits, showing that the stability in things, which is the basic truth, is commensurate with their "being" and is referable directly to eternal and immutable truth.

. . . .

St. Thomas builds up his own doctrine of the actual identity of "being" and "the good" upon an axiomatic definition of the good which is to all intents and purposes that proposed by Aristotle. The essence of the doctrine is set out clearly and succinctly in the *Summa Theologica*[4] as follows: "It seems that goodness differs really from being, but on the contrary Augustine says that inasmuch as we exist we are good. . . . Goodness and being are really the same, and differ only logically; that is clear from the following argument. The formality of goodness consists in this, that it is in some way desirable. Hence the Philosopher says: *Goodness is what all desire*. It is clear that a thing is desirable according to the degree of its perfection; for all things desire their own perfection. Everything is perfect so far as it is actual. Therefore it is clear, that a thing is good so far as it is 'being'; for it is *esse*[5] that makes a thing actual. Hence it is clear that goodness and being are really (*secundum rem*) the same. But goodness states the aspect of desirability which is not explicit in the word 'being.'" Every being, then, precisely in so far as it is being, that is to say, in so far as it is actual, is good. Actuality signifies some sort of perfection and perfection includes the formality of goodness. Hence every being as such is good. Here again we notice the insistence upon the actuality of real existence. Humanity has not the formality of the good or goodness except in so far as it has existence. The relation of all other goods to the perfect Good is that of all beings to the most perfect Being; it is that of the participated to the essential, of imperfect actuality to perfect actuality. The appetible is, in its ultimate analysis, some sort of existence, whether this be represented by life or knowledge or the like, for in each case it is a completer actuality that is desired. Goodness is something intrinsic to each thing, after the manner of an inherent cause. All things are good through their relation to the Prime Goodness, but this is not by a real participation in the divine goodness. The likeness of the cause is to be found in the effect, and thus in all things caused by God, the Prime Goodness, there is imprinted a likeness to Him in their goodness. This is an inherent effect in each thing, but it is true to say, at the same time, that each thing is good by the Prime Goodness which is the exemplary and efficient cause of all created good.

It is important to state, however, without further delay, that the search for "being as such" is the search not for a concept but for a reality, a reality, indeed, which will alone justify the concept. Both Aristotle and St. Thomas maintain that truth is the object of the science of ontology; but it is not the subjective truth of propositions; it is the objective truth of things. If the starting point is the concept of "being" in general, the aim is the discovery of the first and ultimate principle and cause of all "being." Hence for Aristotle implicitly and for St. Thomas explicitly the whole of metaphysics is directed to the proof of God, Who is the First Cause and the Ultimate Purpose of "being" because He is Subsistent Being. Undoubtedly the most important problem in metaphysics which St. Thomas was called upon to resolve was the precise relation and difference between God, the First Cause, and the universe of things caused, for "being" is a predicate common in some fashion to both God and creatures. The difficulty arises from the fact that the metaphysical concept of "being as such"—itself a precision of the confused notion of "being" which is the common object of every intelligence arrived at by abstraction from all concrete and finite examples of "being"— seems either to be identical objectively with the divine "being" or else to be no more than a name. But it must be observed that there is an intermediate possibility, namely, that "being as such" is a *concept* abstracted by the mind but based upon the objective reality of individual beings. This concept of "being" is above all a concept of a proportion between two elements recognizable in all beings.

The nature of "being" cannot be adequately examined, therefore, without an examination of beings, that is to say, of individual objective things actually existing; and the peculiar value of the Aristotelian-Thomist metaphysic is its unswerving recognition of objective reality as the only starting point for all its inquiries into the nature of "being" even in its profoundest implications. The immediate result of such an examination is the recognition (a) of an unending variety of the things constituting 'this objective reality, (b) of their mutability, and (c) in each case of a subject in respect of which divers attributions are to be made. Thus we recognize that this thing we call *John* is a thing that has come into being, now exists as a separate entity, and will eventually pass out of being; and that of it we can predicate humanity, rationality, corporeity, size, shape, color and so on. All these attributions represent the *modes* in which John's being is recognized as qualified and determined, either substantially or accidentally. Besides the more obvious classifications of these modes (such as the predicables and categories of formal logic), there emerges the recognition of a composition in actual "being" which provides the key to the whole problem of "being," that, namely, of a potential and of an actual element whose interaction determines the unending variety of modes of "being" without doing violence to the unity and simplicity of "being" as such. These concepts of potentiality and actuality (*potentia et actus*) and their relationship are absolutely fundamental in the whole philosophy of Aristotle and St. Thomas; and as far as ontology is concerned they are signalized by the signification of the terms "essence" and "*esse*" which represent the two real and really distinct elements in all actual beings other than God.

The word "*esse*" represents the profoundest notion in Thomist ontology and to render it by the usual equivalent of "existence" is to run the risk of missing St. Thomas's solution of the whole problem of "being." The word "existence" is commonly taken to mean the final, common perfection added to things already endowed with many other and diverse perfections. Thus a man's existence is usually understood to be that final perfection, shared in common with all other existing things, which is added to the individual human nature already endowed with all the qualities and powers of body and soul. But for St. Thomas the word "*esse*" has a vastly wider content; for him *esse* and perfection are synonymous terms. Their oneness of meaning is best seen by the introduction of a third term which expresses the point of that oneness, namely "actuality." *Esse* means complete actuality, and actuality means perfection. If a so-called perfection is not actual (and therefore existent) it is not truly a perfection, but at most a capability of perfection; but if a perfection is actual and existent it is a mode of *esse*. If we consider the Archangel Gabriel, Mussolini, Jubilee the ape, and Cleopatra's Needle, we may say of all that they are existing, but there is a great difference between the *esse* of each of them; and this difference consists in the diverse measure or grade of actual perfection in each of these beings: the *esse* of each is the sum total of its own proper perfections. This is true not only of generic or specific perfections, whereby we say that the *esse* of an angel is generically different from that of a man, or the *esse* of a man specifically different from that of an ape. It is true also of individual perfections, so that the *esse* of each individual is different from that of every other individual; or, as St. Thomas has it: *Esse uniuscuiusque rei est ei proprium, et distinctum ab esse cuiuslibet alterius rei.*[6] In brief, therefore, we may say that the *esse* of a thing is the actuality of all those essential qualities or perfections that go to make up that actual thing. The *esse* of a thing denotes (and is) the degree of its actual perfection. The difference of degree may be either individual, specific, or generic; and according as the degree of actual perfection is greater, so is the thing higher in the scale of being.

There are many passages in St. Thomas's works where this notion of *esse* is expounded. We need quote only one here: "Every excellence of anything whatsoever is ascribed to it in respect of its *esse*, for no excellence would accrue to a man from his wisdom unless by means of it he were wise, and so it is with other qualities. Wherefore according to the mode of the *esse* of things so is the mode of their excellence. For things are said to be more or less excellent according as their *esse* is limited to some special mode of excellence, more or less imperfect, not because of the imperfection of *esse* itself (for they do not possess *esse* in the fullest way in which it can be possessed), but because they participate in *esse* in a particular and very imperfect way." It is quite evident that this common attribute is a mental abstraction. It prescinds entirely from the mode or quality of *esse* and from the mode of participation of *esse* and therefore from every kind of individual perfection; it is a useful concept, but it does not represent that constituent element of an actually existing thing which we have to distinguish, by a real distinction, from essence. It is existence but it is not *esse*, in the full meaning of the word. There is the root of my objection to the use of the word existence in this context; it expresses only an abstract concept of the most tenuous kind and takes no account of the actual perfection and mode of perfection that constitutes the actuality of real things.

But when we consider *esse* as a particular attribution (and it is in this sense that St. Thomas uses it in the important phrase we have quoted already: *Esse uniuscuiusque est ei proprium,* as well as in innumerable other passages), we are dealing with the actual perfections of an objective reality. It is clear that every individual thing differs in actual perfection; but from this very difference, and the hierarchy of greater and lesser which it implies, it is possible to effect another abstraction, namely the notion of *absolute* perfection. This notion will include both the completeness and fullness of individual perfections and the sum of all possible perfections; there will be no limit contained in it, neither of degree nor of extension. By this abstraction we obtain a true notion of *esse* in itself, rather in the way that we have a notion of *whiteness* as distinct from that of *white things*: it is perfection unlimited and absolute, actuality without any admixture of potency whatso-ever. It is to be noted, however, that this abstract *esse* cannot be postulated as a reality outside the mind; that would be to fall into the mistake of the Anselmic argument for the existence of God by making an unwarranted transition, as that argument does, from the ideal to the real order. From the *notion* of particular, limited perfections we can arrive only at an abstract *notion* of absolute, unlimited perfection; if our premises represent only some-thing in the mind, then our conclusion will represent only something in the mind. Nevertheless from actual and objective particular perfections we can argue, with metaphysical certainty by means of the principle of causality, to the actual and objective reality of absolute perfection, which is God. In this case our premises represent something in the real order, so that our con-clusion is also in the order of the real. That is the hidden principle, so often not realized, in St. Thomas's fourth proof for the existence of God; and it may be remarked in passing that any attempt to interpret that proof will necessarily fail if it is not based upon an understanding of the significance of *esse* in the thought of St. Thomas.

It is abundantly clear, therefore, that there is a world of difference between the abstract notion of absolute *esse* and the objective reality of absolute *esse* which is God. The former is nothing apart from the particulars from which it is abstracted, except as an idea in the mind. Just as the logical universal, like humanity, is nothing apart from the particular things which are said to share in that humanity, except, I say, as an idea in the mind. Yet there is a true foundation in the particulars for the statement that these latter participate, in their own individual way, in that general perfection which is called by the common name of *esse*. The point to note is that this abstract *esse* has no reality apart from the individual manifestations of it found in all things that are said to *be*.

Though we may justly use the logical universal, like humanity, as an analogy, there is this important difference between it and *esse*, namely, that whereas the universal must be regarded as a potency to be actualized in the individuals, *esse* must be regarded as an unqualified actuality to be limited in the individuals. Here we may remark St. Thomas's answer to the diffi-culty that it seems impossible to distinguish this unqualified actuality from the divine *esse* and that therefore the divine *esse* must be predicated of all things that are; this is pantheism. But, as he points out, while the divine *esse* is in itself unqualified and essentially incapable of any qualification or deter-mination, the abstract *esse* (though also to be considered in itself as unquali-fied perfection) is essentially patient of qualification or determination, and indeed is not an extra-mental reality until it is so determined and limited. Thus the essential difference between God and all other beings is manifest.

The Ontological Roots of Thomism

God *is* absolute and unlimited perfection; He is, therefore, absolute and infinite self-subsistent *esse*, whence He gives His name as "Who is" and it is His alone. In all other beings the limitation of *esse* is an essential element of their reality; without a determinate qualification of "perfection in general" to "this particular sort of perfection" they cannot actually be. Thus we do not say of any being but God: "This is 'Who is' " but "This is what an angel is, what a man is, what Peter is." In other words, such beings have that much perfection, that much actuality, that much *esse*, which is due to them and no more.

If *esse* must be limited thus in all things except God, there must be some principle of its limitation; and if *esse* represents actuality, the only thing that can limit it is potentiality. The relation of potentiality and actuality, and the objective reality of these two as the ontological principles of existing things, is not a discovery of St. Thomas; that was Aristotle's triumph, the groundwork of his whole philosophy of being. It is, indeed, the basis of any theory of causality, and therefore the justification of all science, whether speculative or practical. This Aristotelian thesis, and its corollary doctrine of "becoming," was adopted by St. Thomas in its entirety. But he was not content with it in the form he found it; he pushed the inquiry further and discovered a much more profound truth to which the Greek did not succeed in penetrating. He perceived that potentiality and actuality were not merely the principles of becoming but remained as the actual constituents of things that have come to be, and even of things, like the angels, which cannot be said to have come to be. In other words these principles have a static as well as a dynamic rôle, being actually constitutive of all existent things that are not pure actuality.

There is a twofold implication to be remarked in potency, namely, the capacity to receive perfection and the limitation of the perfection received. To use a rather crude example in the material order, an empty quart jug is capable of receiving a quart of liquid but its very capacity to receive a quart limits its receptivity to that amount; it could not receive more than a quart. Similarly a given potency is capable of receiving a given degree of perfection and excludes all other perfection. The point to be observed here is that once the capacity of any potency has been fulfilled, or actualized, this capacity obviously remains no longer; but in its rôle of principle of limitation the potency does remain, and it is in this respect that potency is to be regarded as a static constituent of actually existing things.

The other principle, namely, act or actuality, denotes perfection unqualified by limitation, but brought into connection with a given potency it is limited by the very fact of fulfilling the capacity of that potency. The relation of these two principles is, therefore, sufficiently clear. Our business now is to translate this relation into terms of essence and *esse*, which, according to the teaching of St. Thomas, are the constituent principles of all beings other than God.

Since we have already indicated the synonymity of actuality and *esse*, it remains to consider the term "essence." Essence is normally understood to be that which is expressed by the definition. But this is essence in the sense of the universal, whereas we are concerned here not with the universal but with the particular; we are not concerned, for example, with the constituent principles of humanity, but with those of Peter, James and John. Each of these, taken to be actually existing men, has a particular essence which can be known but cannot be defined by us. It is this individual essence that is in question when we are dealing with the real distinction of essence and *esse*. The individual essence is normally taken to mean the sum of all the actual and necessary perfections pertaining to this individual. But according to the teaching of St. Thomas, if he is read accurately, it is rather the *capacity* for these perfections; it is the real potency making these perfections possible, but not making them actual. Though in the realm of abstract thought essence is represented as an actuality, in the order of objective reality it represents a potency which is actualized only by conjunction with its complementary principle *esse*.

We have noted that whereas in God *esse* is self-subsistent and absolutely unlimited, in all other beings it is necessarily limited and therefore not self-subsistent. All created things are thus distinct from God and from each other precisely by the fact and mode of this limitation. The *esse* of each individual thing is proper to it and distinct from that of every other thing; but this distinction cannot be due to *esse* itself, for *esse* represents unlimited perfection and does not contain within itself any principle of distinction, which can only be effected by limitation. Therefore, according to St. Thomas,[7] this distinction in the *esse* of things is due to the fact that they have diverse essences or natures whereby they acquire or receive *esse* diversely. *Esse* is limited, therefore, by the essence which receives it, and their relationship is that of actuality and potency. Both are real principles and necessarily distinct from one another, otherwise the essence could not exercise a real limiting function in respect of *esse*. As far as created beings are concerned, *esse* is not precisely actuality but the principle of actuality. Essence, considered apart from *esse*, is a real capacity to receive that measure of perfection due to it; considered in conjunction with *esse*, as a joint principle of an existing reality, it is that which limits *esse* to a given grade of perfection.

In material beings there are two modes of composition: (1) that of matter and form, which constitutes the essence (specific or individual) but not the actuality of that essence; (2) that of essence and *esse*, to be found not only in beings composed of matter and form but in all created things, which constitutes the actual reality. In the angels there is no composition of matter and form; each angel is its own essence and therefore differs specifically from every other angel. In this the angel resembles God in a way not shared by lesser creatures. But that the angels should actually be in the world of objective reality does not belong to them by their essence, otherwise they would be uncaused, absolutely necessary, and independent of God; further, their own perfection would be unlimited and they would be in no way distinct from God. But if their perfection is limited there must be in them, as in all other finite things, a principle of limitation as well as of perfection or actuality; in other words there must be in them a composition of essence and *esse*. In God alone is there no such composition; in Him these two are one, or better, in Him there is no essence in the sense we now use the term but only *esse*. We may speak of God in terms known to us in their created significance; indeed we have no other way of speaking of Him. But we must take care to eliminate from them any element of defect or limitation. If we use the term "essence" of God, it is only because it is often employed to signify the sum of perfections pertaining to a particular being; in this sense the essence of God merely denotes the totality of divine perfection. But in its relation to *esse* it inevitably connotes defect and limitation, as we have explained. Thus we find in St. Thomas such phrases as these: "God has not a quiddity except His *esse*," "God has not an essence which is not His *esse*."[8]

It is possible, therefore, to establish a hierarchy of being in terms of essence and *esse*. At the summit is God, self-subsistent *esse*, absolute actuality and perfection in Whom there is nothing of potency or limitation of any kind. Below Him, separated by an infinitude, is the highest angel in which there is unimaginable perfection (*esse*) limited however by the potency (essence) into which that perfection has been received. As we descend in the scale of being perfection or *esse* becomes more and more restricted, the potential or limiting element more and more pronounced. With man a new and narrower element of restrictive potency appears because of the inclusion of matter in his essence; and from man downwards the restriction of the content of *esse* is continued until the lowest grade of perfection is reached in the world of inanimate reality. In the ascending scale the perfection of the lower is included in that of the higher and exceeded by it; and in the highest created being is contained all the perfection of all the rest. In each degree the appropriate perfection results from *esse*, while the capacity for and delimitation of that perfection pertains to the essence.

It has been necessary to give a somewhat technical summary of St. Thomas's doctrine on this point in order that its significance may be the better understood. *It is the philosophical basis of the whole of Thomism.* This latter is an investigation into reality, into God and creatures and the relation of creatures to God. To establish contact with reality the human mind must begin with those instances of reality immediately known to it; it must discover their perfections (or *esse*); and in discovering these perfections it discovers at the same time their limitations. From both these it can further conclude with absolute certainty to the objective reality of their causes, which alone will explain the actuality of those things whose *esse* is participated and therefore received from some other thing already itself actual. But the principle of causality includes this vitally important element, that there is a likeness, though not necessarily an adequate likeness, between effect and cause; and this likeness (as far as the efficient cause is concerned, above all) is a likeness of *esse*. The basis of this is clear; it is crystallized in the familiar Thomist phrase, *operatio sequitur esse*. It would be a great mistake to imagine that this is to be interpreted merely in the sense that that *esse* must be presupposed to operation. This is true, of course, and it establishes the necessity of a real and objective cause for every reality that is not self-caused; it is indeed, the root principle of all the proofs for the existence of God. But it implies more than the mere fact of the existence of the cause; it implies also that the mode or quality of the operation, and therefore of the effect, follows upon and reproduces in some way the mode or quality of the *esse* of the cause. So that, because the fact of existence and the mode of existence are indistinguishable in reality, the fact and mode of the existence of an effect, that is to say, its *esse*, gives knowledge of the fact and the mode of existence, i.e., the *esse,* of its cause. This necessary relation of similitude of *esse* or perfection between effect and cause does not give complete knowledge of the cause, even when the *esse* of the effect is completely known, except in the case of univocal causality. It gives a true, but inadequate, knowledge— knowledge expressed in analogy. By this means we are able to establish with apodictic certainty (1) the fact of the existence of God, (2) the absolute unchangeableness, necessity, and limitlessness, of the divine *esse*, (3) the universal causality, efficient, final and exemplary, of the divine *esse*, (4) the distinction of all other beings from God and their absolute dependence on Him, signified in their limited perfection, that is in their entitative composition of essence and *esse*, and (5) something of the modality and nature of the divine *esse*, by a recognition of the actual perfections of all known beings through their diverse essences which make these perfections possible by their real potentiality, and by the mental exclusion of all the limitations which those same essences imply. This catalogue alone would justify the contention that as profound an understanding as possible of the doctrine of the real distinction of essence and *esse* is of superlative importance to those who seek to follow the Angelic Doctor in his investigation into reality.

The Ontological Roots of Thomism

St. Thomas Aquinas is a metaphysician *par excellence* because he is concerned entirely and only with the real. He has no use for, nor interest in, speculation for its own sake. He does not consider a thesis or a system to be true because it happens to hang together logically. For him, truth is not merely a thing of the mind, but it is the correspondence of the mind to the thing outside the mind, to something that is real, to something that *is*, quite apart from the mind that knows it. Things are vastly more important than thought, unless thought is the outcome of contact with things, in which case thought becomes valuable because it is true. And truth itself is of value only when it is used in the pursuit of wisdom, and wisdom consists not only in the knowledge of the First Cause but also in the effort to reach the Last End, and the First Cause and the Last End is God. That is the value of reality, of things, as far as we are concerned. From contact with the reality immediately known to us, we can make contact with a whole universe of created reality, and even with uncreated reality itself, and so fulfill the purpose of all knowledge and of life itself. And the primary principle to be recognized is that of the real distinction of *esse* and essence, because that is the common condition and constituent of reality in all created things.

Thus Aquinas begins his synthesis of wisdom by registering certain obvious modifications of material reality, like movement or change, causality, contingence, grades and limits of perfection, and order. From these he proves the fact of God's existence and something of its content; but he could not do this unless he started with real things, existing material things. By starting with things that are and by keeping clearly before his eyes the implications of their potential and actual principles with their interaction one on another, he is able to develop a logical synthesis in which every detail has its counterpart in the world of reality. He does not theorize as to what God might be or could be; he establishes facts about God, His goodness, His infinity, His omnipotence, His intellect, His will, His providence and premotion. Given the divine revelation of supernatural truth, he even probes marvellously into the mystery of the divine Trinity itself. He is so sure of himself because he is so sure of the difference and relation of uncreated and created *esse* expressed in the analogy of proportion and proportionality which he sees must exist between them. As far as St. Thomas is concerned, this analogy can be established only by means of the real distinction of essence and *esse*. Similarly in his analysis of creation, of the multiplicity of created things, of the angelic spirits, and of man, the same principle underlies and guarantees his investigations and conclusions. Indeed, to exhaust its content one would have to introduce every treatise in the *Summa Theologica*.

The intention here is not to defend or expound a thesis of Thomism, but to indicate an approach to reality, an approach that is connatural to the human mind for it is by way of a principle that embodies the basis of composition and division, and the method of human knowing is *componendo* and *dividendo*. It is therefore a principle that enables us (1) to know in a human way, (2) to know with metaphysical certitude, and (3) to know the real. After all, we are, or should be, like St. Thomas, interested not in theses or systems but in reality and truth; and these two are one. Stated as a mere philosophical principle, it may seem to be an arid and unhelpful piece of mental subtlety; but translate it into terms of grass and trees and flowers, of birds and animals, of the sun and the stars, of men and angels, and the whole universe of created perfection; get from all these some understanding of what *esse*, actuality, perfection, really stands for, and go on from this to learn something of what God is, *Esse Subsistens,* absolute and unlimited perfection, to learn how all these came from God, are the products of the divine mind, replicas (however inadequate) of the divine beauty, dependent on God, created not for themselves but for Him.

There is this to be said for the humanism and realism of today; they recognize the value of real things, at any rate those that are immediately perceptible. Their perniciousness lies in this, that they do not recognize the limitations of those realities nor the further and more important realities which those limitations imply. We might well say that they are concerned with *esse* and ignore essence, but by the ignoring of essence they fail to appreciate *esse*. It is not sufficient to say: "God saw all the things that He had made; and they were very good," and then confine oneself to a few material things and think they are good in an absolute sense. Perhaps the most important word in that quotation from Holy Scripture is the word *"all"*; for the true perfection of created things is appreciated only when they are seen in their distinction and relation to one another, and their hierarchic subordination to Him Who made them. But for those who are interested in the sciences of philosophy and theology the temptation is to err in a contrary sense. Because intellectual knowledge comes to us through the medium of universal essences abstracted from material realities, we may tend to become enclosed in a world of thought and ideas which are not related to life and activity. Through our excessive interest in essence we may lose sight of *esse*, ignoring in practice the fact that it is the complementary interaction of both these that alone constitutes reality as we can know it.

Sixth Essay

THE ROLE OF HABITUS
IN THE THOMISTIC METAPHYSICS
OF POTENCY AND ACT

by

Vernon J. Bourke

The Role of Habitus in the Thomistic Metaphysics of Potency and Act

THE theory of potency and act lies at the very foundations of the metaphysics of St. Thomas. Its ramifications spread throughout all the branches of his thought. From it Thomism derives much of its characteristic specificity as a philosophy. But the part played by the concept of habitus in this theory is, perhaps, not sufficiently recognized in many of the recent expositions of Thomistic metaphysics. It is the purpose of this study to situate habitus within this dualism of potency and act.

The term potency was first used to name a capacity of men or animals to operate.[1] Then it was extended to cover the notion of any physical force. Of course, potency is not known directly, in itself, but in function of the act to which it is directed.[2] Thus, there are two types of act, first act which is form, and second act which is operation, and the potency which is directed toward the first act is passive potency, while the potency which corresponds to operational act is active potency. There are, then, two basic sorts of potency: (i) *potency for existence,* and (ii) *potency for action.*[3]

If we consider first that potency which is directed toward operation (because it is the easier for the human mind to understand)[4] we find that it, too, can be subdivided into active and passive operational potencies. This was a division which Aristotle had stressed, when he defined active potency as: "the principle of change, which changes something other than itself, insofar as it is other," and passive, operative potency as: "the principle of passive change, by which a thing is enabled to undergo a change caused in it by another agent, insofar as it is other."[5] Every natural operation requires these two principles; active potency is the source of the action, but it cannot act upon itself; passive potency is the recipient of the actuation from the active potency and it is in the passive potency that the change occurs, which constitutes the action. This analysis is taken over by St. Thomas.[6] He points out that, even in the case of a self-moving agent, the metaphysical principle which initiates the action cannot be identical with the principle which receives the actuation.

This prepares us for the interpretation of a remarkable text at the beginning of St. Thomas's *Question on the General Nature of Virtue.*[7] He begins by describing three different kinds of operative potencies. The first is wholly active in its original state; it requires, and can have, nothing added to it to bring it to the apex of its power. It is a *virtus* because its potency is metaphysically complete within its species.[8] Examples of this type of wholly active potency are: the divine potency, the agent intellect, and physical forces. There can be no question of the development of habitus in these potencies, because they are metaphysically perfect in their original condition. A second kind of operative potency is wholly passive; it does not act unless actuated by an active potency. This sort of passive potency is perfected for the action proper to it by the advent of a quality which is present only during the time of actual operation. This quality is called a passion and it does not belong to the same species of quality as habitus.[9] Since these passions do not remain in the passive potency after the actual operation has ceased, there is no possibility of metaphysical development in these wholly passive potencies. The sense powers (considered simply in themselves without rational control) belong to this second type of wholly passive potency, in which no habitus formation is found.

It is only when we come to the third kind of operative potency that the possibility, and need, of habitus is found. These last potencies are a sort of metaphysical scandal; they are of a nature which seems to go beyond the limits of the simple theory of potency and act. They are at once active and passive, *agentes et actae*. It is true that they must be actuated by their corresponding active potencies, but this actuation does not, as in the case of wholly passive potencies, determine them to one, and only one, sort of operation. Even under the influence of active potency, these powers retain, within well-defined limits, their ability to control their own operations. What is produced in these potencies, under the actuation of active potency, is not merely a passion but a quality, of the nature of a form, which remains after the period of actuation has ceased. The rational powers of man are examples of potencies which can be thus metaphysically developed, or brought to the condition of *virtus*, by the growth of acquired qualities which are called *habitus*.[10]

St. Thomas, himself, suggests at the end of the text from the *De Virtutibus in Communi* that there is more in the historical background of his theory of habitus than the few remarks about *hexis* to be found in Aristotle. The definitions of Averroës and St. Augustine are cited. Of these, the

Augustinian concept and usage of habitus in the definition of virtue[11] is the less important in the field of metaphysics, precisely because Augustine knew habitus only as a *logical* subdivision of quality (from his reading of the *Categories*, c. 8, and through Cicero's somewhat misleading use of the term in his famous definition of virtue[12]) and was unaware of its function in the theory of potency and act. Among Christian authors up to the end of the twelfth century (i.e., those whom St. Albert, for instance, groups together as the *Sancti*), habitus does not appear to advance beyond this rather shallow, categorical usage.

So, it is to the *Philosophi*, the Greek Commentators on Aristotle, and the Arabian philosophers, that we must look for a metaphysically significant notion of habitus in the period between Aristotle and St. Thomas. The *Commentary on the Categories* by Simplicius, written in the sixth century, was translated from Greek to Latin in the year 1266.[13] Through this work St. Thomas was presented with an analysis of habitus which seems to owe something to Stoic antecedents as well as to the theory of Aristotle. In the course of his discussion of the first species of quality, which includes disposition and habitus, Simplicius emphasized a definition given in the *Metaphysics* of Aristotle.[14] "Disposition," wrote Simplicius, "means a sort of arrangement of that which has parts, either in regard to place, or potency, or form."[15] In the *Prima Secundae* (which postdates the year 1266) this passage from Simplicius is cited as a means of clarifying the relations between disposition and habitus. St. Thomas points out[16] that the first kind of dispositions, which order their subject in regard to place, belong properly in the category *situs*, and they are merely corporeal arrangements. Those which dispose their subjects in regard to potency are dispositions belonging to the first species of quality, but since their end is the imperfection of potency, rather than the perfection of act or form, they are not habitus. The third kind of disposition, orders its subject in regard to form and it is a perfect disposition, i.e., a habitus. Basic in all of this is the idea that the subject of a disposition, on any of the three levels, *must have parts*. Now, St. Thomas adds that science and the perfected virtues are examples of habitus, and the question arises: how can the subjects of science and the virtues have parts?

Since we are here dealing with potencies, such as the possible intellect in the case of science, the will and the sense appetites participating in reason in the case of the moral virtues, which are without physical parts, it is clear that "parts" has a special meaning in this case. St. Thomas understands it in reference to the multiplicity of acts toward which these potencies are naturally ordered, and a plurality of agencies which eventually occur in the determination of the subject toward one specific end.[17] Thus, these potencies, which are capable of habituation, have parts in the sense that they are not by nature determined to act in one way only, but can act in a variety of ways. In this lies their essential freedom; they may be used well or badly, with varying degrees of expertness and accuracy. That these, as it were "extrinsic parts," are unified by a sort of commensuration which results in the state known as habitus, is a rather static concept, which St. Thomas seems to owe to Simplicius, and behind it lies, very probably, the Stoic idea of *schema*, a structural ordering of a complex material subject.[18]

For reasons inherent in the Mohammedan religion the early Arabian philosophers developed a highly complicated theory of "stages" of the human intellect. They stressed the dependency of human intellection on higher, celestial intelligences to such an extent that in some cases very little power of native understanding was granted man. From the time of Al Kindi (ninth century), many Arabic treatises were written to show how the human soul, possessed at birth of little more than the apprehensive potencies of internal sense, could be so influenced by the immediate actuation of an Agent Intelligence that it would rise to moments of actual understanding. After this transitory actuation had ceased, the original capacity of man for understanding did not necessarily revert to its first state of pure potentiality. It was thought to be prepared and perfected by actual intellection, thereby acquiring an improved capacity for re-actuation. Obviously this opened the way for a theory of different levels, or stages, of potency for understanding in the human soul. The stages intermediary between the intellect in pure potency and the intellect wholly in act were called perfections, or habitus, of the original power.[19]

That this Arabian theory represents an important development of the original Aristotelian teaching on the potential and agent intellects is beyond doubt. When St. Thomas read Avicenna and Averroës, he encountered and profited by this amplification of Aristotle. It provided him with a dynamic notion of habitus, to which his citation of Averroës[20] makes due reference and acknowledgment. Habitus becomes, not a mere automatic conditioning of a power as the modern term "habit" connotes but the metaphysical growth of a basic potency for operation. It does not decrease the activity of the intellect, or tend toward the semi-conscious repetition of a routine action as is suggested in much of the recent literature of habituation. It does not diminish the element of voluntary control, or verge upon involuntary, automatic, and so non-human, activity. Rather it represents an increase in the power of intellect and will, a vital growth of originally imperfect potencies. It is a metaphysical perfectant, heightening man's rational capacities to such an extent that he who acts with a habituated intellect, and will, approaches the optimum performance of the strongest and most perfect human being.

This is the key to the oft-repeated statement of St. Thomas, that habitus is a mean between potency and act: *habitus medio modo se habet inter potentiam et actum purum.*[21] If the original state of an operative be that of pure potency, then habitus is a new state of that potency in which it is somewhat in act without being wholly in act. As a principle of operation, it is in potency in regard to the act which is operation; as a quality, it is already in act.[22] This introduces the need of a terminological distinction of acts. The act which is operation is called second act, or second perfection; that which brings the potency to the state in which it can perform its specific operation perfectly is called first act, first perfection, *virtus,* or habitus. Thus we have the development of a term, intentionally complex in meaning, denoting a condition in which its subject is at once in act and in potency. This is neither ambiguous, nor paradoxical, for that to which it is in potency (i.e., perfect operation) is quite different from that to which it is in act (i.e., pure, indeterminate potency).

All that has been said up to now, has had particular reference to operational potency. Did St. Thomas assign an equally important rôle to habitus in the sphere of potency for being, for *esse?* It is well known that St. Thomas regarded potency for being as metaphysically prior to potency for operation, though it is not prior in the order of cognition. It is a commonplace in Thomistic philosophy that there is no half-way house between existence and non-existence. Hence it would appear that there is no room here for that sort of mediation which habitus supplies between operative potency and act. From this point of view we should be inclined to say that there are no entitative habitus.[23]

However, Aristotle had used examples of such states as health and sickness in his explanation of habitus.[24] These states of the body are not the proximate principles of action, and thus it appears that there are some habitus which are not immediately operative. St. Thomas does not admit, however, that these bodily states should be called habitus. He suggests that at most they would be *habitual dispositions.*[25] Their causes are not such that they can provide these bodily states with the permanence necessary to habitus. Hence, though we have conditions of the body which approach the notion of entitative habitus, there are in fact no entitative habitus in bodies.

On the other hand, if we consider the soul as the possible subject of entitative habitus, we meet with the obvious difficulty that the soul is a *forma completiva.* In itself the soul is the only existential perfection naturally possible to a human being.[26] It is only with regard to a super-nature that the soul could become the subject of an entitative habitus. This does occur in the case of habitual grace, which raises the soul to a supernatural level of existence, in which the soul participates in the divine Nature.[27] Thus, from the point of view of Christian theology, which obviously has wider horizons than the purely Aristotelian philosophy of nature, there is a place for a type of habitus which perfects the essence of the human soul and not merely its potencies for operation.[28] Of course, grace is a habitus in an analogical sense. The Aristotelian concept of habitus is that of a species of quality, i.e., a category of natural being. The meaning of the term habitus is enlarged, and changed considerably, when applied to a supernatural quality.

There are also applications of the theory of habitus higher than those to be found in the philosophy of man. Among the Greek Fathers, in whose teaching the angelic world plays a prominent part, there was a tendency to think that the angels could have no habitus, since habitus is an accident and they thought that angels were essences without accidents.[29] But, as St. Thomas pointed out in this connection, the angels are not pure acts, they are limited in all cases by some potency though they are not limited by the potency of matter. Hence, their intellects and wills do require some perfecting by habitus in order to attain to the knowledge and love of God.[30] These angelic habitus are not, of course, identical with those of the human soul, but they are perfectants which fall within the range of the general metaphysics of habitus.

Finally, we reach the peak rôle of the habitus concept in St. Thomas's speculations upon the Soul of Christ. In answer to the question: Does the Soul of Christ see the Word through some habitus? St. Thomas offers a terse, metaphysically magnificent, summary of his teaching on habitus.[31] He says that habitus, in its primary aspect, signifies something super-added to a potency, by which the potency is perfected in regard to its operation. Now a potency may require such a super-added complement, either because of the natural limitations of its subject, or because of the imperfection of the potency itself. An added perfectant is needed, for the first reason, if the potency is to be elevated for the performance of an operation which completely exceeds the natural capacity of its subject. Thus, the human soul needs the supernatural habitus of charity in order to rise to a sort of "social love" of God, which is the supernatural destiny of the human soul according to Christian theology. On the other hand, a habitus may be needed to perfect a potency, simply for the perfect performance of an operation which is entirely within the natural capacity of its subject. However, not all of the potencies of man, as has been seen already, are perfectible by habitus. The potency of vision, for instance, is actuated by a species which belongs in the type of qualities called *passiones*. These momentary perfections do not remain in the potency after it has ceased to be actuated. Properly speaking, it is only the intellective potencies of the human soul, or those participating in the life of reason, such as the sense appetites and some of the internal senses, which can be perfected by a super-added quality of the nature of habitus. The result of such habituation is the performance of operations which are enjoyable to the agent, quick in their execution, and easily done.[32]

The *anima Christi* needs something super-added to it for both of the foregoing reasons, that is, as a perfectant to make it capable of actions exceeding its natural powers, and as a complement to render its natural operations easy, prompt, and enjoyable.[33] For the first reason, it is clear that the Soul of Christ requires something added to it, to lift it above the limitations of the creature so that it may see the divine Essence. The supernatural light, fitting Christ for this vision and coming from the Creator, is, then, like a habitus (*ut habitus*) in the Soul of Christ.[34] And for the second reason, the Soul of Christ needs habitus also. Every created intellect achieves actual understanding by the addition to it of intelligible species. In the human intellect, these species are acquired through abstraction from the phantasms of sense. In the angelic intellect, the species are concreated or infused. But in the Soul of Christ, all these are present through the plenitude of grace. Through these species, the Christ-Soul knows, not the Word, but the world of created things. Two habitus, then, are added to the Soul of Christ: the first is the *lumen* elevating it to the knowledge of what lies above it; the second is that collection of intelligible species enabling it to know other creatures.[35]

Habitus has been seen to play the rôle of a mean between the imperfection of potency and the perfection of act. It is a supple, metaphysical principle, participating in the nature of both actuality and potentiality. The study of its essence leads us to the very core of Thomistic metaphysics. The investigation of its applications would take us over the whole of St. Thomas's philosophy of man; into the theology of the supernatural organism which is man elevated to a new level by habitual grace, an organism with its own operative habitus, the infused moral and theological virtues, and the Gifts of the Holy Spirit; finally to the very door-step of God, where we would find the habitual perfectants of that nature which is above all other creatures, the Soul of Christ.

Seventh Essay

THE NATURE OF THE ANGELS

by

John O. Riedl

The Nature of the Angels

I

THE primary purpose of this paper is to analyze the *De Substantiis Separatis* which is unique among the treatises of St. Thomas on the angels. St. Thomas had written on the subject beginning with the *De Ente et Essentia* and his commentary on the *Sentences* and continuing through the two *Summas* and the *De Spiritualibus Creaturis*. In all of these works he made use of the opinions of other men, but in the *De Substantiis Separatis*[1] he set down as his primary purpose to gather from every source material about the excellence of the holy angels. The result is that he considered in detail the opinions of men from ancient times and bequeathed to later ages a source book which is an excellent indication of the writings that were available in Latin in his own day. The only difficulty is that he did not always record the exact source, but left it for his readers to discover what books he used. To trace these sources will be the secondary purpose of this paper.

The *De Substantiis Separatis* is dedicated to Reginald of Piperno, a Dominican who was friend and companion to St. Thomas from 1261 until the latter's death in 1274, and it must therefore have been one of his later writings. Grabmann,[2] arguing from St. Thomas's use of William of Moerbeke's Latin translation of Proclus's *Elements of Theology*, concludes that the *De Substantiis Separatis* was written after July, 1268. Mandonnet[3] gives 1272-1273 as the probable time. In the prologue St. Thomas states merely that he was unable to be present at the solemn celebration in honor of the angels[4] and, since he did not want to spend the time of this devotion idly, he intended to make up for his omission in the chanting of psalms by a more diligent application to the task of writing.

St. Thomas also states in the prologue that he is making the survey of the opinions of others in regard to the angels, "so that we may accept any views we find that accord with our faith, and refute whatever views are opposed to Catholic doctrine." His intention of using Holy Scripture as the criterion, however, does not prevent him from coming to grips philosophically with those men whose opinions he evaluates, and from employing in his criticism the very principles to which they themselves either assented explicitly or would have to assent in order to remain true to their basic philosophy. The result, therefore, which St. Thomas achieves is not an agglomeration of instances in which his predecessors were found to have disagreed with a revelation which most of them either did not know or did not recognize as divine, but a unity of truth attained in the light of Holy Scripture by means of a progressive series of philosophical decisions regarding the doctrines of his predecessors.

The treatise itself is divided into eighteen chapters.[5] In chapters 1 to 3 St. Thomas deals with the early naturalists, who tried to explain the universe by a purely material cause without any intelligences whatsoever, and with the more satisfactory doctrine of the Platonists and of Aristotle as regards the existence of intelligences between God and man. In chapters 4 to 6 he expounds and criticizes the doctrine of Avicebron that angels are constituted of matter and form. In chapter 7 he treats of those who hold that the intelligences are uncaused; in chapter 8 of Avicenna's doctrine of intermediate creators; in chapter 9, of the Platonist doctrine that the intelligences were all created simultaneously and equal. In chapters 11 to 14 he has an elaborate discussion and refutation of those who deny to the intelligences and to God a proper knowledge of singulars and providence over them. In chapter 15 he deals with the egregious error of the Manichaeans. Finally, in chapters 16 to 18 he gives the Catholic doctrine as found in Holy Scripture and in Dionysius the Areopagite.

II

St. Thomas begins his consideration of the "opinions in regard to the angels which were held by men in ancient times," with those who were first to philosophize about the natures of things. These men, he says, were of the opinion that only bodies existed and that the first principles of all things were certain corporeal elements, either one or several or an unlimited number. Among those who held that the first principle was one are Thales of Miletus who made it water, Diogenes of Apollonia who made it air, Anaximander who made it fire, and Heraclitus who made it vapor. Empedocles is among those who insisted on a limited number of elements; he said that there were four, together with the two moving forces of friendship and strife. Democritus and Anaxagoras are among those who said that the principles were unlimited in number, and thus it is easily explained why "none of these men nor any of their followers believed in the existence of incorporeal substances such as we call angels." All agreed, however, that their corporeal principles were divine.

The similarity of this enumeration with that in the first book of Aristotle's *Metaphysics*[6] can be seen at a glance. The only disturbing factor is the erroneous attribution of the doctrine of fire to Anaximander and of vapor to Heraclitus. The Latin phrase is "aut ignem, ut Anaximander; aut vaporem, ut Heraclitus." If the words, "ut Anaximander; aut vaporem," are stricken, the remaining words are correct. Since Anaximander is not in Aristotle's enumeration, the words referring to him may be an interpolation. Heraclitus would then properly be credited in the text with the doctrine of fire, and Anaximander would properly be credited in the interpolated portion with the doctrine of vapor.

St. Thomas extends Aristotle's enumeration by referring, first, to the Epicureans who, he admits, "held to the existence of certain gods, but they made these gods corporeal since they gave them human shape";[7] and second, to the Sadducees who "taught that there was no such thing as an Angel or a Spirit."[8]

Instead of attempting in his own name a refutation of the position of these ancient naturalists, St. Thomas lets a discussion of the doctrines of Anaxagoras, Plato and Aristotle[9] suffice to show that the world cannot be explained merely through material causes.

Anaxagoras, he says, introduced intellect, "which was in itself altogether unmixed and had nothing in common with corporeal nature," as a principle of distinction among things,[10] for, since all corporeal elements were mixed together, there seemed to be no other way in which bodies could be made distinct from one another. St. Thomas says that Anaxagoras is nearer the truth in that he appealed to something other than material causes, but since the intellect is unique in being entirely unmixed he should have made it a universal principle of existence and not merely a principle of distinction. At all events his doctrine fails to yield any information in regard to "the separate, incorporeal substances which we call angels."

Plato developed more adequate arguments[11] against the opinions of the early natural philosophers. He substituted an order of unchanging natures for the flux of corporeal things which the early naturalists had tried to make the basis of man's knowledge. These unchanging natures are of two kinds: the mathematicals; and the universals, which Plato also calls ideas and species.

At this point St. Thomas turns from Aristotle's analysis of Plato to an elaboration of the Platonic philosophy which would be hard to find either in Plato or in Aristotle.[12] The significant feature is the division into gods, intellects and souls which is the identical division in Proclus's *Elements of Theology*, thus leaving very little doubt that the *Elements* are the source.[13]

The passage begins with St. Thomas's statement that, according to Plato, the idea of the one-and-good is supreme, and thus corresponds to the notion of God,[14] and that under this highest God are different orders of substances which participate and are participated in. The first of these orders is that of the lesser gods which St. Thomas identifies with the order of ideas and species.[15] Now these lesser gods are differentiated one from the other according as they in their own individual natures participate more closely in the unity of the one-and-good. Below this order of lesser gods or species is an order of separate intellects which participate in them. The highest of these intellects most accurately in its own nature participates in the species which it knows. Below this highest intellect are ranged the other intellects in proportion as each is most participative of the highest. Below the order of intellects is a series of orders of souls. These souls all animate bodies.

The order to which they belong will depend on the degree to which they participate in intellect, and to an extent also on the kind of body in which they are incorporated. Thus there is an order of souls which inhabit the highest heaven and the heavens below it.[16] Then there is an order of souls which inhabit bodies which are of an aërial stuff and entirely free from the element of earth; these souls are the demons.[17] And then there are orders of souls inhabiting earthly bodies, beginning with men and extending to the lowest levels of living things. Below all these orders of souls are the orders of bodies which participate to a greater or less degree in the order of souls; thus some bodies are animate to a high degree, e.g., the bodies of the heavens, and some are not animate at all.

St. Thomas summarizes this discussion with the observation that "the Platonists" held to the existence of four orders of intelligences between God and man: the lesser gods or ideas or species, the separate intellects, the souls of the heavens, and the demons. He questions whether the last two groups can be identified with the angels of the Holy Scripture. As regards the souls of the heavens he follows the opinion of St. Augustine,[18] that if there are souls of the heavens—and it is a doubtful matter that the heavens are animate—then they could be called angels. As regards the demons, he follows the authority of Holy Scripture[19] in which they are called angels.

He then reverts in the beginning of chapter 2 to the text of Aristotle, and shows by the reasoning of Aristotle[20] that Plato is wrong in holding that universals have a separate and subsistent existence apart from singulars and that mathematicals exist apart from sensible things, for universals are nothing more than essences of particular things, and mathematicals the certain limits of sensible bodies.

St. Thomas then investigates the "clearer and more sound" method of Aristotle who proceeds from a consideration of motion,[21] by way of the two principles that everything which is moved is moved by another, and that there cannot be an infinite series of movers and things moved, to the conclusion that there is a first mover unmoved, and also a first moved which is moved by itself in the sense that one of its parts moves another and thus accidentally moves the whole. Now the thing moved is moved with an eternal motion, and therefore the power that moves it must be infinite and, since infinite, incorporeal. Furthermore,[22] since into the discussion about movable things that which is desirable enters as something which moves without being moved whereas that which desires moves and is moved, the first immovable mover must hold the position of a desirable good whereas the first mover that moves itself must be moved by a desire of the first immovable mover. And since the highest in the order of desires and of objects of desire is the intellectual desire of the good-in-itself, the first moved must have desire and intelligence. But since only bodies can be moved, the first moved must be a body animated by an intellectual soul, and this is the first heaven. All the lower spheres of the heavenly bodies have a similar nature, and each has its separate object of desire which is the proper end of its motion. But some heavenly bodies have several motions and so Aristotle concludes that the number of separate substances which are objects of desire must be equal to the number of motions.[23] Since, however, there are no animate bodies below the heavenly bodies other than those of animals and plants,[24] Aristotle puts only two orders of intelligences between God and man, namely the separate intellects and the souls of the heavens.

St. Thomas criticizes Aristotle's position as less adequate than the view of Plato on two points: The first of these is that it does not afford a rational explanation of many phenomena such as in the case of men who are possessed by demons and in the operations of magicians. Some followers of Aristotle have attempted to supply the rational explanation by an appeal to the influence of the heavenly bodies, as can be seen from the *Letter of Porphyry to Anebantes the Egyptian*.[25] Thus it is claimed that under certain constellations magicians can produce extraordinary effects, such as predicting future events. While it is conceivable that some of these things could occur through the heavenly bodies, there are some which cannot possibly be explained by a corporeal cause, such as: (1) in cases of possession, absolute idiots speaking a foreign language gracefully; and (2) in the operations of magicians, the inducing of apparitions which, it is said, answer questions and move about. The Platonists by their doctrine of demons, afford the possibility of a satisfactory explanation of effects such as these.

The second point of inferiority in Aristotle's doctrine is the limitation of the number of immaterial substances to the number of the corporeal. It is not fitting that this be done, for it implies that the higher exist for the sake of the lower, whereas the opposite is true. It would be a mistake to attempt to determine with accuracy the nature of an end by considering the things which are directed to that end, or to attempt to estimate the greatness and power of higher things by considering the greatness and power of lower things. Now it is not unreasonable for Aristotle to assume that every motion of the heavens is ordained to one star, and that all higher substances which are impassible and immaterial are final causes, but it does not necessarily follow that the number of the immaterial substances must therefore be the same as the number of the heavenly movements. There is no reason to suppose, for example, that the highest heaven must have as its proximate end the highest immaterial substance which is the supreme God. It is more probable, since everything must in some way be proportionate to its proximate end, that some intelligence that is lower than the first is its proximate end. And as the difference between the intelligences and the bodies which are directed to them becomes greater, the possibility of their having the highest substance in any order as their proximate end decreases. Thus the number of immaterial substances might very well be much greater than Aristotle said. In fact, he himself hesitates, for he says, "Let it remain for more courageous intellects to call this necessary."[26]

St. Thomas ends the discussion by showing that there is no cause for objecting to Aristotle's reasoning on grounds of his contention that motion is eternal, for "if one follows carefully the reasoning on which his proof is based he will find that it still holds good when the hypothesis of eternal motion is withdrawn." This ends the section in which St. Thomas expounds the opinions of Anaxagoras, Plato and Aristotle as refutation of the opinions of the ancient philosophers. In the *De Spiritualibus Creaturis*, however, where an exactly similar order has been followed, but not in such detail, St. Thomas rejects the methods of proof of all three philosophers as unsatisfactory, "for we cannot admit the mixture of sensible things with Anaxagoras, nor the abstraction of universals with Plato, nor the perpetuity of motion with Aristotle; and so we must prove the existence of angels by other ways."[27] The only disturbing note is that St. Thomas here seems to connect Aristotle's proof of immaterial substances necessarily with his doctrine of the eternity of motion. Since St. Thomas positively asserts in the *De Substantiis Separatis* that this is not so, he may be trying to give us here a fourth proof for the existence of immaterial substances which is more profound than the three which he gives in the *De Spiritualibus Creaturis*.

III

The third chapter of the *De Substantiis Separatis* is a unit in itself. St. Thomas has already allowed Aristotle to refute the basic doctrine of Plato,[28]

The Nature of the Angels

it he has commended Plato[29] (=Proclus) for having propounded the ghly satisfactory doctrine of demons, and for not having placed undue limits a the number of immaterial substances as did Aristotle. Aristotle, however, clearer and more sound as regards his method of investigation,[30] so that not en his principle of the eternity of motion vitiates his demonstration.[31] His istake is the minor one of having placed more limits on the number of amaterial substances than even his own principles would require.[32] He ade the mistake because of his highly laudable effort not to depart very far om those things which are manifest to the senses.[33] In fact it is not really complete mistake, for he himself says that the number he assigns is not ecessarily so but only probable.[34]

Now St. Thomas may not be entirely satisfied with the demonstration of ristotle. He does not commit himself definitely to it anywhere in the *De abstantiis Separatis*. It involves the doctrine of the animation of the heavens which he is in doubt.[35] But even if he denied that the heavens are animate, there might still be a way, "ad salvandum intentionem Platonis et ristotelis,"[36] of showing that the doctrine is not a necessary part of the emonstration.

Although there may still be reason for doubt regarding St. Thomas's attitude towards Aristotle's demonstration of the existence of immaterial substances, there is no doubt regarding his attitude towards Aristotle's opinion their origin, nature, distinction, and relation to things below them. He is eartily in agreement with him on all points except that of distinction, in hich he says the Platonists are more correct. He shows in chapter 3 that lato and Aristotle agree on the other three points. He then makes this composite doctrine of Plato and Aristotle the criterion for discovering and refuting the errors in the opinions of others which he discusses in chapters 4 to 15. inally, in chapter 16 he sets down as his purpose in this and the remaining aapters to show what Christian belief has to say on each of the four points the teaching of Plato and Aristotle.

It can thus be seen that the composite doctrine of Plato and Aristotle is ot lost sight of throughout the treatise, and that it becomes the means of xpressing St. Thomas's own mind on the subject. It will, therefore, be tting for us to analyze this doctrine in detail.

St. Thomas summarizes the doctrine by the device of listing the points in hich Plato and Aristotle agree, and those in which they disagree.

(1) In the first place they agree on the way in which immaterial substances exist. For Plato held that all the lower immaterial substances are ae and good by participation in the first which is the one-and-good-inself.[37] St. Thomas interprets this participation in terms of causality, and

concludes that according to Plato the highest God is the cause of the unity and the goodness of all immaterial substances.

St. Thomas frequently adverts to the Platonic reasoning that the existence of the partial good implies the existence of the complete good. But he invariably gives the argument a twist—which Plato may or may not have intended—so that the partial in any specific attribute, be it good or hot or luminous or true, is always representative of the partial in being, that is, the contingent. Nowhere is this tendency of St. Thomas more evident than in the fourth of the arguments for the existence of God, which is called the argument from the gradations in things.[38] The argument begins with the more and less good, true and noble; continues with the observation that the more or less in any attribute implies the maximum to give it meaning and concludes that there must therefore be something which is utmost being for according to Aristotle[39] those things that are greatest in truth are greatest in being. The relation of the partial to the complete is then shown to be a causal one, and the conclusion is drawn that there must exist "something which is to all beings the cause of their being, goodness and every other perfection; and this we call God."

Because of this interpretation of Plato, St. Thomas is in a position, when he comes to discuss Aristotle's view concerning the way in which immaterial substances exist, to say that it agrees with that of Plato, and he can quote in support of his contention the passage from the *Metaphysics*[40] that what has being and truth in the highest degree must necessarily be the cause of being and truth for all others.

(2) The second point of agreement which St. Thomas lists is concerning the nature of immaterial substances. For both Plato and Aristotle held that all such substances are absolutely free from matter although they are not all without composition of potency and act. In Plato's doctrine of participating beings, that which they receive as a participation must be act, and thus they must have composition of potency and act. But the highest being does not participate in any other and therefore lacks composition.[41] In Aristotle the notion of the true and the good pertains to act,[42] and therefore the highest true and the good must be pure act, and all others must contain some admixture of potency.

(3) The third point of agreement is as regards the nature of providence. Plato[43] holds that the one-and-good-in-itself must, in accordance with the primary meaning of goodness, exercise providence over everything below it and that each being in each of the orders of being exercises providence not only as regards the beings below it in its own order, but also as regards the beings in the orders which are below its order. Thus the Platonists hold

that the demons exercise providence over men, for they say[44] that the demons are mediators between us and the higher substances.

St. Thomas takes the twelfth book of the *Metaphysics*[45] as the basis of his discussion of Aristotle's notion of providence. Aristotle has just been analyzing the nature of the prime mover who is himself unmoved and has shown that his activity consists in thinking and that the thinking has itself as its object. His next question is how the nature of the universe contains the good and the highest good, whether as something separate and by itself (objective good), or as the order of the parts (subjective good). He answers that it probably does so in both ways, as an army does; "for its good is found both in its order and in its leader, *and more in the latter;* for he does not depend on the order but it depends on him." He then tells how all things are ordered to one end, each in accordance with its nature. He uses a household as an example. The freemen of the household are most subject to rule and regulation and have least liberty to act at random, as opposed to the slaves and the animals who for the most part live at random and do correspondingly little for the common good. Aristotle makes application of this example to the universe, stating that at the very least things come to be dissolved into their elements and thus do their share for the good of the whole. The views of other philosophers are then discussed, ending with that of certain Platonists who "give us many governing principles; but the world refuses to be governed badly. 'The rule of many is not good; one ruler let there be.' "

St. Thomas follows this passage closely, stating first as Aristotle's view that one separate good exercises providence (governance) over all, as one ruler or lord, and that under it are different orders of being arranged in such a way that the higher beings attain the order of perfect providence, and as a result they do not fall short in any respect, but the lower beings receive the order of providence in a less perfect degree, and as a result are subject to many defects. St. Thomas then uses the example of the household. In applying the example, he adverts to the defects of beings in the universe. Lower bodies, he says, display defects of the natural order, but this type of defect is never found in higher bodies. Similarly human souls are often deficient in the understanding of truth and in the proper desire for the true good, but this does not occur in the higher souls or the intellects. For this reason, he says, Plato holds[46] that among the demons and among men some are good and some bad, but that the gods and the intellects and the souls of the heavens are altogether free from wickedness.

With this statement St. Thomas finishes his list of the points in which Plato and Aristotle agree regarding immaterial substances, and begins his list of the points on which they differ.

(1) In the first place, Plato says that there are two orders of immaterial substances above the heavens: the gods or ideas or species, and the intellects which participate in them.[47] But Aristotle denies that there are separate ideas or species and so he posits only the order of intellects; and he has to make the first in the order of intellects God, whereas Plato makes Him the first in the order of species. Now Aristotle's God would have to understand through its own essence and not through the participation of its higher being which would be its perfection.[48] This is Aristotle's opinion, too, of the rest of the good separate substances, under the highest God, i.e., the substances which are the final cause of the movements of the heavens.[49] He makes this reservation, however, says St. Thomas, that in proportion as these substances fall short of the simplicity of the first substance and its supreme perfection, to that extent their understanding can be perfected by participation in the higher substances.[50] But it is still true that the substances which are the final causes of the movements of the heavens are both intellects that understand and intelligible species.[51] They are not, however, the species or natures of sensible substances, as the Platonists held, but altogether higher substances.

(2) The second point of difference is that Plato does not limit the number of separate intellects to the number of heavenly movements, whereas Aristotle does. The reason is that Plato is impelled to posit separate intellects through a consideration of the very natures (=species or ideas) of things[52] and not, as is Aristotle, solely from the consideration of motion.

(3) The third point of difference is that Aristotle does not posit any demons, i.e., souls intermediate between the souls of the heavens and human souls, as Plato does. Neither Aristotle nor any of his followers mentions demons, says St. Thomas.

With this list of points of agreement and of difference St. Thomas ends what might be termed the constructive section of the work. The three points of agreement are all doctrines to which he himself is inclined to assent. On the points of difference he agrees once with Aristotle and the last two times with Plato. Evidence for the importance which St. Thomas attaches to this composite doctrine of Plato and Aristotle is abundantly supplied in the next two sections of the *De Substantiis Separatis*: the first (chapters 4-15) shows that the errors of others are all recognizable by their disagreement with some aspect of the composite doctrine, and that they are usually capable of being refuted by an appeal to the principles underlying it; and the second (chapters 16-18) shows the agreement of the composite doctrine with Holy Scripture and the Fathers. We shall attempt in the next pages a summary analysis of those two sections, but first of that which lists the errors.

The Nature of the Angels

IV

The errors are on three points:[53] (1) nature (*conditio*), (2) origin (*modus existendi* or *origo*), and (3) providence (*gubernatio rerum*). Under the first heading comes the doctrine of Avicebron as found in the *Fons Vitae*.[54]

Avicebron believed, contrary to the opinions of both Plato and Aristotle, that all separate substances under God, are composed of matter and form.[55] He was mistaken in two respects, says St. Thomas. (1) In the first place, he thought that there must be a real composition in things themselves to correspond to the composition in the order of intelligibility which is found in things according to their kinds, as for example a species is composed of genus and difference. Thus in the case of a thing belonging to a genus the genus would be its matter, and the difference its form. (2) In the second place, he believed that the expressions: "to be in potency," "to be a substrate" or "to be a recipient" are used always with the same signification. With these two principles as starting points he investigated the composition of things, even of intellectual substance.

First he noted that in artificial objects the natural substance of which they are made, e.g., wood or iron, is the matter which is related to the artificial form as potency to act.[56] Then he noted that natural substance is composed of the four elements, which are the matter of the natural forms.[57] Then he noted that the elements are all bodies and that body is the matter of the contrary qualities of the elements (dry and moist, hot and cold).[58] But the body of the heavens is not receptive of contrary qualities. Now body, whether of the heavens or not, always signifies substance having length and breadth and thickness, and these three dimensions are as the form to the substance which is the material substrate.[59] But besides substance which has quantity there is also substance which does not have it, and this kind is called separate substance.[60]

If we reverse the process[61] to see how the universe of Avicebron is built up, we find that at its core is a neutral stuff called substance. Substance can be given the form of quantity or the form of opposition to quantity. If it is given the form of opposition to quantity, it is immediately in the class of separate substances. If it is given the form of quantity it is immediately in the class of the visible world of dimension. Granted that it is quantitative, it can be given either any one of the four forms of the contrary qualities or the form of opposition to the contrary qualities. If it is given the form of opposition to the contrary qualities, it is immediately in the class of the heavenly bodies. If it is given any one of the four forms of the contrary qualities, it becomes that element. Granted that it is an element, it can be given the form of any one of many natural bodies, e.g., iron or wood. Granted that it is wood, it can be given any one of several artificial forms, e.g., mallet, Indian, etc. If it actually becomes a wooden Indian, its nature as such would be essentially the primary substance with a series of forms attached to it as accidents in a substrate.

On the basis of a universe such as this, Avicebron gave the following five arguments in support of his opinion that separate substances are constituted of matter and form:

(1) Unless they are so constituted, there can be no diversity among them, for they would then have to be either matter alone or form alone. If they are matter alone, then there would be no diversity, because matter of itself is one and the same, and is diversified through forms. If they are form alone, then there would be no diversity except according as they were the subject of perfection or imperfection. But to be a subject is proper to the notion of matter, but not to the notion of form.[62]

(2) The notion of spirituality is distinct from that of corporeity. Thus corporeal substance and spiritual substance have something in which they differ, and something in which they agree since both are substances. Thus substance functions as the matter, supporting on the one hand corporeity and on the other spirituality. And these spiritual substances are higher and lower in proportion as their matter participates more or less in the form of spirituality.[63]

(3) Being is found alike in both corporeal and spiritual substances. Therefore that which is consequent upon being in corporeal substances will also be consequent upon being in spiritual substances. But in corporeal substances there is a kind of body which has density, that is, the body of the elements, and a kind of body which is the body of the heavens, and besides, body is constituted of matter and form. Now, we find also in spiritual substance a lower kind which is united to a body, and a higher kind which is not united to a body. Therefore, on grounds of the analogy, there must also be matter and form of which spiritual substance is composed.[64]

(4) Every created substance must be distinguished from the creator. But the creator is pure unity. Therefore no created substance can be pure unity but must be composed of two parts, and one of these must be form and the other matter because nothing can be made either out of two matters or out of two forms.[65]

(5) Every spiritual created substance is finite. But a thing is not finite except through its form, because a thing which does not have a form through which it is made an individual is infinite. Therefore every created spiritual substance is composed of matter and form.[66]

After stating Avicebron's case, St. Thomas gives an elaborate refutation.

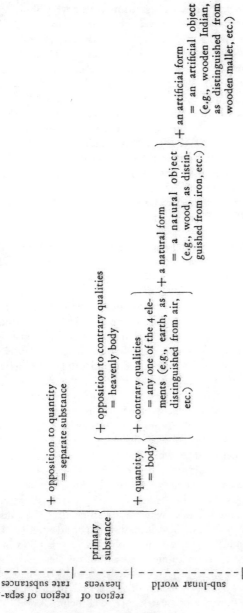

+ opposition to quantity
= separate substance

+ opposition to contrary qualities
= heavenly body

primary
substance

+ quantity
= body

+ contrary qualities
= any one of the 4 elements (e.g., earth, as distinguished from air, etc.)

+ a natural form
= a natural object (e.g., wood, as distinguished from iron, etc.)

+ an artificial form
= an artificial object (e.g., wooden Indian, as distinguished from wooden mallet, etc.)

| – – – – – – – –| – – – – – –| – – – – – – – – –|

region of separate substances

region of heavens

sub-lunar world

In the *De Ente et Essentia*[67] he dismisses him with a very short argument, and also in the *De Spiritualibus Creaturis* he handles him summarily in the answers to two objections.[68] Some controversy must have arisen to call forth the long refutation of the *De Substantiis Separatis*. St. Thomas says in the *De Ente et Essentia* that Avicebron seems to be the originator of this theory, and in the commentary on the *Sentences* that he is one "quem multi sequuntur."[69] He is opposing Avicebron, then, as the father of a numerous progeny. The strength of these philosophical descendents is evident in the efforts of Bishop Etienne Tempier in 1270 to have the doctrine of absence of composition in the angels and in the soul condemned, and in the Averroist condemnations of 1277[70] where three propositions deal explicitly with the subject. But St. Thomas does not mention the names of those whom he is opposing.[71] His refutation is in three parts.[72]

(A) In the first part he shows by four arguments that Avicebron's principle, that potency and receptivity are found in the same way in all things, is wrong.

(1) In the first place, it involves in the analysis of all beings from the lowest to the very highest a reduction to material principles instead of to what is most being. The more we reduce being to material principles the less we find of what being is.

(2) In the second place, it is a reversion in a sense to the ancient natural philosophers who said that all things were one and that their substance was matter. But they at least limited their explanation to bodies, since they were of the opinion that nothing exists except bodies, whereas Avicebron says that the first common matter and substance of all things, corporeal as well as incorporeal, is an incorporeal substance. Thus the differences among species must be for Avicebron by way of the forms, and the forms must belong to the generic matter as accidental passions to substance. Although he holds that all forms considered in themselves are accidents, he nevertheless says that they are substantial in comparison to certain things in whose definitions they are contained, just as whiteness belongs to the notion of white man. (a) But this view destroys the true meaning of prime matter which is to be altogether in potency and hence not predicable of anything actually existing, just as a part is not predicated of a whole. (b) It also destroys the principles of logic because it takes away the true meaning of genus, species and substantial difference, and makes all predication accidental. (c) It further destroys the foundations of natural philosophy because it takes away true generation and corruption from things, just as the ancients did when they posited a single material principle. (d) It destroys even the first principles of philosophy, because, by the doctrine of accidental forms, it takes away unity from individual things and consequently true being as well.

(3) In the third place, Avicebron's method of proof makes it necessary to proceed into infinity in the consideration of material causes so that it would be impossible ever to reach a first matter. For there must be in matter a differentiation as to the receptivity of the two forms of spirituality and corporeity and thus there would have to be differentiation prior to the reception of different forms, and so on into infinity. Thus, whenever we should arrive at a matter that was altogether uniform, in accordance with the principles under discussion, such matter would be able to receive only one form and that equally throughout its entire extent.

(4) In the fourth place, Avicebron's view is improbable because the primary matter is without quantity and hence there is no possibility of division among things except through the forms. But division according to forms would require that there be prior distinction in matter according to other forms which undifferentiated matter receives throughout its whole extent, and thus to infinity.

(B) In the second part of the refutation St. Thomas shows by the same reasoning that there cannot be one common matter for spiritual and corporeal substance.

(1) In the first place, there would have to be in the common matter of both a prior distinction. This cannot be according to quantitative division, for quantity is absent from the primary substance. Nor can it be in the forms, for this leads to a regressive infinity of forms. Hence the matter of spiritual and corporeal substances must be altogether different.

(2) Likewise, since receptivity is proper to matter as such, if the matter of spiritual and corporeal substances is the same, both of them should have the same mode of reception. But this is not true, for the matter of corporeal things receives a form in an individualized way, that is, not according to the common notion of form, whereas every intellectual substance receives in its totality the form understood.

(3) A being is higher in proportion as it has more of the nature of being, that is, of act. But spiritual substance is higher than corporeal, and therefore the matter of spiritual substance must differ from the matter of corporeal substance. But the matter of corporeal substance is pure potency, according to Plato and Aristotle. Then the matter of spiritual substance must in some way be actual being. But it cannot be actual being in the sense of being composed of potency and act without an infinite regression. Hence it must be a subsistent form. But to speak of the matter of spiritual substance as a subsistent form would be the same as saying that spiritual substances are simple and not composed of matter and form. Thus the possibility of forms which are not dependent on matter for their existence is established, for form is prior in nature to matter and as such should not be dependent upon it. But

it must still be established that these forms exist. Now, it is known that forms which need matter for their foundation exist. But it is commonly said that whenever there exists an imperfect member of a genus, there exists also a nature which is the perfect embodiment of that génus. Therefore there are above the forms which are received in matter, other forms which are self-subsistent, and these are spiritual substances, not composed of matter and form.

(C) The third part of St. Thomas's refutation of Avicebron is the answer to Avicebron's five arguments. This part constitutes chapter 6.

(1) The first argument concludes that there can be no diversity in spiritual substances if they are not composed of matter and form. (a) This argument is faulty in its attitude towards matter, for things which are only matter can be differentiated as regards the different kinds of potency to which the kinds of matter correspond. Thus the matter of the heavenly bodies is in potency to perfect actualization by the form, whereas the matter of the elements is in potency to an incomplete form. Above these kinds of matter is spiritual matter, that is, spiritual substance which receives forms in their totality, whereas the lower kinds of matter receive forms in an individualized way. (b) The argument is also faulty in its attitude towards forms, for if things composed of matter and form differ according to their forms, these forms must be different. A form which is closer to matter is less perfect and, as it were, in potency with respect to a higher form. Therefore, the fact that spiritual substances are pure forms does not constitute an objection to the existence of multiplicity among them, since there are different grades of perfection among them. Thus the less perfect is in potency with respect to the more perfect until we come to the very first of them, which is pure act, that is, God. Avicebron's difficulty lies, first, in his thinking of perfection and imperfection as accidents, as if there could not be a perfection which itself designates the proper species of a thing; and second, in his not realizing that to be a subject is an attribute not only of matter as a division of potency, but it is a universal attribute of all potency.

(2) Avicebron's second argument is faulty because he thinks of spirituality and corporeity as accidents compared to a subject, instead of as differences compared to their genus. Thus spiritual substance by itself is simple, not through anything added to its substance, but through its very substance. For the form which gives it the predication of genus is no different than the form which gives it the predication of species. Therefore there is no need of anything such as matter or a substrate to act as the subject for the spirituality of a spiritual substance.

(3) The third argument is based upon the false supposition that being is predicated univocally of all. There is no need to have the same mode of

being in all things which are said to be, since some participate in being more perfectly and others less perfectly, as for example substance compared to accident, and immaterial substance compared to the substance of the heavenly bodies or to the substance of elements.

(4) The fourth argument is based upon the false assumption that if spiritual substances are free from matter, there is no distinction among them. There is, however, still a kind of potency in them, even after the potentiality of matter is taken away, because of the fact that they are not being itself but merely participate in being. But they do not participate in being universally as it is found in the first principle, but particularly in the special determined mode of being which is suited to this particular genus or species. Substances composed of matter and form take their mode of being from their form which places them in certain species, and thus they participate, through their form, in being from God in a manner proper to themselves. But this implies a two-fold relationship: the one of matter to form; the other of the thing already composed, to the being in which it participates. For the being of a thing is neither its form nor its matter, but something accruing to the thing through the form. Now, since the form is that by which a thing participates in being, there is no reason why there should not be a form which would receive its being in itself and not in a subject. Thus it can be seen that the potency of a spiritual substance has to do only with its relation to being, whereas the potency of matter has to do with its relation both to form and to being. To use the term matter for both of these is clearly an equivocation.

(5) The fifth argument confuses the different kinds of finiteness. Material substances are finite in two ways, both from the point of view of the form which requires to be received in matter, and from the point of view of being itself in which they participate in the manner proper to them. Thus they are finite both from above and from below. Spiritual substance, however, is finite only from above inasmuch as it participates in being from the first principle in the manner proper to itself, and it is in a manner infinite from below since it is not participated in a subject. But the first principle, which is God, is infinite in every way.

V

St. Thomas, after refuting Avicebron whose error concerned the nature of spiritual substances, turns his attention to a group of errors on the subject of the origin of these substances. He divides his subject into three sections, devoting a chapter to each: (A) the errors of those who hold that these substances have absolutely no cause of their being; (B) the errors of others who hold that they do have a cause of their being, that all of them, however, do not proceed immediately from the supreme first principle, but rather that the lower ones derive their being from the higher in a certain series of orders; (C) the errors of a third group who are ready to admit that all these substances derive their origin immediately from the first principle, but claim that certain attributes which are found in them, for example, life, intelligence and other qualities of this sort, are caused in the lower substances by the higher.

(A) The first group is unnamed by St. Thomas, but it is not unlikely that they were certain Averroists at Paris. It would be more satisfactory if we were able to name them and to give reference to specific works of theirs, but I am afraid that we shall have to be content to refer to the list of condemnations of 1277 as most closely approximating the doctrine which St. Thomas opposes. The doctrine of these men is, according to St. Thomas, supported by four arguments:

(1) Nothing is produced from nothing. Now a thing which has a cause of its being would seem to be produced. Therefore whatever has a cause of its being must be produced from something. But that out of which a thing is made is matter. Therefore if spiritual substances do not have matter, it would seem to follow that they have no cause of their being whatsoever.[73]

(2) To be produced is the same as to be moved, or to change. Now for every change and movement there must be a subject. Therefore if spiritual substances are immaterial, they cannot be made.[74]

(3) In every act of making, when we arrive at the end of our making, there remains nothing further to be made. This is the case when the form is the end of generation. Thus spiritual substances which are subsistent forms must have their own being and hence do not have a cause of their being.[75]

(4) Plato and Aristotle hold that spiritual substances are everlasting. But it would seem that nothing everlasting can be made, for what is made must be in a state of non-existence prior to its being made.[76]

In the response, St. Thomas states that this doctrine emanates from the same source as the doctrine that there is matter in spiritual substances. The common source of both is the attitude of mind which is unable to pass beyond the limits of the imagination and rise to the contemplation of anything except material things. In the present case the difficulty lies in thinking of all things in terms of the kind of causality which is appropriate to material things. St. Thomas reviews the account of the ancient naturalists given in the first book of Aristotle's *Metaphysics* and shows how Plato and Aristotle found it necessary to posit another and higher kind of becoming over and above that of material change. The proofs of the existence of this higher kind of becoming are four of which we will here give merely the outline:

(1) The first principle must be of the greatest simplicity and hence must be existent being itself and only one. Hence all other beings must exist through a kind of participation in being. Therefore above and prior to that mode of becoming by which a thing comes to be through the advent of a form in matter, we must understand another origin of things according to which being is given to all things by the first being which is its own existence.

(2) The universal cause must be prior to the particular. But the cause which produces its effect through motion is particular. Therefore above this mode of becoming there must be another mode of becoming without any change or motion, through the inflow of being.

(3) That which exists accidentally must be reduced to what exists essentially. Now in every becoming which is the result of motion or change, a thing which is essentially being becomes this or that particular being. It becomes being considered in its generality only accidentally. For it is not brought from a state of non-being, but only from not being this particular thing. Thus if a horse were to become a dog, it would become a dog essentially, but an animal accidentally, because it was an animal previously. We must therefore take thought of a kind of origin of things by which being itself considered in its generality is given to things.

(4) The being which possesses a certain quality in the highest degree is always the cause of that quality in those things which come after it. Now the first principle, which we call God, is being in the highest degree. The first being must therefore be the cause of being in all things.

St. Thomas then answers the four arguments which were advanced in support of the doctrine that spiritual substances are uncaused. The difficulty with the first two arguments, he says, is that their proponents were unable to conceive of a becoming which is through the influx of being and which therefore requires no subject prior to the making. The third argument fails to take into consideration that causes which are directed to determined forms are not causes of being except to the extent to which they are so directed by a first and universal principle of being. The fourth argument fails to note that in the case of things which are produced without change or motion, through a simple emanation or inflowing of being, it is possible for a thing to be made regardless of whether there was ever a time when it did not exist. For when change or motion is done away with, there will be no sequence of before and after in the action of the inflowing principle. The kind of agent responsible for such a becoming would be able to act in this way always, else it would acquire a new ability and thus be changeable.

Hence it is possible that an effect produced by it should always have existed. We must not think, therefore, that Plato and Aristotle, in holding that immaterial substances or even heavenly bodies always existed, denied that there is any cause of their existence. The Catholic faith, as St. Thomas points out, holds the opposite view on this point, namely that these substances had a beginning. But, as St. Thomas also shows, this does not constitute an irreconcilable point of difference, for even though these substances derive their origin from an immovable principle without motion, this is no reason why their existence *must be* everlasting. For things proceed from the first principle by way of intelligence and will. Thus the whole duration of things is contained under His intellect and power so that He bestows upon things from eternity the measure of duration which He wills.

(B) The second opinion regarding the origin of immaterial substances is attributed by St. Thomas to Avicenna, who propounded[77] what has been aptly called "cascade creation." St. Thomas says that those who held this doctrine are of the opinion that, since the first principle of things is absolutely one and simple, then what proceeds from it would have to be one. This one, although it is simpler and more one than all other inferior things, nevertheless falls short of the simplicity of the first cause inasmuch as it is not its own existence, but is a substance having existence. They call this being the first intelligence and say that a plurality of beings can proceed from it. For according as it turns to the understanding of its simple first principle, the second intelligence proceeds from it; when it understands itself under the aspect of the intellectuality it possesses, it produces the soul of the first orb; and when it understands itself under the aspect of the potency which is in it, there proceeds from it the first body, that is, the body of the highest heaven. And so the procession goes on in order even to the lowest of bodies. St. Thomas says that this same doctrine seems also to be supposed in the *Liber de Causis.*

His refutation is in four parts and constitutes a dissertation on the relationship of the causality of the first cause to that of secondary causes. In summary it is as follows:

(1) Since things proceed from the first principle as from an intellective principle which acts according to forms conceived, there is no reason for saying that this first principle, even though its essence is simple, produces only one effect; and that this, in turn, in accordance with the mode of its composition, produces a plurality in order. To hold such a position would mean that the distinction and the order in things proceed not from the intention of the first agent but from a certain necessity of things. However, it should not be imagined that secondary causes can bring a being into existence without any motion, through a simple influx of being itself. For

a universal effect must have a universal cause. Thus when a thing is made simply being, this effect must be traced to the universal cause of being, which is God. It is not true, therefore, that the prior among substances can be the cause of existence in those which come later.

(2) In proportion as a cause is higher, it is more universal and its power reaches out to more things. But that which is found first in any being whatsoever is most common to all, and any additions that are made contract what is already there. Therefore that which subsists as the first in anything, as matter in corporeal substances, and the potential element in immaterial substances, must be the proper effect of the first power and universal cause. Thus no secondary cause can bring into existence a thing in its totality.

(3) Every nature or form is found to have a two-fold cause: one, which is essentially and simply the cause of that nature or form; the other, which is the cause of this particular nature or form in this particular thing. Thus the parent horse is the cause of the form of the offspring, but is not the cause of the form of horse as such; for if it were, it would be the cause of its own specific equine nature. Thus the Platonists made the form a species existing apart from matter, but Aristotle was of the opinion that the universal cause of the species was in one of the heavenly bodies, e.g., the sun in the generation of man. Now it is possible that a thing which participates in a nature in a particular way should be the cause of something by way of motion. But when the existence of a thing is caused without motion, its cause must be the first cause of being, which is God.

(4) In proportion as a potency is farther removed from act there is need of a greater power to reduce it to act. But between no potency and some potency there is no comparison. Therefore, a power which produces an effect without any pre-existing potency infinitely exceeds a power which produces its effect out of some potency. But only God is infinite simply with respect to all being, and hence He alone can produce beings with no potency presupposed, such as immaterial substances.

(C) The third opinion regarding the origin of immaterial substances is attributed by St. Thomas to "the Platonists," and is definitely traceable to the *Liber de Causis*[78] of which he spoke[79] in connection with the opinion of Avicenna. Its proponents held that immaterial substances, and in fact all existing things, have God as the immediate cause of their existence according to that mode of production which is without change or motion. However they posited a certain order of causality in these substances according to other participations of the divine goodness. Accordingly, an immaterial substance[80] which is intelligent, living and being, will be being by virtue of its participation in the first principle which is being itself; it will be living by virtue of its participation in another separate principle which is life; and it will be intelligent by virtue of its participation in another separate principle which is intellect itself.

St. Thomas in his refutation says that there is some truth in this position. In the case of accidental modifications there is no reason why that which comes first should not proceed from some more universal cause, whereas that which comes later, from a later principle. But all things which are predicated substantially of anything are essentially and absolutely one. But an effect which is one is not reducible to several first principles. Thus Aristotle says[81] against the Platonists, that if animal were one thing and two-footed another among the separate principles, a two-footed animal would not be absolutely one. Now in the case of immaterial substance their very being is their life, and their life is not a different thing than their intelligence. Hence they do not derive their life and intelligence from a different source than that from which they derive their being, that is, God. But in regard to anything that comes to them over and above their essence, for example intelligible species or anything of this sort, the opinion of the Platonists can be true.

VI

The next error is in part concerned with the origin of immaterial substances and would for this reason seem properly to be a fourth error (D) under that heading. But St. Thomas does not include it in his list of those errors.[82] It is also in part concerned with the problem of the distinction among immaterial substances and would for this reason seem to constitute a distinct class of error. But St. Thomas does not include such an error in his general classification of the errors.[83] It would, therefore, be best to treat it as an appendix to the section on the errors which have to do with the origin of immaterial substances. It is distinguished from the others in the section because it holds that the entire nature of immaterial substances came immediately from the first principle. The man whom St. Thomas names its originator is Origen.[84] Though the work is not mentioned, it is the *De Principiis*.[85]

Origen wished to safeguard the procession of immaterial substances directly from the first principle, says St. Thomas, so he did away altogether with any order of gradation in their natures. He was of the opinion that different and unequal things cannot proceed from one creator who is also just; hence all things first produced by God were equal. And because bodies cannot be equal to incorporeal substances, there were no bodies in the first production of the universe; but later on, after the production of things by God, diversity arose as a result of the different ways in which the first substances used their freedom of choice. Some of these substances turned towards their principle with a proper movement of their will, and thus became good; and even among these some became higher than others. But others turned away from their principle, and these fell into a lower state. And this was the occasion for the production of bodies, in order that the immaterial substances that had turned away might be bound up in them. The diversity of bodies came from the diversity of the disorderly movements of the will among those who had turned away, so that those who had turned away less were bound up in nobler bodies. St. Thomas's refutation is in five parts:

(1) Since spiritual substances are immaterial, any diversity among them would have to be according to a difference in form. But among things which differ formally no equality can be found. There is, however, nothing to prevent differences from being found among things which differ materially, for different subjects can participate in the same form, either to exactly the same degree, or more, or less. Thus it would be possible for all spiritual substances to be equal, if they differed only according to matter and had the same specific form. And it is possible that Origen believed that they were of such a nature, for he did not clearly differentiate spiritual natures from corporeal. But since spiritual substances are immaterial, there must be an hierarchical arrangement among them.

(2) We do not find many equal beings in one grade or nature unless it be because of the imperfection of any one of them, or so that things which cannot have permanence individually may attain permanence through being multiplied. But things with perfect power and with permanence in the order of their nature are not multiplied numerically in the equality of a single species, for since one is sufficient, others would be superfluous.

(3) The perfection of an effect consists in its likeness to its cause. Now in the first principle we have to consider, not only that it is good and being and one, but also that it possesses these attributes in a pre-eminent degree and that it leads other things to participate in its goodness. The perfect similarity of the universe to God would therefore require not only that each individual thing be good and being, but also that one thing be higher than another, and that one thing move another to its end. The good of the universe is thus a good of order, which Origen's view made impossible by its positing an absolute equality in the production of things.

(4) It is not fitting to attribute to chance that which is best in the universe, namely the good of order, which is a general good. But Origen's view does attribute this order to the chance that one immaterial substance will be moved in a certain way by its will, and another, in a different way.

(5) The function of justice does not require that all things be equal, when it is concerned with the constitution of some whole out of different parts, for

if all the parts were equal, the whole would not be perfect. This is evident both in natural objects and in the state, for the human body would not be perfect if it did not have different members of unequal dignity, and neither would a state be perfect unless there were in it unequal ranks and a diversity of functions. Now when there is a question of the distribution of some common good among individuals, the demands of justice are met if the good of each individual is taken into consideration by having different individuals assigned different things suitably corresponding to the antecedent diversity in the individuals themselves. In the original production of things, therefore, God looked to the perfection of the univërse and brought unequal things into being. But in the retribution at the final judgment He will render to each man according to his deserts.

VII

The third class of error concerns the very complex problem of the relation of spiritual substances to the beings below them. In introducing this division of his subject St. Thomas points out that the source of the errors in the other two divisions was that judgments about spiritual substances were made from the point of view of inferior beings. He then states that the errors regarding the knowledge and providence of spiritual substances were also because men tried to judge of the intelligence and activity of these substances according to the standard of human intelligence and activity.

The men that he has in mind are quite probably certain Averroists at Paris whom we are unable to name. Their doctrines are given briefly in the condemnation of thirteen propositions at Paris in 1270,[86] and more fully in the condemnation of 1277.[87] St. Thomas seems to be referring to the condemnation of 1270, for he states the contents of propositions 11 to 13 in the same order and with similar phraseology, when he says that these men held, "that God and other immaterial substances did not have knowledge of singulars nor of beings below themselves, and in particular that they did not exercise providence over human acts."[88] The only important difference is his addition of the words, "and other immaterial substances," and this is easily explained by the fact that he is discussing immaterial substances. It is noteworthy that in his judgment these Averroist propositions applied as well to immaterial substances as to God.[89]

The Averroist arguments which St. Thomas gives are five:

(1) Since singulars are for men the objects of sense knowledge, whereas intellectual knowledge because of its immateriality is not of singulars but of universals, the Averroists think that the intellects of spiritual substances which are much simpler than our intellects cannot have knowledge of singulars.[90]

(2) In human knowledge the thing understood is the perfection and act of the one who understands. The same should then be the case with God, they say. But there is nothing nobler than God that could be His perfection. Hence they think it follows necessarily that nothing is understood by God except His own being.[91]

(3) Results that proceed from the providence of anyone cannot be fortuitous. Therefore, if everything that happens in this world proceeded from divine providence, there would be no fortuitous occurrences in the universe.[92]

(4) As Aristotle says in the sixth book of the *Metaphysics*,[93] if we must posit a necessary cause of every effect, and if, once the cause is posited, the effect must be posited necessarily, it would follow then that all future events would happen of necessity. For if everything in the world is subject to providence, the cause of all things would not only be present or past, but would precede them from eternity. Nor could it be said that divine providence is rendered vain either through ignorance or the impotence of the one exercising it, for there is no imperfection in God. Thus all things would happen of necessity.[94]

(5) If God has providence over things, it should proceed according to goodness. But we see many evils happen to individuals, especially to men who, in addition to natural defects and corruptions common to them and to other corruptible things, suffer also from the evils of vices and of disorders, as for example when misfortunes beset the just whereas the unjust prosper. Thus some people are led to believe that divine providence extends to immaterial substances and to the incorruptible heavens in which they see no evil, but they say that the lower beings are subject to providence, whether of God or of other spiritual substances, only as a genus and not as individuals.[95]

St. Thomas's refutation of these arguments is in three parts, in the first of which he discusses the divine knowledge, in the second he treats of the divine providence, and in the third he gives the answers to the five Averroist arguments. These three parts constitute chapters 12 to 14.

(A) As regards the divine knowledge St. Thomas sets down the thesis that, "We must of necessity hold firmly that God has an absolutely certain knowledge of all things knowable at any time whatsoever and by any knower."[96] He gives three proofs:

(1) The substance of God is His very being. In Him being is not one thing, and intelligence another,[97] for if this were so He would not be perfectly simple and hence not absolutely first. Therefore, just as His substance is His being, so also His substance must be His knowledge, as Aristotle also concludes in the twelfth book of the *Metaphysics*.[98] And just as His substance is separate being itself, so also His substance is separate knowledge itself. Now if there were a separate form, nothing which could

belong to the notion of that form would be lacking to it. For example, if there were a separate whiteness nothing which is included in the notion of whiteness would be lacking to it. So also the knowledge of everything knowable must be in the universal notion of knowledge which is the divine substance.

But knowledge must always be in accordance with the mode of the knower, just as any activity is in accordance with the mode of the agent. To an even greater degree, therefore, God's knowledge which is His substance is in accordance with the mode of His being. But His being is one, simple, unchanging, and eternal. It therefore follows that by one simple intuition He possesses eternal and unchanging knowledge of all things.

Now that which is abstract cannot be other than one in any nature whatsoever. For example, if whiteness were abstract, there would be only one abstract whiteness, and all other whiteness would be a participation of it. But, just as God's substance is alone abstract being itself, so also His substance is alone altogether abstract knowledge itself. Now just as His being is His very essence and not His by participation in another, so also His knowledge is His very essence and not by participation in another. But what belongs to a thing by participation is found more perfectly in that being which is of its very essence what the others are by participation. Therefore God must have knowledge of all things that are known by anyone whomsoever, as Aristotle implies in the first book of the *De Anima* and in the third book of the *Metaphysics*.[99]

(2) If God knows Himself, he must do so perfectly for His knowledge is His substance and whatever is in His substance must be included in the knowledge of it. But this will imply that His power also is known perfectly. Therefore He must know everything to which His power extends, that is, everything which in any way exists or can exist, whether it be proper to Him or common, whether it be produced directly by Him or through the mediation of secondary causes. Therefore He must have knowledge of all things which exist in any way whatsoever.

(3) Just as every cause is in some way in the effect through a participated likeness to the cause, so every effect is in a more excellent way in the cause according to the power of the cause. Therefore all things must exist in the first cause more eminently than they do in their own nature. But whatever exists in another does so according to the mode of the substance of that other. Now God's substance is His knowledge. Therefore everything which in any way exists must exist by way of knowledge in God, and so He knows all things perfectly.

After giving these three proofs, St. Thomas states that the occasion for the Averroist errors concerning the divine knowledge of singulars is the demonstration of Aristotle in the twelfth book of the *Metaphysics* that the object of the divine knowledge is the divine being itself.[100] In a very long and extremely detailed analysis, St. Thomas shows that the Averroist interpretation of the passage is inaccurate and that "it was not Aristotle's intention to exclude from God a knowledge of other things."[101]

He ends the passage with the statement that the lower separate intellects whom we call angels understand themselves as individuals through their own essence. But according to the Platonic doctrine they understand other things through the participation in the separate intelligible forms, which Plato calls gods, while according to Aristotle they understand other things partly through species, partly through their own essence, and partly through the participation in the separate intelligible forms of that first intelligible being which is God, by whom they participate in both being and knowledge.

(B) The second part of St. Thomas's criticism of the Averroists has to do with the divine providence. Just as the divine knowledge must be thought of as extending even to the least of things, so also must the divine providence include everything under its care. In proof of this St. Thomas gives the following five arguments:

(1) Good is found in all things in a certain order according to which things serve one another in turn and according to which they are ordained to an end. Now just as every being is derived from the first being which is its own being, so every good is derived from the first good which is its own goodness. Therefore the orders of the individuals must be derived from the first absolute truth. Now providence consists in this that an order is instituted by an intelligent being in the things which are under its care. Thus the divine providence rules over all things.

(2) The first mover is the principle of all motions, just as the first being is the principle of all being. In necessarily arranged causes, that cause is the greater which is higher in the order of causes, for it exercises causality over things which are themselves causes. Therefore God is even more fully a cause than individual movers are. He, however, always exercises His causality intelligently, for His substance is His knowledge, as is clear from what Aristotle says.[102] Thus by His intelligence He must move all things to their proper ends, and this is providence.

(3) If all things in the universe are disposed for the best so that they all depend upon the highest goodness, it is better that they be in a necessary rather than in an accidental order. Therefore the order of the universe cannot be an accidental one. But this requires that the intention of the first cause be transmitted from one cause to another even to the last, and this is providence.

(4) Whatever is proper to a cause and an effect is found more eminently

in the cause, for it flows from the cause into the effect. Now we must attribute a certain providence to God, unless we want to claim that the universe is ruled by chance. Therefore the divine providence must be most perfect.

(5) Two things must be considered in regard to providence: a plan for disposing things, and the execution of the plan. Now in the planning, a providence is the greater the more it is done by a single mind. But in the execution, it is the greater the more universally it is applied through a greater number of means and by a greater variety of agents. But the divine providence makes an intelligent plan for every individual thing, and carries it out by the greatest number and variety of causes. Among these causes are the spiritual substances which we call angels. They carry out the divine providence more generally because they are nearer the first cause. That is why they are given the name of angel which means messenger.

(C) In the third part of his criticism of the Averroists St. Thomas answers their arguments.

(1) The first argument of the Averroists is the result of a comparison of the divine with human knowledge. But this comparison is faulty. The order of knowledge is according to the order of things in their being, for the perfection and truth of knowledge consists in a similitude of the things known. Now the order in things is such that the higher beings have goodness more universally. This does not mean that they receive being and goodness only according to a common notion, in much the same way as a universal is said to be what is predicated of many, but rather that whatever is found in lower beings exists more eminently in higher ones, as is evident from their power of operation. For lower beings have powers which are restricted and determined to particular effects, whereas higher beings have powers which are capable universally of many effects; and yet the higher power is operative to a greater degree even in the production of particular effects. Thus it is evident that the power in higher beings is called universal, not as though it were incapable of particular effects, but because it can produce more effects than can a lower power and because in the production of any one effect it is operative to a greater degree. In the same way the power of knowing is the more universal the higher it is, not as if it knew only universal nature—for in that case it would be more imperfect the higher it was, since to know something in a universal way is to know it in a way intermediate between potency and act—but because it extends to more things and knows the individuals among them to a greater degree. Now in the order of knowing powers, the sensitive power is the lower, and so it cannot know singulars except through the proper species of singulars. And because the principle of individuation in material things is matter, the sensitive power knows

singulars through individual species in organic bodies. Moreover, in the order of intellectual knowledge the knowledge of the human intellect is the lowest. Therefore the intelligible species are received in the human intellect according to the weakest mode of intellectual knowledge, that is, a knowledge of things according to the universal nature of genus and species. This representation of things according to their universality alone, requires that things be determined and contracted by abstraction from the phantasms of singulars. Thus man knows singulars through sense and universals through intellect. But higher intellects have a higher power of knowing, so that through the intelligible species they know both the universal and the singular.

(2) When it is said that the thing known is the perfection of the intelligence, it must be recognized that the reference is not to that which is known, but to the intelligible species which is the form of the intellect inasmuch as it is the intellect in act. Now every derived form proceeds from an agent, and the agent is more honorable than the recipient. Thus in man the agent intellect is nobler than the possible intellect. Now the superior intellects of the angels attain the intelligible species either from the ideas, as the Platonists say, or from the first substance God, as follows from the position of Aristotle. The intelligible species of the divine intellect, however, through which it understands all things is its substance which is its knowledge. Thus it must be admitted that there is nothing which is higher than the divine intellect, through which it could be perfected. But rather from the divine intellect itself the intelligible species proceed, as from something higher, into the intellects of the angels. In the case of the human intellect, however, the intelligible species come from sensible things through the action of the agent intellect.

(3) Regarding the third argument which had to do with chance events, St. Thomas says that nothing prevents it being said that fortuitous or chance events occur as long as they are thought of in reference to the intention of a lower agent. But when they are thought of in reference to the intention of a higher agent, they are ordained and not fortuitous. For example, if someone with evil intent sends another to a place where the former knows there are robbers or enemies, the meeting with the robbers is chance as regards the person who was sent, for he had no intention of meeting them, but it is not chance as regards the one who sent him. Similarly there are events which can be called fortuitous as regards human knowledge, but they must be spoken of as ordained from the point of view of divine knowledge.

(4) St. Thomas answers the fourth argument, which has to do with future contingents, by showing that the divine providence pre-existing from

eternity is the cause of all effects which are produced according to it and which proceed from it by an immutable disposition. However, effects do not all proceed from it as necessary, but rather as providence disposes. Those that are disposed as necessary have proper causes assigned which act of necessity, and those that are disposed as contingent have proper contingent causes assigned to them.

(5) The argument concerning the existence of evil is answered by a similar reasoning. Just as contingent effects can because of the condition of their proper causes proceed from God who is essentially and absolutely necessary being, so also there can proceed from Him who is the supreme good certain effects which because they are from Him are good, but which are called evil because of certain defects due to the condition of their causes. Thus God out of His very goodness allows certain defects to occur in things, (a) because it is suitable to the order of things and for the good of the universe that effects follow according to the condition of their causes; (b) because from the evil of one the good of another proceeds, as for example in natural things the corruption of one is the generation of another, and in moral matters the patience of the just arises from the persecution of the tyrant. Therefore it is not fitting that divine providence should completely eliminate evils.

VIII

With the Averroists St. Thomas has completed his projected discussion of the three kinds of errors. But he adds another chapter on the error of the Manichaeans which he says transcends all the other errors. It was not suitable for classification with the others because it involves serious errors on all three points thus far discussed.

St. Thomas's knowledge of the Manichaeans is quite probably derived from St. Augustine, who criticizes them in several of his works, notably in the *De Natura Boni contra Manichaeos*.

The doctrines which St. Thomas attributes to the Manichaeans are: (1) That they appeal to two principles to explain the origin of things, the principle of good and the principle of evil;[103] (2) that both of these principles are corporeal, the principle of good being thought of as a corporeal light which has an infinite power of knowing, and the principle of evil as infinite corporeal darkness;[104] (3) that things are not subject to the providence of a single principle, but to that of contrary principles.[105]

St. Thomas criticizes these doctrines in order as follows:

(1) It is decidedly unreasonable to think that there has to be a principle of evil as the contrary to the highest good. For nothing can be active except insofar as it is being in act because one thing acts upon another to the extent

of its own being, and contrariwise a thing is acted upon by what is in act. Now a thing is called good when it has its proper perfection and activity; and bad when it lacks the activity and perfection which is its due. But nothing either acts or is acted upon except insofar as it is good. Inasmuch as a thing is bad it is lacking in that which perfectly acts or is acted upon. Thus, a house is called bad if it does not have its proper perfection, and a builder is called bad if he is not expert in the art of building. Therefore evil does not have an active principle, nor can it be an active principle. It follows rather from a defect in a certain agent.

(2) It is impossible for a body to be in any way intelligent, for intellect is neither a body nor the act of a body; otherwise it would not know all bodies, as Aristotle establishes in book III of the *De anima*.[106] Therefore if the first principle is intelligent it cannot be a body.

(3) As regards the third point it must be admitted that the good has the nature of an end, for we call that good which we desire. Now all governing is an ordination to a certain end, and hence is according to the nature of good. Therefore there cannot be any governing or ruling or regulating which is evil as such. Two governing or ruling powers, one for good and one for evil, are thus impossible.

These errors arise, says St. Thomas, because their authors observe that in particular cases effects proceed from contrary causes, and then they try to transfer their findings to the universal cause of things. In doing this they err in regard to the nature of contraries, for contraries are not absolutely diverse, but have a common basis of agreement for the aspect in which they differ.

IX

After having shown in the preceding chapters what the philosophers, "especially Plato and Aristotle," thought as to the origin, nature, and order of distinction and government among spiritual substances, and the mistaken views of other philosophers who differed from them, St. Thomas proposes to consider the teaching of the Christian religion on each of these points. This consideration occupies the remaining three chapters, 16 to 18, of the *De Substantiis Separatis*, and is left in an incomplete state since the section treating of the "order of government" promised in the opening paragraph of chapter 16 was never given.

To establish the Christian belief relative to the angels, St. Thomas announces that he intends to use principally the works of Dionysius who has treated the subject of spiritual substances more excellently than any other writer. The works of Dionysius upon which he draws principally are the *De Divinis Nominibus* and the *De Coelesti Hierarchia*.[107] In addition to these, texts from Holy Scripture are cited, and very often St. Augustine or some other of the early fathers.

(A) The teaching of "Christian tradition" relative to the origin of angels forms the matter of chapter 16. The several aspects of this problem as they appear in the light of faith and of the teachings of Dionysius are presented under the following points.

(1) All spiritual substances as well as all other creatures have been produced by God.

(2) All spiritual substances, and not only the highest ones, have been produced *directly* by God.

(3) Spiritual substances derive not only existence but all their *perfections* from one and the same principle, God. The belief that those substances derive being from one principle, and goodness and life and other perfections from other distinct principles, is contrary to the Christian religion. The scriptural grounds for the refutation of this "opinion of the Platonists" who held that the highest God was the essence of goodness, and that under Him was another God who was being itself, and under this one still others, is a series of texts[108] to the effect that God is all these things: goodness, and being, and life. This same truth is expressed by Dionysius who says that sacred doctrine does not regard the good as one thing, and being as another, and life or wisdom as another, nor does it hold that there are many causes and different Godheads producing different effects and subordinate one to another, but that one God is the source of all the emanations.[109]

(4) It is contrary to Christian doctrine to hold that spiritual substances take their origin from God in such a way that they have existed from *eternity*, as the Platonists and Peripatetics held.

(5) The exact *time when* the angels were created cannot be determined from Holy Scripture. That they were not created after corporeal creatures both reason and Holy Scripture attest; reason, since it would not be fitting for the more perfect beings to be created after the less perfect. As to the precise time of their creation, St. Thomas refuses to decide between the conflicting views of various fathers of the church, notably that of St. Augustine whose opinion it was that spiritual creatures were created at the same time as corporeal creatures; and that supported by St. John Damascene, St. Gregory of Nazianzus and St. Jerome, which held that angels existed long before corporeal creation. Neither of these opinions is adjudged contrary to sound doctrine by St. Thomas who feels that it would be "too presumptuous to assert that such distinguished doctors of the Church had deviated from sound doctrine."

(6) The question *where* the angels were created has no meaning on the supposition that they were created before corporeal creation, since place is

something corporeal. On the supposition, however, that they were created along with corporeal creation, the question is valid but place must be understood in the way in which it is proper to angels to be in a place.[110]

(B) The condition or nature (*conditio* or *conditio naturae*) of spiritual substances, in the light of Catholic doctrine, is summed up in chapter 17 in two points:

(1) Angels do not have bodies.

(2) Angels are not composed of matter and form.

The consideration which has prompted some to attribute bodily character to angels is found in Scriptural expressions which seem to imply the existence in them of bodily attributes. These expressions, however, are purely figurative, and the Scriptural intent to hold that angels are incorporeal is clearly demonstrated in the application of the word "spirit" to angels, since this word in Scriptural usage always designates something incorporeal.

Angels are not only incorporeal but *immaterial* as well, having no composition of matter and form. Scriptural authority for this immateriality of the angels is found in the fact that Holy Scripture speaks of angels as powers.[111] A material thing is never spoken of in this way. It may be said to *have* power but never to *be* a power. Just as a material thing *is* not an essence but is something *having* an essence. For power follows upon the essence. The same is true of a thing composed of matter and form. So it is clearly the intention of Holy Scripture to designate angels as immaterial.

Dionysius[112] expresses his belief that angels are immaterial by the fact that he frequently speaks of them as "heavenly intellects" or "divine minds." These words, intellect and mind, signify something incorporeal and immaterial.[113]

(C) The question of the distinctions among the angels forms the subject matter of the final chapter[114] of the *De Substantiis Separatis*. The question of the difference between good and bad angels, announced as the first point to be considered, is the only one that is taken up. The belief that there are good and bad spirits is commonly accepted and is proved by the authority of Holy Scripture as well, St. Thomas shows. While some writers speak of both good and bad demons St. Thomas considers preferable the usage which confines the term demons to the bad angels. He finds different causes assigned by different writers for the wickedness of the demons:

(1) The one view, which is the error of the Manichaeans, is that they are naturally evil, as having been produced by an evil principle. This view is effectively disproved by Dionysius[115] on five counts.

(a) If demons were naturally evil we should have to say that they were neither produced by a good principle nor to be numbered among existent

[145]

things. For evil is not a nature, and if it were a nature it could not be caused by a good principle.

(b) If demons were naturally evil they would have to be evil either to themselves or to others. If to themselves they would corrupt themselves, since it is of the nature of evil to corrupt; but this is impossible. If they were evil to others they would corrupt these others. But a thing which is naturally of a certain constitution, is such towards all and in every respect. They would accordingly have to corrupt all things and in every respect. But this is impossible since there are incorruptible things, and even things that are corrupted are not entirely so.

(c) If naturally evil they could not be produced by God since the good produces good things, and God has been proved to be the principle of all things.

(d) If the demons are always in the same state they are not evil by nature.

(e) They are not entirely devoid of good, since they are, and live, and understand and desire some good.

(2) A second view held that the demons were naturally evil in the sense of having *a natural inclination to evil*, although their nature as such was not evil. This was the view of Porphyry in his *Letter to Anebantes* where he speaks of "a kind of spirits by nature deceitful, many formed, feigning to be gods and demons, and the souls of the dead."[116]

On the supposition that demons are pure intellects with no admixture of corporeal nature, such an hypothesis is impossible, according to St. Thomas, since intellect as such is naturally ordered to the common good. With a mixed nature it is possible that the good of the lower nature should go counter to the good of the nobler nature.

In fact the Platonists did hold to a dual nature and made the demons corporeal animals having intellects.[117] And there was even some doubt among Christian writers, Dionysius himself seeming at times to attribute to demons sensible qualities.[118]

This second view does not commend itself any more than the first to St. Thomas who finds it impossible to believe that there should be "in a whole species a natural inclination to something evil to that species," just as there is not in all men a natural inclination to concupiscence or anger.

The correct opinion relative to the bad angels, says St. Thomas, is that not all were by nature bad or always bad but that some of them became bad through following of their own free will the inclination of their passions.

On the question whether these angels who became bad were recruited from all ranks and orders or just from the lowest order St. Thomas records disagreement among his Christian authorities, some of whom seem inclined to hold with the Platonist Apuleius that the demons occupied only the lower places of the air (*aerea loca*) while the angels or "gods," as Apuleius calls them, inhabited the aetherial regions.

Others insist that these bad angels or demons came from all orders even the very highest. This position, St. Thomas says, has many difficulties and with the enumeration of these difficulties[119] the *De Substantiis Separatis* ends.

X

One of the outstanding features of the treatise which we have just finished analyzing is the manner in which St. Thomas treats the Platonists. Here we see him using Proclus's *Elements of Theology* to make the *Liber de Causis* more intelligible, and then using both works as an addition to his meager knowledge of Plato. We see him searching through St. Augustine's *De Civitate Dei* for references to Apuleius and other Platonists. And then we see him affirm the authority and approve the doctrines of Pseudo-Dionysius. Most certainly St. Thomas sees some dangers in Platonism and he is doing his best to expose them. Nevertheless, he sees much good in it, and he is not slow to say so. But the fact remains that its basic principle of a world of ideas is wrong.

Aristotle, on the other hand, is correct in his basic principles. It is true that his doctrine is not always extended as far as it might be, and that he makes minor mistakes, but he does not err fundamentally. The only times he is seriously misleading are when followers of his attempt to make him a Platonist. Avicenna is one who does this, for the kinship of Avicenna's doctrine with that of the *Liber de Causis* is not hard to see. The practice of treating the *Liber de Causis* as Aristotelian should also be stopped, St. Thomas seems to say.

Having thus tried to save Aristotle from the Platonists, St. Thomas turns to the Averroists and shows that there are among them, too, serious misinterpretations of Aristotle. This effort leads him to give a series of commentaries on crucial parts of the twelfth book of the *Metaphysics* which go far towards justifying St. Thomas's faith in Aristotle.

But the justification of Aristotle is not St. Thomas's main purpose. There was a controversy at Paris between the faculty of arts and the faculty of theology. The faculty of arts took an Averroist Aristotle as their guide, and the faculty of theology in combating the Averroist danger were running into what was probably the worse danger of a too great reliance on Platonism. St. Thomas, therefore, busied himself with a search for the basic difficulty in the way of the truth.

This difficulty could very judiciously be represented by the doctrine of Avicebron. It was he who was unable to rise above his imagination. It was he who thought that things could be explained by material causes. It was he who revived the spirit of the early Greek natural philosophers whom Plato and Aristotle so successfully combated. And so St. Thomas could make him bear the brunt of the criticism. But there is no mistaking the current against which St. Thomas was struggling. Its spirit was that of Bishop Étienne Tempier and his condemnations of 1270 and 1277. And far more important than what was actually condemned, is what the bishop wanted to have condemned.[120]

Now most of these points could be nicely connected with the subject of the angels. And so the treatise of St. Thomas on separate substances is an effort to seek out historically and doctrinally the narrow course between the Platonism in control at Paris, and the Averroism which it condemned. Thus St. Thomas might well be thought to say of these two factions what Bishop Etienne Tempier in the preface to the condemnation of 1277 says of the Averroists, that "it is nct a legitimate excuse for them to say that in an effort to avoid Scylla they were caught in Charybdis."[121]

Eighth Essay

THE DILEMMA OF BEING AND UNITY

by
Anton C. Pegis

The Dilemma of Being and Unity

A Platonic Incident in Christian Thought

I

" ALL *that which, in the history of philosophy, can be traced back to non-philosophical causes is itself irrelevant to philosophy as such.*"[1] Because this judgment of an eminent historian is true, the historian of philosophy must needs be a philosopher in order to be a faithful historian, and the philosopher must needs scan the record of history for philosophical lessons which are as permanent as is the philosophy which he professes. It is inevitable, therefore, that the philosophical continuity between the history of philosophy and philosophy itself should be an increasingly important meeting-ground between the philosopher and the historian. It is equally inevitable that those who are not only disciples of scholasticism as a philosophy but also students of its history during the Middle Ages should confront these two experiences with one another and seek in history itself some understanding of the meaning of scholasticism as a philosophy. This is particularly true in our day when the traditional notion of a universal medieval scholastic synthesis is being replaced by the notion that there were several and mutually irreducible such syntheses; though it may still be true that even in their irreducibilities some of these syntheses betray the influence of common causes.

Such a state of affairs is bound to raise the question as to the *unity*, the *truth* and *meaning* of scholasticism. What sort of unity has it as a philosophy if it is the heir of rival and conflicting syntheses? And since this question is raised under the supposition of a *philosophical* continuity between medieval and modern scholasticism, nothing less than the very significance and coherence of scholasticism is at stake. More than this, since medieval philosophy ended in exhaustion and decline by the middle of the fourteenth century, and since with Professor Gilson we are driven to seek philosophical causes for this decline, the philosophical continuity between medieval philosophy and present-day scholasticism raises the further question of the philosophical health and purity of the heir of a movement which ended in failure. So long as Ockhamism remains a strange and distant phenomenon, somehow outside the pale of the golden successes of the thirteenth century, questions of meaning, of unity and of truth within scholasticism might not appear with all the acuity that they really possess. But just as soon as there are any reasons for thinking that the thirteenth century laid the foundations for the fourteenth, then the present-day scholastic cannot scan his medieval predecessors too closely or too critically.

Within this large problem the present essay is a very modest contribution. The problem with which I am concerned may be called the problem of the *beginnings* of scholasticism. Historians have often remarked that there are no absolute beginnings in history. It is not with such a notion of beginnings that I am here concerned. In philosophy there are absolute and decisive beginnings and these consist in how, and with what justice, a generation of thinkers understands the doctrines of its predecessors. In this sense, what Greek philosophy really was, acting as a remote and ultimately conditioning cause, plus what thirteenth century thinkers thought it to be, acting as a proximate and immediately determining cause, are the absolute beginnings of scholasticism. In these beginnings the essential development of medieval philosophy, down to and including Ockham, is contained with the necessity and inevitability of a continuous deduction. I am suggesting that there were causes within Greek philosophy itself as well as within the thirteenth century experiences of Greek philosophy which were bound to lead to Ockham; which is another way of saying that we shall not understand properly the meaning of medieval scholasticism unless we see that its conflict with Hellenism issued, with philosophical justice and necessity, in the nominalism of William of Ockham.

What I am asserting, therefore, comes to this. There is a common and unchanging problem in the history of Greek philosophy. This problem was understood and accepted by Christian thinkers in ways which were at odds with their Christian convictions concerning the nature of God and of the universe. But the problem presiding over the history of Greek philosophy carried with it implications far beyond the confines of the Greek world. That the Platonic problem of the one and the many should raise all the paradoxes that it has in the history of philosophy is scarcely surprising. But the presence of this problem in doctrines which we might suppose to be far removed from the influence of Plato may possibly prove surprising. And thus a Platonic influence on the epistemologies of Christian thinkers is not at all strange, however it may be unfortunate. But that Plato should be capable of shaping, even as a distant cause, Christian doctrines of the divine liberty may strike us as unexpected. Yet, there is even more. For the supposition that I am advancing contains as its essential feature the notion that we must seek in Platonism itself the origins of the nominalism of Ockham, including his radical voluntarism. By this conclusion I do not mean merely that Platonism offered Ockham the *occasion* to formulate his distinctive doctrines at the very moment of pursuing mercilessly all the errors of Platonic realism. One has only to read the Ockhamist attack upon the Scotistic formal distinction in order to see that, in Ockham's own eyes, the philosophical beginnings of nominalism are to be sought in an attack upon realism. I mean more than this, however. For it is only on the basis of a Platonic assumption that Ockham escapes from Platonism in the particular way that he does; which is the escape of a thinker who also remains a disciple. This is to say that the historical meaning of the nominalism of Ockham, whether we consider the doctrine of the singularity of individuals or the doctrine of an omnipotent divine will as it is understood by Ockham, verifies to the letter the deepest demands of the most persistent dilemma of Greek philosophy. To use a mode of expression which I shall try to explain later on in this essay, in the essential doctrines on the nature of singulars and of the divine will, Ockham is a disciple of Platonic realism, but for the realism of essences he substitutes, in the name of the Platonic principle of non-being, *a realism of the unintelligible.*[2]

The Greek dilemma itself can be put very briefly. It consists in the doctrine of the radical opposition between being and unity. From Parmenides to Plotinus there is no more ultimate problem than this for Greek philosophers, and there is no more unresolved problem. It is the merit of Plotinus as a Greek philosopher that he raises this dilemma to the status of an ultimate principle, explores its consequences and implications, and develops a doctrine of the organization of reality whose very significance is to maintain the antinomy between being and unity in all its purity. And it was the peculiar fortune of Christian thought to feel the effects of this dilemma even when it did not know or properly understand the dilemma itself. To understand the opposition between being and unity, its causes as well as its implications, is to understand the most important lesson of Greek philosophy as well as the unifying problem of the development of medieval philosophy. And because medieval thinkers did not succeed either in transforming or in transcending this opposition between being and unity, they bore within themselves the traces of an issue which had either to remain unresolved or to be resolved in a violent way.

There are two facts which give to this conclusion its proper significance. The first is concerned with the meaning of the transition from the thirteenth to the fourteenth century. The second is concerned with St. Thomas Aquinas.

Externally, the transition from Henry of Ghent and Duns Scotus to William of Ockham appears to be a violent reaction against Platonism. Internally, this transition amounts to the elimination itself of metaphysics. Nominalism, one of the historians of Ockham has said, renders useless the metaphysics of abstraction which was so dear to the thirteenth century.[3] For realism, another historian has observed, the world of Forms in the mind of God stands behind the world of sense, measuring its truth as well as the truth of knowledge. For realism there is a certain analogy between *concept*, *essence* and *idea*. The particular and individual beings of our sensible experience are copies in which the mind can see and abstract the original. On the world of intelligibility which is revealed in our experience of singulars we can then build the whole structure of metaphysics. With nominalism all this was lost. The divine ideas disappear and the sensible world, inhabited now by barren and naked singulars, must bear the full burden which the realism of essences had borne in the thirteenth century. Ideas and concepts are now nothing more than copies and representations of sensible singulars. Their truth is measured by the impervious individuality of these singulars— an individuality which is so radical that the intellect must constantly verify the truth of its concepts by a return to singulars.[4] In short, the effort to drive out Platonism and its world of Forms succeeds, in the hands of William of Ockham, in eliminating intelligibility both from things and from knowledge. Even the historian who does not evaluate Ockhamism in this way nevertheless agrees that these were the facts. And thus, one historian, having accepted the radical empiricism of Ockham as a philosophical conquest, looks back upon the thirteenth century and sees in its various realisms an unbridgeable gulf between the universality of knowledge and the singularity of things. "A realistic epistemology, therefore, found that it was unable to explain the knowability of individual things, even though it was perfectly aware of the necessity of admitting such a knowability. Given a clear separation between reality and thought, thought in its abstract universality and reality in its concrete individuality are destined to remain on opposite sides of an unbridgeable abyss, without the possibility of a meeting or a reconciliation. It was this abyss which Ockham sought to remove by effecting the conciliation of the two extremes. In the prologue of the *Commentary on the Sentences*, which is probably the first of his works, he establishes, as a sort of introduction to his whole doctrine, the theory of intuitive knowledge. In this knowledge, the dualism of reality and spirit is overcome through a decisive return to experience, that is, to the immediate intuition of the actual and individual reality of things."[5] For the moment let us not argue with this historian as to whether he has properly understood the realism of the thirteenth century. Let us note only that even in his interpretation the elimination of realism is *the* accomplishment of Ockham. The only unresolved question is, then, whether this elimination was a victory, as he holds, or a defeat, as do other historians.

The peculiarity and the uniqueness of St. Thomas Aquinas in these vicissitudes of Platonic realism have been brought out recently by Professor Gilson. "Coming after the Greeks, Christian philosophers had asked themselves the question: How obtain from Greek metaphysics an answer to the problems raised by the Christian God? After centuries of patient work, one of them had at last found the answer, and that is why we find Thomas Aquinas using the language of Aristotle in order to say Christian things."[6] But in saying these Christian things, St. Thomas Aquinas was perpetrating a veritable metaphysical revolution: ". . . a decisive metaphysical progress or, rather, a true metaphysical revolution was achieved when somebody began to translate all the problems concerning being from the language of essences into the language of existences. From its earliest origins, metaphysics had always obscurely aimed at becoming existential; from the time of St. Thomas Aquinas it has always been so, and to such an extent that metaphysics has regularly lost its very existence every time it has lost its existentiality."[7] These are remarkable words, for they throw a flood of light not only on St. Thomas Aquinas but also on those of his contemporaries and successors who sought an existential metaphysics by way of Platonism, failed to discover it by such a route, and endangered and ultimately destroyed metaphysics itself because Platonism could not yield even the least support for any existentialism. It is at the moment when Platonism was allowed by medieval thinkers to ruin metaphysics that St. Thomas Aquinas was formulating a doctrine of being of which the same historian has said that "the metaphysics of Thomas Aquinas was, and still remains, a climax in the history of natural theology."[8]

These judgments of the historians give us some perspective on the meaning and the magnitude of the problem before the thirteenth century and on the place of St. Thomas Aquinas in it. I know that to insist on the peculiarity of St. Thomas Aquinas has sounded and will doubtless continue to sound like a partisan and unphilosophical prejudice. Even Professor Gilson, whose extraordinary historical objectivity and understanding have been the admiration of his contemporaries, has found it necessary to defend himself against the ridiculous charge that he is measuring history by a Thomistic yardstick simply because he expresses a philosophical preference for St. Thomas Aquinas.[9] And yet, only those who dream of some private and privileged world of Thomistic truth are guilty of misplaced loyalty and deserve that excellent term of censure coined at the turn of the fourteenth century: *Thomatistae*.[10]

Nevertheless, in spite of such family quarrels, the facts remain unchanged. In its barest outlines, the problem facing Christian thinkers from the thirteenth century and after was the construction of an existential metaphysics. That the idea of God as being is at the center of this metaphysics has been proposed in a now classic work.[11] But whether such an existential metaphysics could be constructed out of the principles of Greek philosophy was precisely *the* problem of the thirteenth century. Christian thinkers differed from one another in their understanding of Greek philosophy as the vehicle of this existentialism in metaphysics. In time, under the pressure of the experiences they had with Greek philosophy, they came even to be divided on the notion itself of an existential metaphysics; (and it is not exactly a secret that they are still divided). What metaphysics is in terms of its object, its method, its manner of transcending the world of sense, is a question that finds only disagreement in such philosophers as St. Thomas Aquinas, Henry of Ghent, Duns Scotus and William of Ockham. The differences among them affect in a decisive way the very reality of an existential metaphysics. But the differences, be it noted, are themselves caused by what they found or what they thought to find in Greek philosophy.

These reflections, however general they may be, help us to understand the deep and lasting issue in the philosophical conflict between Hellenism and Christianity. That conflict is a living problem today, for the precise character of an existential metaphysics is, to say the least, a bone of contention among scholastics. And Greek philosophy is there today, even as it was in the Middle Ages, to lead scholastics down different paths in their explanation of the nature of being. In a word, present-day scholasticism, like its medieval parent, bears within it the marks of all the ways in which Greek philosophy could both help and hinder Christian thinkers in their pursuit of metaphysics. If such is the case, it is not at all surprising that the central problem of Greek philosophy, the problem of the relation between being and unity, should be as contemporary an issue for us as it was for medieval thinkers.

II

That the One is above being in the philosophy of Plato and Plotinus is a doctrine whose influence is too pervasive in history to be treated lightly. Every aim of Platonism is here at stake, for this doctrine is the complement of the Platonic doctrine of the ultimate nature of being. With Plato himself let us call the doctrine of being which he professes the alphabet theory of reality.[12] Being in its ultimate nature is an organized whole of distinct and hierarchically arranged Forms. Each Form is the same as itself and different

The Dilemma of Being and Unity

from all others; each Form introduces into the very heart of being that character of sameness and difference which is necessary to the preservation not only of the interior intelligibility of Forms but also of the intelligibility of their exterior relations and therefore of the whole in which they are found. By nature being is, therefore, a system of determinate essences. By nature being is possessed of what may be called the principle of interior diversification or otherness. Being *is* in such a way that it could not be intelligible and be a unity: the abstract and silent immobility of the Parmenidean One is as foreign to the intelligibility of being as is the restless otherness of the Heraclitean flux. Being is such in its essential nature that it could not be intelligible without being primarily diverse as well as the same; and in the very assertion of its intelligible nature we must assert the reality of non-being in order to maintain the ordered intelligibility of what is. Without a share in unity being would be an unrelated and unintelligible multiplicity; but without a share in non-being and otherness being would be no less unintelligible and chaotic. Somewhere between the chaos of pure difference and the no less chaotic wilderness of pure sameness and unity we must maintain a sort of middle way by proclaiming that *being is only relatively identical with itself*, i.e., that no Form is the same as itself without being also different from every other Form; which also means that the whole of being must be considered not only as being but also as non-being, for non-being is the mysterious co-principle of its interior intelligibility.[13]

It will scarcely be contested that such is the message of the *Sophistes* of Plato. Nor should it be contested, however, that the fundamental notion which leads Plato to steer such a middle course between the immobilist disciples of Parmenides and the disciples of the Heraclitean flowing philosophy[14] also leads him to sacrifice being to its perfections at the moment of endowing it with intelligibility. If being is as it is intelligible, and if it is diversely and determinately intelligible, why then being is primarily diverse, determinate and many: the same determinism which makes it to be intelligible forces it also to be a plurality. Being a plurality, it can have only the relative unity of an ordered whole which maintains within itself the distinct articulation of its members. And because the very requirements of intelligibility thus force being to be as essentially diverse as it is same, they also force it to be a participated and relative unity which preserves the plurality and diversity that is written in the determinate nature of the Forms.

The consequences of this conclusion are as far-reaching as they can possibly be. What Plato is really saying is that the intelligible character of being makes radically impossible the identification of being and unity. By nature, a being can be a whole, but it cannot be one. For the intelligibility of being, indeed *the intelligibility which is being*, is, as we have seen, primarily determinate and diverse. This diversity, which is essential to being, is also not only the cause of the isolation of unity from being but also the measure of its meaning. It is the very meaning of the One of Plotinus that it is above being in order to save itself from this plural determinateness of being; but it is the misfortune of the Plotinian One that the same indeterminateness which saves it from plurality also empties it of intelligibility. A barren unity whose eminence over being is also an isolation from the intelligibility of being: behold the paradoxical fate of the highest Plotinian divinity.[15]

It is inevitable that the approach to the state of intelligible formlessness should be the condition of unity. This is true whether we deal with that curiously silent union of the soul with the One,[16] with the nature of the One itself, or even with the natures of beings considered as sharing in unity. That beings less than the One should only share in unity might seem to be a reasonable enough assertion.[17] But let us notice what is peculiar to this assertion among Platonists both pagan and Christian. *For a being to be less than unity is for it already to be a whole rather than an individual:* it is the sum of its intelligible parts, and to be such a sum or composite is for it not only to be a being but also to be the *systematized intelligibility* that each being is. The opposition between *simplicity* and *composition*, as it is understood by such Christian Platonists as St. Augustine and Boethius, is entirely in the line of the Platonic doctrine of being. If the Boethian God is a *simple* Form rather than an *unlimited* Being, it is because Boethius is seeking to evade the Platonic determinism of being which he admits fully in his conception of creatures.[18]

That the Platonic theory of being should both attract and repel Christian thinkers is no more than what we might expect. How could the Platonic theory of being operate in a world in which God is perfect being and *therefore* one? Exactly what being is Plato describing when he describes the world of Forms? St. Augustine, in a text which has had a remarkable history throughout the Middle Ages, thought to baptize the Platonic Forms and to make them ideas in the mind of God.[19] But this was easier to assert than to accomplish philosophically. For the perplexing mystery of the Platonic Forms is that in a Christian world they can be neither God nor creatures. They cannot be creatures because they are immutable and eternal; and they cannot be God because they are a real plurality of distinct and distinctly determined essences. And yet they rose before the minds of Christian thinkers again and again, and they hovered somewhere on the horizon between God and creatures, strange aliens both from heaven and from earth, and yet aliens whose message proved so enduringly dear to Christian thinkers that, rather than forget it, they exhausted their energies in pursuing it. At the end of the fifteenth century Gabriel Biel does no more than confess the sad experiences of Christian thinkers with the paradoxes of the Platonic Forms. In spite of St. Augustine, the Platonic Forms have succeeded in introducing a war among their Christian partisans. And the discussion, needless to say, centered on this recalcitrance of the Forms. How could they introduce their plurality into God? And yet how could creatures bear their immutability and their eternity? Here are words which, because of the history which precedes them, report no mere academic quarrel but the root issue which had already sealed the fate of medieval philosophy itself:

> *Et quia haec duo, scilicet incommutabilitas sive aeternitas et multiplicitas sive pluralitas non videntur uni posse convenire (essentia enim divina quae immutabilis est et aeterna non recipit pluralitatem illam quae inter ydeas ponitur. Ponitur enim quod quaelibet res creabilis habeat propriam et distinctam ydeam. Et quamvis haec pluralitas creaturae convenit, tamen non incommutabilitas et aeternitas quae solius dei est.):—idcirco duae sunt opiniones extremae in hac materia, licet et multae aliae sint quodammodo mediae.*[20]

It remains, however, that even when, as with Ockham, we are as far from Platonism as we can possibly be, we are still under the shadow of its influence. It was the purpose of Ockham to pursue those who were disciples of Platonism and to expose all the antinomies of their thinking. But it was also the fate of Ockham thus to carry on a war against Platonism only on Platonic grounds. Like the Platonists against whom he fights so valiantly, he is beset by the antinomy between intelligibility and unity; but because he labors this antinomy so much and so persistently, he enables us to understand not only that the road out of Platonism which he chose was itself a concession to Platonism, but also wherein the efforts of St. Thomas Aquinas in the conflict between Hellenism and Christianity were the veritable revolution that Professor Gilson has proclaimed them to be. I hope it will not be thought flippant if I say here that Ockham's manner of avoiding Platonism consists in closing his eyes in a Platonic heaven, whereas the manner of St. Thomas Aquinas consists in laying the ghost of Platonism. But let us turn to the texts.

III

In turning to some of the texts of Ockham, my only aim is to indicate that there exists a philosophical frontier between him and St. Thomas; that that frontier is established by their different relations to Platonism; that these relations are such that it can be said that St. Thomas is separated from Platonism by a principle, whereas Ockham is separated from Platonism only by the manner in which he localizes the Platonic antinomy, which he accepts, between intelligibility and unity; that the Thomistic notion of the individual and the Ockhamist notion of the singular are consequently as far apart from one another as they can possibly be, for whereas the former is freed from the Platonic conflict between being and unity, the latter is the very consequence of that conflict; and that while the thought of St. Thomas on the nature of being develops in the direction of autonomy and independence, that of Ockham develops in the direction of radical indistinguishability and pure contingency. It is the notion itself of what being is which separates St. Thomas from Plato, whether we deal with the problem of individuality or the problem of liberty. But Ockham remains a disciple of Plato on those very points in which St. Thomas Aquinas had effected the metaphysical revolution of which Professor Gilson has already spoken. For on such crucial questions as, what is meant by the unity of each being? what distinction is there among the divine attributes? whether a plurality of divine ideas is compatible with the simplicity of the divine essence? whether the divine essence, intellect and will are in any way distinguishable from one another?—on such crucial questions, one fundamental principle dominates the attitude of Ockham and relates him as much to the Platonic tradition as it separates him from St. Thomas Aquinas. I have already referred to a "realism of the unintelligible." I should like to relate the Ockhamist attitude on these questions to such a realism and to say that the identification of the individual *with the indistinguishable* governs their solution.

Realism in the question of universals is the enemy of Ockham, and it would seem he found enemies everywhere. After a lengthy discussion of Scotus, in the *Commentary*, Ockham, having eliminated the formal distinction from creatures entirely, asks a last and most embracing question: *"utrum illud quod est universale et commune univocum sit quomodocumque realiter a parte rei extra animam?"*[21] *Quomodocumque realiter* is evidently an effort to reach the last stronghold of realism. Ockham finds it everywhere:

> *In conclusione istius quaestionis omnes quos vidi concordant dicentes quod natura quae est aliquo modo universalis, saltem in potentia et incomplete, est realiter in individuo; quamvis aliqui dicant quod distinguitur realiter, aliqui quod tantum formaliter, aliqui quod nullo modo ex natura rei, sed tantum secundum rationem vel per considerationem intellectus.*[22]

However these thinkers may disagree with one another's explanations of

The Dilemma of Being and Unity

their realism, they are agreed in this, that *"universalia sunt aliquo modo a parte rei, ita quod universalia sunt realiter in ipsis singularibus."*[23] Against this realism the position of Ockham is rigorously uncompromising: *"Ad oppositum. Opposita non possunt competere eidem. Sed omnis res extra animam est simpliciter singularis. Ergo nulla res est aliquo modo universalis."*[24]

Nothing appears more uncompromising than this conclusion; and nothing, at first glance, seems more evident than its significance. Clearly, if "everything outside the mind is absolutely singular," and if the same reality cannot be the subject of opposed characteristics, then without any doubt no thing which is the *same reality* in the sense of being *absolutely singular* can be, in any way, universal. But it is equally clear that the demonstration hinges on the meaning of sameness and singularity which characterize *res.* Let us come to the issue, therefore. What exactly is the point of this deceptively simple demonstration? The critique which Ockham directs against Scotus is the clearest location of the answer to our question.[25]

But that location must itself be located. When Ockham reaches Scotus, he has already eliminated two realistic answers to the question of universals. Both of these answers hold that the universal is really distinct from the singular in which it is found. The first of these holds, however, that the universal remains one and identical amidst the multiplication of singulars; while the second holds that it is multiplied according to the multiplication of singulars. As to the first of these two realisms, Ockham reports it as follows:

> *Ad istam quaestionem est una opinio quod quodlibet universale univocum est quaedam res existens extra animam realiter in quolibet et singulari et de essentia cuiuslibet singularis distincta realiter a quolibet singulari et a quolibet alio universali, ita quod homo universalis est una vera res extra animam existens realiter in quolibet homine, et distinguitur realiter a quolibet homine et ab animali universali et a substantia universali, et sic de omnibus generibus et speciebus sive subalternis sive non subalternis. Et ita secundum istam opinionem, quot sunt universalia praedicabilia in quid per se primo modo de aliquo singulari per se in genere, tot sunt in eo res realiter distinctae, quarum quaelibet realiter distinguitur ab alia et ab illo singulari, et omnes istae res in se nullo modo multiplicantur quantumcumque singularia multiplicentur quae sunt in quolibet individuo eiusdem speciei.*[26]

But since Ockham qualifies this opinion as *"simpliciter falsa et absurda,"*[27] we may consider in it only the motivations of those who held it. These

[161]

motivations are as old as Plato: this real universal *"non esset ponenda nisi ad salvandam praedicationem essentialem unius de altero vel ad salvandam scientiam de rebus et diffinitiones rerum, quas omnes innuunt arguentes pro opinione Platonis."*[28] A realism of things known is without question too much to pay for a real knowledge of things. Could we possibly save the realism of knowledge by multiplying universals according to the plurality of singulars? Could we hold the doctrine of universal *and* distinct humanities in Plato and Socrates? This is the doctrine in question, and it brings us nearer the problem of singulars:

> *Ad quaestionem est una opinio quae imponitur doctori subtili a quibusdam, sicut ab aliis opinio recitata et improbata in praecedente quaestione sibi imponitur. Et est opinio quod universale est vera res extra animam distincta realiter ab una differentia contrahente, realiter tamen multiplicata et variata per talem differentiam contrahentem.*[29]

Let us confine ourselves here to the problem we really now meet for the first time, namely, the mysterious relations between the universal and the individual of which it is a part: how, asks Ockham, is a part of a singular whole itself not singular? In fact:

> *Ideo dico ad quaestionem quod in individuo non est aliqua natura universalis realiter distincta a differentia contrahente, quia non posset ibi poni talis natura nisi esset pars essentialis ipsius individui. Sed semper inter totum et partem est proportio, quod si totum sit singulare non commune quaelibet pars eodem modo est singularis proportionabiliter, nec potest una pars plus esse singularis quam alia. Ergo vel nulla pars individui est singularis vel quaelibet; sed non nulla, ergo quaelibet.*[30]

These are already ominous words for Scotus. If the nature of a thing is an essential part of that thing, it cannot be really distinct from it. What is more, there is a proportion between the whole and the part in a thing, such that each part is as singular as the whole, and as each other part. Now it might appear that the position of Scotus, by not holding a real distinction between the universal and the individual, might avoid Ockham's censure on the first count. For, as reported by Ockham, Scotus holds that the universal is something *"realiter extra animam ex natura rei distinctum ab individuo, quamvis non realiter."*[31] But instead of succeeding, this Scotistic position fails. In a word, the position of Scotus, as understood by Ockham, is a half-way house between a Platonic realism of essences, which it accepts, and a strict acceptance of real singulars which it also defends. The position of

The Dilemma of Being and Unity

Scotus is thus peculiarly interesting: there is in it an interior conflict between Platonic essences and unplatonic singulars. Hence the inevitable question: in which direction will Scotus resolve the conflict? Will he take the road back to Platonism or the road forward to Nominalism? Such is the dilemma that Ockham proposes. We may see, from the following text, both the position of Scotus, as understood by Ockham, and the particular care that Ockham takes in expounding it.

> *Ad istam quaestionem dicitur quod in re extra animam est natura eadem realiter cum differentia contrahente ad determinatum individuum, distincta tamen formaliter, quae de se nec est universalis nec particularis, sed incomplete est universalis in re et complete secundum esse in intellectu. Et quia ista opinio est ut credo opinio subtilis doctoris qui alios in subtilitate excellebat, ideo volo totam istam opinionem quam sparsim ipse ponit in diversis locis hic recitare distincte verba quae ponit in diversis locis non mutando. Et est de intentione istius doctoris quod praeter unitatem numeralem est unitas realis minor unitate numerali quae convenit ipsi naturae quae est aliquo modo universalis.*[32]

Quoting from the *Opus Oxoniense*,[33] Ockham considers the Scotistic notion of the common nature from four different points of view. He compares it with the singular, with numerical unity, with universality, and with that lesser than numerical unity which it possesses.[34] His effort in this discussion is to disengage the exact manner in which the common nature is identical with and distinct from the individual in which it is found. The common nature has a unity of its own formally distinct from the numerical unity of the individual; it is of itself not individual; community belongs to it by nature, but not universality or singularity, and therefore it is necessary to seek both the cause of the universality which the common nature has in the intellect and of the singularity which it has in things.[35]

This rapid summary of Ockham's own compact summary of Scotus is sufficient to indicate the critical point at issue. Here is a common nature formally distinct, but not really distinct, from the individuating conditions as well as from the numerical unity of the individual in which it is found. Now, whatever be the motives which inspired this doctrine, Ockham will have none of it: *"Ad oppositum. Nulla natura quae est realiter individuum est realiter universale. Ergo si ista natura sit realiter istud individuum, non est realiter universale."*[36] In fact, in the order of creatures, only where there is a real distinction can there be a formal distinction. Hence the trouble begins when we are asked to make a formal distinction at a moment when Scotus grants that it is not a distinction between realities. It is the impossibility of this position that Ockham belabors. If the nature and the contracting difference in the individual are not absolutely the same, then something can be truly affirmed of one and denied of the other. But of the same reality, in the order of creatures, the same thing cannot be truly affirmed and truly denied. Therefore, assuming the absence of complete identity between nature and contracting difference, Ockham can only conclude that these are not one reality. Shall we deny this conclusion? It would then follow that every way of proving a distinction of realities in creatures would be lost, for contradiction is the strongest way of proving a distinction of realities. If, therefore, reality is such that it does not permit anything absolutely identical to be truly affirmed or truly denied within it, then no real distinction in creatures can be proved.

> *Contra istam opinionem potest argui duplici via. Primo quia impossibile est in creaturis aliqua differre formaliter nisi distinguantur realiter. Ergo si natura distinguitur aliquo modo ab illa differentia contrahente, oportet quod distinguantur sicut res et res, vel sicut ens rationis et ens rationis, vel sicut ens reale et rationis. Sed primum negatur ab isto, et similiter secundum. Ergo oportet dari tertium. Ergo natura quocunque modo distinguitur ab individuo non est nisi ens rationis. Antecedens patet quia si natura et illa differentia contrahens non sunt idem omnibus modis, ergo aliquid potest vere affirmari de uno et negari de reliquo. Sed de eadem re in creaturis non potest idem vere affirmari et vere negari. Ergo non sunt una res. Minor patet quia si sic, periret omnis via probandi distinctionem rerum in creaturis, quia contradictio est via potissima ad probandum distinctionem rerum. Si igitur in creaturis ab eadem re nihil ab eodem pro eadem re potest omnino idem vere negari et vere affirmari, nulla distinctio realis potest probari in eis.*[37]

(We should ask at this point whether the principle of contradiction is the test and the measure of the meaning of unity and identity in things, or whether, were there no such unity and identity, the principle itself would not operate. In any case, let us notice that it is the former of these two possibilities which Ockham is accepting.)

Every reality outside the mind, Ockham continues, is according to the assumption of Scotus himself really singular and numerically one. It follows that no reality outside the mind is really common, nor can it be one with the unity which is opposed to the unity of singularity. Hence, on the principle that if one of two opposites can be attributed to a reality, the other cannot, it follows that there is only a singular unity in each thing.[38]

Having, in the name of their singularity, eliminated community from

The Dilemma of Being and Unity

things, Ockham arrives at two conclusions. These are that every singular reality is singular through itself: *"quaelibet res singularis seipsa est singularis"*; and that every reality outside the mind is really singular and one in number: *"omnis res extra animam est realiter singularis et una numero."*[39] In the language of the *Expositio Aurea*:

> *Est autem tenendum indubitanter quod quaelibet res imaginabilis existens per se sine omni additione est res singularis et una numero, ita quod nulla res imaginabilis est per aliquod additum sibi singularis, sed illa est passio insequens immediate omnem rem, quia omnis res per se vel est eadem vel diversa ab alia. Secundo tenendum est quod nullum universale est extra animam existens realiter in substantiis individuis nec est de substantia vel esse earum, sed universaliter est tantum in anima, vel est universale per institutionem, quomodo haec vox prolata* animal, *et similiter* homo, *est universalis quia de pluribus est praedicabilis, non pro se sed pro rebus quas significat.*[40]

Every being outside the mind, therefore, is singular through itself. Every reality outside the mind is singular and one in number; or, to put the point otherwise, no universal exists outside the mind in individual substances or in any way as part of their being.

Let us assume for the sake of argument that there exists outside the mind a reality which is not of itself singular. Call that reality *a*. Then Ockham argues as follows. Either that reality contains essentially many realities, or it is one reality. Taking up the first alternative, we inquire first whether the realities included essentially within it are finite in number or not. It cannot be held that they would be actually infinite. Hence, on the supposition that they are of a finite number, each one of them is one in number and therefore the resultant whole is one in number. So, on the assumption that the reality which is not held to be of itself singular contains essentially many realities, we have proved that each one of the included realities is one in number and, therefore, that the resultant whole is also one in number. Here is, therefore, a singular whole containing singular realities: the idea of a non-singular reality breaks down. Assume now that that reality *a* is not many realities and that it does not contain essentially many realities. Ockham's point is then established, for "when there is some reality which does not include within itself many realities in any way distinct, that reality is one in number, and consequently, that universal reality is one in number and consequently singular." Again, therefore, the notion of a common reality breaks down. For it is shown now that *a*, which is not assumed to be *de se res singularis*, turns out to be a singular and one in number:

[165]

Si sit aliqua res, quae non sit de se res singularis, cum quaelibet res possit habere nomen, vocetur illa res a. Tunc quaero: aut continet essentialiter plures res aut est praecise una res. Si detur primum, quaero de illis rebus inclusis essentialiter: aut sunt in certo numero aut non. Non potest dici quod non sint in certo numero quia tunc essent infinita in actu, quod est impossibile; si sunt in certo numero, quaelibet illarum est numero una, et per consequens totum resultans est unum numero. Si detur quod illa res non est plures res nec continet plures res essentialiter, tunc habetur propositum, quia quanto est aliqua res quae non includit multiplicitatem rerum quantumcunque distinctarum, illa est una res numero, et per consequens illa res universalis est una numero et per consequens singularis.[41]

Let us pursue this supposed universal reality a little longer. If we add *a* and Socrates together, the result will be either many realities or one reality. If one, and Socrates is a singular reality, then *a* also is a singular reality; if many, and not infinite in number, and indeed they can be only two in number, it follows that, since they are two in number, each one of them is one in number. Wherefore the conclusion: that universal reality is one in number and consequently singular. This can be proved, for every reality which is one and not many is one in number (for that is what being-one-in-number means). Now we have shown that that universal reality is one and not many. Therefore, it is one in number and hence singular:

Praeterea. Accipio illam rem universalem, scilicet a. Tunc quaero: aut a et Sortes sint plures res aut una. Si una, et Sortes est res singularis, ergo et a est res singularis; si sunt plures res et non sunt infinitae, igitur, sunt finitae, et per consequens sunt in aliquo certo numero—et non potest dari quod sint plures res quam duae. Igitur sunt tantum duae res. Sed quando sunt tantum duae res, utraque illarum est una secundum numerum. Igitur illa res universalis est una secundum numero et per consequens est singularis. Confirmatur, quia omnis res quae est una res et non plures est una numero (hoc enim est quid nominis istius quod est unum numero); sed illa res universalis est una res et non est plures; igitur est una numero; igitur est singularis.[42]

The peculiarity of this conclusion is not so much that every reality outside the mind is singular or that the reality of the singular cannot be derived by the method of contracting universals. In saying that each reality is singular, as is its every part, Ockham has arrived at an extraordinary result: *in the name of the singularity of things he has eliminated every vestige of the realism of essences.* Let us even suppose that behind Ockham's attack upon Platonism there lies a certain awareness, however dim, that the individual, existentially considered, contains a uniqueness and an incommunicability which no Platonic method of unlikeness will ever produce. He perceives that to say of each being that it is and that it is itself is a different sort of question from the question of its likeness or unlikeness towards other things. But he never really says that diversity is not difference, and the enormous tenacity with which he contends that each reality is *seipsa singularis* labors under the inability to do more than run away from Platonism. For Ockham has said no more than that the individual is the non-common, and he has left it to the principle of contradiction to bear the burden of proving this non-community. And yet, what is the value of the principle of contradiction in a world of impervious singulars? Granted, therefore, that Ockham avoids rigorously every Platonic effort to people the world with logical intentions, it remains that, in the process of separating the logical from the real, he also deprives the real of an inherent order of natures. And the question that remains is why this supposed rescuing of logic from the notorious "villainy" of a Neoplatonic Porphyry should deprive reality of its intelligibility?[43]

In the *Summa Logicae* Ockham deals with Scotus rather brusquely. Of the opinion that the universal is really outside the mind but only formally distinct from the individual in which it exists, Ockham says flatly that "*haec opinio videtur esse irrationabilis.*" And not only do the reasons go to the very core of Ockhamism, they also answer our question: "*. . . in creaturis non potest esse aliqua distinctio qualitercunque extra animam nisi ubi sunt res distinctae. Si ergo inter illam naturam et differentiam sit qualiscunque distinctio, oportet quod sint res realiter distinctae.*"[44] What, therefore, is a singular being in the light of this precise text except that which is one in the sense of being indistinct and indistinguishable from the standpoint of the intellect? Ockham is here saying that to be a *res*, one in number and singular, is equivalent to being nothing more and nothing less than radically impervious to the intellect. Who would deny that this is the death of Porphyrianism? And yet, did Porphyry have to be put to death so violently? Is it only in a world of atomic and indistinguishable singulars that we are safe from the logic of Porphyry? In Platonism, only a plurality of distinct realities—distinct in the order of intelligibility itself—can guarantee the difference and the plurality which is necessary to the intelligibility of knowledge. Yet, how does it happen that the Ockhamist answer to this Platonic alphabetism of reality consists in holding, not that the Platonic conception of being is wrong (because, in fact, the Platonic conception as to how being is intelligible is wrong), but that we have disarmed Plato by the expedient of declaring that each reality is one because it is impervious to the intelligence?

Such questions have, so far as I can see, one and the same answer. And since that answer is verified abundantly elsewhere in the thought of Ockham, there is every reason to believe that it is correct. That answer, put in the historical terms which give it its proper significance, is that the method which leads Ockham thus to base the individuality of things on their supposed indistinguishability is the same method which has led Platonists and Neoplatonists, Greek and Arabian, to the doctrine of the One. This is to say that the method which raises into a principle an open war between intelligibility and unity in being is a method which can lead to a violent victory in one of two directions: with Platonism it drives unity to a formless isolation above being, and with Ockhamism it maintains unity by driving out intelligibility. This means that for Ockham, as for Plato and Plotinus, there is one standing paradox which reality offers and that it is the conflict between essence and individuality, intelligibility and unity. In the presence of this paradox, we can maintain a world of singulars only by suppressing essences from being; which means also that our notion of what a singular is includes within itself, *as a constitutive principle,* such a suppression.

Declaring the world dark, however, in order to avoid Plato is conceding that it is Plato's conception of the world which governs us: *he* set the antinomy, and from the same antinomy we simply choose a different alternative and consequence. And precisely, what is this to say but that, if the Platonic sun of intelligibility shines too brightly and too hotly upon the world, we have only to darken the world and to close the eyes of our intelligences in order to avoid the glare? If this conclusion is true, it cannot be said of Ockham that, however much he was opposed to Platonic realism, he succeeded in avoiding it. On the contrary, he lived under its influence, and the Ockhamist notions of unity, identity and simplicity, whether applied to creatures or to God, are freighted with the burden of the Platonic conflict. For Ockham's notion of God, of the divine unity and attributes, of the divine will and its omnipotence, is a notion which, such as it has been described by his historians,[45] reveals all the effects of an antinomy that can be seen to persist by the very violence of its resolution. Exactly what is the meaning of a divine nature whose unity must be. measured by that very indistinguishability which is the price of avoiding Platonism?

The Dilemma of Being and Unity

IV

This is the question which relates the natural theology of Ockham to Platonism and which separates St. Thomas Aquinas as much from Ockham as it does from Platonism itself. From one point of view, there is nothing peculiar or new about the question. The enormous concern of Ockham with the simplicity of the divine essence is notorious enough. In the name of that simplicity, understood after the manner which led Ockham to the notion of indistinguishability as the mark of individuality, we arrive at a simplicity whose imperviousness to analysis and distinction is the means of maintaining its unity. Indistinction rules Ockham's conception of the perfections of God. Let the divine essence be silent and opaque in order that it be one: *"dico quod non sunt plures perfectiones attributales, sed tantum est ibi una perfectio indistincta re et ratione, quae proprie et de virtute sermonis non debet dici esse in Deo vel in divina essentia, sed est omnibus modis ipsa divina essentia."*[46] Is not this a conclusion which fears the pluralism and the determinateness of the Platonic notion of being? And is not Ockham transcending this pluralism in a direction which is itself Platonic, namely, the direction of emptying being of its perfections in order to reach unity?

The point is a crucial one. If we refuse to accept the contention that Ockham is making concessions to Platonism,[47] how shall we explain his attack upon what may legitimately be called the traditional doctrine of divine ideas? In formulating his own doctrine of ideas Ockham is conscious of opposing his predecessors in a decisive way. And yet that very opposition is made possible for him by the dissociation between divine ideas and *essences* which the thirteenth century itself, under the influence of Avicenna, had already accomplished. As a remarkable historical work has proved, and as I shall indicate presently, this sundering of divine ideas into *ideae* and *ideata* may have preserved what Henry of Ghent was anxious to have preserved, namely, the distinct essences of things within eternity itself. From the standpoint of essences this is a Platonic victory, but from the standpoint of the nature of God this is the source of serious conflicts for Christian thinkers.

What is it, to be more specific, that leads Ockham to interpret the famous Augustinian text of the *Liber de diversis quaestionibus LXXXIII* (p. 46) in such a distorted way? And what is it that leads Ockham to deny that, in the sense in which God is said to be eternal, the divine ideas are not eternal? Here is the proper meaning of eternal: eternal is said *"uno modo proprie pro eo quod vere et proprie et realiter est actualiter existens aeternaliter."* Now this is the sense in which the ideas are not eternal, but God alone is eternal: *"primo modo dico quod ideae non sunt aeternae, sed solus Deus sic*

Essays in Thomism

est aeternus."[48] Why does Ockham resolve the problem of ideas, not in favor of identifying them with the divine essence, but in favor of identifying them with creatures? Is not this, too, a fear of Platonic pluralism? *". . . essentia divina non est idea, quia quaero: aut ideae sunt in mente divina subiective aut obiective. Non subiective, quia tunc essent ibi plura subiective, quod est manifeste falsum; ergo sunt ibi tantum obiective: sed essentia divina non est tantum obiective; ergo non est idea."*[49] With Ockham we seem to proceed not out of fear *for* the divine ideas, but out of fear *of* them. And is not this to say that, since the Platonic pluralism has captured the divine intellect itself through the Avicennian persuasions of Henry of Ghent, we now stand in awe of the very essences whose distinctness we had thought to guarantee? For how can we prevent the conflict between the divine simplicity and an order of essences which are too creaturely in their determinateness to live peacefully, and to allow God to live peacefully, in eternity?

My purpose in asking these questions will be misunderstood if it is not seen that I intend them, not at all as a demonstration of the truth of Thomism, but as a sort of historical propaedeutic to an understanding of the significance of Thomism in terms of the doctrinal conflict between Hellenism and Christianity. We must grasp the conflict itself in its philosophical implications in order to understand the exact meaning of the issues at stake and therefore the requirements of a true solution. The Thomistic notion of God is, in more ways than one, a monument to the meaning and the successful resolution of the oppositions and antinomies contained in the Platonic theory of being; and it is in this sense that we may very properly consider the metaphysics of St. Thomas Aquinas to be a climax in the history of natural theology. Intelligibility minus unity; intelligence minus autonomy; being which is fighting a continual war against interior forces of division, plurality and even disintegration; being which therefore stems the barbarism of eternal matter by a transcendence which is a confession that the barbarians are continually threatening at the gates of reality as well as at those of the Roman Empire: such is, in its simplest outlines, the intellectual message of the ancient world. It is not at all surprising that intelligence should rule as permanently, as determinately, yes, and even as despotically as it possibly can in order to maintain an imperfect and compromised dominion over being. If, from one point of view, this is the picture of a necessitarian world, from another point of view, it is the picture of a dismembered world; it is the picture of a world which is as lacking in individual beings as its intelligibility, sealed in determinateness, is lacking in unity. This is a world of order, but it is also a world which sacrifices its reality to order.

The Dilemma of Being and Unity

The open mystery of the philosophy of Plotinus is that God has no independence of action whatever. The mystery is an *open* one because in a philosophy in which the world itself has been divinized God must be a stranger to his own being. Now it is abundantly clear that Ockham has transcended the determinism which led, in Plotinus, to a God who is an intelligence without autonomy, as well as a being without unity. What is not at all clear is whether, in avoiding the determinism which immobilizes the Plotinian God, Ockham is not proposing a mystery of his own. The Plotinian determinism requires finally that God take refuge in the formlessness of a unity above being. The question is whether Ockham has a successful answer to the Plotinian determinism in the doctrine of the radical indistinctness of the divine simplicity. The divine simplicity, as understood by Ockham, leaves the divine will embarrassingly free. However we may conceive the will of the Ockhamist God, and even supposing that the notion of voluntarism in Ockham still remains to be clarified, what we can now say with certainty is that Ockham is distinguished from St. Thomas, not by any doctrine of an *arbitrary* will, but rather by a doctrine of a divine essence which, in the name of its own simplicity, is as barren of order and wisdom as the Plotinian One is barren of the intelligible nature of being. It is a mystery why the world which proceeds from the will of the Ockhamist God contains more than the stability of a pure *fiat*, and why the divine will itself can contain the wisdom, the independence and the necessity of an infinite being. For the nominalist fear of essences has made the divine will their master, until with Biel we come to this: *"nec enim quia aliquid rectum est aut iustum, ideo Deus vult, sed quia Deus vult, ideo iustum et rectum."*[50]

In the world of Plotinus, necessity and contingency do not and cannot penetrate one another: they can only give place to one another, and they can only limit one another. Contingency, as a vehicle of autonomous activity, is as unknown to Plotinus as necessity is unknown to Ockham. Such is the opposition: Plotinian necessity, which excludes autonomy and liberty, versus Ockhamist omnipotence, which excludes necessity in order to retain liberty, but in which autonomy has surrendered to radical contingency. It is clear that the Plotinian God has no independence and autonomy of action: he is the victim of his own intelligence and being; it is both a fact and an inexplicable mystery that the God of Ockham has. Just so. But my point is that the Ockhamist mystery must be understood as a reaction against, and indeed a defiant reaction against, the necessity which ruled the Plotinian God. Such a defiance means not only that it is standing in the presence of Greek intelligence and a Greek notion of the intelligible nature of being, but also that it is standing in fear of them. For the ancient enemy of intelligence minus unity we are substituting, with nominalism, a new mystery: autonomy versus intelligence. And this is true because for the equally ancient enemy of a doctrine of being whose determinateness casts out unity, we are now forced to substitute a unity which casts out intelligibility. From Platonic realism to nominalism the line of descent is both direct and inevitable. If we accept current interpretations of Ockham,[51] and if we make an effort to see his thought as a philosophical phenomenon produced by fundamentally philosophical causes and antecedents, then we are led to see in it the old antinomies of Greek philosophy repeating themselves. This is the only contention that I am here advancing. It enables us to understand both the age of St. Thomas and St. Thomas himself. It enables us to see that both our view and our solution of the problems of the thirteenth century must be as radical as the range and the depth of the problems themselves.

With such a conclusion we are at the doorstep of St. Thomas, as well as at the origins of his age. The transition from the twelfth to the thirteenth century was a transition from a logical view of the famous question of universals to a metaphysical appreciation of the Platonism which lay behind this question. Early medieval thinkers were dominantly concerned with genera and species, but with the thirteenth century the problem becomes one of generic and specific essences. The point of view of extension is replaced by the point of view of comprehension. It has been thought, and with great justice, that the Avicennian doctrine of the *absolute essence* was responsible for this metaphysical coming of age of the problem of universals.[52] Quite clearly, the thinkers of the thirteenth century were considerably beyond the position of reifying the logical universal—if only because the Aristotelian critique of Plato, in insisting that the universality of knowledge needed a ἕν κατὰ πολλῶν and not ἕν τι παρὰ τὰ πολλά, and in laboring mercilessly the difficulties of the participation theory, forced Platonists themselves to argue out their case in metaphysics and to propose Platonism primarily as a theory of being and not as an exorbitant effort to say the universality and the necessity of knowledge.[53] Henry of Ghent, for example, not only accepts the Aristotelian critique of universals reified apart from singulars, but also argues against Aristotle himself that Plato never thought any such thing.[54] More than this, following a tradition made famous by St. Augustine, Henry identifies the Platonic Forms with the ideas in the mind of God.[55] The Platonic *separatism* is gone, but Platonism remains entrenched in Christian thought more strongly and more dangerously than ever.

It is only when we see that in the thirteenth century the Platonic theory of Forms succeeds apparently in finding a home in the Christian world of God and creatures that we are really in the presence of what is at once exciting and decisive in the relations of Christian thinkers to Platonism. Have Christian thinkers thus really succeeded in explaining, within the framework of a Platonic theory of being, the nature of God, of creatures and of their relations? Have the Platonic Forms found at last a resting place *both* in the natures of things *and* in the mind of God? Had Plato ever thought of this and had he ever intended that the world of Forms should somehow become doubled? Is it Platonic thus to describe the divine ideas and the essences of created beings by means of one and the same theory of being? To a Christian looking at Plato there is every invitation to translate the *Timaeus* into a doctrine of a free creation and thus to endow the sensible world with a far greater share in reality than Plato had ever intended and than his philosophy really permits. Plotinus, the great disciple of Plato, overcomes the Platonic opposition between the intelligible and the sensible, the eternal and the temporal, in a way which cannot at all lend itself to a doctrine of God and creatures.[56] The more Plotinus analyzes the world of sense, the more he discovers the intelligible and the divine. Somehow the intelligible and the divine comes down into, and is found in, the world of sense itself. If Plotinus is any criterion at all, Platonism should resolve the apparent discontinuity between the sensible and the intelligible by uniting the two so intimately that the last outpost of the reign of divine intelligibility is formless matter itself. This is to say that what we call God and creatures so merge with one another in Platonism that it is impossible to avoid a confusion of their respective attributes. For Christian thinkers, the great stumbling block that Platonism offers is that, being strictly neither an analysis of the nature of God nor an analysis of the nature of creatures, but rather an analysis of being in which there is no such distinction between God and creatures, it cannot be used successfully to describe either the nature of the Christian God or that of His creatures.

The very inappropriateness of Platonism in a Christian world, therefore, arises at the moment that it is called upon to explain the nature of God and of creatures by means of a metaphysics of being in which there is, strictly speaking, neither the one nor the other. To put the point otherwise: the eternal and the temporal are related as the divine and the changeable, but *not* as God and creatures. In brief, the dividing line in the order of being is for Plato, not between God and creature, but between intelligibility and matter. It is therefore inevitable that what is divine in Platonism should have some of the attributes which, in a Christian world, belong to creatures; and it is equally inevitable that the temporal should have some of the attributes which, in a Christian world, belong to God. We witness here that dismemberment of reality which the doctrine of the eternity of matter finally produced and which becomes the root principle of the philosophy of Plotinus. God and the world so penetrate one another in the philosophy of Plotinus, and the imperfections of the world so capture the divine intelligence, that the famous flight of the One from being is the only way in which God can find freedom from the world and the world itself a resting place from its own divisions.

V

The Platonic conflict between intelligibility and unity must be seen as proceeding from such a view of being before the meaning of the Thomistic reconstruction can be fully appreciated. What is needed is not a new theory of knowledge, or a new theory of the relations between logic and metaphysics. The need is deeper. What is needed is a theory of being which, having measured the Platonic conflict for what it really is, *and having seen the Platonic inability to speak of being in a universe of God and creatures,* rebuilds the notion of being itself within the framework of a world in which the divine and the temporal are related as God and creatures. This is a change in metaphysical perspective which is at once radical and decisive. The antinomies between intelligibility and being were, in fact, born of a confusion—a confusion which allowed neither God nor creatures *to be,* but which sacrificed the existence of both to the orderly reign of a war between them. What must be done? Evidently, we must first ask: what is it for a being to be? We must not sacrifice the being of things either to Platonic essences or to Aristotelian species. We must therefore see, secondly, that the frontier of *existence* is opened to things by the doctrine of a God Who is by nature Being. In this doctrine of God as *Being,* and in the meaning of His *unity* as an infinite Being, we must see the radical basis of the answer to Platonism which St. Thomas proposes. That there is a God Who is one and Who, in the infinity of His Being, possesses in a unique and unitary way all the perfections of being—*this* is a doctrine which separates St. Thomas from Platonism by a principle which is a decisive elimination of the Platonic determinism.

To understand this conclusion, let us limit ourselves to the problem of the divine ideas such as it presented itself to the thirteenth century. The simplest way to put the problem is to see that, so long as St. Augustine could be used to curb the fundamental dispersion in the doctrine of ideas which is found in Avicenna, the influence of the illustrious Arabian philosopher remained at once limited and compromised. "Let us observe again that the theologians of the thirteenth century are unanimous in taking from the Arabians the entirely un-Aristotelian thesis of an *universale ante rem*; that with equal unanimity they locate this transcendent universal in the divine ideas; and that finally—it is *this* point on which I am insisting—the Idea is for them not at all distinct from the very substance of God, the highest and all-inclusive Intelligible. From St. Augustine to St. Thomas, by way of John Scotus, St. Anselm, William of Auvergne, Alexander of Hales, Robert Grosseteste and many others, one and the same doctrine, continually refined and perfected, dominates the theological teaching concerning the foundation of essences. Multiplicity belongs to them alone, and their common foundation lies in the unity of God and of His Word: seen from the side of God, the Ideas become identified in a single reality which is none other than the divine essence."[57]

But the peculiarity of thinkers such as St. Albert the Great and, more especially, Henry of Ghent, is that in their doctrine of divine ideas Avicenna has the ascendency over St. Augustine. And this ascendency means, precisely, an introduction of the Platonic Forms into the divine intellect as an order of essences, really distinct from the divine essence and really distinct in their essential being, in order to satisfy the intelligible requirements of the divine activity and the intelligible natures of creatures. Apparently, Albert and Henry think to maintain an emanation of essences within the divine intellect in order to safeguard the old intelligible alphabetism of being that Plato bequeathed to European thought. Here is Henry of Ghent, true Avicennian, distinguishing in the doctrine of divine ideas the *respectus imitabilitatis in divina essentia* and the *rerum essentiae in divina cognitione.* Why? Because the traditional Christian doctrine of the divine ideas is insufficient, in his eyes, to express the objective and distinct character of the essences which are the objects of the divine knowledge: *"modus . . . theologorum magis consuetus est appellare ideas ipsas rationes imitabilitatis . . . sed positionem idearum secundum quod essentiae rerum appellantur ideae . . . optime exponit Avicenna, in sua Metaphysica . . ."* Elsewhere Henry distinguishes in the divine ideas these two aspects: *"rerum essentiae in divina notitia . . . ut quaedam objecta cognita (comprehensae) . . . quae secundum rem sunt aliae a divina natura; rationes cognoscendi illas quae secundum rem sunt eaedem cum natura divina"*! The enormous Platonism of this distinction requires reflection. When we turn to creation, Henry therefore argues that there is first a *production* of the *essential* being of creatures in the divine intellect which is followed by an external production of their *existential* being: *"quia igitur ideae in Deo causalitatem omnimodam habent super res quarum sunt formae, in constituendo illas in esse essentiae et existentiae, et hoc secundum rationem causae formalis exemplaris, idcirco respectus ideae ad ideata . . . (est) . . . penes primum (genus relationis) quod est inter producens et productum . . . ex perfec-*

tione divina provenit quod a ratione ideali in Deo fluit in esse essentiae primo essentia creaturae, et secundo mediante dispositione divinae voluntatis in esse existentiae."[58] This conclusion, be it observed, allows to the Platonic intelligibilization of being an honored place in the Christian world. For the multiplicity and the atomism of the Platonic Forms surely now disturbs the unity and the simplicity of God in a way which is no less serious for taking place within the divine intellect. But, more than this, having captured such a high citadel of being, the Platonic atomism is henceforth bound to be felt wherever beings are called upon to assert and maintain the intelligible frontiers of their essences. Within the order of creatures there is an order of essences which requires only the gaze of the human intelligence in order to declare an independence from sensible being which will make the Christian soul dream, however fugitively, of some of the privileges of a Platonic god. And why not? Is not this dream a Greek secret which the Platonic Forms maintain even in the intellect of the Christian God? But however this may be, and however exciting it would be to tell the story of this Greek god seeking to recapture his lost divinity in a Christian world, it remains that for St. Thomas Aquinas the Christian world yields no such message, the Christian man is asked to indulge in no such memories, for the Christian God does not bear within His intelligence any such Greek secret.[58a] For His name is Being.

One should scarcely be accused of—may I say it?—*Thomatism* if he urges that St. Thomas Aquinas is distinguished from his contemporaries by that very principle which distinguishes him from Platonism and which, in effect, eliminates all the pluralistic consequences of the Platonic determinism. Hence, the same historian from whom I have cited the above texts of Henry of Ghent can say of St. Thomas that, faithful to tradition, he knows only the essence itself of God as the divine ideas.[59] This is so true that it is scarcely necessary to insist upon it. In making that statement my own, I am concerned only to urge that it separates St. Thomas from Platonism both in fact and in principle.

It is asked: whether there is a plurality of divine ideas?[60] St. Thomas replies that there must be. Since, in fact, the order itself of the universe is intended by God, it is necessary that He should have an idea of it. But a whole cannot be known unless its members are known: as a builder cannot conceive the essence of a house unless the proper nature of each part were known to him. Hence, it is necessary that there be the proper expressions (*rationes*) of all things in the divine mind. As St. Augustine says, "*singula propriis rationibus a Deo creata sunt.*"[61] But there is nothing yet distinctive in this conclusion. Let us, therefore, ask a much more embarrassing question, namely, how this doctrine of many ideas is not opposed to the divine simplicity. The idea of an object which is produced, says St. Thomas, is in the mind of the producer as that which he knows: it is not the intelligible species which informs the intellect and actualizes it in order to know. Thus, the form of a house in the builder's mind is something which he knows and to the likeness of which he fashions a house in matter. Now precisely, it is not against the simplicity of the divine intellect that it should know many things; but it would be against its simplicity if it were informed by many intelligible species in order to have actual knowledge. The conclusion, therefore, which St. Thomas wishes to reach and which, in his view, reconciles the divine simplicity with the plurality of divine ideas is that there are many ideas in the divine mind as the objects of the divine intellection: *"unde plures ideae sunt in mente divina ut intellectae ab ipsa."*[62] Now how are we to understand this point, and more particularly, how are we to understand the reconciliation of simplicity and plurality? More particularly still, how does this conclusion make these reconciliations *and* guarantee to God a proper knowledge of creatures?

We must look for an answer in the direction of the famous Thomistic doctrine of the divine imitability. God knows His own essence perfectly, and this must mean that He knows it in all the ways in which it is knowable. But the divine essence can be known not only as it is in itself, but also as it can be participated according to a particular manner of likeness by creatures. Each creature has its own proper form, and thus shares, in a given way, in the likeness of the divine essence. Therefore, inasmuch as God knows His own essence as thus imitable by a given creature, He knows that essence as the proper expression (*rationem*) and idea of that creature. And so it is clear that God knows a multiplicity of proper expressions of a multiplicity of things, and this multiplicity of proper expressions is a multiplicity of ideas: *"et sic patet quod Deus intelligit plures rationes proprias plurium rerum, quae sunt plures ideae."*[63]

This demonstration requires two precisions. The first concerns the character of the *respectus* or relations which multiply ideas in God; the second, an explanation of how this plurality of ideas, so understood, transforms the Platonic determinism and eliminates from the thought of St. Thomas Aquinas any objectification of distinct essences as the means of preserving the distinct natures of the *creabilia*. I am concerned here only with the second of these two precisions. The question we have been asking must now be changed. We must now ask whether God has a proper knowledge of beings other than Himself?[64] The reason for this change is that we are now driven to ask the reason itself for the *proper* knowledge of things which God has.

To suppose, as have the Arabians, that God has only a general knowledge of things is to detract from the nature of the divine intelligence. For if God did not know things in their particularities, it would follow that His knowing would not be universally perfect, and that, consequently, neither would His being. Now, says St. Thomas Aquinas, this is against what I have already proved. And indeed it is, for he has already arrived at the idea of a universally perfect being.[65] How must we answer the question, then? We must say that God has a proper knowledge of other things, and this not only in so far as things agree in being, but also in so far as they are distinguished from one another. This is, in fact, a proper knowledge of each thing. Exactly how is it possible?

I have already shown, continues St. Thomas, that whatever perfection is found in any creature wholly pre-exists and is contained in God in a supreme way. To the perfection of creatures belongs not only that wherein they agree, namely, being itself, but also those things through which they are distinguished from one another, such as, to live and to have intelligence: through these, the living are distinguished from the non-living, and those beings that have intelligence are distinguished from those that do not. Every form, in fact, by which a thing is constituted in its proper species, is a certain perfection. In this way, we are to hold that all things pre-exist in God, and this includes the characteristics by which things are distinguished from one another.[66]

This is to say that God contains within Himself all perfections. But there is much more that we must say. Since God contains all perfections, His essence is compared to all the essences of things, not as the general to the particular, but as a perfect actuality to imperfect actualities: *sed sicut perfectus actus ad imperfectos actus*. The whole issue with the Platonic Forms is here at stake. Through a perfect *act* imperfect *acts* can be known with a proper knowledge. Thus, to use an analogy, he who knows man has a proper knowledge of animal. So too in the case of God. Since the essence of God possesses in itself whatever perfection is possessed by the essence of any other being, and indeed possesses greater perfection still, God can have in Himself a proper knowledge of all beings. *For the proper nature of each thing consists in this, that it participates the divine perfection in a certain way.* Now, God would not know Himself perfectly unless He knew every way in which His perfection is capable of being participated by other beings. What is more—and this is the peak of the demonstration—God would not have a perfect knowledge of the nature of existing, unless He knew all the ways of existing: "*nec etiam ipsam naturam essendi perfecte sciret nisi cognosceret omnes modos essendi.*"[67]

The Dilemma of Being and Unity

VI

It might not appear that in reaching this conclusion we have achieved our objective. It remains, however, that we have. In spite of Platonic essentialism in Christian thought, we must insist that the answer for which we have been looking is to be found in this doctrine of God as perfect actuality. It is not for nothing that St. Thomas looks back to the earlier discussions in the *Summa Theologica* as the key to the very meaning of what he is here saying. *Only if we begin with a God Who is infinite Being can we solve the problem of how the divine self-knowledge can include within itself a proper knowledge of all other beings.* I italicize this conclusion because St. Thomas Aquinas insists on it as the cornerstone which both founds his doctrine and separates it from Greek philosophy in general and from Platonism in particular. More than this, St. Thomas insists also that the conversations between Greek and Christian thought must take place at this frontier if Christian thinkers are to maintain the integrity and the purity of their own doctrines in the presence of Greek philosophical speculation.

It may be that familiarity can dull the freshness of our awareness. It may be that, never having had to face the necessity of meeting Greek philosophy as did the thirteenth century, we have both too easy a view of its significance and too easy a view of its place within Christian thought. One of the great lessons of the thirteenth century is that the Christianization of Greek thought was neither easy nor painless, and that the Platonic theory of Forms was not an extravagant defense of the truth of knowledge but a thoroughgoing theory of being which knew its own nature and its own root principle. In this respect, the commentary of St. Thomas on the *Liber de Causis* deserves to be better appreciated for it contains a diagnosis of Platonism which is throughout sensitive to the most enduring principles of the Platonic tradition. To interpret, in fact, the thought of St. Thomas Aquinas in relation to his conception of the nature of Platonism is to see the veritable revolution which must take place in philosophical thought before a philosophy which is authentically Christian and therefore consciously existential can be established.

Here, however, let me insist only on what may be called merely the theme of this revolution. It is a theme which, were we to consider it in itself, would indicate how Plato and Aristotle had a greater and a deeper possession of philosophical truth than they themselves really knew. For in distinguishing between the sensible and the intelligible, both in the order of being and in the order of knowledge, they came to stand, after all, in the presence of a mystery which they did not properly understand and yet on which they were gazing even at the moment of not understanding it.

Indeed, how can it be that one who holds that there are intelligible realities in existence, which are somehow *produced* realities, is not asserting a doctrine of production within the order of being that can ultimately be *only* a doctrine of creation? At the moment, therefore, when Plato and Aristotle transcend *generation* as the explanation of the origin of being, however waveringly and hesitatingly they may do so, however weakly they may look beyond *becoming*, it remains that the only true and stable position in which their vision can find a resting place is the doctrine of creation. Hence, it is true to say both that they arrived, and that they did not arrive, at a doctrine of creation. They did not arrive, for they never asserted it; they did arrive, but they never knew it.[68]

This conclusion resolves, from an exegetical point of view, a rather famous difficulty presented by the texts of St. Thomas Aquinas on the subject of Plato and Aristotle in relation to the doctrine of creation. The *De Potentia* affirms, and the *Summa Theologica* denies, that they arrived at the doctrine of the universal origin of being.[69] Those who might be inclined to think that St. Thomas changed his mind on this question will find in the *De Substantiis Separatis* that he adopts both the position of the *De Potentia* and the position of the *Summa*.[70] The positions are not mutually exclusive, though I can do no more here than simply assert the fact. This is not to deny the errors of Plato and Aristotle. On the contrary, the same St. Thomas who is at pains to point out these errors is likewise at pains to show *to Plato and to Aristotle* themselves the deepest implications of a doctrine of being which has arrived at a notion of production that transcends matter and generation. This is what Plato and Aristotle never said and yet what they were open to saying:

> *Sed ultra hunc modum [i.e., generation] fiendi necesse est, secundum sententiam Platonis et Aristotelis, ponere alium altiorem. Cum enim necesse sit primum principium simplicissimum esse, necesse est quod non hoc modo esse ponatur quasi esse participans, sed quasi ipsum esse existens. Quia vero esse subsistens non potest esse nisi unum, sicut supra habitum est, necesse est omnia alia quae sub ipso sunt, sic esse quasi esse participantia. Oportet igitur communem quamdam resolutionem in omnibus hujusmodi fieri, secundum quod unumquodque eorum intellectu resolvitur in id quod est, et in suum esse. Oportet igitur supra modum fiendi quo aliquid fit, forma materiae adveniente, praeintelligere aliam rerum originem, secundum quod esse attribuitur toti universitati rerum a primo ente, quod est suum esse.*[71]

Who shall say that St. Thomas is not here saying *to* Plato and *to* Aristotle that this is what they should have said? He is correcting them in the name of their own transcendence of matter. And yet, who shall say that, though he thus corrects Plato and Aristotle in their own name, he is not also making them share in truths that they never asserted? For what does this text mean except that God is Being and *therefore* one, that produced beings are creatures because production means the production of being, and that if there is a mode of production higher than that of generation, that mode is the creation of beings by Being?

But the road from Platonism to this conclusion is a long one. Platonism has even a sort of interior history until it finally becomes absorbed in the doctrine of creation. Nothing is more dramatic than to see the insistence with which St. Thomas Aquinas traces the slow stages and steps by which Platonism haltingly and stubbornly threw off, one by one, its dearest errors until finally it discovered that it could, after all, save its most cherished intentions in the doctrine of creation. The existence of spiritual substances is a crucial issue for Platonism and an instructive issue for its historians. St. Thomas knows very well that just as soon as Platonism faces the issue of explaining the existence of spiritual substances it faces the problem of creation in an aggravated form. For, in a way, the existence of spiritual substances is a sort of test case for Platonism. What is being tested is whether Platonism will successfully maintain itself *above* the order of generation and corruption in its explanation of the origin of being. Evidently, if there are spiritual substances which are *also* produced substances, and if generation is the only mode of production in being that we know, then the existence of these spiritual substances becomes embarrassing in the extreme. This is, in fact, the point where, as St. Thomas looks at the situation, the Platonic story becomes both interesting and crucial. But let us let St. Thomas·tell his own story. In citing the following text I shall insist only that, with particular reference to the existence of spiritual substances, it contains the interior history of the transformation of Platonism into a doctrine of creation.

We have reached a moment when philosophers have realized the immateriality of spiritual substances. At this moment we meet the following three and successive stages in the efforts of philosophers to discuss the existence and the origin of these spiritual substances:

> *Sicut autem praedicta positio circa conditionem spiritualium substantiarum a sententia Platonis et Aristotelis deviat, eis immaterialitatis simplicitatem auferens; ita et circa modum existendi ipsarum aliqui a veritate deviasse inveniuntur, auferentes earum originem a primo et summo auctore: in quo inveniuntur diversi*

*homines tripliciter errasse. Quidam enim posuerunt praedictas sub-
stantias omnino causam sui esse non habere. Quidam posuerunt eas
quidem essendi causam habere, non tamen immediate omnes eas
procedere a summo et primo principio, sed quadam serie ordinis
inferiores earum a superioribus essendi originem habere. Alii vero
confitentur omnes quidem hujusmodi substantias immediate essendi
habere originem a primo principio; sed in ceteris quae de eis
dicuntur, puta quod sunt viventes, intelligentes et alia hujusmodi,
superiores inferioribus causas existere.*[72]

The vicissitudes contained in this 'text simply indicate, as St. Thomas
wisely remarks, that the human reason advanced *slowly* in its investigation
of the origin of things. What caused philosophers to maintain the first position? We might have guessed the answer; for, though they stood above
the order of generation, they yet could not see a mode of production which
was above it:

> *Sic et ista opinio ex hoc videtur procedere quod elevari non potest
> intellectus ad intuendum alium modum causandi quam istum qui
> convenit materialibus rebus.*[73]

We are still at the barrier of matter, therefore. And yet, how could it be
that these spiritual substances are unproduced? Hence it is that we find other
philosophers taking a step, a halting step, towards creation:

> *Haec igitur et hujusmodi alii considerantes asserunt quidem
> omnia essendi originem trahere a primo et summo rerum principio,
> quem dicimus Deum; non tamen immediate, sed ordine quodam.*[74]

This is the moment when Greek and Arabian necessitarianism arrives at
the notion of the divine unity but does not know its true nature as Being
and its true dominion over being:

> *Cum enim primum rerum principium sit penitus unum et simplex,
> non aestimaverunt quod ab eo procederet nisi unum.*[75]

The Platonic pluralism now asserts itself in all its distinctiveness. Let us
suppose that because of the very nature of the realities to be produced we
must say that their being must be *immediately* produced by God. Creation,
therefore? Not at all, for Platonism has still a device left before it yields up
its alphabetism. We shall make God the immediate cause of being, *but* we
shall now empty being of its perfection:

> *His autem rationibus moti, Platonici posuerunt quidem immate-
> rialium substantiarum et universaliter omnium existentium Deum*

esse immediate causam essendi secundum praedictum productionis modum, qui est absque mutatione vel motu; posuerunt tamen secundum alias participationes bonitatis divinae ordinem quemdam causalitatis in praedictis substantiis. Ut enim supra dictum est, posuerunt abstracta principia secundum ordinem intelligibilium conceptionum: ut scilicet sicut unum et ens sunt communissima, et primo cadunt in intellectu, sub hoc autem est vita, sub qua iterum est intellectus, et sic inde; ita etiam primum et supremum inter separata est id quod est ipsum unum, et hoc est primum principium, quod est Deus, de quo jam dictum est, quod est suum esse. Sub hoc autem posuit aliud principium separatum, quod est vita; et iterum aliud, quod est intellectus. Si igitur sit aliqua immaterialis substantia quae sit intelligens, vivens et ens, erit quidem ens per participationem primi principii, quod est ipsum esse; erit quidem vivens per participationem alterius principii separati, quod est vita; et erit intelligens per participationem alterius separati principii, quod est ipse intellectus: sicut si ponatur quod homo sit animal per participationem hujus principii separati quod est animal; si autem bipes per participationem secundi principii, quod est bipes.[76]

The last step lies ahead. If indeed the Platonists have really said that God is the immediate cause of the being of immaterial substances, then they must say more. They must include within the unity of that being all that that being is and all the essential perfections that it has: *"Nam omnia quae substantialiter de aliquo praedicantur sunt per se et simpliciter unum."*[77] If *to live* and *to have intelligence* were accidents of spiritual substances, the Platonists might escape at this point. But even on their own contention this is not the case, in spite of their famous *separatism*. Hence, they must bow to the inevitable union between being and unity and to the recognition of God as the total cause of the total being of spiritual substances: *"Si igitur omnes immateriales substantiae a Deo habent immediate quod sint, ab eo immediate habent quod vivant et intellectivae sint."*[78]

We are here as far beyond the Platonic dismemberment of being as we can possibly be, however it may be true that we are teaching Platonism the logic of its own vision. In asserting and exploring the nature of a God Who is Being, we are beyond the dangers of the Platonic Forms. But we are beyond such dangers only if we see how it is that in the unity of a God Who is Being we have transcended the reign of *otherness* and *difference* within being. For we are in principle beyond the Platonic conflict between unity and intelligibility. We have reached a notion of being in which being and unity are reconcilable in the order of creatures because they are identified in God.

Ninth Essay

PRUDENCE,
THE INCOMMUNICABLE WISDOM

by
Charles J. O'Neil

Prudence, the Incommunicable Wisdom

SINCE the days of Socrates and before, moral philosophy has never escaped the problem of knowledge and virtue. We are accustomed to think of Socrates as one who solved the problem boldly by identifying the two. For, we are told, he thought all the virtues were practical wisdoms, or rational principles.[1] The Christian conscience, however, with its more penetrating awareness of human liberty, seems always convinced that some energy deeper than knowledge enters into every moral act.[2] Thus Christian moral philosophy cannot forget that human liberty—even in the light of philosophical knowledge—retains its awe-inspiring dominion over its act. If it were as simple a problem as this, one might be tempted to solve it as radically as Socrates did by a complete separation of liberty from knowledge. But that would be an unhappy solution and foreign to man's rationality, one which consigns moral philosophy to a vague and inane realm of the unreal entirely separated from the existential realities of man's daily activity.[3] The moral philosopher avoids this difficulty not only by remembering that his science is fundamentally—if remotely—ordained to action but also by maintaining that there is a knowledge which is a virtue and a virtue which is a knowledge: the virtue of prudence.

With a request to impart this knowledge, however, the moral philosopher cannot comply. He can establish and defend the first principles of moral wisdom; he can supply the principles needed by a variety of moral sciences. But he cannot give the knowledge which is virtue. He cannot communicate the wisdom which guides the good life in concrete completeness here and now from day to day. If he is asked to tell us where we can find the abstractions and universalizations of moral philosophy reduced to the concrete singularity of good living he can only point to the virtuous life of the prudent man.

Why is such the case? Why, in fact, does the moral act stand in need of this knowledge? What unique mastery of truth does it possess which permits it to carry truth into the sacred and inviolable precincts of man's free choice? The answers to these questions can teach us much about moral philosophy, for they make us examine closely the good action to which it is ordered from afar. St. Thomas's answers to these questions will bring us closer to his solution of the problem of knowledge and virtue.[4] And his answers to these questions can be had if we direct our attention to his teaching on the virtue of prudence.

I

St. Thomas gives a very high place to prudence in his hierarchy of virtues. The eminence of a virtue is determined by the greatness of the good to which it is ordered. This gives a unique pre-eminence to the theological virtues, for they have God as their object. But among the rest

prudentia est maxima quia est moderatrix aliarum.[5]

The greatness of prudence and its title to a kind of sovereignty are not hard to justify. Rectitude in human acts is a matter of conformity to rule. And the proper and—so to speak—familiar (*homogenea*) rule of human acts is right reason. To this a man attains through prudence

quae est recta ratio agibilium.[6]

There is nothing surprising in the eminence of prudence over the other virtues if prudence itself is simply "right reason in things to be done."

"Live according to reason" is, however, an ancient and venerable counsel. The familiar and amazingly simple formula we have just mentioned seems but its conterpart; and thus prudence becomes a mere vague summation of human virtues[7] rather than one which is distinct and pre-eminent. We cannot, therefore, explain the greatness of prudence by pointing to its rational rectitude. We must penetrate more deeply into its nature precisely as a virtue. To do this we must ask ourselves the questions which will lead us to examine the prudential operation itself: Why is such a virtue necessary? How is it distinct from all others? How does one explain its relation as *moderatrix* to the others?

Prudence is a virtue because it does what every virtue does; and virtue, as St. Thomas often says (following Aristotle) makes him good who has the virtue and renders his work good.[8] The virtue of the agent, however, cannot be understood apart from the nature of the agent;[9] and thus the limitations of the nature of the agent are also those of its virtue. The good, then, which the virtue gives and the work which it renders good will not be beyond the reach of the natural inclination of the agent. In the case of brutes and of men that inclination is naturally accompanied by knowledge. Nature, in other words, has set as object of appetite for both man and brute cognized

[188]

or apprehended good. Now what strikes us about the good for the brute is precisely its "brute uniformity." The swallow builds its nest and the spider weaves its web but the unfailing similarity shows us that the operation proceeds not according to the swallow's own determination but that of its nature.[10] This uniformity is true of the brute throughout the entire range of its operations. But its entire range is narrow just as its performance is uniform. For the debility of the active principle limits it to a few objects and a few operations. Its virtue calls for no more than a natural judgment and a natural appetite.[11]

Brute uniformity and narrow limits are by no means characteristic of man's activity. His operations are, in fact, many and diverse. The multiplicity and diversity of his operations are indications of the nobility of his active principle. Its range seems to know no limit. For in man the active principle is his rational soul *cuius virtus ad infinita quodammodo se extendit.*[12]

The difference of nature between brute and man gives us a difference of work and a difference of virtue. The debility of the brute's active principle *limits* its operation to such an extent that the natural inclination orienting its appetite and the natural judgment guiding its appetite are *sufficient* for its good work. In the building line one expects from a good swallow only a good swallow's nest. Precisely, however, because of the *nobility* of his active principle, man is *not* limited in the range of his objects. He can build and weave; and these are noble things. He can know the truth and love the good; and these are far nobler things. Since he can know the truth and love the good in the endless multiplicity and diversity in which they are discoverable, a natural appetite for the good and a natural illumination of that appetite are *not* sufficient to produce in its marvelous variety that good work which is good human work. In the doing line we are entitled to demand a great many skills before we call a man a good man, hence the nobility of man's active principle leads us through the variety of its objects to the assertion that a natural appetite for good and a natural judgment on right action are not sufficient for man *without further determination and perfection.*[13]

The need for that further determination and perfection to render good the human work is the basic need of prudence. But before we proceed to it we should observe that there is in man a natural appetite and a natural judgment. They may be insufficient but they are there. The comparison to brutes is not a mere convenient parallelism. In each case the appetite is oriented and the judgment is enlightened through a natural endowment. Before we proceed to the "further determination and perfection" we may profitably investigate that appetitive and intellectual natural endowment, which is insufficient but necessary for the good work of man.[14]

The appetite which is bestowed on man by nature is, of course, a rational appetite. And since this rational appetite is bestowed by nature it is not opposed to nature but is itself natural and even "a nature,"

quia omne quod in rebus invenitur natura quaedam dicitur.[15]

Since the rational appetite of man is a nature—and like man a created nature—what is true of every created nature will be true of the human will: that there be in it by divine ordination a natural and naturally necessary inclination for the good which befits it.

What is the good which is befitting to the will?· It is the good, of course, which is fitting to the will as a nature; and as a nature the will is the principle of human operations, of man's movement to good. The multiplicity and diversity of man's objects and operations makes us aware of his mobility and indetermination. But the indeterminate is reduced to the determinate; and "every mobile is reduced to the immobile" from which every motion proceeds. Since the will is the first and natural principle of human movement to good, the good or appetible corresponding to the will as a natural principle will be the *first* good, the appetible which is the "principle and foundation of all others."[16]

The human appetible which is the principle and foundation of all others is man's completion in goodness: to be, to live, to be happy; in other words, his beatitude and those things which it includes. This is the befitting good to which natural necessity inclines the will; in respect of this good, the ultimate end, the will is a natural appetite.[17]

Thus far, therefore, the will is determined and even, like any natural appetite, determined to one. But *this* natural appetite is a rational appetite; and hence the will is rationally determined to one. Man is able, in other words, to single out this or that "special good" as constituting the beatitude to which natural necessity universally inclines him.[18]

This special good, whether it be the true beatitude or some other, is principle and foundation with respect to all other appetibles.[19] It is the ultimate end in which other goods participate; it will be desired by natural necessity and with it whatever is indispensable to it. Here again we must remember the multiplicity and diversity of man's operations. For the wide range of his acts and their objects clearly indicate that man is neither constantly nor exclusively concerned with the naturally necessary object of the will, his ultimate end. There are many appetibles not the ultimate end; and to these also as included in the universal good the rational appetite is in potency. These, however, are not desired of necessity; and to these the natural ordination of the will is not sufficient. To that further ordination, that "further determination and perfection" prudence, of course, contributes. We have here only briefly adumbrated the foundations of that ordination which nature has laid in the rational appetite.

The natural necessity which is in the appetite belongs to it precisely as rational. It does not, therefore, separate it from knowledge and the habits of knowledge. On the contrary we must expect this natural inclination to be illumined by a knowledge which has a proportionate necessity and is equally a natural endowment. For "nature in all her works looks to the good and to the conservation of those things which the operation of nature accomplishes."[20] And if the appetite inclines to a good which is the first of appetibles, nature must provide a knowledge from which operations may begin, a knowledge characterized by stability and certainty, a knowledge of principles which, because they must be first, must be permanent and immutable. Moreover, such knowledge (if it is to principle and conserve operation in its rectitude) must be universal; it must resist all evil and assent to all good.

Et hoc est synderesis cuius officium est remurmurare malo et inclinare ad bonum.[21]

When we say that this natural habit inclines to good and resists evil we seem to have no distinction—save a name—from the natural inclination of the will to the first principle of good. Let us remember that the harmonious co-ordination of these fundamental tendencies is rooted in the fact that they are the origins of action of a *rational* nature. And let us not forget that synderesis is nature's endowment of *knowledge*, but of the knowledge related to doing. For synderesis is nature's primary[22] ordination of the practical intellect; and the practical intellect does not have truth as its object, for it is not directed to conformity with things as they are in their essences; nor does it have good as its object, for although practical it is still an intellect. The object of man's practical intellect is the truth relative to the work of man.[23]

The truth relative to the work of man includes many truths, many principles, many judgments. Synderesis is a habit which produces some of these truths with ease, promptness, and certainty. It makes man know certainly and immutably that God is to be served and obeyed, that one must live according to reason, briefly that one must do good and avoid evil.[24] For synderesis is the perfectant of the practical intellect which holds it in easy readiness to affirm the precepts of the natural law.[25] With regard to these first and universal principles of action the light of synderesis is steady and clear: habitual, inextinguishable, infallible. The soul cannot lose this light so long as it continues to be a human soul![26]

All would be well in practical knowledge, then, if it were confined to these universal affirmations. But almost anyone who has tried it will assure us that the life of virtue does not consist in the continuous affirming: "good is to be done." The life of virtue consists in virtuous doing, in doing the things a man does in that almost bewildering multitude of circumstances in which from year to year, in fact, from moment to moment a man finds himself. The very constancy and immutability of the first principles *prevent* their being of immediate usefulness. For the operations which a man performs, the operations which bring his nature to the fulness of goodness, take place in contingent and concrete circumstances—of times and places and persons and things, of weakness and strength, of past achievement and future promise, of all those things in all men's lives which conspire to make every human situation different from every other.[27]

For action of this kind universal practical knowledge is clearly insufficient. Nature's universal illumination and fundamentally right ordination are indeed generous, but in that bewildering multitude of circumstances it is not the nature but the man that acts. His nature fixes his end; his nature enlightens him with respect to his end. But he himself must end his bewilderment, he must introduce reason's order into the welter of circumstances; he must put reason's stamp of unity on their multiplicity and diversity. This is no easy task. He needs a habit to give him just this skill, a virtue of *knowing* the right here and now. This very necessary virtue is prudence.[28]

We have now found the answer to our first question. Prudence is necessary for human goodness because of what prudence does. And the prudential act is "right discernment about human good in single things—to be—done" (*recte dijudicare de bono humano secundum singula agenda.*) We need not allow the prosy tone of our formula to obscure either the necessity or the importance of this virtue. The right caress at the right moment to soothe a sick and fretting child is a single thing to be done. And "incapacitating an enemy aircraft" at the risk of one's own life is a single thing to be done. We speak of the virtuous life in abstractions; in fact we tend to obscure it in abstractions, to "distinguish it" to death. But it is neither abstract nor moribund; prudence is its assurance of fully rational life in every moment of its justice, and courage, and temperance. But how is it different from these? How, in fact, is it different from all other human perfections? In answering this our second question we shall have further opportunity to explore the characteristic prudential act.

Let us begin by setting off prudence from the natural practical knowledge of which we have spoken. Synderesis is concerned with universals. Prudence goes much further.[29] For practical knowledge is not confined to knowledge of ends, ends that are determined by nature, but extends to "those things which are for the end in human affairs." And these are no determined by nature but are varied and multiplied according to the seemingly endless variety of human persons and human interests. Prudence, therefore, is unlike synderesis in this: prudence is not a natural endowment; it does not give a certain judgment proceeding from a habit given by nature. And the reason for this lies in the fact that prudence is directed toward means. It includes more than universal cognition, it belongs to prudence to know the *singular operable* that is for the end.[30]

Human ends are determined, means are not; means are, in fact, indeterminate and variable. This difference in its object seems to set prudence off not only from synderesis but also from the habitual speculative knowledges. Unlike wisdom, understanding, and science it is not concerned with the necessary but with the contingent. In this, of course, it resembles art. But art and prudence do not coincide further: they are *practical* perfections concerned with the *contingent*. But the object of art is the thing-to-be-made, a thing constituted in exterior matter; and prudence

est circa agibilia quae scilicet in ipso operante consistunt.[31]

Prudence, therefore, is unlike the habits of the speculative intellect thanks to its object; it is unlike art thanks to the perfection which it gives to the agent in his very operation; it is unlike synderesis, for synderesis is a gift of nature. Finally, prudence is distinct from the virtues with which it is most commonly associated, the other cardinal virtues. For justice, courage, and temperance are perfectants of man's appetites; prudence perfects his intellect. For it is a *practical* knowledge, a knowledge of "those things which are for the end" in the concrete, singular, human activity.

We should observe, however, that no knowledge whatever is entitled to the name of virtue unless it has its own proper rectitude. It is not the mere demonstration which makes demonstrative knowledge a virtue but demonstration which issues in a conclusion which is right. In speculative matters— for science belongs to the speculative intellect—the conclusion is right when it has the truth proper to the speculative intellect: conformity to things as they are. Truth in the practical intellect, and hence rectitude or truth for prudence is another conformity: conformity to right appetite, conformity to a desire for those things which the nature of the agent demands.[32] The very goodness and rightness which prudence establishes in human activity is, therefore, related to right appetite. Prudence, therefore, is much more fully entitled to be called virtue than any speculative knowledge for it deals not merely with that which is good but with the good in its own formality; by its conformity to right appetite it is concerned with the appetite as such.[33] Among all the habits of the intellective and appetitive potencies which we have mentioned the uniqueness of prudence is this: it directs desire; it enters into appetite itself. We saw previously that it fixes on the means "here and now." The special conformity of the practical intellect leads us to say that it directs desire to "those things which are for the end." Here we are speaking, of course, of prudence as *moderatrix*; and to appreciate fully this aspect of the prudential operation we must continue with the third of our initial questions (p. 188): how does prudence "direct" right appetite? What, in other words, is the relation of prudence and the moral virtues?

II

In approaching this problem there are two fundamental points that we may quite profitably bear in mind. The first is that the fulfillment or act of the intellect as such is knowing the truth. The object of intellect is always the true.[34] The second is that an appetite as such is determined to good. And the good or end of any appetite given by nature is, precisely as natural, determined by nature. Now there are natural inclinations of just this sort corresponding to the moral virtues. The fact that they are natural endowments is conformed by the observation that in some they are discernible from earliest childhood. Thus Job wrote:

> . . . *from my infancy mercy grew up with me and it came out with me from my mother's womb.*[35]

These inclinations, however, to the works of justice and courage and the rest are entirely imperfect as virtues. They attain to the more perfect status of virtue by "attaining to right reason." But it is well to note that they are nevertheless—from the point of view of appetite—natural endowments. They incline to an end which nature itself requires.[36]

What is this end? Since these are the appetites of man, it cannot be other than the good of man. And the good of man will be in accord with the distinctive characteristic of his nature: his rational fulfillment in being.[37] The moral virtues, as appetitive inclinations, have as end man's "being according to reason." But of itself this would not call for a group of operative habits distinct from one another. Each of these habits has its own concern, its own field wherein it seeks the human good. Considering their concerns globally the matter of the moral virtues is human passions and operations;[38] and to the good of reason in this matter the moral virtues are naturally inclined. The good of man as a rational being "consists in his adequation to rule and measure." Hence the good for him in passions and operations is that these attain the "rule and measure" of reason for such precisely is the good of reason.[39] And what is the good of reason in such matters? Its name is as unique as it is venerable. It is the mean, the mean which is not measured by material things or their quantities, not arithmetically or geometrically, but the mean of reason in action.[40] This "modus" or mean of reason is the very mark, the stamp, the impress which reason puts on passions and operations to make them her own, to set them off as contributing to the whole good of man.

Both success and failure in these inclinations cannot be understood apart from reason: "the excess, the defect, the mean are understood with reference to the rule of reason."[41] And reason gives her rule not by measurement of things but according to her nature as a practical intellect. Courage, for example, is not measured by the weight of the tank or the speed of the bomber but he is brave "who faces the gravest dangers according to reason, *that is to say when he* should, *as* he should, and for *sound* motives."[42] Virginity, again, may seem an extremity from the point of view of measurement, for it makes a complete renunciation. Nevertheless, the virgin is not at the extreme but achieves the mean of reason because virginal abstinence is "for sound motives and as one should."[43] The mean of reason, in other words, is achieved by fully rational action here and now and with knowledge of particulars in human passions and operations. This is the very knowledge in which the perfection of the prudential operation lies. Completely virtuous operation, therefore, in human passions and operations calls for a perfectant of the intellective together with a perfectant of the appetitive potency.

Human passions and operations include the whole of man's human activity. Perfected operation calls for prudence and the moral virtues. These have their matter in common, they also have in common that mean of reason which is the human virtuous good. And hence both prudence and the moral virtues enter into virtuous operation. But the unity of that operation is both maintained and understood by the distinction of the intellective and appetitive potencies and their proper habits. For the mean of prudence is the mean of moral virtue,

sed prudentiae est sicut imprimentis, virtutis moralis sicut impressi.[44]

St. Thomas's profound distinction shows us also that prudence does not enter into the essence or definition of moral virtue. Prudence is not the form, or mark, or stamp of reason, *which is impressed*. Prudence is rather reason giving itself, granting a *participation in itself* to the appetitive potencies.[45]

And prudence is, therefore, rather an effective than a formal cause; it is not the mean but bestows the mean.[46] Prudence is, in fact, like the natural agent which confers a form on the appropriate matter: without the form the matter will not achieve its good, without the agent the whole will not achieve its being. But prudence acts after the manner of a natural agent; that is to say, without prudence there will be no mean, without prudence the good of reason will not be achieved in the operation of moral virtue; but it does not fall within the scope of prudence to determine whether or not the moral virtue shall seek the mean.[47] It does fall within its scope to *discover* the mean, for it specializes so to speak in knowledge; and it discovers that very mean which the appetite of man desires.

Our brief consideration of prudence and the other cardinal virtues has given us a new view of the characteristic operation of this virtue. In examining the need for prudence we discovered it as the virtue which perfects the agent and his work "in this that he determines rightly about human good with regard to single things-to-be-done." We now see prudence as the virtue effective of the mean, the virtue which grants a participation in rational goodness by signing and sealing the virtues of the appetitive part of the soul with the mark of reason itself. Here again prudence is rightness in knowledge, the right knowledge of what is to be done here and now in circumstantial concreteness. And when we reflect that in those singular things to be done we must include the whole of man's human activity we can agree with the high praise which calls "felicity in action" that "prudential act by which one governs himself and others."[48] A governor, however, is a pilot; and a pilot should know the port as well as the channel.[49] And thus we are brought to our last questions: does prudence set the end before those moral virtues which perfect man's activity? Does prudence know the end of human activity?

III

In this matter also our work can be simplified by recalling a fundamental point. Let St. Thomas express it for us:

> *Principium autem totius ordinis in moralibus est finis ultimus qui ita se habet in operativis sicut principium indemonstrabile in speculativis.*[50]

The ultimate end is the ultimate principle; and this simple emphasis advises us that we have not done with prudence until we have discovered its relation to the ultimate principle. We cannot claim a place for prudence in the moral order nor a place for its act in the moral life until we have established its relation to the ultimate end of man.[51]

St. Thomas is also directing us here to explain the act of prudence in the moral life by the operations of reason in the speculative life. In terms of that very analogy he often explains the relation of prudence and the other cardinal virtues: "As there can be no speculative science without the understanding of principles, so there can be no prudence without the moral virtues."[52] Now the understanding of principles is the primary habit of the speculative life, and the order of intelligibles demands that all the intellectual virtues depend on the habit of understanding "as prudence depends on the moral virtues."[53]

There may be some obscurity, however, in this analogy. Prudence was set off from the moral virtues because the former was the perfectant of an intellective potency, and the latter of appetitive potencies. Does this habit of knowledge depend on habits of desire? Does perfection of knowledge for St. Thomas depend on perfection of appetite? Or are we perhaps to say that the *will*, for example, in which justice resides, gives us the judgments from which prudence derives, just as the demonstrative habit depends on the understanding of principles? We may then say that the *appetite* is prior to the reasoning about means, as the understanding of principles is prior to the reason syllogizing to conclusions.[54] And since the end is the principle from which the process begins it seems to follow that the moral virtues propose the end to prudence which is, in turn, exclusively preoccupied with means.

Quite contrariwise St. Thomas himself says:

> *prudentia non solum dirigit virtutes morales in eligendo ea quae sunt ad finem sed etiam in praestituendo finem.*[55]

Perhaps St. Thomas will solve for us the difficulty his language seems to create. Some all-out aid—and effective at that—toward the solution of our broader question of prudence, the whole of human activity, and the end of man can be had from his own answer to a narrower question: does prudence set the end for the moral virtues?[56]

If we are searching only for verbal formulae a very pat answer is at hand: "It does not belong to prudence to set the end before the moral virtues but only to dispose of those things which are for the end."[57] But we must be more generous with ourselves and St. Thomas concerning his answer. And that for two reasons: *first,* the prudential act, as we have seen it thus far, is not constrained to being dispositive of means. It has means for object, yes, because for the sake of operation it knows the contingent variables, and it impresses on them the order of reason; its character in so doing is its knowledge of 'when one ought,' 'just how one ought,' and 'because of what one ought.' *Secondly,* he who disposes of means in moral activity is not a mere inventory clerk, nor a semiskilled worker on an assembly line: he is the builder of the whole, he is the *man* rendering good himself and his work; and he cannot dispose of means without knowing the end. In studying virtues we must not lose sight of the whole in assembling the parts.

St. Thomas begins his solution precisely by avoiding this shortsightedness.

"The end of the moral virtues is human good, and the good of the human soul is to be according to reason." Now we have just seen a most characteristic function of prudence: assisting the moral virtues to this end by granting them participation in reason. To be according to reason, of course, is to operate according to the law of rational nature. And to operate rationally is to proceed from the end, from the end *known*. "Hence it is necessary," so St. Thomas continues, "that the *ends* of the moral virtues preexist in the *reason*." (Italics added.)

We now have the ends situated in the reason, that is to say *known*; but we must further see how they are present and how they are to operate; and St. Thomas has recourse to the familiar analogy:

> *In the speculative reason there are certain things present as naturally known, and to these the understanding of principles pertains; and there are certain things which* become known through the former, *namely conclusions, and to these science pertains.*[58]

We must not, however, lose sight of the fact that the conclusions become known thanks to the principles. Without conclusions there is no science; for conclusions issue from demonstrations, and science is the demonstrative habit. But the habit of demonstration is that in which the premises together *effect* the conclusion. And the habit of understanding must supply the indemonstrable principle into which the valid conclusion must be resolvable.[59] Hence without the habit of understanding the habit of science simply cannot act, i.e., conclude. The distinction of these two habits is not intended to sever the conclusion from the principle on which it depends!

We are ready to apply the analogy to prudence:

> *Thus in the practical reason certain things pre-exist as naturally known and the ends of the moral virtues are of this sort; because the end is to operation what the principle is to speculation . . . and certain things are in the practical reason as conclusions: and of this sort are those things which are for the end to which we come thanks to the ends themselves, and with such prudence deals.*[60]

The ends of the moral virtues are, therefore, in the practical reason as *naturally known*, and thus all confusing questions of knowledge in appetite are eliminated. Since they are present to the reason as naturally known they belong to that habit, that natural endowment, which knows the operable principles corresponding to the equally natural determinations of appetites. We have already seen and named that habit; it is not a virtue but the enlightening preamble to virtue.[61] Since the appetite moves to its naturally determined good through a naturally apprehended principle it is rather

[198]

that "natural reason which is called synderesis" which sets the end before the moral virtues.[62]

Prudence, however, is not a mere natural habit but a complete virtue. Prudence is man's reason working here and now on man's task by "applying the universal principles to particular conclusions in matters of operation." The application in particular matters may fail of the mark, but the natural endowment of the soul cannot fail. When then, there is question of prudence, the end, and the moral virtues we will not say that the virtue of prudence sets the end before the moral virtues. The establishment of such ends is not the task of prudence. Neither is it the task of any other virtue. It is the work and the prerogative of the author of man's nature. He shows man the goods of his nature by the natural endowment of reason itself.[63] Of prudence, therefore, we must say that it does not devolve upon it as a virtue to set their end before the moral virtues but rather to make disposition of the things which tend to that end.[64]

Clearly, however, these virtues are helped to their end by prudence:[65] prudence prepares their ways, disposes or sets in order means, in fact *moves* them as the natural agent moves matter; for the contingent and variable, the particular and operable cannot acquire—save through prudence—the impress of rationality apart from which there is no human good.[66] This impress of rationality is the good which prudence offers those virtues, the good which they owe to its direction. Prudence, therefore, still remains clearly preeminent over the moral virtues, moving them to their good, it is still moderatrix as directing them.[67]

Prudence directs the moral virtues, we must remember, because it is the syllogizing habit of practical conclusions. A practical syllogism can no more *conclude* without its principles than a speculative syllogism can. In other words, a moral virtue which is a habit of choice is directed in its choice by the habit of practical demonstration; and there can be no demonstration without the solid ground of principle. In this work synderesis moves in prudence, supplying a premise; and this premise effectively linked to another in the syllogizing habit produces the conclusion. The characteristic work of prudence, then, is "to dispose of means," but in that very activity it leads the moral virtues rationally to end. Prudence is concerned with the means and with the end: with the means, because the variability of means demands this unique knowledge; with end, because it is knowledge for operation.[68]

Such is the answer of St. Thomas to our question about the relations of prudence and the ends of the moral virtues. If, then, there is obscurity or confusion in the analogies used by St. Thomas it is through no fault of his. Rather it arises from forgetting that prudence is a *practical* knowing, a knowledge which is for operation and, therefore, for end. In such knowledge prudence is the demonstrative habit; and we now see that in its operation we have a practical syllogism which brings the universal knowledge of the good to bear on the particular and contingent. By examining that knowledge a bit more closely we may discover the answer to our broader question: the relation of prudence and the end of man.

IV

Good or end, we should recall once more, is not merely the principle which prompts operation as such but the principle *in operativis*, a principle for the intellect which directs all operation. St. Thomas puts it:

> *bonum est primum quod cadit in apprehensione practicae rationis quod ordinatur ad opus.*

If good is in the first apprehension of this intellect, the first natural judgment of this intellect will be the first truth about good: "that good is to be done and'pursued and evil avoided." For the truth about the good is its "to-be-done-ness"; and the intellect would fail us if in the presence of the good it did not assert the truth about it. He has simply not intellectually grasped operable good who does not see it as the object which invites appetite to its fulfillment in that existential fulness to which it is always in potency. Therefore whoever grasps good knows immediately that it is to be done; and *all* those things will be seen as to be done which the practical reason naturally apprehends as human goods.[69]

Since nature itself provides the apprehension of those goods and the natural preceptive judgments which follow on such apprehension, we may look also for an order of nature in those precepts. That order will correspond to the inclinations of nature, for practical knowledge answers to natural appetite. Let us consider that order very briefly.

Both reason and nature put first things first. And first of all for man must come that which he has in common with every nature: the inclination for the first and basic appetible: "the conservation of his being according to nature." Man's second inclination is "more special" and tends to the continuity of his nature. This he has—at least in part—in common with other natures which also require continuity. But man's third inclination is his very own (*sibi propria*). It is his inclination to the fulfillment of his nature precisely and distinctively as rational: to know the heights of truth, i.e., to know God; to dwell with others in society, in short, to use his reason to the full. The sum total to which the precepts corresponding to these inclinations come is this: to pursue the good proportionate to nature. Since such pursuance is but the doing of good and avoiding evil all precepts are referable to the first and nature is that common root in which all meet.[70] How shall we express that precept? Insofar as it applies to every natural appetible and to every operable we have expressed it already: "that good is to be done and pursued and evil avoided."[71] But if we need to express it from the point of view of rational operation proceeding from principles to conclusions we formulate it: "the end must be achieved."[72]

That the end must be achieved, although not the most abstract principle of synderesis, is in truth the first principle in the order of operation. For the order of operation is what we may call the order of joint action of reason and appetite. And of it St. Thomas says:

> *Every operation of reason and will in us derives from that which is according to nature . . . for every reasoning is derived from principles naturally known, and every appetite of things for the end is derived from the natural appetite of the ultimate end.*[73]

The knowledge of the variable, contingent means is thus derived, but not without right appetite, from the knowledge of the necessary and the end. And the appetite for that which is for the end is derived,[74] but not without right knowledge, from the appetite for the end itself. The end is the initial principle, the principle to which appetite is fundamentally inclined and the principle for which reason bestows order. The end, therefore, is as truly a principle for prudence as it is for any practical knowledge; and knowledge of the end is as indispensable to prudential demonstration as knowledge of the indemonstrable verities is to speculative demonstration. But is this the whole story of the relationship of prudence to the end of the whole of human life? To answer that question satisfactorily let us reexamine the prudential operation once more.

We have now seen that the prudential operation is one which brings the practical principles to bear on the matters subject to practical conclusions. Prudence is the virtue which stabilizes and expedites that process of reasoning which issues in a good human act in the matter of passions and operations. Prudence, in fact, is the habitual principle which assures that reasoning process the consequence which every demonstration must have. The prudent man is successful in that operation because he takes his departure from the first of precepts; he deliberates concerning lesser goods with his vision fixed on the greatest good. And he judges well, that is to say, his vision is also sharp with respect to the particular good which in the circumstances in which he finds himself, is most consonant with the greatest. Clearly his specialized practical demonstration calls for both these knowledges. And it is genuinely conclusive, truly demonstrative, when his knowledge issues in a command, that is to say, when he gives the ultimate, almost creative, word, the *fiat* of action here and now which for the sake of the greatest good bestows rationality on his human act.[75] Briefly, prudence deliberates, prudence judges, prudence commands. How is each of these diverse acts which contribute to the prudential whole related to the end of human life?

With respect to deliberation the answer is not far to seek. St. Thomas had understood Aristotle too thoroughly and well to forget that it is:

> *the mark of a man of practical wisdom to be able to* deliberate well *. . . about what sorts of thing conduce* to the good life in general.[76]

Counsel, for St. Thomas, is not worthy to be called good unless it seeks for good means to a good end. And this is necessary to good counsel as it is to the whole of prudence, for direction to an end which is not the end of man destroys that ordination without which there is no virtue.[77] On the contrary, the good deliberation which begins from the end helps to win for prudence the noble title of wisdom. For good deliberation is the act which leads the way in the ordination "to the whole of living well." And the whole of living well is the "common end of the whole of human life," and thus the highest of causes with respect to human acts. This cause prudence considers and thus we may well call it wisdom.[78] Prudence is, of course, not the highest wisdom, the wisdom without qualification, directed to the highest object. But it is man's own wisdom, his rationality in passions and operations. It is human action's wisdom as it is human action's felicity.

On good counsel follows judgment for ceaseless deliberation is useless to action. The rightness of practical judgment, like the rightness of any cognoscitive judgment, lies in this: that "one apprehend a thing as it is in itself."[79] That which is to be apprehended by this judgment is a contingent principle, a singular extreme. This is the judgment which bears directly on the means, on that which is for the end. The man whom nature has rendered sensitive to truth will be sensitive also to the truth of action. The man who is naturally rather clever at discovering means to ends may be quicker at discovering good means to good ends. But it is not his native quickness which makes his judgment right; for it will not be right without rightly oriented appetite. It will not be the judgment characteristic of the virtue of prudence unless it be right judgment "toward the good end of the whole of life."[80]

The relationship of each of these acts to the end of man may be characterized as remote. This is not because the end does not stand to deliberation as principle; for a consideration leading from end to means would be a blind wandering and not a rational discourse if it did not have end as its point of departure. And it is not because the end is alien to the right judgment; for the disorderly *is* alien to the rational, and it would be a disorderly procedure, indeed, which knew means but could not relate them to end, or which knew a particular end but not because it saw in that particular end its relation to the first of all goods. Each of these acts is an act in the moral order in which the ultimate end is the first principle. We do not call their relationship remote because it is real and vigorous! It is remote in comparison to the last and strictly prudential act: the precept itself. For the practical intellect does not rest content with the searchings of deliberation; nor is it satisfied to pass judgment on the things it has discovered. To be true to its end as a practical intellect it must go further: it must complete its direction of operation; it must not only search out the good, it must not only point out the good discovered, it must illuminate that good for appetite as the good which here and now *must be embraced*. And this is to command, this is the "application of the things deliberated and judged to operation itself,"[81] and to this the previous acts are ordained. Beyond this act the intellect, even the practical intellect, cannot go. Man's desire for the end has prompted his practical discourse, and now his practical discourse terminates in its conclusion here and now on that which is for the end. It remains for appetite to embrace the good for in human operation the will must give substance to that movement to good, that election which makes the human operation a man's very own.[82] This last act of prudence is, therefore, not remotely but immediately related to the ultimate end. The precept is immediately related to the end because the practical intellect has now completed its own operation for the end: "the good must be done" is now concreted in "this good must be embraced"; "the end must be achieved" is here and now embodied in "this means must be taken for the end."[83]

Prudence, therefore, in its principal act most truly merits its title of felicity in action for in its principal act its direction "of oneself and others" is truly complete. And prudence throughout its operation merits the title of human wisdom for prudence never loses sight of the most profound of causes in human activity, the ultimate end of man.

Those very characteristics which elevate prudence to the dignity of wisdom make it an incommunicable wisdom. Human operation in the temporal order is the human person in his ultimate fulfillment: in my act of union with good I am most fully myself; but my act is my own and no other's act can be mine. And as I am myself incommunicable so is the rational perfection of my act incommunicable. For only the human individual can resolve the last doubt that calls for counsel; the human individual has only his own native ability and experience to sharpen his intuition of the practical situation; only the human individual himself can issue that ultimate moral precept, for that command is heard in that inner realm wherein, under God, he alone is master.[84]

It is the very incommunicability of prudence which puts it beyond the competence of the most learned and devoted teachers. The most inspiring lecturer cannot impart it, and the most carefully wrought book cannot contain it. For prudence is a man's very precious possession, his own and incommunicable wisdom. Moral philosophy may be learned, moral sciences may be taught. Prudence must be lived.

Tenth Essay

A QUESTION ABOUT LAW

by
Mortimer J. Adler

A Question About Law

I

THE false issues and confused controversies of modern jurisprudence must be shocking to the Thomist who finds the Treatise on Law in the *Summa Theologica* an almost perfect expression of wisdom about the nature, sources, and kinds of law. Anyone who, having commenced with typically modern discussion of these matters, comes subsequently to a study of the Treatise on Law is equally perplexed by the contrast. St. Thomas appears to know the answers to problems which, since his day, have been raised again and again, each time with less clarity in the problem itself and consequently less definiteness in the answer. This is especially true in the case of natural law—whether it is, what it is, and how it is related to positive law. And the consideration of natural law has generated the central issues of modern jurisprudence—whether law is discovered or made, whether law is a work of reason or of will.

Positivism which is the prevailing mood of modern thought generally, is also found in the special field of legal theory. In jurisprudence, the positivist denies natural law, affirming the contingent and variable enactments of political communities to be the only laws there are; as, more generally, the positivist denies the necessary truths of philosophical knowledge, affirming the contingent and variable conclusions of scientific research to be the only valid knowledge there is. And, in both cases, the same result occurs: positive law, like positive science, becomes unintelligible; positive law, like positive science, tends toward the dangerous extreme of being entirely conventional, entirely man-made and arbitrarily imposed.[1]

The sympathetic historian can undoubtedly cite numerous causes, operating in the decay of mediaeval culture and in the transition to modern times, sufficient to explain the loss of Thomistic wisdom; but precisely because such explanations usually place all the blame on modern shoulders, they fail to help modern thinkers recover the truth they have lost. Some historians of thought who also happen to be Thomists tend to be historical about every human thinker except St. Thomas. Though historical evidences plainly suggest that every human thinker suffers from the limitations of his cultural location, and has defects peculiar to the time and circumstances of his work, these historians often seem to extricate St. Thomas from the impurities of history, while at the same time accounting for the failure of later ages to understand St. Thomas's teaching in terms of causes which must somehow apply to St. Thomas himself and which, if applied, would lead us to look for errors and inadequacies in Thomistic doctrine—defects appropriate to the historical circumstances of its development.

If St. Thomas were approached in this way, it might be possible to bring him more effectively into the circle of contemporary disputation. It is not difficult to understand why Thomists must be heard to say "*Peccavi*"—for themselves or for their master—before their criticism of modern doctrines will be listened to by moderns. With this in mind, I am going to try to suggest defects in the Treatise on Law which may help modern minds to examine their own errors. The misinterpretations of natural law are not entirely of modern origin. I am inclined to think that if the doctrine, as expounded by St. Thomas, had been utterly and simply clear, it could not possibly have been so grossly misunderstood and so variously confused. As a matter of fact, the Thomistic exposition is too simple, and therefore unequal to the subtlety and complexity of the points that are involved.[1a] A more adequate statement may not only remove misunderstandings which have led to denials of natural law, but it may also have merit as a more explicit understanding of what is involved in Thomistic principles. In the field of law, as in every other case, Thomism becomes more intelligible in itself by trying to become more intelligible to its modern opponents. It is not a new and different truth that is discovered, but an old truth that is extended and better understood.

Relative to readers who are competent students of modern jurisprudence, the Treatise on Law has two defects which account for the difficulties about natural law. In the first place, considering it as a part of the *Summa Theologica*, it is, as it should be, primarily theological. It is not primarily concerned with human positive law, or even with natural law, but with Divine positive law, and with natural law as a human participation of Eternal Law.[2] In contrast, human law, as positively instituted and as naturally founded, is the primary concern of the philosopher of law. St. Thomas does not pretend to write the philosophy of law in a manner that is adequate to its principles and problems. Here, as elsewhere in the *Summa*, he uses philosophical knowledge and analysis in the service of theology, as an instrument to achieve some understanding of revealed truth.[3] This does not

A Question About Law

mean that philosophical truth is not present in the *Summa*; it is neither lacking, nor obscured. But it is subordinated, and many points are treated too briefly and too simply which, if the aim were exclusively philosophical, would demand much more extensive discussion and much more complicated analysis than is needed or justified in a theological work. We have no right to complain, we can only regret, that St. Thomas did not write about human and natural law with the fullness proper to philosophical discussion in itself and apart from theology. Nor need we rest there, for within the scope of a few compact questions St. Thomas has given us enough to enable us to do a job which, under the exigencies of his life and times, he was not called upon to do. We not only can, but should, write about law in a purely philosophical manner, so that Thomistic principles may become effective in modern discussions. That sort of work is our historical vocation, as St. Thomas had his.

In the second place, in the Treatise on Law, there are ambiguities in the use of some of the principal words, such as "common good" and "law" itself. These ambiguities are relevant, not only to the distinction between natural and positive law, but to all the other basic distinctions among kinds of law, Eternal and temporal, Divine and human, *ius gentium* and *ius civile*; furthermore, they bear on the difference between the spheres of ethics and politics, for law is differently related to private and public conduct. Now these ambiguities, fundamental though they are, do not affect or mar the Treatise on Law in so far as it is primarily a theological work dealing with Divine positive law, with the Old Law and the New. That may be one reason why St. Thomas did not make the effort to increase the precision of his language. Even apart from the theological context, St. Thomas may have felt no need for making certain distinctions in meaning more explicit, not because he did not see these distinctions, but rather precisely because he saw them so clearly that it never occurred to him that anyone could misread his words.

On this last point, however, the historical evidence is painfully clear. His words have been misread, sometimes even by his followers who use the word "law" as if it were univocal, simply because St. Thomas does not explicitly say the contrary. All questions of fault aside, the fact remains that modern misunderstandings of the natural law arise, in large part, from the supposition that what is signified by the phrase "natural law" is law in exactly the same sense as what is signified by the word "law" when it is used to refer to the positive enactments of human legislators. Since the philosophy of law is primarily concerned with human law, and since it must consider the nature of such law, or, in other words, the natural and the conventional components of legal justice, it becomes a matter of the first importance, in philosophical discussion, especially in the context of modern problems, to clarify the ambiguity of the word "law." If the modern followers of St. Thomas had always insisted explicitly on the non-univocity of "law"—if they had carefully explicated the ambiguity of this one word as it is used in such phrases as "natural law" and "positive law"—they might have saved the Treatise on Law from being misunderstood, and made the doctrine of natural law contribute its proper light to modern legal theory. It is unfortunate that some of them understood St. Thomas too well and others not well enough, for in either circumstance they failed to see the need for such explication, a need that becomes greater as the general context shifts from theology to philosophy, and almost imperative in terms of the mentality of modern readers.[4]

Within the brief compass of this essay, it will be impossible to do more than indicate the analogy of law. Because my aim is philosophical, I shall deal primarily with human law, as natural and positive, though other kinds of law may be mentioned for comparative purposes. No one will deny that the point under consideration is crucial to the philosophy of law, but some may think that it is too obvious to deserve discussion (the whole matter being one of verbal clarification, rather than an explication of real distinctions), whereas others may insist that it is St. Thomas's thought, as well as his speech, which affirms the univocity of law. My argument must be mainly directed against the latter, although I shall try to show the former that more than verbal clarification is involved; thus, for example, the character and scope of *ius gentium* will be more precisely defined when natural and positive law are fully disinguished.

Briefly to accomplish what I have in mind, I herewith propose a question which is not asked in the Treatise on Law. But it might very well have been asked, as one of the articles of Question 91 on the kinds of law. The question is: whether the word "law" is said univocally and unambiguously in speaking of law as natural and as positive, or as Eternal and human. I think St. Thomas would have answered this question in the negative; and, once his reasons for this answer were given, he would have proceeded positively to explain in what way or ways the word "law" is used analogically or equivocally.[5] It is always necessary to establish, first, that a term is not univocal, before one inquires whether the word expressing it is equivocal or analogical in significance.

Within the limits of this discussion, I shall find it necessary to use the terms "analogical," "equivocal" and "univocal" as they have been traditionally and are currently used, despite the fact that such traditional and current usage is analytically unclear. Thus, for example, the word "univocal" is sometimes used to signify that a word is being used unambiguously in two impositions, and sometimes to signify that a word is imposed by way of intrinsic denomination upon a nature that can be defined; similarly, the word "equivocal" is sometimes used to signify that a word is being used ambiguously in two impositions or that it is being imposed by way of extrinsic denomination in a single instance; and what is called "attributive analogy" is sometimes also called "equivocation by intention" to distinguish it from "strict equivocation" or "equivocation by chance." I shall presently publish a book, devoted to a critique of the traditional doctrine of analogy, in which I have tried to clarify these confusions, and to show that, strictly speaking, there are no "modes of analogy"—that what is traditionally called "analogy of proportionality" refers to the only true case of analogical usage (on the part of names) or analogical predication (on the part of concepts), and that what is traditionally called "analogy of attribution" or "analogy of metaphor" are cases of equivocal speech.

The analysis which the book presents is too elaborate and too unfamiliar to be employed here. For the sake of raising and discussing this question about law, I must use the traditional and familiar language, even though it makes a precise and refined discussion impossible. The reader will, how-ever, understand that when I say that the word "law" is not used univocally in reference to natural and positive law, I mean that it does not express one and the same definition in these two impositions. Furthermore, if the "mode of analogy" which here obtains is what is traditionally called "at-tributive analogy," then the word "law" is used *ambiguously* when it is used to refer to both natural and positive law and, in that ambiguous usage, the word "law" must be said *equivocally* (albeit *by intention*) of natural law, if it is said *univocally* of positive law. Only if there are kinds of law which fall within what is traditionally called an "analogy of proportion-ality," will the word "law" be used unambiguously of both kinds, ex-pressing a truly analogical concept, and imposed on both kinds, therefore, by way of intrinsic denomination.

I shall proceed, first, to give Thomistic reasons for maintaining that the word "law" cannot be said unambiguously of both natural and positive law, i.e., that it cannot be said univocally of both, in the sense of expressing *the same definition* when imposed on both. And, then, I shall try to show that the word "law"—when imposed on natural and positive law—is said univocally of the latter, and equivocally of the former, the type of inten-tional equivocation here being what is traditionally called "analogy of attribution." In this second connection, I shall also briefly consider whether any kinds of law—such as Eternal and human—are unambiguously sig-nified by the word "law" as expressing a truly analogical concept; or, in other words, whether there are any types of law which fall within what is traditionally called an "analogy of proportionality." To show that the meaning of "law" does not embrace both natural and positive law under a strictly univocal concept is the first and most important part of this analysis. To show that natural and positive law are not embraced under a strictly analogical concept (that natural law is called "law" as medicine is called "healthy"), is the second and subsidiary part of my argument.

Neither of these tasks can be discharged adequately, for demonstrative reasoning requires an elaboration of analysis impossible in a short essay. I must content myself, therefore, with a bare citation of the evidences one could use to demonstrate the negative answer to the question proposed. Even so, it is necessary to place a great deal of the analytical elaboration, as well as textual commentary, in the footnotes which I must ask the reader to consult for the expansion of many points that cannot be adequately discussed in the essay itself. I trust he will forgive me for the extra burden of careful reading which this imposes upon him.

II

Let me begin by contrasting *ius naturale, ius gentium,* and *ius civile* with one another according to the type of practical judgment in which each consists. The judgments of the practical reason (and here, of course, in the sphere of action, not production) are, in the first place, either concerned with ends or with means; and in the second place, they are either (1) primary and indemonstrable practical truths or secondary and derivative practical truths, and if secondary, they may be (2) necessary conclusions from the primary truths, (3) contingent general determinations of these conclusions, or (4) singular applications of these determinations. Now it is clear at once that the first principles of the practical reason (the primary and indemonstrable truths held by *synderesis*[6]) are concerned with ends, whereas all the other judgments, held as conclusions, determinations, or applications, are concerned with means—the conclusions with the means universally considered, the determinations with the means qualified by reference to the generality of contingent circumstances, and the applications with the singular means *hic et nunc*. Let me use the word "principle" to name the primary and indemonstrable judgments about the ends of action, "precept" to name the implied conclusions about the means universally considered, "rule" to name the determinations of these means by reference to contingent circumstances, and "decision" to name the applications of rules to the case at hand in which a singular means must be chosen.[7] Of these four types of judgment, the last, because it is singular, cannot be a law in any sense of the word. Herein lies the distinction between laws and decrees.[8]

Laws, strictly speaking, are not commands directing particular actions; commands are always applications of law, and as such are immediately proximate to action. Commands follow acts of choice by the will and put to use the last judgment of the practical reason (the typically prudential judgment which I have called "decision"). They occur on the boundary line between intention and execution.[9] As opposed to commands, laws are always practical judgments having universality or at least a certain degree of generality.[10] Of the three remaining types of practical judgment, there can be no question that *rules* correspond to the propositions of *ius civile* (municipal or positive law); for positive laws are determinations of the principles and precepts of practical reason, determining the means in a general way by reference to the generality of contingent circumstances.[11] If one uses the word "law" to name only positive law, it becomes redundant to say "rules of law" for positive laws are rules; but if one uses the word "law" without such restriction, then to speak of "rules of law" indicates that the reference is to the propositions or enactments of positive law.

The only difficulty in classification arises with respect to *ius naturale* and *ius gentium*. In so far as the *ius naturale* is said to consist of the indemonstrable first truths of the practical reason, and in so far as the *ius gentium* is said to consist of conclusions drawn from these first principles,[12] it would appear that *principles* correspond to the propositions of *ius naturale* and *precepts* correspond to the propositions of *ius gentium*, as *rules* correspond to the propositions of *ius civile*, and *decisions* to the propositions which apply rules. But, unfortunately for clarity, the conclusions from the principles are sometimes called the secondary precepts of the natural law, in which case the propositions of *ius gentium* become propositions of *ius naturale*.[13] This is not only unfortunate with respect to precision of language; it is also erroneous analytically. *Synderesis*, which is the habit of the natural law, cannot be at once the habit of both indemonstrable principles and of conclusions drawn therefrom (as understanding and science cannot be one habit). Furthermore, if the conclusions are said to belong to natural law because they are derived therefrom, then the determinations should also be said to belong to natural law (even though they cannot be said to "belong" in the same way); to the extent that they are just rules, they must also be derived from the natural law, though this derivation be mediated by the conclusions.[14] In fact, this is said when it is said that the natural law is changed by the addition of positive determinations;[15] although here it is admitted that what is thus added to natural law can be said to belong to natural law only in an improper mode of speech.[16] Finally, the principles in which natural law consists are judgments about ends, whereas the conclusions derived from it (the so-called secondary precepts) are judgments about the means, albeit universally considered. For all these reasons, I think it is analytically inaccurate to extend the meaning of "natural law" to include more than the first or indemonstrable˙ principles. Strictly speaking, there are no secondary precepts of natural law; rather we should speak of the precepts of law which, as the propositions of *ius gentium*, are derived from the principles of law (the propositions of *ius naturale*) by way of conclusion therefrom. And the propositions of *ius civile*, as rules of law, are derived from the natural law not immediately, but mediately, by way of determination of the precepts.[17]

Precepts, rules, and decisions, are divided against principles in that the former are all directions of action with respect to means (universally, generally, singularly), whereas the latter are directions of action with respect to ends. Furthermore, precepts, rules, and decisions are the result of practical reasoning, though these different types of judgment are not reached by practical reasoning of the same sort, whereas principles are the work of intuition on the part of the practical intellect—the same sort of intuition by which self-evident speculative truths are known. There is as much reason, therefore, to divide the precepts of *ius gentium* (or, for that matter, any conclusions from natural law whether or not they belong to *ius gentium*) against the principles of *ius naturale*, as there is for separating the rules of *ius civile* from the principles of *ius naturale*.[17a] When such divisions are made, it becomes necessary to clarify the notion of *ius gentium*, both in itself and in relation to the notions of human and positive law. The philosopher must disengage the meaning of *ius gentium* from its restricted usage in the tradition of Roman law.[18] The propositions of *ius gentium* are all those practical precepts which are common, and must be common, to diverse bodies of municipal law (*ius civile*), for they are indispensable to every body of municipal law as mediating between the principles of natural law and the rules of *ius civile*.[19] What is meant, then, by "the law of nations" is not what moderns understand by international law, nor what the Romans understood to be an adjunct of their municipal law, whereby the *Praetor Peregrinus* could justly administer transactions between Roman citizens and subject peoples having their own local customs or positive laws; rather "the law of nations," philosophically understood, names what is common to the bodies of law of diverse nations or states. For though the rules of law are diverse in diverse municipalities or states, the quality of justice in them, without which they would be laws in name only, is due to their derivation from the principles of natural law by way of determination of those precepts which must be common to all bodies of municipal law because they are necessary conclusions from natural law about the universal means which men must employ to live peacefully and justly with one another in a political society. When the *ius gentium* is thus understood, there can be no distinction between the precepts in which it consists and what are sometimes called the secondary precepts of natural law, at least in so far as these secondary precepts of natural law are conclusions about universal means in the sphere of social, as opposed to private, conduct.[20]

The question then arises whether the precepts of *ius gentium* should be properly called human law or positive law. The word "human" as qualifying "law" may signify the status of law as *made* by man, as Divine law is made by God, or it may signify the status of law as somehow *received* by man. In the latter signification, natural law is human, in so far as the principles in which it consists are actually known by men through processes of discovery on their part;[21] similarly, the precepts of *ius gentium* are human law, for these, too, can be discovered by men through reasoning, and are received by them in so far as they are thus known; the rules of *ius civile* are also human law, though here the manner of reception is different, for these propositions are known by men not through discovery, but only as formulated by legislators and promulgated to those they govern. So far, then, these three types of law are all human, differing only in manner of reception, with respect to which difference *ius naturale* and *ius gentium* are sharply divided against *ius civile*. This division is further accentuated when the other signification of "human" is considered, for only the rules of *ius civile* are strictly made by man in his capacity as a legislator, an official to whom is entrusted, in part, the care of the community. In contrast, *ius naturale* is made by God as the creator of human nature, whose natural inclinations toward the good are reflexively recognized in the first principles of practical reason; and, in a subordinate sense, *ius gentium* is also made by God to the extent that necessary conclusions are implicitly contained in the premises by which they are entailed. Both the *ius naturale* and the *ius gentium* are active participations (through the activity of human reason) in the Eternal Law by which God governs the created universe. When one considers the difference between the Eternal Law, which proceeds from God as creator and is received by man through the understanding of his own created nature (in which that law is implicit) and the Divine positive law, which proceeds from God as legislator and is received by man through Revelation as a mode of promulgation, the meaning of "positive" becomes clear as a qualifier of "law."[22] Strictly speaking, only that sort of law which is made by man as a legislator, which carries with it not only the authority of the sovereign community but also the coercive force of its *vis major*, is positive human law. The principles of *ius naturale* and the precepts of *ius gentium* have no coercive force; they do not proceed from human officials who exercise extrinsic authority conjoined with power over the individual man who is subject to such laws.[23] In the sphere of human law, only the rules of *ius civile* have the coercive force of law. If institution by politically constituted authority exercising power over members of the community, and reception through extrinsic promulgation (by word, in the case of written law, or by deed, in the case of custom), are the notes which define positive law as man-made, then, in strict usage, what is properly human law (man-made as well as humanly received) is identical with positive human law, and both are identical with the rules of *ius civile*. The principles of *ius naturale* and the precepts of *ius gentium* are certainly not positive law at all, and they can be spoken of as human law in only one respect; namely, that they are humanly received through reason's activity in discovering what God has ordained for man (as to his ends and the universal means thereto) by creating him to be of a certain nature. It is erroneous, therefore, (1) to speak of *ius gentium* as positive law, (2) to speak of *ius gentium* and *ius civile* as human law without a sharp distinction in the meaning of "human," and (3) to speak of *ius gentium* as human law without also speaking of *ius naturale* as human law, distinguished, as *ius gentium* is distinguished, from *ius civile* in that it is human without being positive.

Analytically, these distinctions are plain, but verbal difficulties still remain, for if we divide human law, loosely speaking, into natural law and positive law (which is human law, properly speaking), then it would appear that we must call *ius gentium* natural because it is not positive, although, as we have already seen, there is good reason for distinguishing between *ius naturale* (the indemonstrable principles of practical reason) and *ius gentium* (the necessary conclusions drawn from these principles). This verbal difficulty cannot be solved because the precepts of *ius gentium* are genuinely a mean between the principles of natural law and the rules of positive law: they participate in the characteristics of the opposed extremes. These precepts can be said to belong to natural law because they are necessary conclusions from its principles, because they are discovered by man rather than made by him, because they are not relative to political constitutions, because they are not changeable or variable with time and place, because they are above the sovereign state and, since they do not proceed from its authority, lack the coercive force of political power. But these precepts can also be said to belong to the positive law because they deal with means rather than ends, because in certain cases, albeit rare, dispensation from obedience to them can be granted by the political sovereign,[24] and because, like the positive law, they direct human action toward the social common good (the well-being of a particular political community or of the society of nations), whereas the natural law directs human action toward the individual common good (temporal happiness) primarily, and toward the social common good

A Question About Law

only as a means to happiness.[25] Although strictly speaking the precepts of *ius gentium* are neither natural law nor positive law, it is clearly possible to speak of these precepts both as the "secondary principles" of natural law and as the "proximate principles" of positive law, for this indicates their status as conclusions in the one case, and their status as premises in the other.[26] Since I am chiefly concerned here with the distinction between natural and positive law, I can proceed despite the verbal difficulty of naming what is intermediate between them. It will be necessary, however, to remember the difference between the natural law strictly understood as constituted only by indemonstrable principles and the natural law loosely understood as including the precepts of *ius gentium* which are demonstrable conclusions.

We are now prepared to consider the main problem: whether in our discourse about natural and of positive law, we use the word "law" univocally, equivocally, or analogically? By "positive law" I understand (a) the rules of social conduct, (b) which have been made by duly constituted political authority in a particular community, (c) which are promulgated to all who may be subject to this authority, and (d) which exact obedience, not only by binding in conscience but by the enforcement of sanctions which the community has the power to impose. By "natural law," strictly said, I understand (a) the principles of practical reason itself, (b) which express reason's speculatively-practical knowledge (i.e., prescription) of the natural end of human life (the good which is the object of natural desire), (c) which knowledge can be in every man's possession by natural habit (*synderesis*), and (d) which, possessed, is the proximate source of knowledge of the means universally (by way of conclusion) and the remote source of determination of the means particularized by reference to the contingent circumstances of this community or this individual.

The only further clarification of meaning that is required concerns the unity and plurality of the principles constituting the natural law. The natural law can be stated in a single principle or in several. The single principle is: *Seek the good, and avoid evil.* This is a practical truth that is self-evident to any mind which has the notions of good and evil and which understands the nature of appetite. But the good, which is the end of all human seeking, can be truly or falsely conceived by men. The natural law does not direct man to seek any good, real or apparent, for such a statement would be a description of what, in fact, every man does seek; it would not be a prescription of what should be sought.[27] As directive, the natural law must be properly prescriptive; as a descriptive statement, it would be purely speculative, not practical, knowledge.[28] Hence the natural moral law, or what is the same, the first principle of the practical reason is: *Seek the real good, avoid real evil.* And the distinction between the real and the apparent good must

[217]

be understood in terms of natural desire: the ultimate objects of natural desire are really good. Not all truth in the practical intellect is by conformity to right (i.e., *licit*) desire; with respect to the end, practical judgments are true by conformity to natural appetite: the good which is the object of such appetite is the real good to be sought.[29] Furthermore, since the natural law directs man to his end, the good to be sought must be understood as the complete good: the whole of natural goods. This, of course, is happiness, temporal, natural happiness.[30] But happiness, as a whole of goods, as the possession of all good things, is constituted by an order and variety of partial goods, each of which is a part of the end and may, therefore, be regarded as *an* end or as a constitutive means to *the* end.[31] Hence the natural law may be expressed in a single principle or in several principles, according as the end is conceived as the whole itself or as the orderly structure of the parts constituting this whole. "Seek happiness" is analytically equivalent to "seek every type of good which is essential to the constitution of happiness." Precisely because human happiness is itself a complex unity, the natural law can be expressed in a single principle which derives its singleness from the unity of the end, or in several principles which derive their multiplicity from the complexity of the end. When it is said that the several principles are reducible to one, or flow from that one, what is indicated is, not the deduction of the many from the one (for then the several principles would be conclusions, whereas they are as genuinely indemonstrable as the single principle), but rather that the one and the many are analytically equivalent expressions of the same truth.[32] When the natural law is expressed in several principles, the order of these principles is according to the order of man's natural inclinations which arise from the ordered complexity of man's nature as a corruptible being, as a living being, and as human.[33] Now, man is not only a social animal (having gregarious impulses and need for cooperation with others of his kind, in which respect he is like other social animals), but, being also rational, he is rationally rather than instinctively social. The good of social life is, therefore, not merely an object of man's natural desire (and, as such, a partial good, a constitutive part of his happiness), but it is also an end for the attainment of which reason must discover and determine the means to be employed. One of the several principles of natural law is, therefore: *Seek the social good:* i.e., the good of the community, domestic or political. This principle is sometimes expressed in the following manner: *Do good to others, avoid injuring others, and render to each his own.* It is of the utmost importance to realize that this principle is not equivalent to the natural law, when that is expressed as a single principle (*Seek the good, and avoid evil*), for though the whole good which is to be sought includes the social good as a part, the whole (happiness) cannot be identified with

[218]

one of its parts (the "common good" in the sense of the good of a human community).[34]

The full understanding of this point requires a sharp distinction between two senses of the ambiguous phrase "common good"—the sense in which the happiness of each individual man is a good common to every member of the human species, and the sense in which the good of a human community is a good commonly enjoyed by its members as a part of, and a means to, their individual happiness.[35] When this point is understood, it will be seen that the one principle of natural law which is the foundation of the precepts of *ius gentium* (as conclusions therefrom) and of the rules of positive law (as determinations of these precepts) is the principle which can be expressed either by "Seek the *common good*" or "Do good to others, avoid injuring others, and render to each his own."[36] This principle is, of course, implicitly contained in the unitary expression of natural law in the single principle "Seek happiness"; but its explicit statement as one of the several principles by which the natural law is analytically expanded is, nevertheless, indispensable for discovering the natural foundation of positive law, since positive law determines means to the common good proximately, and to happiness only remotely. The other principles, which belong to the natural law as analytically expanded from one to several principles, provide the natural foundation for the precepts (conclusions) and rules (determinations) of private morality—concerned with all the means, other than the common good, for achieving happiness.[37]

These things being understood, the reasons should be clear why we must conclude that the word "law" is not used unambiguously when we speak of natural and positive law. The foregoing analysis has already revealed most of them, though one or two remain to be indicated. For the sake of adequacy and by way of summary, I shall, therefore, now enumerate all the points which could be used if one were undertaking to demonstrate the conclusion. This can be done briefly except for the few points which have not so far been mentioned.

1. The principles of human conduct are divided into the intrinsic and extrinsic. The intrinsic principles are power and habit, and here virtue is the principle of good acts.[38] The extrinsic principles are twofold: help or actual assistance, and direction, whether by command or counsel. But both help and direction, as extrinsic principles, involve the relation either of God to man or of man to man. Hence, the extrinsic principles can be divided either according as a man is helped and directed to good acts by God or by other men, or according as the extrinsic source proceeds by the way of help or of direction.[39] Considering God as source, we understand Divine help as grace and Divine direction as law. So far as men are concerned, Divine

direction takes the form either of Divine positive law (the Old Law and the New), or of natural law in so far as, through reason's discovery of it, men participate in the Eternal Law which governs all creatures. I shall not pause here to ask whether the Eternal Law and the Divine positive law are both law univocally, or whether they are analogical modes of Divine direction.[40] My concern is with human law, whether it be human as discovered by man or human as made by him. Men *help* one another to good acts, and to the attainment of happiness thereby, through social cooperation. Men *direct* one another either through counsel or command, the distinction here being that counsel or advice is effective direction only in terms of the moral authority of him who gives it as speaking with the voice of reason, whereas command is effective direction in terms of the political authority of the community, or its representatives, combining coercive force with instruction. Now it is clear at once that human positive law like Divine positive law, is purely and primarily law, for it is extrinsic direction whereby a sovereign (the State, like God), combining authority and power, commands acts to be done at the penalty of sanctions to be enforced if the rules of conduct are violated. In both cases, such rules (enacted by the State or made by God) are received by those who are subject to them through promulgation by their extrinsic source (whether this take the form of human communication or Divine revelation). In sharp contrast, the natural law, in so far as it is received by man through processes of rational discovery, is an intrinsic principle of human conduct, for it is possessed by way of a natural habit (*synderesis*) and this habit is like the virtue of understanding. But virtues are, as we have seen, intrinsic principles of good conduct. Hence, the natural law as operative in human life (and its being operative depends on its active reception through rational discovery) operates as an intrinsic, not as an extrinsic, principle. The natural law is an extrinsic principle only in the sense that its extrinsic source is God as creator of human nature and human reason, but it is no more extrinsic, in this sense, than human powers are; in fact, it is even less so, because human powers are in no way the result of man's own activity, whereas the natural law as habitually possessed is in part the work of man's own activity (the work of discovery). Hence, if powers are said to be intrinsic principles of human conduct (though they can also be called extrinsic in that their ultimate cause is God as creator), how much more so must the natural law—so far as it is actually operative— be said to be intrinsic rather than extrinsic, especially when the primary meaning of an extrinsic principle is understood in terms of Divine help and direction (grace and Divine positive law) or human help and direction (social cooperation and political regulations).[41] That which is primarily an extrinsic principle of conduct, by way of direction, is not only a rule made by another as to explicit formulation, but also, in those it governs, this rule is received by way of instruction rather than discovery.[42] Furthermore, the natural law and the positive law stand in a different relation to the moral virtues and to prudence. The habit of the natural law is itself a virtue and also the nursery of all the moral virtues,[43] whereas the positive law is, at best, an extrinsic cause of the moral virtues in those who act according to its rules.[44] This difference confirms the insight that natural law operates as an intrinsic, whereas positive law operates as an extrinsic, cause of good conduct. And the natural law cannot be obeyed except by those who have and exercise the virtue of prudence in determining the means to be chosen for attaining the ends appointed by the natural law, whereas the positive law can be obeyed both by the prudent and the imprudent man, as well as by those who are in the process of becoming morally habituated.[45] This last point is related to a difference between natural and positive law with respect to their violability: for the principles of natural law can be violated in two ways (both by intellectual errors of judgment in conceiving the end to be sought and by defections of the will from the end, even when rightly conceived), whereas just rules of positive law can be violated only willfully, for the extrinsic promulgation of positive law precludes violation by intellectual error (though, of course, ignorance of the law or misunderstanding of its intention, due to unclear formulation, may lead to involuntary violation of it). All of these considerations support the main insight that, as causes of human conduct, natural law and positive law differ in operation as intrinsic and extrinsic principles, and therefore they cannot be univocally law. (To say that "they cannot be univocally law" is to say that the word "law" is here being used ambiguously in such a way that if it is imposed univocally on positive law, it cannot be imposed univocally on natural law.)

2. In the practical order, the end is the first principle. The indemonstrable first truths of the practical intellect must, therefore, be about the end—as a whole and as constituted by its essential parts. Hence it follows that the natural law is not *direction* in the same sense as positive law, for the former directs only by prescribing the end, or ends, of conduct for which all means shall be chosen; whereas the latter directs by prescribing certain types of acts to be done or avoided, which acts are among the variety of means to the end appointed.[46] Since direction is of the essence of law, and since natural law and positive law differ radically in their mode of direction (as radically as the end differs from the means), they cannot be univocally law.

3. The propositions of the natural law being principles (prescribing the end), they cannot be directly applied in action, because action always follows a choice of singular means *hic et nunc*. Nor can the propositions of *ius*

gentium, regarded as belonging to the natural law by way of necessary conclusion therefrom, be directly applied in action, for though they are precepts (prescribing means), they define the means universally in terms of the nature of man and of what is natural about society. But individual men differ accidentally and particular societies differ in what is conventional about their constitution. Hence the universal means must be somewhat particularized with reference to the generality of contingent circumstances before the universal precepts can be applied in action by particular men in a particular society. Such particularization of the means is accomplished by the rules of positive law which prescribe means that are fitting and feasible in a given community. The rules of positive law can, therefore, be directly applied in action by those who, being subject to this law, must obey it, and by those whose executive or judicial duty is to administer this law in particular cases. Strictly speaking, only the rules of positive law can be administered by executive decree or judicial decision; only the rules of positive law can be directly applied by reason's act of command to action in the singular case. The principles of natural law and the precepts of *ius gentium* are not capable of political administration by magistrates (executive or judicial), nor can they be directly applied in action, for the former are about ends, and the latter are not sufficiently determinate with respect to means.[47] These principles and precepts are inadequate *practically,* and it is this practical inadequacy which the determinations made by rules of positive law supplement. Since application to action by reason's command is of the essence of law, and since the natural law (even including the precepts of *ius gentium* as secondary principles) and the positive law differ radically in their applicability (indirect and direct), they cannot be univocally law.

4. The end we are bidden to seek by the natural law is natural, temporal happiness.[48] As we have seen, this end, because it is a whole of goods, can be analytically expanded into an order and variety of constitutive parts, among which the common good is one—both an end *secundum quid* (in the order of political activity) and a constitutive means to temporal happiness (which is the end *simpliciter* in the natural order).[49] Now, the rules of positive law prescribe determinate means to the common good as the proximate end, though, of course, this proximate end is, in turn, a means to happiness as ultimate end. And here the precepts of *ius gentium* must be associated with positive, rather than with natural, law, because the means they universally define have the common good as their proximate end.[50] For this reason, the precepts of *ius gentium* can be regarded as the principles of positive law, their proximate rational foundation. In contrast, the natural law, as expressed in a single first principle, is the rational foundation for

both ethical and political determinations—for ethical precepts defining the virtues as means to happiness, and for rules of positive morality prescribing ways of becoming virtuous, as well as for the precepts of *ius gentium* defining means to the common good, and for the rules of positive law.[51] There is only one proposition of the natural law (when the natural law is expressed by several principles) which prescribes the common good as an end for which means must be defined and determined.[52] Since it is of the essence of law to be concerned with the common good, since the meaning of "common good" is not the same when it signifies now happiness and now the welfare of the community, and since the natural law is concerned primarily, and as a whole, with happiness, and only secondarily, and in part, with the common good, whereas the positive law is concerned primarily and entirely with the common good, they cannot be univocally law.

5. Virtuous acts are means both to happiness and the common good. But an act can be said to be virtuous in two ways: extrinsically, because it is good, or intrinsically, because it proceeds from the right intention of a good habit.[53] Furthermore, the virtues, and their acts, can be divided as perfecting or as social, according as they aim at the happiness of an individual or at the common good of a community.[54] And with respect to the common good it is sufficient if acts be virtuous extrinsically, whereas with respect to happiness, acts must be virtuous intrinsically. Now the natural law, appointing happiness as the end, demands that every virtue be ordained as a means and requires that acts be intrinsically virtuous, though it does not prescribe these acts determinately.[55] In contrast, the positive law, though it prescribes virtuous acts determinately, does not repress all vices and prescribe all virtues, but forbids vicious acts and requires virtuous acts only so far as such acts can be ordained to the common good, and hence only as virtuous or vicious extrinsically.[56] Since it is of the essence of law to direct men to virtuous acts, and since the scope of natural law and of positive law, with respect to the prescription of virtue and the prohibition of vice, is radically different (both in the end and the character of virtuous acts), they are not univocally law.

6. In order to be applied in action, law must be effective in moving the will of agents. But law can be effective in two ways: either through binding the conscience of those who assent to it on rational grounds and exercise their will accordingly, or through extrinsically enforceable sanctions which coerce the passions through fear of pain. In so far as they are just, the rules of positive law are effective in both ways, for they bind virtuous men in conscience and coerce all others by the threat of extrinsic sanctions.[57] In contrast, the natural law (and with it the precepts of *ius gentium*) is effective only through binding the conscience of the virtuous.[58] Since its effectiveness

is a property of law, and since positive law is effective in a way that is totally lacking to natural law, they are not univocally law.[59]

7. In order to be effective, law must be known to those whose acts it regulates. Now anything can become known to a man in two ways: either through discovery or under instruction by another. As speculative instruction is accomplished by teaching, so practical instruction is accomplished by giving counsel (or setting an example), and by the promulgation of law, through word or deed.[60] Discovery is, however, the same in both the speculative and the practical spheres—the unaided work of reason in learning the truth by induction or deduction. The natural law (and with it the precepts of *ius gentium*) becomes known to men through discovery—the natural law inductively, the precepts of *ius gentium* deductively.[61] But the positive law becomes known to men only through promulgation, whether by official enactment or by public custom. Furthermore, that which is communicated to others must itself first be actually known by those who instruct. In the speculative sphere, what any teacher has as actual knowledge, someone must first acquire by discovery. In the practical sphere, however, those who instruct others about law may do so either by helping others to discover the natural law which they themselves already know, or by making rules of positive law, which they then promulgate. In short, in so far as law is, strictly speaking, promulgated, it is made, not discovered; and in so far as it is discoverable, it can be discovered by all men, with or without the aid of others. Since communicability is a property of law, and since the natural law is commonly known through discovery by all (though, in certain cases, the discovery may be aided by those who instruct, albeit in a speculative manner), whereas the positive law can be commonly known only through promulgation and is discovered neither by those who make it nor by those who receive it, they are not univocally law.

8. Because of the differences already noted, it follows that natural law becomes operative in human life primarily through the work of reason in discovering it, and the will is involved only so far as the reason is voluntarily exercised; whereas, in contrast, positive law becomes operative in human society only in so far as it is first made and then promulgated. But the making of positive law is not purely a work of reason. Though it is never independent of the will with respect to exercise, reason is not moved by the will, in specification to object, when that object falls within reason's proper sphere. Herein lies the distinction between knowledge and opinion: with respect to its proper objects, the intellect knows, which means that it is moved to affirm or deny by the object itself and not by the will; whereas with respect to all other objects, the intellect only opines, which means that its affirmations or denials are caused by the will.[62] Now, practical knowl-

edge, as well as theoretic knowledge, is strictly discoverable. But, as we have seen, the rules of positive law are not discoverable because they are not practical knowledge—being neither self-evident principles nor necessary conclusions therefrom. Hence, the rules of positive law are, in the practical sphere, like opinions in the speculative order. That this is so is further attested by such facts as that they are only generally, not universally, true, that they consider contingent circumstances, that they are susceptible to variation relative to changing circumstances, that they are not simply just but are mixtures of natural justice with conventional determinations on points that would be otherwise indifferent.[63] Therefore, rules of positive law, as conventionally instituted by political authorities, are the work of reason, not purely, but as moved by the will, with respect to specification as well as exercise. This is another way of saying that natural law is purely natural, whereas positive law is partly natural (in so far as it is founded on reason's knowledge of natural law) and partly conventional (in so far as the determinations, in which it exceeds what can be strictly known by reason, are practical judgments which, like opinions, are subject to the causality of will). These things being so, positive law and natural law are not univocally law.[64]

9. Because the positive law is both natural in its implicit foundations, and conventional in its explicit determinations, because it is a work of reason as moved to specification by the will, and not the work of reason purely, the authority of the positive law must derive in part from the authority of the legislators who make it, which in turn derives from the authority that a sovereign community naturally exercises over its members, to direct them to the common good which is a means to their happiness. But the authority of the natural law is the authority of reason itself, deriving only from the sovereignty of God as reason's creator. Though the natural authority of the sovereign community also derives from God as creator of man's social nature, the proximate sources of obligation are not the same in the case of natural and positive law. A man is obliged to obey the natural law only because what it ordains is known to be practically true; but a man is obliged to obey the positive law because it has been instituted for the welfare of the community to which he belongs. In so far as its rules are just, made by duly constituted officials, and directed to the common good of a particular community, the positive law obliges those who are subject to it. A number of consequences follow: a man is obliged only by the positive law of the community to which he belongs (whether as resident or as visitor), whereas all men everywhere are obliged by the natural law; the positive law is law only in so far as its conventional determinations conform to natural law and through such conformity have the quality of justice, whereas natural law is itself intrinsically

[225]

just or, at least, in one of its principles is identical with the principle of political justice.[65] These things being so, positive law and natural law are not univocally law.

10. Finally, because the positive law is, in the practical order, comparable to opinion in the speculative order, whereas natural law is comparable to knowledge, the rules of positive law have certain intrinsic defects or limitations from which the natural law escapes. The justice of positive law is not only by conformity to natural law, but also by conformity to the constitution or political type of a particular community: rules which may be just or useful in one community may not be so in another;[66] in contrast, the natural law is prior to political constitutions and is that whereby their justice is measured. In short, the natural law measures the justice of all political constitutions, whereas the constitution of a given community measures the justice of positive law in that community. Furthermore, the rules of positive law not only differ from community to community,[67] but also are mutable in a given community from time to time; in contrast, the principles of natural law are absolutely immutable.[68] Moreover, with respect to the variability of positive law, it must be noted that custom has the force of written enactments, and can make ineffective, or abolish, such enactments as are contrary to well-established custom; whereas, custom neither has the force of natural law, nor can it abolish natural law.[69] Strictly speaking, natural law cannot be abolished from the hearts of men,[70] whereas rules of positive law can and should be entirely abolished whenever their usefulness in service of the common good decreases to the point where more harm is done by keeping the law fixed than by changing it.[71] Finally, the rules of positive law being intrinsically defective because they are practical opinions dealing with contingent circumstances, it is necessary to do justice in certain cases by equitable dispensation from these rules, for greater justice is done by equity where positive law is defective due to its generality, than can be done by strict observance of the law in every case.[72] But the principles of natural law are not defective in this way, and there can be no dispensation from them, though in certain rare cases there may be dispensation from the precepts of *ius gentium*, but these cases always involve international transactions and never the affairs of a single community.[73] These things being so, natural law and positive law are not univocally law.[74]

III

Suppose it be granted that the foregoing arguments demonstrate (or outline a demonstration) that the word "law" cannot be said unambiguously and univocally of both natural and positive law. This conclusion being negative, there still remain three questions which must be answered on the positive side: (1) whether the word "law" is here being used in a manner that is strictly or absolutely equivocal? (2) if not, whether the type of analogy involved is what is traditionally called "attribution" or "proportionality"? and (3) if what we have here is an "analogy of attribution," which is the primary analogate, i.e., is the attribution from natural law to positive law, or conversely?

To answer these questions adequately would require a full statement of the doctrine of analogy. More than that, as I indicated at the beginning, it would require an elaborate critical revision of the doctrine of analogy as that has been traditionally expounded and is currently accepted. For that I must refer the reader to a book about the subject which I have just written and which I hope will shortly appear. Here I can do no more than suggest some of the reasons for the answers which have to be given. I can, however, make the intention of the three foregoing questions clear by restating them in the light of traditional examples.

(1) Is the word "law" said of natural and positive law, as the word "pen" is said of a writing instrument and a place for pigs? The word "pen" as said of these two objects exemplifies strict or absolute equivocation, or what is called "equivocation by chance."

(2) Is the word "law" said of natural and positive law, as the word "healthy" is said of medicine and man, or as the word "being" is said of God and creatures? The word "healthy" as said of medicine and man exemplifies what is sometimes called "equivocation by intention" and sometimes called "analogy of attribution." The word "being" as said of God and creatures exemplifies what is called "analogy of proper proportionality."

(3) Is the word "law" said of positive law primarily and essentially (by intrinsic denomination) as "healthy" is said of man, and is the word "law" said of natural law secondarily and attributively (by extrinsic denomination) as "healthy" is said of medicine; or is the reverse the case? In the so-called "attributive analogy" of the word "healthy" as imposed on man and medicine, man is the so-called "primary analogate" because man possesses health as an intrinsic or formal constitutive of his nature, whereas medicine is not healthy at all (in any intrinsic manner), but is only called "healthy" as being a cause of health. This question, therefore, is whether natural law or positive law is intrinsically and formally law, and, in consequence, which is called "law" only in virtue of a causal relationship to the other.

I shall now proceed to answer these three questions, with the hope that the reader will understand their meaning, even though I have not been able to give the complete account of modes of signification which I have in mind in asking them. Nevertheless, in order to make my discussion intelligible to those who employ traditional language, I shall continue to speak of *equivocation by intention* (whether attributive or metaphorical) as a "mode or type of analogy" and I shall use the phrase "type of analogy" to cover the modes of signification traditionally classified as "analogy of proper proportionality" or "proportional analogy," "analogy of attribution" or "attributive analogy," "analogy of metaphor" or "metaphorical analogy," etc.

(1) The first question is the easiest to answer. The fact that there is a causal relationship between natural and positive law—natural law being the formal cause of justice and legality in positive law—shows at once that the word "law" is not *absolutely equivocal* here. We know, therefore, that some type of analogy must prevail. To sharpen the significance of this point, let us consider a case of (a) strict univocity on the one hand, and a case of (b) strict equivocation on the other.

(a) In the notion of positive law are included many different kinds of positive law, such as codified and common law, written and unwritten law, substantive and procedural law, criminal and civil law. Conceived as a genus including these kinds which are subordinately distinct, the notion of positive law is strictly univocal.

(b) What the natural scientist calls the "laws of nature," such as the "law of gravitation" or "Mendel's law" or "Boyle's law," are, *as known by man,* not law at all. To speak of such theoretic propositions as "laws" and to speak of the first principles of the practical reason as "laws" is strict equivocation. And if the scientist's "laws of nature" and the moralist's "natural law" involve an equivocation, how much more so is this the case when the scientist's theoretic formulations are contrasted with the legislator's conventional, practical rules.

But it may be objected that what the scientist calls "laws of nature" are knowledge of the natures of infra-human things, as what the moralist calls "natural law" is knowledge of man's nature, and in both cases what is known is the participation by creatures in the Eternal Law. Hence, a common cause being involved, there is no equivocation. The objection, it seems to me, is answered by pointing out that what is being compared is not human nature and the natures of other corporeal creatures, but scientific knowledge and the principles of morality. So far as the notion of nature goes, there is, of course, analogical participation in the Eternal Law as governing all things, the main negative point of this analogy being that man's participation is active, rational, and free. But we are considering man's knowledge of the Eternal Law as that is manifested in the nature of things and is capable of being discovered by human inquiry. And here, it seems to me, strict equivocation is perfectly apparent in the use of the word "law" to name both propositions of theoretic knowledge and principles, precepts, or rules of practical conduct.[75]

(2) The second question is the most difficult to answer, not in itself, but with respect to certain difficulties that arise in consequence. Let us first consider it in itself, the narrow question being about the type of analogy that obtains between natural and positive law. There are, as we know, three possible answers: the analogy of metaphor, the analogy of attribution, and the analogy of proportionality. The very fact which showed that the word "law" is not absolutely equivocal as imposed on natural and positive law also shows that the mode of analogy is attributive, namely, the fact of causal relationship between the two. As medicine or exercise is called healthy as a cause of the body's health, so natural law is called law as a cause of legality in the enactments of human legislators.[76] Clearly, the analogy is not metaphorical, for whereas the lion and the moon are in no sense rulers when they are called, respectively, "the king of beasts" and "the queen of the night," natural law has something of the essence of human law: it consists in practical judgments; it is concerned with the ends, and implicitly with the means, of human life; it directs human conduct, even though from afar, and not proximately as do the rules of positive law; it relates, in part, to the common good which is the whole object of positive law.

But, though the same analogy cannot be both attributive and metaphorical (and here there is no question about which type prevails in the case of natural and positive law), it may be supposed that the same analogy can be primarily proportional, and implicitly, or secondarily, attributive; thus, for example, the fact that Divine and human knowledge are analogous by the proportionality of an infinite and a finite intellect does not preclude Divine knowledge from being a cause of human knowledge, and hence, in this connection, analogous by ,attribution from effect to cause.[77] I have tried to show, in the book already mentioned, why an attributive analogy is *never* virtually contained in an analogy of proper proportionality, as John of St. Thomas supposed. But here let us accept the supposition, for the dialectical purpose of considering the question it raises.

The question is whether natural and positive law are primarily analogous by proportionality, and only secondarily by attribution. Taking both as human law, i.e., considered as in man's possession through his own activity, the answer seems to be clearly negative. Every analogy of proportionality is founded in the prime proportionality of being. But, as actively possessed by man (whether through rational discovery or through voluntary institution), both natural and positive law belong to the same being—man's intellect as practical. "Natural law : human intellect : positive law : human intellect" does not formulate an analogy of proportionality. Therefore we must con-

that, as human law, natural and positive law are analogical in only an attributive way; or, in other words, that the univocal notion of human law is attributed from positive law, *which is what that notion primarily signifies,* to natural law, as from effect to cause. This indicates at once the answer to the third question, but before we turn to it, it is necessary to mention certain difficulties which follow from this solution of the second problem. In a sense, all of these difficulties belong to the theologian rather than the philosopher because they concern the Eternal Law and the Divine positive law in relation to human law, natural and positive. Yet they may throw some light on the main points here being considered in the philosophy of law. I shall state them as questions.

(a) *Are Eternal Law and human law analogous by proportionality to the Divine and human intellects?* The answer would, at first, seem to be Yes, for as knowledge in the Divine and in the human mind is analogous proportionally, so is law. But, then, a difficulty arises when it is pointed out that the natural law is to the Eternal Law, as the positive law, as received by those who are subject to it, is to the positive law, as instituted by the human legislator. The natural law, as human law, would thus appear to be proportionally analogous to the Eternal Law, on the one hand, and also, as a part of (i.e., a participation in) Eternal Law, it would appear to be proportionally analogous to positive law, on the other hand. This difficulty can be solved, I think, by noting a duplicity in the notion of natural law, a duplicity already pointed out in our consideration of the sense in which the natural law is and is not human law.[78] As signifying a passive participation in the Eternal Law, the natural law is human only in the same way that it is also brutal or vegetable or simply corporeal. But as signifying an active participation in the Eternal Law through the discovery of practical truth about the ends of human life, the natural law is human in the same sense that the positive law is human, i.e., as resulting from the work of intellect and will in making sound rules about the means to be employed. Hence there is a sense in which the natural law is divided against human law, and in this sense it is proportionally analogous to positive law (which as made by human legislators is analogous to the Eternal Law, and which as received by those subject to it is analogous to the passive participation by created natures in the Eternal Law); but there is also a sense in which the natural law is a part of human law and is thus divided against the Eternal Law. In this latter sense, the natural law is not proportionally analogous to the positive law; it is rather the human law in its entirety which stands in this relation to the Eternal Law.[79] There are still certain difficulties about this analogy, because whereas the human legislator is subject to positive law in the same way and to the same extent as every other member of the community he helps to govern,[80] the Divine legislator of the Eternal Law is not subject to that law in the same way as created natures are by passive participation;[81] or, in other words, we must distinguish, in the one case, between the Eternal Law and the natural law (in its non-human sense), whereas, in the other case, there is no need to distinguish between the positive law as made and as received, because, though it be given by some, it is equally binding on all members of the community.

(b) *Are the Divine positive law and human positive law univocal or analogical?* Here, it seems to me, the answer is that both are univocally law. The truth of this answer depends on restricting the signification of "Divine positive law" to what is strictly positive law, namely, to the judicial and ceremonial precepts of the Old Law, and to the ceremonial precepts of the New Law. Certainly, the New Law is not positive law in so far as it is actually identical with Grace, or in so far as it consists of counsels, and not commands;[82] and the Old Law is not positive law in its moral precepts, for these are nothing but the conclusions of natural law (the precepts of *ius gentium*) as Divinely revealed instead of naturally discovered by the work of reason.[83] But the Mosaic law is, strictly speaking, positive law, civil in its judicial precepts, and religious in its ceremonial precepts.[84] It consists in a determinate set of rules which can be immediately applied to action by individuals, and administered by officials of the community; in its judicial precepts, it is exactly like municipal law, directing the members of a community in those acts which are useful to (means to) the common good. It may be objected, however, that Divine positive law, in this precise and restricted sense, cannot be univocal with human positive law, because of the profound difference in source (God and man), and hence in the authority which the law expresses, the character of the sanctions it imposes, etc. The objector here should be asked to face another question: whether the theoretic truth which men hold by faith in Divine revelation and the theoretic truth they discover by their own inquiries are univocally truth as a rectitude of the human intellect in conformity with being? If the answer is affirmative, then so must it also be with respect to the practical truth of sound positive regulations, whether such truth be revealed or humanly instituted.[85] In short, it would seem that positive law is the same in essence whether Divinely or humanly made, though, in consequence of different origins, certain *accidents* of human positive law are not found in Divine positive law, and conversely.[86]

(c) *Are Eternal Law and Divine positive law univocal or analogical?* Everything that has so far been said seems to indicate that they are not univocal. And it seems equally clear that they are analogical as two kinds of Divine law, the one proportionate to the natural end of all creatures, the other proportionate to the supernatural end of man.[87] If it be objected that

clude the Old Law, strictly conceived as positive law, and in its judicial precepts, has the temporal well-being of a particular community (i.e., the society
of the chosen people) as its end, it can be answered that, while this is true, the
ultimate end of the Old Law is eternal salvation in so far as it prepares for
the reign of the New Law.[88] The only difficulty here lies in the fact that
when its ultimate and supernatural end is its only end, the Divine positive
law is, strictly speaking, not positive law, and in a sense, not law at all, for it
consists either in the counsels of the New Law or in Grace itself, which is
help and not direction.[89]

(3) However these theological difficulties be solved, the main point in the
philosophy of law seems to be sufficiently established: that natural law (as
human through active discovery on man's part) is law only by attributive
analogy with human positive law. *But which is the primary analogate, the
cause or the effect?* As I have already indicated, the answer seems to me to
be that, within the sphere of human law, the univocal notion of law signifies
positive law primarily, and natural law secondarily, only by attributive extension from effect to cause. (In other words, when we call the first principles of the practical reason "law," we signify them as *causes* of law, and
not *formally* as laws, just as "healthy" said of medicine expresses the concept 'cause of health.') The primacy of cause over effect does not require
the cause to be the primary analogate in an attributive analogy; thus, for
example, health is said primarily of the body and not of medicine or exercise as causes of health. The decision between cause and effect depends on
the essence of that, the name of which is attributed from cause to effect, or
from effect to cause.

The analogy of truth is helpful here in understanding the analogy of law.
Truth in the Divine intellect and truth in the human intellect are analogous
by proportionality. But the truth which is said to be in things is not truth
by proportional analogy with either the Divine or the human intellect.
Things have truth only by attributive analogy; their truth is identical with
their natures as efficiently caused by Divine truth, for Divine knowledge is
creative;[90] but the truth of their natures is, in turn, the formal cause of truth
in the human mind, which has rectitude through conformity to the nature
of things. Thus, when things are said to have truth, there is a twofold attribution: from the Divine intellect as from cause to effect, and from the human
intellect as from effect to cause. And, in the one case, truth in the Divine
intellect (the cause) is the primary analogate, whereas, in the other case,
truth in the human intellect (the effect) is the primary analogate.

Now, the analogy of law can be explained in the same way. Eternal Law
and human positive law are analogous proportionally. Now the natural law

is both an effect of Eternal Law and a cause of human positive law. Hence, a law is said to exist in the natures of things both by attribution from the Divine cause and by attribution from the human effect. In the one case, the Eternal Law is the primary analogate; in the other, the human positive law is the primary analogate. There is one difference, however, between the analogy of truth and the analogy of law. The truth which is identical with the natures of things is the same whether it be viewed as cause or as effect; but the law which is identical with the natures of things is not the same as cause and as effect: for, as effect, natural law is a purely passive participation in Eternal Law and so, even in the case of man, is not, strictly speaking, human law; whereas, as cause, natural law, in the case of man, must be an active participation through reason's work of discovery, and is, therefore, human as well as natural law.[91]

That the univocal notion of human law signifies positive law primarily (and that, within the sphere of human law, natural law can be called law only by attribution therefrom) is confirmed by the definition which St. Thomas gives of law. The rules of positive law are "nothing else but an ordinance of reason for the common good, made by him who has the care of the community, and promulgated."[92] This definition, strictly interpreted, does not apply to the principles of natural law (or even to its necessary conclusions, the precepts of *ius gentium*); for though the "common good" which is mentioned in the definition can be understood either as happiness or the social welfare, nevertheless the element of the definition which says that "the making of law belongs either to the whole community or to a public personage who has care of the whole people,"[93] indicates absolutely that that which is signified by "common good," as the prior element in the definition, must be the welfare of the community, and not individual happiness.[94] The definition, as given by St. Thomas, is imprecise, however, with respect to the first element named. An "ordination of reason" can be either a practical judgment which is knowledge (in making which the intellect is specified by its object) or a practical judgment which is opinion (in making which the intellect is moved to its specific act by the will). Now those rules of conduct which are made by the whole community (customs) or by public officials (enactments), for the social welfare (i.e., for the common good), are ordinations of reason in the second, not in the first, sense. We are, therefore, faced with the following dilemma: either the third element in the definition (made by the whole community or by a public official) must be omitted from the definition (in which case positive law is not defined), or the first two elements must be made more precise accordingly—"common good" to be understood as social welfare, not happiness, and "ordination of reason" to be understood as a practical rule conventionally instituted, not as a practical principle rationally discovered—in which case, the definition applies properly only to positive law. Whichever choice is made, it follows necessarily that natural law and positive law cannot be comprehended in the same definition, which must be the case, of course, if they are not univocally law.[95]

The choice to be made is plainly indicated, it seems to me, by the rest of the Treatise on Law which shows positive law to have the essence of law.[96] If the definition of law were precisely formulated to express the univocal notion of human law, and hence primarily to signify positive law, all of the properties of law would follow from the definition: its need for promulgation, its mutability, its coercive force, its relativity to political constitutions, its extrinsic and limited causality with respect to virtue and virtuous acts, its relation to custom, its deficiencies which require correction by equity. All of these properties have been shown to belong strictly to positive law, and to natural law either not at all or only in some special and different sense.[97]

Two consequences would follow from such precision in definition. In certain connections (I am thinking of contemporary discussion of the philosophy of law), it might be helpful to use words with a corresponding precision. No harm would be done, and some clarity might be achieved, if the word "law" were used only to signify the rules of positive law, and never the principles of natural law. *The rules of positive law are laws. The propositions of natural law are not laws.* They are *only* principles, sources, or foundations *of* law.[98] Such verbal usage is always desirable in relation to univocal concepts whose signification is extended by attributive analogy. Thus, by strict grammar, it is incorrect to speak of anything except the body as healthy: the medicine which is a cause of health or the urine which is a sign of health is not healthy, for neither has health. It may be necessary to use a phrase in place of a single word in order to speak the truth precisely: we should call the medicine "a cause of health," and the urine "a symptom of health." Similarly, only rules which are conventionally instituted and publicly enacted have the status of laws; the principles of practical reason, without which such rules could not be rightly formulated, should be called "principles of law" or "sources of law," but never "laws" or "propositions of law." In short, our speech should reflect the fact that the rules of positive law are law by intrinsic or essential denomination, whereas the principles of natural law are law only by extrinsic or causal denomination.

Much futile controversy would be avoided by such accuracy of speech to correspond to precision in analysis. Nor would the dignity and importance of natural law in human affairs suffer thereby, for we would be insisting that the essence of legality in positive enactments derives from their rational foundation in the principles of natural law. (Positive enactments which are absolutely arbitrary can be nothing but the impositions of a tyrant's will, and are, therefore, laws in name only.[99]) But though natural law is the source of legality and justice in positive laws, the essence of legality is in the positive rules, and not in their source.[100] This can be said another way: positive laws are *conventional*, but not purely so; they are also *natural* in the sense of having a foundation in nature; and what is natural about positive law (i.e., the *natural* that is found in them underlying conventional determination) is what is derived from the natural law.

The other consequence of the clarification which I am proposing (both in speech and thought) is that we can discover the origin of all the confusions about natural law in terms of the Roman distortion of the Greek analysis. Aristotle never speaks of the natural law.[100a] In fact, the opposition of the Greek words for nature and law (*physis* and *nomos*) made such speech difficult, for *nomos* signified not only law, but also that which is essentially conventional and hence opposed to the natural. This does not mean that Aristotle fails to see the nature which underlies conventions in so far as they are just. The terms of his analysis are natural justice, legal justice, and political justice, for the justice of laws (political enactments) is partly natural and partly legal or conventional.[101] And when Aristotle says that equity is better than legal justice, but not better than absolute justice, he is indicating that positive laws are, at best, only an imperfect expression of natural justice.[102] Analytically, there is a strict equivalence between what Aristotle means by the principles of natural justice (which are not laws) and what St. Thomas means by natural law in so far as it is the principle of law. In both cases, what is signified is that first principle of the practical reason which directs men to the common good, and perhaps also the necessary conclusions to be drawn therefrom about the means universally considered; for, in both cases, the rules of positive law have legality and justice through serving this end and particularizing these means by determinations relative to the particular community. But although there is an analytical equivalence here, it is not indifferent which words are used to express the analysis, because, unfortunately, the Latin phrase "*ius naturale*" is infected with erroneous conceptions about God, man, reason, and nature, due to the influence of stoicism on the traditions of Roman law. This can be readily seen by anyone who compares Cicero's discussion of natural law with Aristotle's discussion of natural justice.[103] The whole tradition of what is called "natural law theory" in the Middle Ages and down to the seventeenth and eighteenth centuries cannot escape the coloring and distortion which stoicism and Roman law gave to jurisprudence through using the phrase "natural law."[104]

I am not suggesting that the phrase be abandoned—history cannot be undone so easily—but I am recommending that the theory of natural law be purified by returning to the Aristotelian analysis, and by understanding Thomistic doctrine as its analytical equivalent, *so far as both are philosophical.* A philosophy of law might then be written which had a certain autonomy apart from theology. Both in the precision of its thought and the restraint of its language, it might satisfy contemporary students of jurisprudence that all the facts about law could be accounted for, conceding the conventionality of positive law, yet not so as to deny that natural justice without which political enactments are laws in name only. Legal positivism (currently called legal realism or pragmatism) is not wholly false. Legal naturalism (or what is the same, legal idealism or rationalism) is not wholly true. The truth is contained only in a doctrine which recognizes the natural foundations of positive law, yet which understands the essence of law to be positive and its properties to follow from the origin of law through political institution. The truth is epitomized in the insight that it belongs to the nature of law for its rules to be *formulated* by ordinations of reason and *instituted* by acts of will. The jurist or legislator is a man of prudence using knowledge but also obliged to exercise a free will.

Eleventh Essay

THE ECONOMIC PHILOSOPHY
OF ST. THOMAS

by

John A. Ryan

The Economic Philosophy of St. Thomas

SUBSTANTIALLY all of St. Thomas' economic teaching is found in the moral part of his *Summa Theologica*. The doctrines to be examined fall under seven heads:

1) the virtue of justice;
2) private ownership;
3) use of wealth;
4) duties of wealth: almsgiving and liberality;
5) just price and just wage;
6) trade;
7) usury.

Numbers 2, 5, 6 and 7 are treated according to the principles of justice; numbers 3 and 4 mainly on the basis of charity. The virtue of justice is expounded in questions 58 and 61 of the *Secunda Secundae*. There, St. Thomas describes the three kinds of justice, namely, general or legal, distributive, and commutative. While he makes no mention of social justice, the omission is not surprising, since this phrase did not begin to appear in Catholic moral treatises much before the beginning of the present century. The first Pope to use it was Pius XI.[1]

I. THE VIRTUE OF JUSTICE

In his discussion of justice as a general virtue, St. Thomas points out that the members of a community are related to the community as the parts to the whole, and that the good of a part is subject to the good of the whole. Insofar as it is the function of justice to direct all actions to the common good, it comprises the good of every virtue whether the virtue be other-regarding or self-regarding. Justice directs all the acts of all the virtues to the common good. In this sense, justice is a general virtue; inasmuch as it impels men to conform to the law which ordains the acts of all virtues to the common good, it is called legal justice.

Evidently, general justice, or legal justice, as described by St. Thomas, includes one element of social justice. Indeed, some writers identify the two concepts. That does not seem to be the teaching of Pope Pius XI:

> *Now it is of the very essence of social justice to demand from each individual all that is necessary for the common good. But just as in the living organism it is impossible to provide for the good of the whole unless each single part and each individual member is given what it needs for the exercise of its proper functions, so it is impossible to care for the social organism and the good of society as a unit unless each single part and each individual member—that is to say, each individual man in the dignity of his human personality —is supplied with all that is necessary for the exercise of his social functions.* (Atheistic Communism, *par. 51*)

Rev. André Rocaries, S.J., declares that Pope Pius XI added a new element to Catholic teaching, when he defined the common good as comprising not merely the good of the whole community but the good of all and each of the members.[2] The late Holy Father emphasized the distributive as well as the collective element in the common good; the distributive as well as the collective element in social justice. He specified not only the good of the whole community as a unified entity but the good of all its constituent social groups and all its individuals. This conception of the common good is not explicitly stated in St. Thomas' treatment of general justice. General justice, or legal justice, as he explains it, covers the common good as a whole but does not specify individuals or social groups.

In his treatment of distributive justice, St. Thomas says that when common goods are distributed among the members of a community, each individual receives that which is, in some sense, his, inasmuch as what belongs to the whole belongs in a certain way to the part. Here, again, we have one element of social justice, namely, the duty of the state to promote the good of members of the community; but there is no mention of the other element, namely, the duty of social groups and individuals to participate in the task of making a proper distribution.

By way of summary, then, we observe that, as described by St. Thomas, neither general justice nor distributive justice nor both together cover the whole ground of social justice. General justice takes in only one of the two *objects* of social justice, while distributive justice includes only one of its two *subjects*. General justice aims at the common good collectively considered; it does not explicitly comprehend the common good taken distributively, as individuals and social classes. The subject of distributive jus-

The Economic Philosophy of St. Thomas

tice is exclusively the state, while the subject of social justice is not only the state but social groups and individuals.

Nevertheless, the notion of social justice may be said to be to some extent implicit in St. Thomas' exposition of general justice and distributive justice. The concept of social justice represents the evolution or unfolding of a germ which existed in the treatment of these two kinds of justice by the Angelic Doctor.

St. Thomas' discussion of commutative justice contains nothing suggestive of social justice. There is not even the germ of the concept, such as may be said to exist in his statements about the relation between the whole and the parts where he deals with legal and distributive justice. From the nature of the case, that could not be expected: commutative justice governs the relations between independent entities, while social justice is based upon the relations between the whole and its parts, or between parts and parts as such, not as mutually independent. However, social justice may ordain the performance of acts which are also required by commutative justice, as the payment of a family living wage.[3]

II. PRIVATE OWNERSHIP

St. Thomas discusses this subject mainly in two places in the *Secunda Secundae*: question 57, article 3, and question 66, article 2. In the former article, he asks himself whether the *jus gentium* is the same as *jus naturale*. Answering in the negative, he uses in the course of his argument the example of private ownership, *proprietas possessionum*. Considered absolutely, a given field, he says, exhibits no reason for belonging to one person rather than to another; considered in relation to its cultivation and peaceful possession, it has a certain adaptability to possession by one man rather than another. This is a matter to be decided by natural reason and therefore, pertains to the *jus gentium*, not to the *jus naturale*. In the latter of the two articles cited above, St. Thomas declares that, although natural law does not itself make a division of goods, neither does it dictate that they should all be held in common and nothing held privately. The division is made by human agreement and this pertains to positive law. Hence, private ownership is not against natural law, but is superadded to it through the intervention of human reason. In a word, private ownership is neither directly commanded by, nor contrary to, natural law. Hence, it is morally lawful for man to hold goods as his own.

However, St. Thomas goes beyond this negative and neutral position; he declares that private ownership is not only reasonable and lawful, but that it is necessary for human life on account of the following three reasons:

First, because everyone is more solicitous about procuring what belongs to himself alone than that which is common to all or many, since each, shunning labour, leaves to another what is the common burden of all, as happens with a multitude of servants. Secondly, because human affairs are conducted in a more orderly fashion if each has his own duty of procuring a certain thing, while there would be confusion, if each should procure things haphazardly. Thirdly, because in this way the peace of men is better preserved, for each is content with his own. Whence we see that strife more frequently arises among those who hold a thing in common and undivided.

In the article which immediately precedes the one from which this quotation is taken, St. Thomas declares that the *use* of external goods is necessary for every individual. He makes no such assertion concerning ownership. In the excerpt given above, he is talking about a social group, a community. In effect, he declares that private ownership is necessary as a social institution. He does not say that it is necessary for every member of a social group.

Does he mean that private ownership is absolutely necessary, or only conditionally so, in certain social conditions? Referring to the three reasons, Father Bede Jarrett says:

This is a purely conditional necessity, and depends entirely on the practical effect of the three reasons cited. Were a state of society to exist in which the three reasons could no longer be urged seriously, then the necessity which they occasioned would also cease to hold. In point of fact, St. Thomas was perfectly familiar with a social group in which these conditions did not exist, and the law of individual possession did not therefore hold, namely, the religious orders. As a Dominican, he had defended his own Order against the attacks of those who would have suppressed it altogether; and in his reply to William of St. Amour he had been driven to uphold the right to common life, and consequently to deny that private property was inalienable.[4]

The conditional element in the necessity for private ownership is expressed in substantially the same terms by all the moral theologians. Father Tanquerey's statement is fairly typical: "Permanent and exclusive private ownership of external goods, even lands, circumscribed by just limits, flows from natural law and in present conditions is morally necessary."[5]

Do the three arguments of St. Thomas exclude state and community ownership, or are they directed merely against a complete absence of ownership, a situation in which there would exist indiscriminate use of everything by everybody?

The Economic Philosophy of St. Thomas

The usual argument for private ownership found in Catholic treatises seems to go beyond the three reasons specified by the Angelic Doctor. It lays principal stress upon the impossibility, or unworkableness, or undesirableness, of government ownership, socialized ownership, or any form of collectivism. The three reasons given by St. Thomas do not explicitly set forth this modern argument. The second reason is directly opposed to economic anarchy rather than any system of social or government ownership. However, the first and third do contain an implicit rejection of such a system. As Bede Jarrett remarks:

> Of course it was perfectly obvious that for St. Thomas himself the idea of the Commune or the State owning all the land and capital, and allowing to the individual citizens simply the use of these common commodities, was no doubt impracticable; and the three reasons which he gives are his sincere justification of the need of individual ownership. Without this division of property, he considered that national life would become even more full of contention than it was already. Accordingly, it was for its effectiveness in preventing a great number of quarrels that he defended the individual ownership of property.[6]

Both the advocates and the opponents of socialism usually distinguish between private ownership of the goods of production and private ownership of the goods of consumption. As a rule, the former admit that consumption goods cannot and should not be socialized, that the individual should be permitted to own the food that he eats, the clothes that he wears, the furniture in his house, and possibly the house itself. This concession is not always made by the Communists. The opponents of socialism and collectivism and Communism hold that private ownership is necessary even for the instruments of production, with a few exceptions which mostly fall under the head of public utilities. Speaking of the tenets of mitigated socialism, Pope Pius XI said, in *Quadragesimo Anno*:

> For it is rightly contended that certain forms of property must be reserved to the state since they carry with them an opportunity of domination too great to be left to private individuals without injury to the community at large. Just demands and desires of this kind contain nothing opposed to Christian truth, nor are they in any sense peculiar to socialism.

The three reasons given by St. Thomas do not make this distinction between the goods of consumption and the instruments of production. Nevertheless, he was undoubtedly aware of it and intended his statement to cover both kinds of goods as they then existed. In his day, there were no machines or factories or railroads. The instruments of production were all comprised in land, the tools of the artisan, and the equipment of the merchant and the trader.

By way of summary, we may assert that St. Thomas' teaching on the philosophical basis and the necessity of private ownership contains in substance the traditional Catholic doctrine as taught by the moral theologians and the Popes.

III. USE OF WEALTH

In addition to the power of "procuring and dispensing" external goods, man possesses the power of use. In the latter respect, he ought not to hold goods as his own, "but as common so that he may readily share them in the need of others."[7] The same principle had been expressed by Aristotle in substantially the same terms:

> It is evident that it is best to have property private but to make the use of it common; but how the citizens are to be brought to this mind it is the particular business of the legislator to consider.[8]

Enunciated by a pagan philosopher upwards of twenty-three centuries ago, these propositions constitute a striking rebuke to the neo-pagans of our age who assert that a man may do what he pleases with his own and that the state has no right to regulate the use of private property. On the other hand, Pope Pius XI was following the tradition of Aristotle and St. Thomas when he wrote in *Quadragesimo Anno*:

> That we may keep within bounds the controversies which have arisen concerning ownership and the duties attaching to it, We reassert in the first place the fundamental principle laid down by Leo XIII, that the right of property must be distinguished from its use. It belongs to what is called commutative justice faithfully to respect the possessions of others, not encroaching on the rights of another and thus exceeding one's rights of ownership. The putting of one's own possessions to proper use, however, does not fall under this form of justice, but under certain other virtues, and therefore it is "a duty not enforced by courts of justice." Hence it is idle to contend that the right of ownership and its proper use are bounded by the same limits; and it is even less true that the very misuse or even the non-use of ownership destroys or forfeits the right itself.
> Most helpful therefore and worthy of all praise are the efforts of

those who, in a spirit of harmony and with due regard for the traditions of the Church, seek to determine the precise nature of these duties and to define the boundaries imposed by the requirements of social life upon the right of ownership itself or upon its use. On the contrary, it is a grievous error so to weaken the individual character of ownership as actually to destroy it.

It follows from the two-fold character of ownership, which We have termed individual and social, that men must take into account in this matter not only their own advantage but also the common good. To define in detail these duties, when the need occurs and when the natural law does not do so, is the function of the government. Provided that the natural and divine law be observed, the public authority, in view of the common good, may specify more accurately what is licit and what is illicit for property owners in the use of their possessions. Moreover, Leo XIII had wisely taught that "the defining of private possession has been left by God to man's own industry and to the laws of individual peoples."

In article 7 of question 66, St. Thomas says:

According to the order of nature instituted by Divine Providence, the goods of the earth are designed to supply the needs of men. The division of goods and their appropriation through human law do not thwart this purpose. Therefore, the goods which a man has in superfluity are due by the natural law to the sustenance of the poor.

The last eight words of the foregoing quotation are a translation of *"ex naturali jure debentur pauperum sustentationi."* From the context and for other reasons, it is evident that *"naturali jure"* means "natural law," not "natural right," and that *"debentur"* indicates a moral obligation, indeed, but not an obligation of strict justice.

It will be recalled that private ownership had been defended by St. Thomas precisely because the end of external goods would thereby be most effectively attained.[9] That end is the satisfaction of human needs. In a regime of common ownership there would be too much disorder and too much uncertainty. But, he says, private ownership can attain this end only if goods are held in common as to their use. This obligation of using one's goods so as to supply the needy reflects the traditional Christian conception of ownership as stewardship. It also calls to mind the equally ancient doctrine that the primary right of property is not private ownership, but common ownership, in the sense of common use, so as to effectuate the right of all persons to subsist upon the bounty of the earth.

In this same article (question 66, answer 7) St. Thomas emphasizes the superiority of the common right by declaring that in necessity all things are common, that in *extreme* necessity a person may take as much as he needs from his neighbor and that this will not be, properly speaking, theft: *"Non habet rationem furti, proprie loquendo."* He repeats these propositions in substantially the same words in question 32, answer 7.

More than fifty years ago, Cardinal Manning declared: "The natural right of every man to life and to the food necessary for the sustenance of life prevails over all positive laws," and "a starving man has a right to his neighbor's bread." Although this assertion was merely an application of the traditional doctrine to the abysmal destitution of London, the Cardinal was severely criticized by contemporary champions of liberalism and unlimited rights of property.

IV. DUTIES OF WEALTH: ALMSGIVING AND LIBERALITY

In question 32, article 1, St. Thomas declares that almsgiving is an act of charity if performed from the right motive, that is, on account of God. It also pertains to the virtue of liberality inasmuch as this virtue removes that obstacle to almsgiving which is created by an excessive love of one's riches. In other words, the virtue of charity governs and produces the act of almsgiving, but the virtue of liberality sometimes prepares the way for the act by creating a favorable attitude in the mind of the possessor.

In question 32, article 5, the Angelic Doctor shows that almsgiving is not merely a matter of counsel but a matter of precept, as is clearly indicated in the words of the Gospel according to St. Luke: "What remaineth, give alms." (XI, 41)

Alms are to be given out of one's superfluous goods; and superfluous goods are those which remain to a person after he has supplied the needs of himself and his dependents. To the objection that it is lawful for a man to retain that which is his own instead of distributing it in alms, St. Thomas replies that temporal goods which are divinely given to man belong to him, indeed, as regards ownership, but as regards their use they belong not only to him but to those other persons who can be sustained out of one's superfluous possessions.

In question 32, article 6, St. Thomas points out that there is no obligation to give alms out of what is necessary for oneself or for one's dependents. On the other hand, goods which are regarded as necessary for the maintenance of a person's station in life can be diminished somewhat without endangering the essentials of such station or standard. To give alms from these possessions is a good work; but it is one of counsel, not of precept.

owever, it would be inordinate to give so much that a man would not
ve enough left to live in accordance with his station or to carry on his
fairs: "for no one should live unbecomingly."
The foregoing propositions are all practical applications of the principle
at the use of goods should be common. The central thought is that a
an's superfluous goods must be held subject to distribution among the
edy. It seems clear that St. Thomas would have *all* superfluous goods
ble to this obligation if the needs of the non-possessors were sufficiently
tense and sufficiently extensive. However, neither St. Thomas nor any of
e other medieval writers formulate precise rules for determining the
agnitude of the obligation as it rests upon any individual in any given set
conditions. Hence, Father Bede Jarrett remarks:

> To give out of a man's superfluities to the needy was, they held,
> undoubtedly a bounden duty. But they could make no attempt to
> apprize in definite language what in the receiver was meant by
> need, and in the giver by superfluity.[10] How much "need" must
> first be endured before a man has a just claim on another's super-
> fluity? By what standard are "superfluities" themselves to be
> judged? For it is obvious that when the need among a whole popu-
> lation is general, things possessed by the richer classes, which in
> normal circumstances might not have been considered luxuries,
> instantly become such. However then the words are taken, however
> strictly or laxly interpreted, it must always be remembered that
> the terms used by the Scholastics do not really solve the problem.
> They suggest standards, but do not define them, give names, but
> cannot tell us their precise meaning.[11]

)ne statement made by St. Thomas would seem to require some qualifica-
n if applied to the social and economic conditions of today. According
this statement, it is possible to give some alms from the goods required
the maintenance of social position without essential injury to the stand-
d itself. Since these requisites are not precisely and mathematically de-
mined, something may be subtracted from them consistently with the re-
tion of sufficient "to conduct life according to one's station." However,
Thomas continues, to give alms from this source is not a matter of
cept but only of counsel. Why so? Suppose the needs that might be re-
ved are very grave and could not otherwise be supplied? The general
nciple of right use would seem to render giving in these conditions a
tter of strict obligation.
\t any rate, such action in such circumstances would seem to be morally
igatory and not merely a counsel of perfection today. Current concep-

tions of social position are much more elastic than they were in the thirteenth century. In many cases the standard of living to which men cling in our time is measured not so much by what they have as by what they desire and hope to have. Moreover, many of the standards currently maintained are too expensive, too luxurious, and cannot be defended on any rational ground. Finally, many of the current outlays for the maintenance of social position could suffer much greater diminution than at the time of St. Thomas without lowering the standards in any considerable degree. Suppose that a family is maintaining three automobiles, and suppose that by giving up one of them it will be able to relieve very grave need in the family of a neighbor, for example, destructive and long-continued illness. In such circumstances, it would seem that giving alms at the expense of social position would be required under the head of strict precept and not merely of counsel.

Probably St. Alphonsus would approve this judgment, for he says that there is some obligation to relieve a person who is in grave necessity at the cost of moderate injury to the social position of the one who gives the relief. While some theologians seem to take a different position, they apparently mean that one is not obliged to give alms in these conditions if such giving would cause a total loss of social position or a decline to a lower social level. This is obviously in accord with the fundamental principle of charity that a person is not obliged to remove grave inconvenience from a neighbor at the cost of grave inconvenience for himself. In general, it is important to remember that the content of a given standard of living or social position is not rigid but flexible, and contains many elements that can be discarded without fatal injury.

More than twenty-six years ago, I summed up the teaching of the moral theologians on the distribution of superfluous goods in the following sentences:

> *When, however, the distress is grave; that is, when it is seriously detrimental to welfare; for example, when a man or a family is in danger of falling to a lower social plane; when health, morality, or the intellectual or religious life is menaced,—possessors are required to contribute as much of their superfluous goods as is necessary to meet all such cases of distress. If all is needed all must be given. In other words, the entire mass of superfluous wealth is morally subject to the call of grave need. This seems to be the unanimous teaching of the moral theologians. It is also in harmony with the general principle of the moral law that the goods of the earth should be en-*

joyed by the inhabitants of the earth in proportion to their essential needs. In any rational distribution of a common heritage, the claims of health, mind and morals, are surely superior to the demands of luxurious living, or investment, or mere accumulation. (Distributive Justice, *Third Edition: p. 239*)

In question 117, article 1, St. Thomas shows that liberality is a virtue because it regulates the right use of those external things which are necessary to sustain life. In article 3 of the same question, he points out that liberality impels men to put aside an immoderate love of money which might deter them from making proper expenditures either upon themselves or in the way of gifts to others. In article 5, he declares that liberality differs from justice inasmuch as the latter connotes a legal debt while the former implies only a certain moral debt, arising out of a certain decency or becomingness. Hence liberality exhibits a minimum degree of the concept of debt. Question 118, article 1, declares that liberality is directly opposed to the sin of avarice, and avarice is an immoderate love of riches or wealth. The main differences between liberality and charity seem to be two: the former connotes a benevolent attitude of the mind and will; second, the obligation carried by liberality is somewhat stronger than that of charity, since it connotes a debt which is somewhat akin to the debt of justice. According to St. Thomas, it is a part of justice. Hence, it is mid-way between charity and strict justice. Pope Leo XIII declared that the obligation of distributing surplus income was a duty not of strict justice but of charity. Speaking of the same obligation, Pius XI in *Quadragesimo Anno* declared that it pertains also to the virtues of beneficence and liberality. This is one of the few references to liberality which occur in modern practical discussions of the duties of wealth.

V. JUST PRICE AND JUST WAGE

In question 77, article 1, St. Thomas declares that it is wrong to sell a thing for more than it is worth, for more than its value. Since buying and selling exist for the common utility of both parties, the contract or transaction ought not to burden one more than the other. If the price exceeds the quantity of value, or if the value exceeds the price, the equality demanded by justice is destroyed; hence, to sell for more than or to buy for less than the value is essentially unjust and unlawful. *Per accidens,* however, the seller may demand a somewhat higher price in order to compensate him for some peculiar damage which he suffers from the transaction. On the other hand, the seller may not raise the price merely because the buyer derives from the contract some advantage that is peculiar to himself; for this would, in effect, charge the buyer for a utility which is attributable to him alone.

That one should not sell an article for more than its value may seem little more than an identical proposition: the price should not be more than it ought to be. Equality is, indeed, of the essence of justice in buying and selling as in all other onerous contracts. But to be told that there must be equality between the thing and the price is not very informative unless one has some means of knowing how this equality is to be measured or ascertained.

The solution of the difficulty is to be found in the concept of just price. St. Thomas says in effect that the price should be just; he does not say how the just price is determined, apparently assuming that his readers understood the current rules employed in this process. In his time, the immediate ethical measure of such prices as were not fixed by law was the common estimate of prudent and competent men. It was what such men pronounced to be just with regard to any given commodity. Nevertheless, the common estimate was neither arbitrary nor entirely subjective. It was a judgment which had to be guided by such objective considerations as scarcity, diversity of place and time, and cost of production. In question 77, reply to the second objection of article 2, we are told that the prices of commodities necessarily differ according to place, abundance and scarcity; that where the prices are fixed by public authorities or by custom, it is not lawful to ·depart from them. Custom in the middle ages always recognized the cost of production as the most important determinant of the just price. And cost of production was in the main the cost of living of the laborer according to the customary and accepted standards of his class. Economic historians usually take as typical of this doctrine the statement of Langenstein, Vice Chancellor of the University of Paris in the fourteenth century, to the effect that everyone can determine for himself the just price of the goods he sells by reckoning what he needs to support himself in the status which he occupies.

Those who are disappointed in the failure of St. Thomas to give in question 77, article 1, a specific measure of just value and just price, should recall that in this place he is not professedly dealing with those subjects. He is answering the particular objection that one is permitted to sell a thing for more than it is worth because deception in such a transaction was permitted by the civil law, that is, the Roman law. To this he replies that the law cannot effectively prohibit all vicious conduct. In his reply, he seems to assume that his readers knew how value and just price were determined, or he may have avoided it as something with which he was not then concerned.

The Economic Philosophy of St. Thomas

St. Thomas has very little to say on the subject of just wages. Probably, his most specific statement is the following: "That is called a wage which is paid to anyone as a recompense for his work and labor. Therefore, if it is an act of justice to give a just price for a thing taken from another person, so also to pay the wages of work and labor is an act of justice."[12] This is merely an assertion that the wage should be just. How was justice to be determined? Undoubtedly, St. Thomas would have answered in the terms used by all the other authorities of the middle ages. Very few of them discussed the question of wage justice by itself, for the number of wage receivers was then comparatively small. When medieval writers declared that the commodities produced by the artisan should bring a just price, and that the just price was mainly determined by the artisan's customary cost of living, they were laying down the rule of just wages.

When Leo XIII, in 1891, prescribed as the minimum measure of wage justice the maintenance of the worker in reasonable comfort, more than one of the Catholic authorities in this field were troubled. They thought that the Pope was departing from the traditional rule of commutative justice, namely, that there should be an equivalence between the labor produced and the salary received. As a matter of fact, he was but reaffirming the ancient doctrine and the ancient test.

Léon Polier deals with this question clearly and thoroughly, admitting that the canonists stressed the concept of equality or equivalence between work and pay, but pointing out that they sought in vain to find a fixed base for this equality in the concept of value.[13] The only measure of equality which they could find was that manifested in the "common estimation." This was pretty far removed from that concept of absolute justice which seemed to be latent in their principle of equality.

Nevertheless, the "common estimation" in that time was itself determined by the customary cost of living of the laborer. This was an objective measure. It provided a fixed basis for equality in the wage contract, but the equality which it connoted and demanded was not between wage and work but between wages and the recognized proper cost of living.

"Equality between pay and work" is nonsense. There exists no third term by which to make the comparison. These incommensurate entities can no more be directly compared, as regards their equality or inequality, than sound and color. Nor does "equality between pay and the value of work" mean anything, unless we are told how the value is to be determined. Speaking for the majority of the Supreme Court, Mr. Justice Sutherland declared (1923) that the minimum wage law of the District of Columbia was unconstitutional because it ignored the "value of the service rendered" and disregarded "the moral requirement that the amount to be paid and the

[251]

Essays in Thomism

service to be rendered shall bear to each other some relation of just equivalence." But the learned Justice gave no indication that he had any precise
idea of what he meant by these terms. Did he mean value in a competitive
market? That would be intelligible, indeed, but it would justify starvation
wages. Did he mean value as measured by the dignity of the laborer and his
right to a decent living? Evidently not.

The sum of the matter is that there can be no equality (nor inequality)
between pay and work, but that pay can be equal (or unequal) to the value
of the work; but the value of the work has to be ascertained and determined
by some extraneous factor, such as, the civil law, the higgling of the market,
the decrees of a trade union, or the worker's cost of decent maintenance.

The last mentioned determinant was the one accepted by St. Thomas and
by all the other medieval writers. It was also laid down by Popes Leo XIII
and Pius XI. When they did that, they were returning to the traditional
doctrine and they were repudiating the impossible standard of "equality
between pay and work."

The principle upon which the minimum wage laws of the United States
and several other countries fix remuneration likewise reaches back to the
days of Thomas Aquinas. For these laws either prescribe rates of wages
which will enable the worker to live decently, or, if this is for the time being
impracticable, they keep it in mind as one to be attained as soon as possible.
In the minimum wage laws the value of labor is, in effect, defined as the cost
of decent living for the laborer.

Today, as in the time of Aquinas, the measure of just price is the reasonable cost of production. But it includes an element which was not very
prominent in the economic conditions of the thirteenth century. That is,
interest on the producer's capital. For example, boards of arbitration in wage
disputes today generally aim to allow fair interest on capital as well as fair
wages for labor. In principle and insofar as it is formally recognized, the
conception of just price is, at present, substantially the same as it was in the
days of St. Thomas—the fair cost of production.

VI. TRADING

In the usage of the scholastics trading or commerce (*negotiatio*) denoted
the act or practice of a buyer in selling a thing unchanged at a higher price,
i.e., at a profit.

In question 77, article 4, St. Thomas asks whether it is lawful for a trader
to sell a thing for more than it cost him. Before answering this question
specifically, he discusses at some length the nature, the motives, and the
morality of trading. He points out that trading, or trade, is an exchange of

[252]

money for money, or goods for money, not in order to procure the necessaries of life but for the sake of gain. This practice, he says, is justly censured because so far as its own nature is concerned it promotes greed for gain which knows no limit but tends toward infinity; considered in itself, therefore, trading involves a certain degree of dishonor, because of its own nature it does not connote an end which is morally good or necessary. Neither, however, does it, by its own nature, imply anything vicious or contrary to virtue; hence, there is no reason why gain cannot be directed to some necessary or even morally good end, thus rendering trade lawful; for example, when a person uses the gain which he seeks in trading for the maintenance of his household, or for the relief of the poor, or even for the public good, so that the necessaries of life may not be wanting to his country, and he seeks the gain not as an end but as a reward of his labor. Stated summarily, the foregoing propositions would take this form: it is unlawful to trade for gain alone but it is lawful to seek gain for good ends, such as those mentioned at the end of the preceding sentence.

Suppose, however, that a man trades and seeks gain not, indeed, for its own sake but for some other end than the four mentioned by St. Thomas. A man may engage in trade or business for the sake of economic power and social prestige, or to prevail over his rivals in competition, or merely because he gets more satisfaction from continuing these activities than from any alternative course of conduct. Apparently, these motives are excluded from the class of ends for which it is lawful to pursue trade, according to St. Thomas. On the other hand, here, as in many other actions, the motives are generally not simple. They are usually complex and mixed. Thus a trader's dominant motive may be economic power and social prestige, but he may also intend to dispense some of the profits in charity. Would the dominant motive render the trading illicit? It is difficult to say. If a man who has acquired an ample competence continues in business, continues to seek gain, merely because he would be unhappy in any other occupation, or lack of occupation, are the conduct and the gains morally unlawful? Probably not. To be sure, if this man did not make a proper distribution of his gains, or part of them, as required by the virtues of charity and liberality, he would be acting wrongfully; but that is a distinct consideration which has no bearing upon the morality of pursuing gain from the motive just specified.

The last of the four lawful ends specified by St. Thomas presents some difficulty. The trader must seek gain, he says, "not as an end, but as a sort of reward of labor." As a rule, men do, indeed, refuse to work without some kind of recompense, but they do not look upon the reward as an end which is coordinate with a livelihood or with either of the other two ends which are put down by Aquinas as lawful. Of course, useful work creates a claim to reward, but no one looks upon the reward as a final end. To engage in activity merely in order to get compensation, without any plan or intention regarding the disposition of the compensation, would scarcely be a rational procedure. At best, the reward is a condition rather than an end or motive of work. Possibly this was in the mind of St. Thomas when he wrote this sentence. Possibly he was alluding to the generally accepted principle that all honorable labor was entitled to a reward.

In his discussion of the second objection under this same article of question 77, St. Thomas answers specifically the question about buying cheap and selling dear. A person, he says, who buys a thing not to sell but to hold, and who later sells it, is not guilty of sinful trading, even if he receives for the article a higher price than it cost him. In three situations this will be lawful: first, when the trader has modified the thing for the better; second, when its price has risen because of the change of time or place; third, when the higher selling price is a compensation for the risk which the trader underwent in transporting the article from one place to another, or in causing it to be transported by someone else. In none of these cases, is the buying or the selling unjust.

This is a pretty comprehensive group of justifying situations. They might render lawful speculation in real estate or on the stock exchange, if a profitable change in price occurred some time after the purchase. Of course, St. Thomas was assuming a rise in price brought about by reasonable influences. While there is today no such institution as the "common estimate" which functioned in the Middle Ages, either in the real estate market or on the stock exchange, there exists in its place the process known as competition, or the higgling of the market. Would St. Thomas have recognized an increase in price thus produced at a later time as adequate to justify selling a piece of land or a block of securities at a higher figure than the purchase price? We do not know.

At any rate, his language specifically condemns the action of a person who buys a thing with the exclusive intention of selling it at a higher price, without improving it or undergoing any risk. He would not have permitted stock exchange speculation. Likewise, he would probably have censured a man who sold an article at an enhanced price which was fixed not by the common estimate but by the arbitrary control of the buyer himself.

The propositions laid down by St. Thomas in question 77, article 4, lend no support to the slogan that is so frequently heard in our time, "production for use, not for profit." Aquinas clearly allows trading for profit in certain situations and also production for profit, since he specifically mentions changes made in the article (what the economist calls *form utility*) by the purchaser as a justification for selling it at a higher price. In any case, "production for use, not for profit" is not only impracticable but as used by its advocates is too indefinite and superficial to be helpful.

The Fathers of the Church denounced trade as dangerous to the soul, and the attitude of Christians in the Middle Ages was still one of disapproval. By the fifteenth century, however, the patristic and medieval attitudes had become liberalized, or mitigated. While the moralists still quoted question 77, article 4, they showed a disposition to regard trading as morally colorless in itself but capable of becoming evil through bad motives. As one writer of that time expressed it: "Not commerce itself, but its abuse is a sin."

Two factors were responsible for the low esteem in which commerce was held by Christians before and during the Middle Ages. As carried on in that period, trade and commerce very frequently involved immoral or unworthy motives and practices. The second factor was the high appreciation accorded to labor in the teachings of the Bible and by the example of Christ. Compared with labor as an occupation or a means of livelihood, trading was regarded as less worthy of a Christian, even though it was not always immoral. The very fact that St. Thomas thought it necessary to make a formal defense of trading is a clear indication of its relatively low esteem in Christian thinking.

Today, all that is changed. No one thinks it necessary to set up a formal argument for the lawfulness of commerce. While it may be fairly said that the current attitude departs from that of St. Thomas more in emphasis and detail than in principle and essence, one extremely important condition which he introduces into his discussion is almost universally ignored by the traders and in the business ethics of today. That condition is that the gain from trading should be "moderate" (*lucrum moderatum*). These two words point to a difference between the medieval and the modern attitudes and conceptions whose practical implications and consequences can scarcely be exaggerated. A typical illustration of this difference is seen in the demand made by the United States Chamber of Commerce, in the Spring of 1939, for the repeal of the federal tax on excess profits. Inasmuch as this levy affects only that portion of a man's profits which is in excess of a reasonable, in fact, of a more than average rate, this shameless demand sharply and violently contradicts the Thomistic principle of "moderate gain." In this matter, as in that of just price, the business ethics of today gives full license to the vice of avarice. In the Middle Ages, no other vice was more strongly condemned.

VII. USURY

Question 78, article 1, inquires whether the acceptance of usury for borrowed money is a sin. Of course, usury meant at that time not an excessive rate of interest but any interest at all, any sum exacted by the lender and paid by the borrower in addition to principal. The long answer given by St. Thomas has been translated by Professor George O'Brien as follows:

> *To take usury for money lent is unjust in itself, because this is to sell what does not exist, and this evidently leads to inequality, which is contrary to justice.*
>
> *In order to make this evident, we must observe that there are certain things the use of which consists in their consumption; thus we consume wine when we use it for drink, and we consume wheat when we use it for food. Wherefore in such-like things the use of the thing must not be reckoned apart from the thing itself, and whoever is granted the use of the thing is granted the thing itself; and for this reason to lend things of this kind is to transfer the ownership. Accordingly, if a man wanted to sell wine separately from the use of the wine, he would be selling the same thing twice, or he would be selling what does not exist, wherefore he would evidently commit a sin of injustice. In like manner he commits an injustice who lends wine or wheat, and asks for double payment, viz. one, the return of the thing in equal measure, the other, the price of the use, which is called usury.*
>
> *On the other hand, there are other things the use of which does not consist in their consumption; thus to use a house is to dwell in it, not to destroy it. Wherefore in such things both may be granted; for instance, one man may hand over to another the ownership of his house, while reserving to himself the use of it for a time, or, vice versa, he may grant the use of a house while retaining the ownership. For this reason a man may lawfully make a charge for the use of his house, and, besides this, revendicate the house from the person to whom he has granted its use, as happens in renting and letting a house.*
>
> *But money, according to the philosopher, was invented chiefly for the purpose of exchange; and consequently the proper and principal use of money is its consumption or alienation, whereby it is sunk in exchange. Hence it is by its very nature unlawful to take payment for the use of money lent, which payment is known as usury; and, just as a man is bound to restore other ill-gotten goods, so he is bound to restore the money which he has taken in usury.*[14]

It has been objected that this argument overlooks the fact that while technically the loan of money is a sale, it is a peculiar kind of sale. If the contract called for the immediate repayment of the loan, undoubtedly, the exaction of interest would be unreasonable and immoral. Since, however, the repayment is not required for some time, say a year, the situation for the borrower is changed in a very important respect. In that interval, he can buy a farm, or a factory, or a store and make a profit with the money that he has borrowed or "bought." In brief, the economic value of a loan which is to run for a year is frequently greater than its face value. So, the borrower has "bought" something that becomes worth more to him when he repays it than it was when he entered upon the transaction.

While this objection seems plausible because it assumes that the loan has been used productively, it could be applied in principle to loans for consumption also. Money borrowed to buy food or clothing or objects of pleasure, likewise seems to increase in value during the period of the loan. That is to say, the borrower thinks that he can repay the loan with interest and still be somehow better off than if he had not borrowed the money at all. Medieval authorities (and it should be kept in mind that the argument used by St. Thomas, which he borrowed from Aristotle, was universally accepted at that time) were not ignorant of this apparent increase in the value or utility of money during the period covered by the loan, whether the money was used for the purchase of goods of production or goods of consumption. They were quite well aware that needy persons would sometimes pay interest or usury rather than go without a loan. But they regarded the exaction of this additional payment as taking undue advantage of human needs, in fact, as extortion. Most of the loans for consumption purposes as well as most of those made by artisans for the purchase of tools of their trade, the medieval writers looked upon as properly acts of charity.

Of course, they were right. The utility added by time to borrowed money which was invested in the production of a thing, found recognition some centuries later than the time of St. Thomas in the theory that modern conditions have made money virtually productive. If, in substantially all cases, the borrower can exchange the sum borrowed for a farm or a factory, it means that the virtual productivity of money has become universal. This is the view taken today by probably the majority of moral theologians when they come to discuss the justification of interest on loans. In the time of St. Thomas, however, this practically universal convertibility of money into capital, this virtual productivity of money, did not exist. The opportunities for this kind of investment were comparatively few. One indication of this condition is seen in the fact that St. Thomas apparently did not recognize the title of *lucrum cessans*. He accepted *damnum emergens*, indeed, but that had nothing to do with investment.

In article 3 of question 78, Aquinas replies to the contention that a man who has acquired profit from the use of borrowed money ought to transfer the gain to the lender. St. Thomas rejects this view, on the ground that since the money was really sold, the lender has no claim to anything beyond the principal. The gain which is brought about through the use of the money is not the fruit of the money but the product of the labor expended by the borrower in the productive enterprise. On the other hand, a house or a field which is borrowed does produce fruit, or utility, and this belongs to the man who rents out the house or the field for use but who remains its owner. In these cases the usufruct does not belong to the borrower. It might be objected that the man who operated a field which he had purchased with borrowed money expended no more labor than the man who cultivated a field which he had rented. Why should the gain go to the borrower-cultivator in the former case but to the lender-owner in the latter?

The answer is to be found in the technical fact that the loan of money is a sale, and in the additional fact that the borrower assumes the risks of the enterprise.[15] A man who committed money to an artisan or merchant in a partnership might lawfully exact profit because he retained ownership and risk. He did not transfer these to the borrower as in the case of a loan of money. In medieval discussion, assumption of risk was regarded as an essential test of ownership. To be sure, the gain acquired by the investor in a partnership sometimes exceeded the average risk, just as the gain from a field which one bought with borrowed money sometimes exceeded the average reward of labor, but this did not often happen in the thirteenth century. Risk and labor were regarded as the dominant titles of reward; when both were wanting, gain was looked upon with disfavor. This attitude persisted for decades after the time of St. Thomas, as is evident from the long opposition to the gains reaped by the silent partner in the triple contract.

It has been charged that when St. Thomas and the other medieval writers insisted upon the gains from borrowed money going to labor, instead of to the lender, they automatically rejected the lawfulness of "unearned income."[16] This inference is clearly unwarranted, since the great majority of the authorities of that time recognized the justice of the traffic in rent changes, the extrinsic title of *lucrum cessans*, and the institution of partnership. These frequently yielded some unearned increment, that is, a return which exceeded both risk and labor. However, there can be no doubt that the medieval authorities evaluated the right to gain from mere ownership of property in much feebler terms than do the men of today. As a moral claim to reward, the medieval writers certainly did not put ownership upon as high a level of approval as labor.

To the charge that the opposition of the Church (and of the civil law) to interest-taking, retarded the development of commerce for several centuries, an authoritative answer may be drawn from the words of Sir William Ashley:

Where money was borrowed it was, in the vast majority of cases, not for what is called productive expenditure, but for consumptive; not to enlarge the area of tillage, or to invest in trade or industry, but to meet some sudden want due to the frequent famines, or to oppressive taxation, or to extravagance. The money that was lent was money for which it would otherwise have been exceedingly difficult to secure an investment. The alternative to lending was allowing it to remain idle. There was, moreover, so little loanable capital that those who had control of it could demand any interest they pleased; they were so few in number that each had practically a monopoly in his own district; and when there were several money-lenders in a neighbourhood, they were usually united by a tie of race which served as a sufficient "combination" against the Gentile or the native. . . .

The very fact that we hardly meet in the Middle Ages with such instances of the oppression of the poor by usurers as were frequent enough in modern Europe during the brief period in which there were no restrictions on the usurer's trade would seem to prove that, on the whole, the combined action of Church and State, backed up by popular sympathy, was successful. The mere fact that statutes were passed against usury from time to time, with the usual pessimistic preamble, no more proves that the law was generally broken than the frequent new criminal laws of modern times prove that all men are thieves or murderers. . . .

Speaking of the middle of the fifteenth century,—the conditions a century later we shall discuss in a subsequent section,—we may fairly say that these methods satisfied business needs, and that there was no strong demand on the part of those engaged in trade for the repeal of the usury prohibition. It is altogether misleading and unfair, then, to speak of the prohibition as putting obstacles in the way of the employment of capital. So far as wealth was intended to serve as capital, it found ways open for its employment—ways which were adequate for the time, and against which the canonists had not a word to say.[17]

Obviously, the strict prohibitions laid down by St. Thomas against interest-taking could not have continued operative in modern times. But it is a great misfortune that their spirit did not persist. In one of the early paragraphs of his Encyclical, *Rerum Novarum*, Pope Leo XIII declared: "The evil has been increased by rapacious usury, which, although more than once condemned by the Church, is nevertheless, under a different form but with the same guilt, still practiced by avaricious and grasping men." A distinguished fellow countryman of Sir William Ashley, namely, John Maynard Keynes, is of the opinion that the system of capitalism will not be able to survive unless interest on money is reduced approximately to zero. Probably Keynes is asking for the impossible. Certainly, however, the share of the national income or national product which now goes to capitalists in the form of interest will have to be drastically reduced if the economic machine is to be kept going. Labor will have to get more while capital will have to be content with less. This will be in accord with the spirit of the Thomistic teaching on labor and usury.

In the foregoing pages, the effort has been made to present adequately, even though briefly, all that St. Thomas had to say in the field of economics. The total number of pages which he devotes to that subject is very small but they are sufficient to exhibit clearly his ethical judgments on the economic practices and institutions of his time. Many of these judgments have become obsolete because the economic conditions of that day no longer exist. On the other hand, many of his pronouncements are still pertinent because they are based upon the eternal laws of justice. Such are his statements concerning property, its uses and its duties, the just price and trade. In principle at least, his economic-ethical declarations are permanently valid.

Twelfth Essay

BEYOND THE CRISIS OF
LIBERALISM

by
Yves R. Simon

Beyond the Crisis of Liberalism

DVERSARIES of liberalism, whether conservatives or revolutionists, are agreed that the rise of liberal doctrines was historically connected with the imperialistic development of the middle class. Supporters of liberalism naturally feel inclined to conceal the class-connections of their philosophy: yet, the least they must concede is that the golden age of the middle class coincided with the triumph of liberalism. Liberalism was used as an ideological weapon against the forces of the Old Regime with which the middle class had entered into competition: landed aristocracy, landed religious orders, privileged guilds. Wherever those three elements of the Old Regime were powerful, the liberal movement proved anti-aristocratic, anti-clerical, and anti-corporative.

The destruction of the order-system, achieved through the victory of the liberal middle class, opened the field to the development of a class-system and of a class-struggle. So long as the order-system prevailed, the social elements that were to become the working class remained integrated in the Third Estate, and the tendency to secede, which characterizes class-developments, was unable to materialize.[1] The liberal legislation established by the victorious middle class suppressed the internal organization of the Third Estate (guilds) and granted the workingmen civil and political liberties. As a result of such an emancipation coupled with a complete lack of organization, the Third Estate was bound to split into conflicting classes, the bourgeoisie and the proletariat.[2]

What happened, then, to the ideology which had been the common weapon of the undivided Third Estate in its struggle against the upper orders and the order-system? From then on, the conscience of liberal groups suffered from a constant uneasiness, born from the confused realization of a fundamental antinomy. Liberalism had been held out as a universalistic philosophy: it was, in fact, a universalistic philosophy, pledged to provide all men with the same basic rights. On the other hand, it was the ideology of a particular class and this ideology was bound to serve the

[263]

interests of a particular class, even though it be to the obvious detriment of other classes. This was the great historical singularity of the middle class: its class ideology was a universalistic ideology, and had to be a universalistic ideology, since nothing but a universalistic ideology could achieve the destruction, and prevent the restoration, of the order-system.[3]

So long as the liberal era was not over, people often paid less attention to the value of liberal universalism than to practices of self-interest which gave the upholders of that philosophy a rather hypocritical appearance. It is true that while liberalism proclaimed freedom and equality in contractual relations, its prohibition of labor-organizations caused this freedom and equality to be empty words for several generations of proletarians. It is true that liberal governments, in spite of the fundamental proposition that all citizens should be granted the same civil rights, so long as they have not excluded themselves from the civil community by some felony, deprived whole categories of people of some common rights (expulsion of religious congregations, religious orders forbidden to teach, etc.). It is true that whereas liberal principles excluded imperialistic conquests and the exploitation of conquered countries, the liberal era witnessed a voluminous process of imperialistic expansion and colonial robbery. It is true that whereas liberalism openly condemned every discrimination based upon race or color, the liberal era witnessed enduring facts of race exploitation in all parts of the world. All that is true and it is not astonishing that, *so long as the liberal era was not over,* those facts in open conflict with professed doctrines appeared so shocking as to give these doctrines the sheer appearance of Machiavellian devices.

Now that the liberal era is over, at least in continental Europe, we come to realize that the liberal declaration of equal justice for all, however frequently it was contradicted by facts, contributed most effectively to the reduction of the amount of iniquity in societies. We now realize what a tremendous difference there is between a society whose principles are intended to bring about some kind of justice for all—albeit a very imperfect justice—and a society whose doctrine, spirit and fundamental trends imply the assumption that some categories of people can be lawfully subjected to arbitrary rule. During the liberal era, victims of discriminatory measures could appeal from the actual practice of their government to the principles stated by constitutions. On the contrary, in the "organic states" which succeeded to decadent liberal societies all over continental Europe, such practices as discrimination, denial of rights, arbitrary treatment of hated groups, are as constitutional as anything can be. Personal virtue, services actually rendered to the common good, patriotism, high morality, do not matter.

Beyond the Crisis of Liberalism

For instance, in the "Christian" regime founded in France by Marshal Pétain, whoever is legally defined as a Jew, whether he is actually a Christian or not, whether he behaves as a good citizen or not, whether he did or did not shed his blood for the defense of his country, is legally condemned to a predicament which amounts, in most cases, to destitution, starvation, slow death. Against such treatment, what appeal can be made? This so-called regime never pledged itself to protect the rights of man and of the citizen or to assure equal justice for all. It openly declared its intention of doing away with "equalitarian fallacies."

The martyrdom of the peoples ruled by gang-organizations causes us to realize the worth of a doctrine of government which cannot, without contradicting itself and running the danger of self-destruction, do away with universalistic principles. A philosopher who thinks, as Aristotle did, that the end of moral science is not the perfection of knowledge, but the righteousness of action,[4] cannot discuss the problem of liberalism in a purely abstract way and without regard to the historical results that certain diatribes against liberalism have actually effected. We cannot abstract from the appalling fact that the errors of liberalism have been actually succeeded by incomparably worse errors, that the mischiefs of liberal policies have been succeeded by incomparably more mischievous and devastating policies. The criticism of liberalism, as expedient and necessary today as it ever was, can no longer be carried out in that spirit of nihilistic irony which was popular, not so long ago, in some intellectual circles. Beyond the crisis of liberalism, we are looking forward to a revival of universalism and a new era of liberty.

LIBERALISM: AN OPTIMISTIC NATURALISM

In the most varied circumstances of its adventurous history, the liberal movement showed a persistent interest in the problem of truth. Liberalism never goes without a theory of the liberty of the mind. In the emancipation of the intellect, in the freedom of thinking, a number of theorists saw the very heart of liberalism.[5]

The idea of the freedom of the mind is not necessarily a liberal idea. It is unquestionably an ambiguous idea, whose confusion often protects arbitrary or nonsensical propositions.

The most fundamental operations of the mind are not, by any means, acts of freedom. They are not, either, a matter of authority: they are a matter of objectivity. When confronted by evident truth, the mind is not free to give or refuse its assent; it has just to say, yea, yea, no, no, according as the object commands, "and that which is over and above these, is of evil."[6] It is only with regard to secondary or substitutional factors of its determination that we can speak of the freedom of the mind.[7] We can reasonably speak of the freedom of the mind with regard to passions and prejudices: to say that this mind is free from passional influences, that another mind is enslaved by passions, are relevant statements. We can speak of the freedom of the mind, also, with regard to intellectual authorities: to say that this mind lacks freedom because its assent is wholly based upon the authority of a teacher, to say that another mind enjoys a greater freedom because its assent springs entirely from inner conviction, are relevant statements. We can speak of the freedom of the mind with regard to temporal pressures: to say that this mind is not free because its assent wholly results from the demands of the social environment, to say that another mind enjoys greater freedom inasmuch as its assent is given to the truth of the object regardless of surrounding prejudices, are relevant statements. If liberalism had contented itself with speaking of the freedom of the mind in those particular and limited ways, its claim for the emancipation of the mind would not involve any question of principles. It would be only a matter of prudential expediencies. The point would be to determine under which circumstances the progress of the mind is hampered or possibly fostered by passions, authorities, pressures from without.

But it is a fact that the liberal tradition has constantly sheltered a tendency to understand the intellectual emancipation in a more radical way. Occasionally this tendency went so far as to assert that the mind is free from all necessitating subjection to its object. The most consistent expression of this radicalism is found in the work of Charles Renouvier.[8] According to this theorist of liberalism, who was a great and powerful philosopher, the fundamental operations of the mind are acts of rational and free belief. Such an extreme consistency in the development of an error sheds much light on the nature of this error. It is not true that the mind enjoys any freedom in its assenting to self-evident principles. It is not true generally that the mind enjoys any freedom in its assenting to any evident truth, whether it be immediately evident or demonstrated. When truth is perfectly enlightened, it imposes itself upon the mind, and we should understand that an assent wholly determined by the clarity of the object is of itself better than any assent in which the obscure forces of the appetite have to cooperate.[8bis] The naturally and indefectibly determined assent of the intellect to evident truth is both the strength and the glory of the intellect. It is on the basis of this primordial accomplishment that every freedom of belief and action has to be built up. If the mind were incapable of being determined by evident principles, this incapacity, far from manifesting its ontological nobility, would rather manifest a radical deficiency, an unnatural deficiency, in plain contradiction with the notion of the intellect as a power of knowing the truth.[9]

. . . .

It does not seem that such a radicalism in the assertion of the freedom of the mind pertains to the essence of liberalism. We would rather say that the idea of a free adherence to the first principles of truth has been haunting the liberal movement after the fashion of an evil genius, inconspicuous most of the time, generally loathed when it revealed openly its character, yet ceaselessly inducing the liberal conscience into subtle temptations.

According to the most current forms of liberal thinking, the mind does not enjoy any freedom in regard to logical truth and experimental truth, consequently does not enjoy any freedom in regard to positive science, which is thought to be worked out wholly by experience and logic. As regards the so-called transcendental sphere, that is, the sphere beyond experience and its logical organization, the individual should be granted an unlimited freedom of assertion and denial. He should be free to assert that such a transcendental sphere exists, that it can be investigated, also to publish the result of his investigations; he should be equally free to deny the knowability of the transcendental sphere. Liberties cannot be safeguarded unless society adopts an attitude of complete indifference toward transcendental objects, and professes some kind of agnosticism.[10]

We dare say that this connivance of liberalism with agnosticism has done more than any other factor to turn elevated intellects away from liberal ideas and incidentally from the very cause of liberty. As soon as those who were, by historical destiny, the ordinary supporters of liberty, revealed that there was a link between their philosophy and a certain spirit of indifference toward the most important and sublime truths that the human mind is capable of, uncompromising lovers of truth were bound to look at liberalism with aversion, at liberty with suspicion. The result was a disjunction, altogether unnatural and disastrous, between the spirit of truth and the spirit of liberty.

Liberal agnosticism does not necessarily deny the relevance of any speculation about the transcendental sphere—although it favors such a negation. What specifies, to our knowledge, liberal agnosticism *qua* liberal is the principle that transcendental speculations should be left to the individual mind and conscience. For very significant reasons, it is impossible to trace accurately the limits of what we call the transcendental sphere: let us say that it embraces religious dogmas, metaphysical doctrines, and also the supreme principles of ethics.

The argument underlying the opposition of liberalism to society's taking a stand on transcendental questions is drawn from the lack of any general agreement concerning these questions. For the sake of clarity, the following discussion will be conducted with special regard to metaphysics and natural ethics. Problems connected with the recognition of revealed truth involve particular difficulties and require a particular treatment.

As Kant puts it in the preface to the *Critique of Pure Reason*, metaphysics, unlike some other sciences, has never achieved the general consensus which would enable it to be regularly taught and learned. The temptation is great to take a lack of general consensus concerning a system of statements for a sign that such a system admits of no steady communicability. The temptation is great to assume that there is no universal objectivity where consensus proves actually limited to small groups of kindred minds. Current agnosticism does not exactly deny that metaphysical speculation may have some value: it only states that the value it has, if any, has no character of universality and that consequently civil society must abstract from metaphysics altogether, and from the metaphysical foundation of ethics. Should society uphold any definite position in metaphysics, this could not go without some ill-treatment of the great many minds that hold this position to be untrue.

The whole question depends upon the validity of the reasoning which concludes from a lack of consensus to a lack of universal objectivity. It is perfectly true that whenever universal objects are concerned, objectivity provides a steady foundation for the communicability—or intersubjectivability—of truth. Every universal truth is *de jure* universally intersubjectivable.[11] But, here as elsewhere, contingency causes a gap to take place between what should happen *de jure* and what happens in fact. Some truths are *de jure* intersubjectivable without limit, and yet do not enjoy in fact more than a very limited intersubjectivability. This can be easily verified in some departments of positive knowledge. Many positive theories cannot be assented to by more than a few people. Their validity does not depend on any subjective disposition, but their understanding requires a number of conditions which are not commonly realized (highly specialized training). What happens not so rarely in positive sciences happens generally in metaphysics: the truth is established on an objective basis and in a perfectly demonstrative way, yet it is grasped only by few people.[11bis] The reason is that the understanding of metaphysical demonstrations requires such conditions as an extremely wise education and a rather high degree of moral purity: conditions which have never been current in any society.

It would surely be nonsensical to think of society's taking a position about essentially incommunicable truths. But what about those theoretical truths which are *de jure* communicable without limit, although common mediocrity prevents a general consensus? Two attitudes are possible. It may be said that the social life of the intellect can embrace only those truths which are steadily intersubjectivable both *de jure* and *de facto*. Accordingly, society should abstract from any problem of truth which, for any reason whatsoever, essential or accidental, fails to obtain the general agreement of people normally fit for social life. This is the traditional position of liberalism. It can be said, on the contrary, that the duty of society is to foster all truths which matter for its welfare and, so far as such truths are concerned, to reduce the gap between the *de facto* and the *de jure* possibilities of the minds of men.

Liberalism gives up all interest in truth whenever its general recognition appears exceedingly difficult, whenever, in order to have truth prevail, it is necessary to accept the hardships and risks of a struggle against common laziness and short-sightedness. Considering, furthermore, that the most elevated forms of truth often present exceptional difficulties, we realize that the liberal surrender is inevitably destined to lower the spiritual level of mankind in all fields and to cause extensive processes of decadence. No wonder that the reaction against the liberal spirit of mediocrity takes the form of an aristocratic, individualistic, anarchistic exaltation of heroic values. No wonder that Nietzsche is widely read wherever people make up their minds to overcome the spirit of mediocrity that liberalism, in the last phases of its decadence, has generally brought about. By giving up any effort to have the great number of men adhere to the highest forms of truth, liberalism caused people to take it for granted that no struggle should be fought in order to provide access to the sources of grandeur and sublimity for the great number of men. It was exceedingly easy to draw the conclusion that reaching the higher forms of life was the privilege of a self-appointed elite which, as a condition and a reward for its heroic achievements, would give itself the right of enslaving the rest of mankind.

Modifying slightly our point of view, we shall now pay special attention to the part of the transcendental sphere which concerns ethical life more directly. Liberal agnosticism generally took the view that no general agreement can be required concerning the ultimate justification of concrete duties. Whether you justify the prohibition of murder by appealing to hedonistic principles, or on the ground of the dignity of man, or on the ground of the divine law, matters little for liberal agnosticism: the only thing that does matter is that we are all agreed that murder should be prohibited. The justification of the prohibition is a private affair.

The first upholders of liberalism were little concerned with the practical danger of a doctrine which left to individual consciences the burden of finding the reasons why crimes ought not to be committed. At the time when modern forms of social life came into existence, the consensus of people concerning the elementary duties of justice, temperance, mutual help, etc., was sufficiently assured by a centuries-old set of traditions. Owing to the moral sentiments kept alive by tradition, those elementary duties were, for most consciences, beyond any question and appeared self-justified. In fact, they survived, for quite a while, the collapse of the beliefs that provided their ultimate justification. But a time came when societies were confronted by mass-movements favoring openly such forms of murder as abortion, mercy-killing, the extermination of political foes. As always happens in time of crisis, a reconsideration of principles took place and moralists raised their powerless voices. The folly of the old liberals consisted in their failure to understand that the vitality of traditional mores sprang from the principles with which these mores had been connected in the past. When cut off from their vitalizing principles, those mores were doomed to wither away in the space of a few generations.

．　．　．　．　．　．　．

Although the historical connection of liberalism with agnosticism is fairly general,—although agnosticism, on the other hand, provides an obvious foundation for the most persistent practices of liberalism, it can still be wondered whether agnosticism is of the essence of liberalism. Can a man who is not an agnostic in any way, either so far as the principles of ethics are concerned, or so far as religion is concerned, or so far as metaphysics is concerned, be a liberal?

In fact some typical representatives of the liberal movement were not agnostic in any way. Some great liberals were convinced as decidedly as anybody can be that positive truth *is not* the only kind of truth which imposes itself upon the mind of man and which can, under favorable circumstances, win the assent of a vast number of men.[12] They were convinced that intellectual liberty, full liberty for expression of all opinions, was the most favorable condition for the actual triumph of truth. The root of liberalism, here, is not agnosticism, but optimism. Everything would surely be *for the best* if, in order to have truth prevail, we had nothing to do save giving all opinions a perfect chance to show how they look.

In our analysis of agnostic liberalism we have already been confronted by the optimistic dispositions of the liberal spirit and its characteristic failure to understand the part played by contingency in human affairs. Optimism takes it for granted that nothing can disturb, at least in most cases, the normal development of the powers of man, except the unnatural interventions of society. On the basis of such an assumption it is easy to conclude that if equal chances are given to truth and to error, truth will generally win out over error, for truth is the perfection toward which the intellect naturally aspires. What may be the use of giving truth any kind of protection? Truth has in itself all the strength needed for its actual triumph. Moreover, the silencing of error often implies the silencing of truth, since truth is often mistaken for error so long as it has not undergone the trial of free discussion. It should even be said that silencing error is always silencing some truth, for there is no error so complete as not to involve a partial truth. Finally, protecting truth against denial and criticism amounts to devitalizing the assent of the mind and substituting conventional, superficial, insincere adherences for the heartfelt convictions which alone are compatible with the reverence due to truth.

Such argumentation is developed with great dialectical skill by John Stuart Mill in his famous book *On Liberty*. It is perfectly logical argumentation, which rightly points out what would happen if the logical, or normal, functioning of the powers of the mind were not hampered by any interfering factor. Just as a flower normally, logically, naturally, tends to develop into a fruit, so the mind naturally, normally and logically tends to achieve itself by discovering the truth and adhering to it. Now, most flowers fail to develop actually into fruits because of frosts, storms, insects, etc. Similarly, an undetermined proportion of people (in most instances, the vast majority) will fall into the worst errors, unless they are granted some protection against the innumerable forces which conflict, in the mind of man, with the natural aspiration toward truth.

Psychological literature, in the last generations, has given a new emphasis to the old idea that the human heart comprises a host of disorderly tendencies. Among that crowd, virtue has to fight its way, painstakingly, under such hard conditions that its successes can never be more than precarious achievements, ceaselessly jeopardized by the unexpected revival of untamed appetites. There are similar conflicts within the intellect of man. The light of truth has a hard time fighting its way amidst the crowd of illusions which haunt even the best trained minds. Our adherence to truth, no less than the virtuous disposition of the will, is at best a precarious achievement, possibly undermined by inconspicuous ghosts, and ready to break down, at the very time when we are enjoying the happiness of possessing the truth. In this connection, it is interesting to notice that liberalism has often celebrated Descartes as one of its great spiritual forerunners. As a matter of fact, the rather simplified psychology initiated by Descartes provided an ideal climate for the optimistic assumptions on which liberalism thrived. The identification of mind and consciousness, the at least implicit assumption that a proper education can confer upon all our representations a condition of perfect clearness and distinctness, blinded many people to most redoubtable forces of error. For the working of illusions is largely unconscious.

The indignant reaction of many people to the Freudian discoveries proceeded in part from a pharisaic unwillingness to acknowledge the existence and the redoubtable vitality of infernal desires in the heart of people who know they are reputed to be decent and want to keep their good reputation. It may some day happen that a psychologist will carry out an investigation of the subterranean life of the mind similar to the investigation made by Freud of the subterranean life of the appetite. Then, pharisees will not fail to raise indignant protests. But if the precarious situation of truth in the mind of man is ever the object of general acknowledgment, the kind of optimism upon which liberalism thrives will be a thing of the past. Every liberal will, then, be bound to be an agnostic and to declare openly his lack of interest in the most elevated forms of theoretical and practical truth.

In a period of universal disasters such as our time, we are really compelled to open our eyes to the lamentable weakness of the adherence of the human mind to truth. It has never been so evident as it is today that individual minds, in order not to succumb to the temptation of distorting truth in the most vicious way, need to be unceasingly protected by society against the devils of error that inconspicuously haunt their minds. The word of Holy Scripture, *omnis homo mendax,* has never appeared so appallingly true. Not only ordinary people prove ready to swallow any lie, however gross and stupid it may be, which is presented to them on printed paper, but we see highly educated people, men of culture and science, philosophers, theologians, contemplatives, whose life is actually devoted to effecting subtle distortions that suffice to render truth definitely powerless. Are those people conscious liars? Surely not all of them; probably not the most dangerous of them. We can reasonably assume that many of them are just taken in by a host of mischievous illusions.

In a previous development, we have tried to show that sound mores have no chance to survive indefinitely the oblivion of the principles which justify them. Whoever is interested in the preservation of mores should be equally interested in the preservation of the principles with which they are logically connected. Taking a step farther, we now have to point out that *when ethical principles are given up by society as such, considered as a private affair, and left to the individual conscience, they tend to become inoperative even for those who still recognize them.*[13]

Let us state the question as clearly as possible. An individual decidedly believes in a body of ethical principles. For society, the main thing is to have these principles govern his conduct actually and materialize in good practices. Three possibilities are conceivable:

1. There is a sufficiently regular conformity between conduct and principles.

2. Because of the weakness of the will, conduct is at variance with principles, but the light of truth is not extinguished, conscience is aware of a shocking discrepancy between principles and practice, repentance takes place from time to time, the case is not hopeless, the forces of evil are not totally unchecked.

3. Practice is at variance with principles, and conscience is not aware of this discrepancy. The light of ethical truth is practically put out. Conscience enjoys a fallacious peace and a pharisaical satisfaction. Without having to suffer the humiliations that accompany the practice of virtue, the individual has the privilege of exhibiting a high standard of morality. There is little hope of improvement: the forces of evil are not only unchecked, but sheltered, efficaciously protected by a formal adherence to a doctrine which has become an empty word.

Unless the principles of morality are embodied in the collective life of the group—unless individual conscience is constantly comforted, stimulated, controlled, by the reactions of the group, protected by the power of collective conscience against its own weakness, against its own fallacies, against its own inclinations toward a comfortable blindness, the worst possibility will materialize often. This is a point that has been regularly missed by theoretically-minded moralists: considering the case of a person who knows ethical truth, who has received and accepted the principles of virtuous life, they believe that a consciously mischievous will alone can prevent ethical truth from materializing in actual practices. Such a psychology is surely oversimple. People accustomed to the concrete observation of mores would agree that, all things being equal, the actual enforcement of moral principles varies considerably according as the collective life of the group imperatively demands the enforcement of a certain rule of conduct or is indifferent to it.

When laws permitting divorce were established in France in the latter part of the nineteenth century, it was pointed out that Catholics had no reason to worry, since nothing could compel them to make use of laws regulating a practice forbidden by their religion. The case seemed perfectly clear and a number of Catholic jurists thought it was satisfactory: divorce laws did not concern Catholics, to whom divorce is forbidden, but only people who think divorce is legitimate. Experience showed that this optimism was ill-founded, and that these jurists were ignorant of the sociological conditions of real morality. Divorce laws were used not only by people who already thought, at the time these laws were established, that marriage is not absolutely indissoluble, but also by many people who came to believe, under

the influence of the current practice of divorce, that marriage can sometimes be legitimately dissolved. The exact knowledge of the psychological
conditions of sound conscience affords the most obvious refutation of
liberalism.[14]

PSYCHOLOGICAL AND SOCIOLOGICAL OBSERVATIONS
ON THE CRISIS OF LIBERALISM

Some fifteen years ago, I was living in an intellectual circle where a con-
temptuous attitude toward liberal ideas was fashionable and even obligatory.
The frame of mind which prevailed in this circle has an historical significance insofar as the anti-liberal ideology of our time was given there a
rather sharp and consistent expression.

Among the teachers and companions of my youth, the criticism of liberalism proceeded from two main sources. One of them was an exact understanding of the requirements of truth, a sound aversion for any pragmatic,
symbolic or sentimentalistic interpretation which might jeopardize the
meaning of religious dogmas, a burning realization of the sacredness of
truth, an uncompromising belief that error has no rights and never should
be put on the same footing as truth, a steady awareness that the best is not
achieved by letting things go, a laudable hatred for easy life in the field of
principles.

The other source was a cruel conception of the world and of life, which
mimicked pessimism but really sprang from the emptiness of a disillusioned
optimism.

In this connection, attention should be called to the psychological distinction between genuine pessimism and disillusioned, or disappointed, optimism.[15] At a time when "pessimism" is so much in fashion, it is of a
supreme importance not to be deceived by external similarities between two
dispositions that are so widely different. A genuine pessimist is characterized by an intense feeling of the misery of our species. He knows that
little can be expected from men. He realizes the everlasting character of
the struggle to be fought by mankind against the fatalities of its condition.
His temper is not so sad: any good, any progress, any improvement, gives
him an almost unexpected joy. His dispositions are systematically benevolent,
and he finds around himself plenty of reasons to rejoice and to hope.

A disappointed optimist is quite a different character. He professes pessimism, he is actually mistaken for a pessimist because he speaks all the
time of the tremendous amount of evil he perceives everywhere (except in
himself and in his companions). In fact, he is not so convinced as he seems
to be that our nature is miserable. He preserves at the bottom of his heart

the illusion that things should be better, that mankind should not be engaged in an unceasing and everlasting struggle. Unconsciously he is, just as much as the optimist without qualification, a dreamer of utopias whose thought is dominated by the fiction of stable equilibrium and undisturbed harmony in human relations.

The only real difference between the disappointed optimist and the optimist who has not yet become disappointed is that the former locates his dreams and utopias in the past, whereas the latter locates his utopias and his dreams in the future. Both are inclined to angered resentment and cruelty. How could it be otherwise? Both take it for granted that human affairs should run smoothly and harmoniously. The conflicts, failures, retrogressions which they are witnessing are for them a continual scandal, a confusing riddle that cannot be accounted for except by laying the blame on relatively small groups of extraordinarily vicious people, whose viciousness is depicted as the only possible cause of universal unhappiness. The optimist cannot help nourishing a ruthless and implacable hatred against those few who disturb so perniciously the universal harmony of the human realm.

Of the two, the disappointed optimist is the more obnoxious because his utopia is located in the past—as far away in the past as possible. His hatreds are increased by being combined with an attitude of despair. He knows that the past has not the slightest chance to revive. Since the happy past has been definitively destroyed by the people he hates, the only thing that remains possible is to take a crushing vengeance upon those people.

Thus, the doctrinal criticism which took place as the liberal era was drawing to its close resulted from a catastrophic collusion between an elevated spirit of truth and the most detestable spirit of deception. No wonder that evil had the upper hand in this unnatural collaboration. Those who were bound by vocation to uphold truth became infected by the wickedness of their collaborators. Liberalism underwent great losses. But, what was taken away from liberalism went to increase the strength of the forces of despair and hatred, with little benefit, if any, for the spirit of truth.

.   .   .   .

We have seen that liberal ideology, taken as an historical phenomenon, shows an antinomic character. On the one hand, it is the ideology which properly fitted the biological needs of a particular group, namely the middle class. On the other hand, it is a universalistic ideology, based upon the idea of the right of all men and which makes appeal to the passions and sentiments of all men. Using a universalistic ideology is always, for a particular group, playing a dangerous game. As a matter of fact, liberal men of prop-

Essays in Thomism

erty were often given the following warning by conservatives: the weapons
that you are using today against privileged orders—or their remnants—
will be used against you, tomorrow, by the great mass of the poor. For a
century or so, conservative critics looked with derision at what seemed to
them the suicidal policy of the liberal middle class. The day when the liberal
middle class no longer turned a deaf ear to those warnings, the liberal era
was over.

The middle class ceased to be liberal when it became more preoccupied
with defending actually threatened positions than with taking over new
positions from its old adversaries. It ceased to be liberal when it ceased to
be revolutionary. It ceased to be liberal when revolution ceased to be a
bourgeois affair. Liberalism was doomed the day revolution became exclusively proletarian, or plebeian. This took place in the early nineteen-
twenties, when the enduring character of the Soviet state made it clear that
not every proletarian movement could be smashed so easily as the uprisings
of 1848 and 1871 in Paris, or that of 1919 in Berlin.

So long as the proletarian movement was not powerful enough to strike
propertied classes with panic, both middle class and aristocracy remained
consistent in their opposition to the ideology spontaneously assumed, in
most countries, by the proletariat, namely, socialism. Whenever it was a
question of fighting socialism, liberals and conservatives, in spite of their
divergencies, sealed a tacit agreement. Both for conservatives and for
liberals, socialism meant basically the destruction of private property and
of private initiative on behalf of state property and bureaucratic control
over economic and educational life. So long as the privileged classes, namely,
the old aristocracy (or its remnants) and the bourgeoisie, remained uncompromising in their opposition to state-socialism, societies were efficaciously protected against the all-devouring expansion of the powers of the
state. Strikingly enough, democratic liberties were defended against state-
socialism by people the majority of whom were not democratically-minded.

Now, sometime in the early nineteen-twenties, privileged classes, in most
countries of the world, came to realize, or to believe, that the proletarian
movement could no longer be controlled in the framework of a liberal
society. Then state-socialism began to appear as a possible means of holding
the proletarian movement in check. To unimaginative people, state-socialism
seemed to be the only alternative to this liberal disorder which made possible the always growing menace of proletarian revolution. Little by little,
men of property became reconciled to the idea of a considerable increase
in the powers of the state. The prospect of a totalitarian organization, as an
alternative to a proletarian conquest, did not, in the last analysis, look so

unpleasant to people who believed they would be the masters of such an organization. Propertied classes gave up their opposition to state-socialism.

In order to be possible, such a transformation had to be inconspicuous and generally unconscious: now, making it inconspicuous and unconscious was mostly a matter of vocabulary and emotional coloring. Socialism had to change its name, at least to qualify it, had to call itself Fascism, or National-Socialism, or National Revolution, or Corporativism, or anything like that. The success of the word "Corporativism," one of the most deceiving in today's social and political terminology, calls for special attention.

Corporativism: a word which, in Latin countries at least, evokes a rather well delimited historical reality, the guild-system which was general before the introduction of unchecked competition in economic relations. Let us notice how little known is the genuine history of ancient "corporations." From a true image of the old corporative order, profitable lessons might have been taken; but the advocates of corporativism succeeded in having prevail a romantic and idyllic idea of the happy life of peoples under the regime of "corporations." A propaganda which, otherwise, would have looked thoroughly dull and unattractive, owed a certain lure to its association with fancies elaborated by early romanticists. Such fancies graciously adorn the negativism of disillusioned optimists, who locate their utopias in the past.

To our knowledge, what had to be preserved from the old corporative regime can be summarized in three principles capable of multifarious applications: 1. that rational organization is, of itself, better than an anarchistic scattering of individual initiatives; 2. that occupational grouping is, all things being equal, more natural than class grouping; 3. that the organization of economic relations should be left to private societies whenever the intervention of public powers is not indispensable. As a matter of fact, institutions born from modern corporative movements are constantly characterized by a complete control of state bureaucracy over all branches of economic life.

· · · · · · ·

At the time when the proletarian revolution seemed more redoubtable than ever to the disillusioned middle class, another revolution, plebeian rather than proletarian, was under way. Privileged classes soon came to wonder whether, in spite of their dislike for revolutions, the plebeian revolution should not be encouraged, as an efficacious check on the proletarian movement. In all countries where democratic forms have been replaced by totalitarian institutions, there has been a period of uncertainty during which people in privileged positions felt hesitant, and willing to postpone the day when revolutionary forces were to be unloosed. They got rid of their hesitation as their conviction grew that the ambitions of the working class could no longer be controlled in a regime which granted the workingmen freedom of association, freedom of expression, and parliamentary representation.

Yet, the upper classes, in order to bind up their destiny with that of the plebeian forces which constituted the dynamism of the new revolution, had to overcome strong repugnances. Common opposition to the proletarian movement had easily sealed the reconciliation of the aristocracy with the middle class. It was incomparably more difficult to unite in a common front, on the one hand, the *plebeians-in-chief*[16] who led the Revolution of Nihilism, on the other hand, ex-liberal bourgeois and steadily conservative aristocrats, all gentlemen highly conscious of their respectability and little inclined to mix with adventurers from the lower classes. The cooperation of the conservatives with the *plebeians-in-chief* was the more paradoxical, since all institutions, mores, principles, to which conservatives were attached, were obviously threatened with violent destruction by the nihilistic forces of the plebeian revolution.

Yet all obstacles were overcome and the keys to many cities were delivered by distinguished conservatives. This paradoxical achievement becomes easily intelligible as soon as the blinding power of hatred is given due consideration. The leaders of the privileged classes and those of the rabble had few positive principles in common. But many hatreds were common to them. No wonder that the *Revolution of Nihilism* was made possible by a conspiracy of hatreds.

THE DELIVERANCE OF THE WORLD

In the course of the last few years, while the catastrophes from which the world is now suffering were unfolding themselves with an overwhelming appearance of fatality, people who represented the principles of truth and justice generally felt powerless and confused. Social thinkers who had the privilege of knowing the true principles of ethical, social, political, international life, proved able to criticize many errors of the day, but astonishingly unable to generate any dynamic and appealing idea. Such a failure was not exclusively due to the cowardice of their character and to their occasional connivance with the forces of evil. It seems that a fundamental misunderstanding had taken place concerning the proper conditions of a practical thinking which is to be practically efficacious.

People whose duty it is to prepare in the silence of patient reflection improvements to be realized in society, are ordinarily inclined to believe that their task is over when they have set up a number of unquestionably true principles. Applying those principles is a task to be performed by other people, men of action, social leaders, party leaders, statesmen, etc. Owing to this division of labor, social thinkers assure the peace of their mind at very low price. Have they not said the truth? Their task is fulfilled. It belongs to other ones to carry out in the field of action the principles which they have so nicely formulated.

I must confess that I have shared for many years this view of the problem. It is not until recently, and under the pressure of present catastrophes, that I came to realize that this division of labor between the academic task of elaborating principles and the task of applying them in the field of action was not compatible with the laws of collective action. The reasons why scholars are so generally unwilling to go beyond the statement of principles which are capable of varied applications, interpretations and misinterpretations, is that they are exceedingly afraid of being proved wrong some day by actual events. It is true that easy jokes are made whenever a dignified scholar is shown to have forecast or simply advocated exactly the contrary of what has happened. These jokes are too easy and these scholars too dignified. The only question is whether a concrete investigation of the future of society has some good chance of being useful to the actual realization of a better future.

We can no longer content ourselves with asserting and reasserting principles which can afford to be unquestionably true because they lie on a sufficiently high level of abstraction. We can no longer content ourselves with uttering statements which are so thoroughly disentangled from historical contingencies that no historical occurrence can invalidate them. The only point we have to be particular about is defining a method to direct our speculation about the future.

. . . .

In this methodological connection, the works of Georges Sorel contain most valuable suggestions.[17] According to Sorel's analysis, methods employed in speculations about the future of society can be reduced to two main types. There is a form of speculation which consists in constructing utopias: let us call it the *utopian* method. And there is a method which consists in analyzing myths: let us call it the *mythical* method. Those terms must be defined with great care, since the way we use them after Sorel not exactly the way they are used most ordinarily.

By *utopia* people ordinarily understand an arbitrary construction which implies a fundamental failure to recognize some law of human nature or some regularity of human history, and consequently is thoroughly unrealizable. A utopia in Sorel's sense is not necessarily an unrealizable construction: all we can say is that the most typical examples of utopias in Sorel's sense also fit the common notion of the term. What characterizes a utopia in the sense of Sorel is the fact that it is a construction worked out in an intellectualistic way by a thinker. Such a construction is not necessarily fantastic. Yet, realizable though it may be, it has no chance of being realized unless some enormous power—so enormous that no contingency can hold it in check—is put at the service of what is thought to be the rational way of organizing society. Among the great builders of utopias in the early nineteenth century, some were not at all inclined to favor state-socialism. Witness the phalansterian system of Fourier, which has a distinctly anarchistic flavor. However, the first utopians demanded at least the help of a powerful financier. Fourier himself expected all his life the millionaire who would advance the funds needed for the first application of his system. Later, when the utopian spirit lost its juvenility, its sharers became convinced that relying upon a millionaire to institute some local realizations of an ideal society, and then hoping that those realizations would multiply themselves through the sheer prestige of their success, was exceedingly naïve. The state alone enjoys the uncheckable power which is needed to realize a plan of social reform devised by lovers of ideal and harmonious programs.

It is a matter of history that the utopian method always and inevitably turns to a tremendous increase in the power of the state and the actual bringing into existence of state-socialism. Let us emphasize the fact that words do not matter; what matters is the character of the forces which a system is bound to unloose if it is to be put into practice at all. Whether this system calls itself communism, socialism, collectivism, new order, national revolution, or corporativism, the net result will always be a state-socialistic society. Whatever may be the name, the appearance, and the good intentions of the system under consideration, as soon as this system has the character of a rational construction to be imposed upon the spontaneity of societies, we can be sure that its realization can neither be effected nor maintained without the overwhelming power of the state assuming the control of all sections of social life through an all-devouring bureaucracy.

This is why we think that any use of the utopian method is particularly inadvisable in our time. Since the most immediate of our problems is to do away with the totalitarian state, it would be perfectly foolish to make appeal to a method which generates totalitarianism with the infallible necessity of a law of nature.

It is hard for people trained in theoretical studies to give up the utopian method. Building utopias is surely the easiest way of speculating about the future. It is the kind of speculation which agrees best with our mental

Beyond the Crisis of Liberalism

habits. Giving up the utopian method is for us giving up the spirit of easiness. Moreover, we might believe that a utopia built by us under the light of principles which we know to be true could only bring about felicitous effects. Let us rid ourselves of such illusions: whether it looks reasonable or foolish, a utopia, today more than ever, cannot fail to develop into some state-socialistic and totalitarian monster.

The myth theory was first explained by Sorel in a book devoted to an analysis of the labor movement. Alluding to the future of industrial society, Sorel removes the illusions nourished by some theorists of social science, and declares that there is no scientific method of foreseeing the future with any degree of certainty. Yet Sorel acknowledges that we cannot help going beyond the present and speculating about "the future which seems to escape always the grasp of our reason. We are taught by experience that constructions . . . may be very efficacious and imply few disadvantages when they are of a particular nature. This is what happens when we have to deal with myths in which the most powerful tendencies of a people, a party or a class, find their expression." A myth is not primarily the work of a thinker, it is not an intellectualistic construction. It is collective and social in its origin. It results spontaneously in the mind of a group from emotional stimulations which take place in the daily life of people who are engaged in some great collective achievement. It is an organized, wholistic vision which sums up a set of aspirations, and expresses in an organic unity an indefinite number of emotions and volitions. It is an emotionally loaded vision which springs from the dynamism of the collective will and which in turn assures with an extraordinary efficaciousness the firmness, the steadiness, the unanimity, the discipline and the uncompromising character of the collective will. As examples of myths, Sorel mentions the belief of the early Christians in the imminent return of Christ, the representations that stirred up the early partisans of the French Revolution, the ideal of an Italy united and free which was pursued by Mazzini and his followers. In each of those instances, actual occurrences were widely different from what had been anticipated by the people whose imaginations were inflamed by the myth. On the other hand, the myth proved an historical force of the utmost efficaciousness. "It can be wondered whether the Revolution has not been much more radical a transformation than that which was dreamed of by the people who, in the XVIIIth Century, built up social utopias . . . it has become unquestionable that without Mazzini Italy would never have become a great power and that he has done much more for Italian unity than Cavour and all the politicians of his school."[18]

The purpose of Sorel was to base a conjecture on the future of the labor movement by analyzing the myth which animated that movement. We can

[281]

disregard the result of his analysis; what is relevant here is the method he outlines for the recognition of a myth in the consciousness of a group. Let us observe, he says, people who play an active 'part in the revolutionary movement: "these people can err on many questions of politics, economics, or ethics, but their witness is decisive, sovereign, and final, when the question is to know what the representations are which act upon them and upon their companions with the greatest efficaciousness, and owing to which hopes and particular perceptions seem to constitute an indivisible unity."

The rules for the observation of a myth can be summed up as follows: *First:* define and circumscribe a movement. *Second:* select a number of persons who deserve to be considered as genuine representatives of that movement and carriers of its ideal (an elite). *Third:* listen to the confessions of those people; pay special attention to that which, in their talk, is most spontaneous, most heartfelt, least artificial, least systematic, least prepared; pay your best attention to their spontaneous, unreflective reactions in the face of a number of moving events. You will succeed in discovering the myth which animates the group. Provided you succeed also in understanding the characteristics of the myth, *you will know with an extraordinary certitude where the group is going.* This does not enable you to draw any detailed picture of what is going to happen. *This does enable you to foresee the formal character of the state of affairs bound up with the triumph of the group under consideration.*

Looking backward a few years, let us recall that at the time when the Nazis came into power, many people, in Germany and elsewhere, believed that Nazism was doomed to be a short-lived movement. They thought their anticipation was justified by the extreme poorness of the Nazi ideology, the vagueness, the confusion, the stupidity of the Nazi program. Those gentlemen felt they were much more intelligent than the Nazis, they had rationally elaborated ideas, distinguished interpretations, figures and statistics. They were men of culture and education, but they did not know the myth-theory.

The Nazis had a myth. Everywhere they appeared, either as cultural propagandists, traveling salesmen or soldiers—whether in time of so-called peace or in time of declared war, their myth accompanied them, preceded them, and spontaneously proliferated at an unbelievable speed. Whoever was able to understand the Nazi myth was able to foresee the near future with an accuracy sufficient for all practical purposes.

.   .   .   .

Considering now the recent history of the groups which stand on the side of justice, it is exceedingly plain that their supreme weakness, and the major reason for their failures, consisted in their long-lasting inability to generate a myth. For many years it seemed that the twilight of the myths darkened irretrievably the conscience of the just, doomed to irresolution, confusion, disorder, and despair, while the forces of evil were triumphantly going forward under the infernal light of their stupid and mischievous ideal. It is not until recently that hope was revived in our hearts, as we witnessed the birth of a new myth, but, this time, on the side of the just.

True to the method outlined by Sorel, let us examine the consciousness of people who are really representative of the forces engaged in the struggle for a better future. What are the visions that animate them, inflame their resolution, console their sufferings? All testimonies coincide: whether we have to deal with soldiers on the line of fire, or with statesmen burdened with tremendous responsibilities, or men in the street subjected to the horror of bombings, or isolated citizens who, in the darkness of their solitude, are conducting illegal action against triumphing tyrannies—all these people have in mind, not visions of glory, nor visions of power, but visions of freedom.

In order to understand better what is happening and what we are permitted to hope for, let us say that an ideal can exist in two ways, or, to put it more accurately, is capable of two existential conditions. An ideal can exist in the mind of men as a mere representation of the future, without exercising any noticeable influence on the actual life of those who are carrying it. This is what ordinarily happens with utopias, for the following reason: A utopia is conceived as a rational outline to be realized, some time in the future, through the uncheckable action of some overwhelming power (in practice, the state; more exactly, the totalitarian state). So long as the overwhelming power which is relied upon is not set in operation, the utopia does not demand to be realized to any degree, and thus can very well fail to inform actually any existence. This could be evidenced by many examples.

In countries where parliamentary socialism had lost the character of a violent, dramatic opposition to the existing order, it was often noticed that the daily life of socialists was not at all modified by the fact that they were the upholders of a revolutionary ideal. A socialist lawyer had just the same kind of daily life as a conservative lawyer, a wealthy socialist enjoyed the privileges of wealth as remorselessly as any other member of the wealthy class. Still more enlightening was the particular case of the French royalist group the *Action Française*. This group had been founded to carry out the tasks of restoring traditional monarchy, of destroying all institutions born of the French Revolution, of eradicating the ideas and the spirit of French Revolution. Accordingly the *Action Française* put great emphasis upon the idea of authority, and its extraordinarily stubborn propaganda was, during some forty years, centered around a criticism of liberal politics and an exaltation of authoritarian principles. Yet no movement ever did so much as the *Action Française* to spread the spirit of rebellion, indiscipline and anarchy among the French youth. This contrast was not really astonishing. The utopia of authoritarian society dreamed of by the *Action Française* was thought to be realizable only through the taking over of the state machinery. So long as the royalist gang was not in power, there was not any reason to foster the spirit of obedience; there was every good reason to foster rebellion against the detested Republic.

On the other hand, an ideal can exist in its upholders in such a way as to materialize in their subjectivity before it is given a chance to materialize outwardly in institutions. It happens that an ideal modifies and informs the conduct and the character of its carriers before it is given a chance to modify and inform the structure and functioning of society. Such seems to be the case whenever an elite is engaged in a sublime accomplishment under the guidance of a myth. The very exigencies of the struggle, the spirit of heroism and ingenuity that the struggle demands from everyone in all circumstances of his daily life, causes the ideal to exist really in the psychological subjectivity of individuals and in the sociological subjectivity of their groups. This subjective realization of the ideal establishes a continuity between the present and the future and provides the action for a better future with a steady basis in the present.

· · · · · · ·

After having extensively utilized the method defined by Sorel, I must say how deeply I feel at variance with this irrationalistic philosopher concerning the part that reflective reason and conscious wisdom have to play in the guidance of historical forces. In the making of history, just as in the building up of individual personality, it is equal foolishness to disregard the indispensable power of imaginative and emotional forces, and to fancy that those forces of irrational character can achieve any kind of self-control. With regard to the building up of a strong personality, instincts cannot be too healthy, and it would be foolish to weaken them systematically. Yet they have to be controlled by reason, virtue, prudence, in all their developments and movements, for there is not the slightest chance that they may secure any kind of order if left to themselves. Similarly, there is in every historical myth, however honest and well-founded it may be, an element of instinctiveness which demands to be controlled and ceaselessly purified by the labor of reason and conscious wisdom.

These considerations may throw some light upon the task that social thinkers have to perform today. We remarked earlier that there is too often an unnatural and harmful disconnection between the social thinking of philosophers and the requirements of concrete action. In the last few years we were given many chances to observe that persons who were among the finest products of our intellectual, religious, and moral culture, felt entirely confused, unimaginative, thoroughly powerless when confronted by the duties of immediate action. What was lacking? Neither the spirit of truth nor the goodness of the will. That which was lacking was a point of application, a steadily guaranteed continuity between thought and action, a living intercourse between the spontaneity of social organisms and the reflective organization of rational truth. We suggest that the consideration of the mythical forces which are developing under our eyes might provide social philosophers with such a desirable point of contact, and enable us to do away with the nefarious separation between the investigation of truth and the movement of history.

So far as the problem of liberty and the problems connected with the discussion of liberalism are concerned, the duty of philosophers is clearly indicated. At the very time when the ideal of liberty seemed to be definitively discredited as à result of the crisis of liberalism, we are witnessing a world-wide movement whose driving force is a liberation-myth. The salvation of the world from the Revolution of Nihilism is bound up with the victory of forces which are more and more currently called *the forces of liberty*: this is the only expression that fits their world-wide unity. Nobody can give an outline of the order which will be generated by their victory. The only certain thing is that inasmuch as these forces are driven by a liberation-myth, their victory is bound to open a new era of liberty. This new era has already begun, insofar as the ideal which is generating it has already succeeded in informing the profound life of an heroic elite. The liberation-myth which is now driving the world toward a better future should be, from now on, the main subject-matter of the philosophers who feel any interest in the destiny of mankind. The myth of the deliverance of the world, its forms, manifestations, embodiments and phases, should be ceaselessly observed and analyzed by philosophers, with the definite purpose of assuring the prevalence of truth over illusion. To give a concrete idea of the kind of practical elucidation that I am suggesting, I would call attention to the following problem: it is inevitable and perfectly normal that the present struggle should be assimilated to the wars of liberation carried out, in other times, by several peoples in both Hemispheres; it is inevitable and perfectly normal that the spirit of the Revolutions which brought about liberal societies in America and in Europe, should revive in the fight which is intended to make possible a new birth of liberty; it is inevitable and perfectly normal that the new philosophy of liberty should be conscious of its kinship with the old liberalism. And thus, there is a danger that liberal errors may infect the present movement toward liberty, with the prospect of new disappointments and new disasters. In order to prevent such a danger from materializing, the analytical reason of philosophers has to investigate, more carefully than it has done up to now, the components of the old ideology of liberty. This ideology is far from being homogeneous: part of it can be traced to the idolatrous worship of an ambiguous deity, part of it to the worship of a Divine Name: for God is Liberty, and liberty is among the most glorious names of the true God. Undoubtedly, something can be done in order to have the new current expanded by a revival of the old enthusiasm for liberty, while protected against the errors of liberalism.

Thirteenth Essay

THE FATE OF REPRESENTATIVE GOVERNMENT

by
Walter Farrell, o.p.

The Fate of Representative Government

THE future of representative government is without doubt the most pressing question which engages the attention of modern political thinkers. The steady flow of monographs, articles and books on this question is not a tranquil stream of abstract, disinterested, even idle speculation. There is a note of panic about these treatises. They speak of defects, remedies, fundamental revisions of previous modes of representative government in a way which leaves no doubt of each author's conviction that this form of government is facing a crisis.

To put the situation more bluntly, the student of politics sees a serious threat to representative government on the political horizon. He may gloat over the fact, cower before it, throw up his hands in surrender or search desperately for some means of escaping the danger. But he does not question the fact of the threat to the very existence of representative government. Whatever the sympathies of the individual philosopher of politics, the first step in a rational encounter of such a threat is to discover the precise nature of it.

To accomplish that purpose it will be necessary to glance at the threats possible to a representative government, and of all possible threats, to concentrate on those that fall properly within the field of the political philosopher.

Representative government is subject to threats both from without and from within. We may sum them up under two headings.

Extrinsic Threats: The first and most obvious extrinsic threat to any government is that of military force. It is always possible that a hostile army may overwhelm a government, invading its territory and subjecting its people without reference to law or justice. Such a threat has been an almost constant factor in history. As such it has never been entirely overlooked by any capable government and has been provided against as far as the particular historical circumstances have allowed. Indeed the guarantee of peace from external enemies enters intimately into the very purpose for which the government exists.

Essays in Thomism

The second extrinsic threat is of an entirely different character. It is indeed extrinsic relative to government, though it is intimately intrinsic to the community which that government directs to the community's end. This threat comes about through a gradual change, either slow or considerably accelerated, in what has been called the "pre-political dispositions" of the community. In other words, in the course of time a fundamental change is effected by such factors as education (good or bad), moral invigoration or degeneration, abundance or scarcity of physical necessities, social harmony or discord, cultural refinement or coarsening. As a result, what was formerly a people capable of self-government degenerates, or a people on the bare margin of civilization matures.[1]

Since the particular form of government does not drop down ready-made from heaven, but is rather the fruit of the industry of men, it must respond to the conditions of the people whom it governs.[2] Normally the pre-political conditions of a people are slightly in advance (to good or evil) of the course of a government since it is these dispositions that are met by government. Granted a sufficient change in these dispositions under unchanging government, a new form of government, responding to those dispositions, must ultimately come into existence. A particular form of government threatened by such a change, to better or worse, can thwart the danger if, in time, it recognizes the factors that are making for such a change and limits or eliminates them. However a progressive change of this kind cannot long be hindered except through tyranny.

Intrinsic Threats: From within, representative government may be threatened by an *absolute* defect, i.e., one that is inherent in the very nature of such a form of government. Such a threat is inescapable: it will be found, if it exists at all, in representative government whatever the age, the nation, the political dispositions of the people governed by it. On the other hand, the threat may be only *relative*, i.e., a defect not inherent in representative government as such but consequent on the circumstances of this particular representative government, of this age, of these pre-political dispositions, of this particular country.

THE FIELD OF THE POLITICAL PHILOSOPHER

Obviously there is no point in the philosopher's consideration of the extrinsic military threat. That is a question of fact to be examined and faced by political leaders, military strategists, patriots precisely as patriots. The fact of a change in pre-political dispositions—the other extrinsic threat—is also a question to be determined, not by the philosopher but by agencies capable of and equipped for such observation. However the ascertainment of such facts furnishes the starting point for the analysis of the political philosopher by which he can determine the nature, seriousness and possible remedy of such a threat; from this angle a consideration of pre-political dispositions is definitely philosophical.

If the external threats give the philosopher little material for his considerations beyond a starting point, the intrinsic threats to government fall squarely within his field. He not only may legitimately and fruitfully consider this material, he must give it his most earnest thought if he is not to lose title to his high name of philosopher. If such an intrinsic weakness exists in representative government, it is only by recognizing and diagnosing it that representative government can be saved; in such a case the philosopher's considerations will be by way of remedy. They may, however, in truth's severe kindness, be by way, not of remedy, but of cauterization; for if no remedy be possible, if the particular weakness be of such a nature as to be demonstrably irremediable, it must be honestly faced and the hopeless experiment of representative government be abandoned.[3]

THE INTRINSIC THREAT BY *A POSTERIORI* INVESTIGATION

It would be unfair both to the critics of representative government and to the representative governments themselves to lump all criticisms together and on that score attempt to estimate men's opinions of this form of government. It will be much fairer to make clear the precise meaning of the term "representative government," thereby eliminating much of the criticism that is not in fact directed against this form of government, whatever the terminology used in the criticisms.

This necessity of more precise terms will be evident if we remember that the very word "democracy"—which is one of the constants in all criticism of representative government—is an equivocal term. It has been used to describe an individualistic extreme that is in reality a denial of government; in this sense it has been quite properly claimed by such a wide variety of groups as anarchists, syndicalists, material liberalists and communists. At the opposite limit, democracy has been used to signify an organismal extreme that submerged both the state and the individual in a monstrosity that went by such names as the "general will." In this sense democracy was used by Rousseau and his disciples of the French Revolution. More recently the same term is applied to what might be called a legalistic popular sovereignty which in itself remained indifferent to whether the head of the state was an elected official or an hereditary monarch; but which insisted on the sacred rights of the individual, a régime of law and order to the common good and an active participation by citizens in government.[4] The confusion of these three meanings of "democracy" accounts for much of the muddled political thinking, both for and against representative government, some trace of which is to be found in so many political treatises today; while, as a matter of fact, the bond of union between the three is little more than the thin thread of a single word.

To avoid such confusion in this study we have used the term "representative government" rather than "democracy" to signify a ruling power that includes popular sovereignty, the sanctity of the individual, and the common good. Its signification might be put more briefly by insisting that it includes popular sovereignty, an explicit or implicit social contract, and dependence on and a harmony with natural law. This form of government is of peculiar interest, not by way of contrast between good and bad governments, nor as a study of one governmental device, nor yet by way of comparison with totalitarian forms of government, but rather by way of analysis of one form of good government. There is no particular point in bringing up the distinction between representative monarchy and democracy in the legalistic sense with an elected presiding officer; for the fundamental issue at stake is the individual and the feasibility of his perfection by a participation in government.[5]

Representative government, taken in this sense and seen from this point of view has been subjected, of late, to fundamental criticism by its enemies and has been the object of some serious doubts on the part of its friends. Both the criticism and the doubts turn upon the very nature of representative government and make necessary a clear, reasoned answer to the question: is representative government, by its very nature, doomed to oblivion?

I. *Inimical Criticism:* The inimical criticism of representative government has been summed up briefly by saying that such a form of government is unscientific, ethically unsound and practically impossible—a criticism that is fundamental and sweeping enough, in all conscience.[6] As a matter of fact the accusation on grounds of science—based as it is on such unstable grounds as racial superiority, intelligence tests and the superior influence of heredity—can hardly be taken seriously by any thinking man. It is in itself most unscientific. That representative government is ethically unsound is a criticism that stems from the nineteenth-century ethical theory of a mechanistic natural right, the parent of the *laissez-faire* program as well as of the "general will" myth of the French revolutionists both of which did much to delete any serious consideration of the individual who is the fundamental possessor of natural rights. This latter criticism is a typical product of the confusion of the senses of democracy. That it is practically impossible is a question of fact that is indeed open to serious discussion; if it be impossible in this sense, only sentimentality would attempt its defense.

The Fate of Representative Government

A much clearer insight into the real criticism of representative government on the part of its enemies can be had by looking at the details of that criticism rather than at summaries of those details. Thus this form of government has been attacked as guilty of:

1. fundamental weakness in face of external enemies;
2. being ineffective when confronted with fundamental problems;
3. lacking authority and fostering disorder;
4. constant injustice both towards its citizens and the common good;
5. being undemocratic and capitalistic;
6. being bureaucratic, having very little of popular sovereignty in it through lack of participation in government on the part of its citizens.[7]

It is not our purpose, for the moment, to evaluate this criticism; we shall attempt that later in this study. Here it is sufficient to see the criticism itself clearly, in order that later on we may be able to determine its exact nature and the seriousness of the faults it points out in representative government.

II. *Friendly Criticism:* The friends of representative government have suffered some serious doubts about it these past few years, doubts whose expression comes perilously close to the blunt criticism of its enemies. They claim to have noticed:

1. that it has only a tardy adaptability, particularly when sharp, decisive, immediate change seems essential to continuation in existence;
2. that there is a serious degree of inefficiency in its details of actual government;
3. that it has an appearance of futility and helplessness when faced with fundamental problems;
4. that there is an alarming disinterest and lack of participation in government on the part of the citizens.[8]

A comparison of this criticism with the unfriendly criticisms of representative government, along with the evaluation of both, will be reserved for later pages of this study, principally because for such an evaluation it is essential to have clearly in mind the principles inherent in representative government.

A PRIORI INVESTIGATION OF THE THREAT

Representative government, like all governments, has (1) a basis upon which it rests, (2) a form which differentiates it from all other types of government, (3) the matter which this form specifies, and (4) an operation proper to itself. An intrinsic threat to representative government then must be found in some one of these four: basis, form, matter, operation. To put the possibilities in plain language, we may say that an intrinsic threat to representative government can only come from:

1. the ethical principles which are the basis or foundation upon which it rests;
2. its political principles—whether ultimate or derived—which constitute the form of the government;[9]
3. a conflict or lack of harmony between the political principles or form and the pre-political dispositions of the citizens or the matter; or, in other words, through a disintegration of the unity of form and matter;
4. or, finally, from the execution and application of the political principles, i.e., from the very operation of the government.

The last of these sources of a threat to representative government does not directly involve a philosophical question, but is rather a matter for judicial or police processes. The first is a strictly philosophical question; but since it revolves around necessary and absolutely universal principles, its solution represents no insuperable difficulty and runs nothing like the risk of error to be encountered in dealing with political principles. These latter, which represent the second possible intrinsic threat and with which we shall deal more fully later, are indeed philosophical but they are of the strictly contingent order, intimately involved with the historical circumstances in which they operate. The third possible source of an intrinsic threat—pre-political dispositions of the citizens—is to a great extent a question of fact relative to the actual dispositions among this or that people; but the consequences and causes of the fact are within the territory of the philosopher. It is something to be settled and may, indeed, be crucial. It represents the most fertile field of modern political discussion.[10] The value of an investigation in this field lies primarily in the detection of the factors making for the change or deterioration of the pre-political principles which laid the original ground for the foundation of a representative government.

An investigation of the intrinsic threat to representative government from an *a priori* point of view will therefore involve:

A. an examination of the ethical principles which are the foundation of the political principles of representative government;
B. an examination of its political principles;
C. an examination of the sources of conflict between the pre-political dispositions of the citizens and the political principles;

D. an indication of the possible sources of danger, insofar as such an indication lies within the realm of philosophy, in the defective execution and application of the political principles or in the very operation of the state.

A. Ethical Principles of Representative Government

To avoid all confusion in the course of this discussion of principles it may be well to point out the double sense in which the term can be taken whether it be considered from the point of view of *signification* or of *stability*:

a) in its signification, a principle may be taken either for a root, ultimate origin or basis; or it can signify a fundamental proposition of a science;

b) in regard to its stability a principle can be absolutely immutable and universal, independent of whatever contingent circumstances may arise in the course of the ages; or it can be only relatively stable, possessed of a degree of immutability which makes its change so gradual, even so reluctant a thing as to make its stability stand out as a predominant characteristic.

As will be more apparent in the course of this study, both ethical and political principles are ultimate origins, bases: the first of ethical life, the second of political life as distinct from, but by no means independent of, ethical life. It is in this root sense that we are primarily taking the term "principle." But it is also true that both ethical and political principles are fundamental propositions of a science: the first of the science of ethics, the second of the science of politics.

From the aspect of stability, ethical principles—as flowing from the very essence of things—are absolutely immutable and universal; political principles, inextricably involved in the unfolding of the records of history and containing in themselves an element of human industry, cannot be more than relatively stable.

I. *Ethical Principles of All Government:* The ethical principles which are fundamental to politics will be those that flow from the nature and end of man. They are as universal and immutable as their sources; or, to trace their immutability to its last source, they are as immutable as the intellect of God upon which they depend.[11] Ultimately they are reducible to the principles that are regulatory of the life of man in his common life with other men, that is, to the principles of justice whose immediate effects are some measure of order and peace. In detail they can be radically stated in two propositions and the consequences of these propositions:

1. *Political society is a natural human phenomenon.*

   a) As *natural*, it has common bonds with all else in nature. Certainly, as natural, it does not exist in splendid isolation; nothing in nature does. It does not, in other words, exist *in* itself; there is something immediately beneath and something immediately above it, for, like every other natural thing, it has its orderly place in nature's hierarchy. To both the higher and lower, political society inevitably has relations: to the lower the relation is one of superiority and dominion; to the higher it is one of inferiority and subordination. Political society, as natural, has an origin and a terminus, i.e., it does not exist *for* itself or *by* itself. Rather, in common with all natural things, it exists for something else and by and from something else. It is judged by the same norms that determine hierarchical place in the rest of nature: nature intends that which endures proportionately to the perfection of its being. Nor are these norms the arbitrary rules of a parlor game excogitated by a theorist impatient of observation; they are to be gathered from the objective workings of nature. To "liberate" political society from any of these limitations of natural things is to attempt the impossible. The result of such an attempt is either the irrational insistence that political society is a freak in nature or the monstrous divinization or annihilation of political society. Whatever be the aberrations of the human mind relative to political society, it remains a natural phenomenon and only as such can it be objectively judged.

   b) As *human*, political society stands apart, differentiated from every other natural thing. Whatever human characteristics it has find their source in that which alone in nature is essentially human—the human individual. Consequently political society does not conflict with or destroy but rather flows from, harmonizes with the essentials of human nature, namely:

   1) the end of man:[12]
      a. of man as a moral being, i.e., his individual perfection through the development of the virtues and the perpetuation of the race. These might be called the spiritual and physical ends of the individual if such terminology did not involve the danger of overlooking the fact that both these ends are *moral* ends, being the proper ends of a moral being, the human individual;
      b. of man as a political being, i.e., his communal end, an intermediate end, the common good of the community;
   2) the intrinsic and natural guidance of man to his ends or the natural moral law.[13] That this is a corollary of the preceding is obvious.

A political society ceases to be human when it cuts itself off from the source of all that is human by operating against the human individual; and it cannot pretend to be operating in favor of that individual when it conflicts with the law provided by nature to perfect the individual, to lead him to his end;

3) the characteristics which flow from man's proper and spiritual accidents of intellect and will, namely:

a. freedom,[14] i.e., not the absence of all restraint but at the very least a moral freedom that allows a man to attain his individual ends—surely that freedom which precludes slavery in the sense of one man being used for another's end rather than being directed and helped to his own;

b. equality:[15] for man as a person, a sacred whole with supreme ends proper to himself, is not the subordinate tool of anything else in nature. On the basis of his rational nature alone he is the equal of his fellow men and the superior of all else; in those things that pertain essentially and directly to his ends he needs no state aid—in generation, the ruling of his home, the practice of virtue;

c. inequality:[16] the specific equality of men, the inviolable character of their rights to fulfill the obligations imposed by the very supremacy of their ends, does not demand an absolute standardization of all individuals. It is an absurd denial of facts to pretend that all men have the same intellectual perspicacity, strength of will, inclination to virtue, practical capacities such as ability to govern, to paint, to compose music, and so on;

d. sufficiency:[17] relative to the essentials of life. Men can exist without the help of their fellow men; indeed, through all of history individuals have so existed;

e. insufficiency:[18]—yet men need their fellow men, for their lives are lived not merely on a plane of bare existence but rather of human existence; they have not merely the end of physical existence to the point that will insure the propagation of the race, they have a more personal end of intellectual and moral perfection that can be seriously interfered with, even thwarted, through the absorption of all their powers in a desperate effort barely to hang on to life.

2. *It is the human being that is both beneath and above the state, both its inferior and its superior, both its material and its goal.*[19] This paradox is rooted in the complex nature of the human individual, a nature that is

both material and spiritual. As the grasp on the spiritual nature of man is gradually lost, the capacity to understand the nature of political society is proportionately lessened until it disappears altogether with the disappearance of the insight into the spirituality of man. For to understand political society it is essential to see its ethical basis clearly—an impossible task unless man be seen as a complex creature possessed:

1) of both matter and spirit, body and soul; enjoying only a mortal existence yet living on in immortality;

2) of apparently conflicting properties. While he is self-sufficient in one sense, in another he is insufficient to himself; while in one sense all men are equal, in another sense no two men are equal;

3) of a double end, physical and spiritual (though both are moral) as an individual, communal as a political being. In other words, man exists for the perpetuation of the species, for the common good of the community, but he also, and primarily, exists for the perfection of his individual form or human soul.

3. *Consequences of these two propositions:*

1) Political society, as a natural human phenomenon, takes its rise from nature, not any nature but human nature. So that that *from which* the state proceeds (its origin) will be some elements of human nature itself:[20]

    a. The elements that might be called *naturally* human, as not being subject to the workings of human choice and industry, namely: (1) man's natural inclinations to political life as an intermediate end and so as a means necessary to the attainment of his ultimate and individual goal; (2) man's natural insufficiency which must be supplied for; (3) man's natural inequality for which order, protection and fostering is demanded. These three viewed in relation to man's naturally determined end are the root of the *de facto* necessity of the state.

    b. The elements that might be called *freely* human, as involving the industry and choice of the individual, namely, freedom, equality, and sufficiency, are the root of the form, the extension and the limitation of the state.

2) The end of the state—that *for which* it exists—must also revolve around the human individual, since the end must respond to the beginning, the final cause to the efficient cause.[21]

    a. Its immediate and proximate end will be summed up in the word "peace," a goal attained by protection from external enemies and by the guarantee of internal harmony through provision of necessities and just distribution of burdens, punishments and rewards.[22]

b. But it will go far beyond this to its ultimate end which is "the life of virtue," "the divine life" by which the state is immediately and directly a means to the end of the individual. This final end of the state means no more than the affording of the opportunity to its citizens to live the life of virtue, to fulfill their natural inclinations to individual perfection. This ultimate end of the state is the *common good*,[23] in its fullest sense of final cause (*finis causa*).

3) The *measure* of the state, the determinant of its nature, extent and limit is also to be found in the very essentials of the one essentially human thing in the universe—the human individual. Thus the inequality and insufficiency of man are a statement of the extent of the state, his equality and sufficiency a statement of its limitation. In other words the measure of the state is the end of man and his needs in relation to the attainment of his end.[24]

4) The *means* of the state, that by which it attains its proximate and ultimate ends, are again determined by the nature of the human individual. Because he is a moral being, moving to his end by intellect and will rather than by instinct, the means of the state must be moral means, i.e., authority by which the state moves man by his intellect and will.[25]

a. His insufficiency, his inequality, his capacity of choice of a variety of means to his end are in themselves a demand for the existence of authority.

b. His freedom, equality and sufficiency are a statement of the limitation of that authority.

c. The characteristics of the authority of the state, then, are no more than declarations of the harmony of that authority with individual human nature.

1. Civil authority is thus primarily directive, moving its subjects not by physical but by moral force, by intellect and will. It orders man to his end; the only order in harmony with his nature is a moral order.

2. Secondarily it is coercive by way of protection of the common good against the wicked who choose to act against their own end and against the common good of others.

3. It is distinctly limited by several factors:[26]

a) by the natural moral law which is its source;

b) by the form of the particular civil society;

[299]

c) by the ends of the state which alone give it power relative to the means to be used.

d. The act of authority—i.e., moral movement by civil power—is known as *law* or the duly promulgated ordering of practical reason to the common good by him who has authority.[27]

II. *The ethical principles of representative government* in its generic consideration (leaving aside the specific consideration of good, better, and best) are no whit different from the ethical principles of any other form of good government. These principles stem immediately from human nature itself and, consequently, are of an absolute universality. If there is a generic differentiation of governments, necessarily on the grounds of ethical principles, then one of the governments is not good but bad government. And bad government is no government: it is a tyranny that is not working for the human individual but against him; it has abandoned the end of the state and consequently its title to existence; it has ceased to be human for it has cut itself off from the sole source of humanness in the universe, the human individual.[28]

B. Political Principles of Representative Government

I. *Distinction from Ethical Principles:* The ethical principles are absolute and immutable, flowing as they do from the intrinsic nature of things as they are; moreover they are universal principles. By them the inner life of man can be judged immediately by the mere application of the principles, for the inner moral life of man, its goodness or evil, does not vary. But the political life of man is quite another thing. In dealing with that we are not dealing with an unchanging set of factors but with the infinite variety of historical circumstance. It will always be true that the end of the state is peace and the life of virtue; but the mode in which that peace and life of virtue is to be attained will obviously be different in the small city states of ancient Greece and the far-flung industrial Empire of modern Britain.[29]

St. Thomas put the difference between ethical and political principles succinctly in insisting on the mutability of the conditions under which man lives, the necessity for a determination of the universal ethical principles to meet the contingent circumstances of life and the relative stability of these determinations.[30]

1) Thomas spoke again and again of the immutability and the mutability of human nature. The first embraced the intrinsic principles of that nature and all that flowed immediately (by way of conclusion) from those principles. The latter extended to the external conditions under which a man lived his life: the social, economic, intellectual,

moral and cultural circumstances that obviously vary from age to age, country to country, people to people. In these varying circumstances, the political machinery by which peace and the life of virtue are guaranteed to men has historically varied, indeed must inevitably vary.

2) The universal principles of ethics are brought down to operation in particular instances in a two-fold way: by way of conclusion and application; and by way of determination or the selection of one out of many means conducive to the attainment of ethical ends. This latter particularization of universal ethical principles is the field of political principles and law.[31] Political principles then are less universal than ethical principles; they are general rather than universal judgments, limited to and fitted for a condition subject to change. Yet they are a determination of ethical principles, existing under and subordinate to ethical principles from which they take their rise.

3) Since political principles direct the external, social life of man, stability is one of their essential characteristics, demanded both because they are to serve as guides and because they bring ethical principles down to the conditions under which men *de facto* are living their lives. A guide that varied from moment to moment or from year to year would, of course, be no guide at all but a source of confusion; on the other hand, the conditions under which men live have a relative permanency about them which would make constantly changing political principles defeat the very ends of politics. If these political principles were fitted to this particular people at this time, then a considerable change in them does violence to the people in question and is no longer a suitable means to ethical ends, no longer a determination of ethical principles and consequently no longer has a claim upon the minds or hearts of men. Yet because the historical circumstances do change, the stability of political principles can never be more than relative.

We have then as the contrasting characteristics of these two kinds of principles: (1) the ethical are universal, primary, absolutely stable, dealing immediately with the inner moral life of man; (2) the political are general, secondary and subordinate to the ethical which they determine; (3) political principles are relatively stable, contingent upon the historical conditions in which men live.

II. *The Nature of Political Principles:* From their distinction from ethical principles, political principles may be described, in broad terms, as general judgments about singular circumstances, namely, historical conditions under which men are living, relative to the attainment of the ends of political life. Or, more concretely, it might be said that they make up the stable element in political organization as contrasted with the progressive element furnished by acts of popular sovereignty or representative bodies. As examples of political principles we might mention the Constitution of the United States and its Supreme Court.[32]

Of these two, one, the Constitution, is primary; the other, the Supreme Court, is derivative or secondary. This order is always to be found in political principles. One will be ultimate; all others derived. That is, one will be the first principle determining the political form of the government; from this first determination all the working institutions of the particular political order will flow.

Perhaps this will be clearer if we trace the resemblance between political principles and civil law. The resemblance in regard to the first political principle is especially clear: like law it too is stable, of itself perpetual but not immutable and it too is a determination of the natural law. However, there are some interesting differences flowing inevitably from the relatively universal character of the first political principle. While it is from authority, as all determinations of natural law to common good must be since this end is proper to no individual, yet it is not from politically constituted authority; rather it establishes this authority. It is from the community as a political group *in via*, in the process of formation. Indeed on this score the first political principle is comparable to the first moral principle, the first principle of natural law which does not presuppose but constitutes morality. Just as the first moral principle comes immediately from nature to whose perfection all morality is directed, so the first political principle comes immediately from the community to whose perfection all politics is directed. As nature is the immediate and ultimate source of morality, so the community is the immediate and ultimate source of all political institutions. This is a truth whose importance can hardly be exaggerated for it brings out clearly the power of the community as the ultimate court of appeal with the right to change what it has established. Another striking difference between the first political principle and civil law is to be seen in the fact that while the first political principle, like civil law, is ordained to the common good or end of the state and therefore deals only with means (political means), it precedes, in the order of nature, the state to which this end is proper. And this is but another declaration that the real possessor of the common good is the community to whom alone the end is essentially proper. It is noteworthy that neither ethical nor political principles establish their own ends; their field is limited to means. In the ultimate analysis they are both acts of the practical virtue of prudence whose ends are furnished by the moral virtues. A political principle attempting to establish an end other than that furnished by the moral virtues under the guidance of ethical principles would be an absurdity—though perhaps a tragic absurdity.

As determinations of natural law, political principles cannot be brushed aside without incongruous results. The result of such a rejection would be either a set of wholly indetermined ethical principles as sole basis of the stability of the political organization—in other words, every man left free to do his own choosing of political means to political ends, which would be political chaos; or the denial of the ethical principles at the root of the political principles, and this would be like cherishing the roof as we dynamited the foundations. From the nature of political principles and their necessity some important conclusions follow:

1) Every state must have political principles for every state must have determined bases of stability. Or, in scholastic language, every political society must have a political form.

2) In every state there must be a certain lag in adaptation, the result of the forces of stability (political principles) resisting the effects of progressive forces on the form of the political unit.

3) Complete and immediate adaptability, which turns every emergency to the immediate advantage of the state regardless of the injury done to individuals or other nations, can be had only at the cost of the capitulation of the stable elements to the progressive, i.e., at the cost of political principles. This kind of amoral opportunism is catastrophic in its results, for it means government without principles— the destruction of *human* government; it is the destruction of the form of the political organism and consequently the complete loss of direction towards the ends of the state since end responds to form. The result, visible in our times, is ultimately a disregard of the human ends of the state and a succession of rapidly shifting temporary ends and the adoption of means directly inimical to the individual ends of the citizens of the community.

.4) On the other hand, complete stability is no less disastrous. It means a constant widening of the gap between the political dispositions of the people (the matter of the political organism) and the political form of their government. It is the death by senescence of the political organism. While the surrender of stability is the tyranny of anarchy, the surrender of progressive elements is the tyranny of an anachronism, the forerunner and sure guarantee of revolution.

As these stabilizing and progressive factors approach a more perfect balance, the political life of the community is more vigorous and healthy.

On the grounds of its political principles there is no intrinsic threat to representative government. It does not abandon political principles and thus deny ethical principles or leave them indeterminate, i.e., it does not set up an inhuman government or abandon government to individualistic chaos. It is neither hopelessly conservative through an exaggeration of stability, nor fluctuating with every demand for adaptation through an exaggeration of change or progress. The two are balanced, as they must be for human government. The justice of that balance determines the condition of the particular representative government.[33]

C. Possible Conflict of Political Principles and Pre-Political Dispositions

The necessity for a consideration of what we have called pre-political dispositions can be traced to the fact that "political institutions and arrangements do not exist in a social vacuum, nor are they prior to the society which they constitute."[34] The question of good government, in any practical sense, must always be a question of good government for this particular people at this historical time. It is fitted, in other words, to their actual condition; if it is not, there is conflict between the political principles of that government and the pre-political dispositions of its citizens.

In speaking of the conditions of a people it is well to remember that these can never be merely material. This has been fairly well recognized in the copious treatments of the political dispositions by modern authors; but it has also been superbly ignored by governmental agencies the world over. It is not enough to consider the economic, social, cultural conditions unless these latter are taken in a very wide sense to include the intellectual and moral state in which this particular people exists.

Thus, for instance, it has been said that in modern times these pre-political dispositions have been democratic because they have been working towards an equality of conditions;[35] in the concrete, wealth has been greater and its distribution much more perfect, there has been more widely diffused education and superior living conditions. As a matter of fact the emphasis here is wrong. An equality of physical and social[36] conditions can be an ideal disposition for totally unrepresentative government, indeed that has not been a totally theoretical result of much modern standardization. The intellectual and moral factors are much more important in the disposition of a people to representative government than are the economic and social.

This can be readily understood if we take the sum of present pre-political dispositions for representative government to be present capacities for social direction. Obviously then the intellectual virtue of prudence, with its moral material, and the moral virtues from which it accepts its principles, must always be of primary importance since it is *par excellence* the directive virtue. On the other hand, intellectual and moral decay, whatever the physical and social conditions, strikes at the very roots of the dispositions for representative government. Again this is not mere theory but something that can be seen as a parallel to the levelling factors in the physical and social order in the shape of a steady, strong decline in the appreciation of the ethical foundations of political principles. The consequence of this decline is inevitably a loss of the sense of value, not merely of representative, but of all *human* government.[37] It is encouraging, if startling news that Stanford University inaugurated a course in medieval authors with this reflection: "It is to be hoped that a study of medieval authors such as Thomas Aquinas will make the student a bit more hesitant voluntarily to give up his inalienable rights guaranteed to him by the Constitution. . . ."[38]

A threat inherent in representative government from a conflict of political principles with pre-political dispositions would be through some agency so changing the physical and social, and above all the intellectual and moral, conditions of a people as to demand a change in the form of government because of the impossible gap between the form and the matter of the political organism. Such changes might be brought about, for example: (a) by the reduction of many to poverty through an intense concentration of wealth; (b) by the spread of economic insecurity through decrease in ownership as, for instance, through highly centralized industry in contrast to the small farmer and small operator; (c) by the monopoly of the organs of expression and propaganda by a special interest or group; (d) by the limitation of educational facilities to few or the failure of a widespread educational system to discipline and cultivate the intellects of its pupils, thus contributing to the destruction of intellectual and spiritual liberty; (e) by decline or loss of appreciation of ethical foundations of government.

The play of these factors in the change of pre-political dispositions, however, are all factual questions which can be answered, either negatively or positively, only by comprehensive study of the facts. Here it is enough to indicate the sources from which such changes might arise.[39]

D. THREAT FROM EXECUTION AND APPLICATION OF POLITICAL PRINCIPLES

This consideration is, again, a factual not a philosophical question. Its solution must come only after a thorough study of the facts. But here it will not be inopportune to point out some of the possible sources of danger to representative government that may approach along this avenue.

There is first of all the possibility of the growth of a group or voluntary organization to a power superior to that of the state, thus reducing political organization to helplessness in the matter of the application and execution of political principles. Such a group could defy the state with impunity and thus obtain a *de facto* exemption from the law which is the principal instrument of the political organism. For example, a national or international industrial group, financial clique, political party, or labor union, may in actual fact be too big for the government. In other words, what is representative government's strength and guarantee of progress (voluntary association) can prove to be a serious weakness.

Again political instruments may be seized by some special interest with the result that the political form becomes a mere tool used not for the common good but for a special end which is inimical to the common good. This will not be a matter of defying political power but rather of absorbing it; it will be somewhat less spectacular than open and successful defiance, but will be no less deadly in its result of destruction of representative government.

There is, too, the possibility of complete apathy on the part of the citizens of a representative government, thus automatically eliminating the progressive element and condemning the political organism to the slow death that must follow on complete stagnation. Eventually the gap between the matter and form must widen, the political principles become unsuited to these historical circumstances, to be followed, almost as a matter of course, by revolution.

Finally, and perhaps most insidious as well as most disastrous, there is the possible destruction of the moral force of law through the slow corruption of the moral life of the citizens—a corruption that has historically come about through a variety of causes: lack of discipline, bad education, unbridled passion, corrupt customs.

EXAMINATION OF THE *A POSTERIORI* INVESTIGATION

I. *Comparison of the Two Criticisms:* Of the extrinsic or inimical criticisms (mentioned above on pages 292-293), those which are reducible to abuses may be ruled out of our consideration as being not inherent but decidedly remediable; such are the charges of: being unjust, undemocratic, capitalistic in the bad sense of the term, i.e., abusively capitalistic, of fostering a bureaucracy which absorbs the actual governing of the state. The other extrinsic criticisms are, strangely, reducible to, indeed even identical with, the intrinsic or friendly criticism of representative government, namely: tardy adaptability, inefficiency in the broad sense of fomenting disorder and weakness, an air of futility in face of fundamental problems, disinterest and lack of participation on the part of the citizens in government. (Cf. page 293.)

These intrinsic criticisms are all fundamental, made as a rule by way of contrast with non-representative governments, particularly totalitarian governments. Thus they call into question the political principles (ultimate or derived) of representative government. Indeed, in some of the forms in which they are proposed, they challenge political principles in themselves.

II. *Evaluation of Intrinsic Criticism:* The first two of these criticisms have already been dealt with in the treatment of political principles (Cf. pages 300-304). A challenge to representative government on these scores (beyond a castigation of abuses) is a challenge to political principles in general, and usually to ethical principles; for fundamentally these criticisms are a demand for the total submergence of the elements of stability in a political organization. The latter criticisms demand more detailed examination.

1) On the score of futility in the face of fundamental problems, it must be noted that these problems may be of two kinds:
   a) They may be fundamental problems relative to the *matter* of the political organism, i.e., of pre-political conditions. If a change is to improvement there is no intrinsic reason why representative government should be futile and helpless. It has means of progress as well as of stability. It may be that a change in the details of political organization will go far beyond the conceptions formally explicit in the political principles; but these details should not fall short of the original conceptions for any intrinsic cause. It can be, of course, that there is a real helplessness consequent on incapable officials, but this is transient or at least always remediable. On the other hand, this change in the matter may be in the direction of degeneration rather than progress; but again this is not a result flowing from the intrinsic nature of representative government but the consequent lack of balance between the elements of stability and change or of incapable officials; all of which factors are susceptible of remedy under the political form of representative government.
   b) It may be that the fundamental problems to be faced have to do with the *form* of the political organism rather than with its matter. In such a case the fundamental problem will be either a challenge to the form of representative government in favor of some other form of good government, or it will be a challenge to all human government, i.e., a challenge to political forms and principles as such. If Aristotle's contention that the better government is that which governs least be correct, then a challenge of the first sort is definitely the result of a falling back, a degeneration that has its source in defective governing rather than in any

intrinsic weakness of representative government. The helplessness in face of such a challenge is a remediable helplessness, not a hopeless one.

A challenge to human government, i.e., a challenge to political form as such, is ultimately a challenge to the foundations of the first political principle, a questioning of the ethical foundations of all good government. Before such a challenge, representative government may indeed be really helpless and futile; for in representative government there must be an agreement among citizens on the nature of the state, of man and of the complex of social institutions. In other words, representative government has only one weapon with which to fight against attack on its ethical principles, i.e., right reason and the proofs it can adduce. It is a serious defect on the part of political principles if they do not protect the ethical principles from such an attack by the working institutions established in the political order. Thus, for example, there is a tragic irrationality in a representative government which, by the working institutions its political principles have established, not only tolerates but positively encourages naturalistic education in its state institutions of learning.

2) The lack of citizen participation in representative government, to be properly evaluated, must be carefully interpreted. To this end it is worthwhile to contrast the citizen participation in government in totalitarian states and in representative governments. To grasp the full significance of that contrast it is necessary to distinguish two kinds of citizen participation in government:

a) One participation is by way of regimentation. In this case the citizens are as parts of a great machine, co-operating with machine-like precision but with no choice in regard to the method, extent or purpose of the co-operation. The results have an appearance of perfect order, efficiency and smoothly functioning authority. Actually this is a destruction of human order, human efficiency and authority; it is movement, not by intellect and will (by law), but by force.

b) The other participation is by way of choice. It is a human participation brought about by the exercise of privilege or free obedience to law. It sometimes gives an appearance of disorder, inefficiency and lack of authority. Actually it is preservation of all of these in the human scale.

It is noteworthy that tyranny on the one side and anarchistic or individualistic democracy on the other are both denials of authority (power to move by intellect and will to the common good) and consequently of human government, since authority is the common means of human government. There is complete error in the modern identification of absolutism with order and authority, individualistic anarchy with freedom and representation.

On this score—of participation in government—there is no inherent barrier to the citizen's participation in representative government; but there is an inherent opposition to participation by regimentation and an inherent championing of participation by choice, e.g., through voting, voluntary association or as a member of a political body.

3) Lack of interest on the part of its citizens can be fatal to representative government, indeed much more so than to other forms of government, especially to the non-human forms. Not infrequently this lack of interest is the offspring of long security and the absence of fundamental problems; it is not infrequently reawakened by the threat to security or the arising of some fundamental problems.

III. The *a posteriori* investigation of representative government does not disclose an intrinsic threat to this form of government. Rather it singles out, in a confused medley, some of the virtues of representative government and some of the abuses which feed like so many parasites on its blood but which, however damaging they may prove to be, can never be identified with the political organism itself.

Fourteenth Essay

THE THOMISTIC CONCEPT OF EDUCATION

by

Robert J. Slavin, o.p.

The Thomistic Concept of Education

I. NEED OF THOMISTIC DOCTRINE

THEORIES of education follow closely the pattern cut out by philosophies of life, philosophies constructed from answers to fundamental questions concerning the source of life, the purpose of living, and the means of attaining that happiness which is the driving force of all of our activity. If the latter be of such a nature as to ignore an objective interpretation of man and his place in society, then the former will lose the broad perspective they should have in the training not only of minds and bodies, but also of hearts and souls. This panoramic point of view has been lost in our day with the consequent narrow and lopsided interpretation of life, of man, of the world, even of God. This has brought about the cult of self-made man, the hatred of fellow men, and the degradation of the noble impulses latent in human nature.

There is no dearth of critics of American education both in its underlying philosophy and in its methods of teaching. Even the man in the street, whether it be Main Street or Wall Street, feels that something is the matter. Fact-finding commissions are not certain whether the confusion and chaos in economic, social, political, and religious life are causes or effects of the disorder in educational matters. There is agreement on the negative side, namely, that the products of our schools find themselves unable to cope with the problems of life—poverty and unemployment, horrors of war, racial and religious prejudices, crime and correction. Millions of our people have lost that assurance of moral stability which is essential to happiness. In our social life, the refusal to follow the dictates of reason in the natural order and the authority of God in the supernatural order has subjected individuals to the tyranny of license or the whim of caprice. Economic stability has become an end, not a means to an end, and this inverted pyramid has resulted in the inversion of all other values. At any other time this confession of weakness might have been a good sign but today it is a tragic admission of defeat. Since educators refuse to come to grips with fundamental problems they at least find vicarious satisfaction in talking platonically about truth while fearful of touching it. Facts are piled high upon facts with no attempt at an interpretation in the light of absolutes. Such interpretation is termed "authoritarianism" and roundly condemned with totalitarianism. What the moderns fail to see is that unless education be rectified at all levels by the final goal and subjected to the ends of psychology and ethics, then it is an end in itself and must use its subjects as means which is the tragic error of all forms of totalitarianism.

While there is general agreement on the negative aspects and results of American education there is general non-agreement on the positive steps which are necessary to remedy present evils. Indeed the reformer attitude of mind engenders suspicion and enmity. It frequently rests on a subjective bias, closing its eyes to objective reality in its unrestrained passion for axe-grinding. It is not our intention, in these reflections, to impose statements in the mad desire to club minds into an acceptance of them, but rather to show forth the objective set of truths of one who mirrored in his teachings the great central problem of all time, the relation of man to God. The vigor and exhilarating freshness of his principles must always appeal to open minds.

II. THE FOUR CAUSES OF EDUCATION

It should be clear that no sweeping claim is made that Thomas Aquinas developed a closed system of pedagogy which should be taken over by modern educators. His scientific observations and methods bear the limitations of the age in which he lived. Educational psychology and methods of teaching have developed side by side with the great technological and scientific advancement of the centuries. Thomas Aquinas wrote no "ex professo" work on the philosophy of education but in another sense it may be said he wrote nothing but a philosophy of education. His philosophical and theological system is his science of education. The drawing of the broad outlines of that science is the subject matter of this essay. Aquinas clearly and precisely understood the nature of the educable. Because he had the wide horizons of faith to further his vision he wrote not about an ideal type of man but of man as he actually exists, destined for eternal happiness, created according to the image of God, fallen from grace by original sin, redeemed by Christ, and laboring now in this world for the reintegration of his personality by building within himself good habits. The unity of any science, says Aquinas, is derived not from its material object but from the formal aspect under which the material object is considered.[1] This formal object is man, perfected and consequently educated by the complete development of his natural and supernatural faculties. Integration of personality for complete and wholesome living is then attained by the cultivation of the intellectual and moral virtues. To separate subjective development from objective truth would result in abortive intellectual culture and so under the formal object of education are found the objective truths which constitute for Aquinas the first essential element in his philosophy of education. All the agencies used in instruction—parents, teachers, the Church —form the instrumental efficient cause in education while the personal initiative of the student constitutes the principal efficient cause. Thus, while others may offer instruction, it is the student himself who either advances through discovery or places a barrier to the work of instruction by a passivity which disintegrates faculties rather than develops them. The *terminus ad quem* of all education is wisdom, natural and supernatural. From this goal education derives the power to bear fruit since in every movement the end is of more account than the beginning.[2] Wisdom places us on the heights, lifting us up from facts which stifle to truth which makes us free.

In the exposition of these four causes of education stress will be placed on the material and formal aspects; for once these are recognized, the efficient and final aspects fall into their obvious place in the entire hierarchy of Thomistic education. Moreover, this treatment is envisaged as being of particular help to the student; for once he has grasped the significance of his own nature in relation to the purpose of education, his eagerness for knowledge tempered by docility will be a spur to instructors to make themselves the best possible instruments administering to the needs of students.

III. THE MATERIAL CAUSE OF EDUCATION

The vital problem in education is man himself. The history of philosophy shows that in the solution of this problem the pendulum has swung in opposite directions. Some philosophers have concentrated on man himself until the focus of his place in society and his relationship with God were blurred; or they have emphasized environment to the neglect of man himself. Some have thought of mass improvement exclusively; while others, intent upon themselves, have denied the right of each human being to strive in freedom and under reasonable human conditions for his own perfection —individual, religious, economic and social. Both of these extremes meet on common ground in departing from the essential fact of the dignity of the individual human being. To those submerged in the conviction that man is a pawn in the hands of any society, no matter how praiseworthy that society may be, Thomistic philosophy is firmly opposed. It is just as strongly opposed to the excesses of *laissez-faire* individualism. Both have forgotten the human way of looking at man. An honest effort to know the nature of man will bring together the truths in both positions. We readily admit that a healthy outlook produces sanity but in order to know the source from which the outlook proceeds introspection is necessary.

Things have specifically different activities because they have specifically different natures.[3] From the observations of his own activity, his accomplishments, his reflections, man is gradually led to an understanding of his nature. It takes no mental acrobatics to perceive that man has both material and spiritual activities. In common with plants, he is distinguished from non-living substances by the functions of nutrition, assimilation, growth and reproduction. Like other animals, he is superior to mere vegetative life by his powers of sensation. He is marked off from brute animals by his ability to reason.[4] Man is not a duality but a unity, a unity effected by the rational soul being the source of all his activity. He is not an animal with a rational soul superadded like the superstructure of a house, any more than an animal is a plant with sensation added to it. Nor is man a mixture of elements gathered from the terrestrial kingdom, but a distinct type of being whose inner life is spiritual although manifested materially.[5]

In virtue of his ability to attain truth he rises to a conception of God, to ideals of virtue, to a consciousness of right and wrong. He knows that he has a spiritual soul as the principle of all his activity for he knows material things in an immaterial way. The conflict that takes place between the material and spiritual part of human nature does not doom man to inactivity but rather gives greater zest to accomplish things since the solution of the conflict is likewise found within his spiritual nature. It is possible for man to perfect himself through the development of his potentialities because of the freedom that is his. Because the universal good is all embracing, lesser goods can never force him.[6] Hopes and dreams are more than things that can be mixed in a test-tube. The engine of an automobile may react to the pressure of a foot on the self-starter but stimulus and response will never satisfactorily explain human activity. Educability is a gift from above rather than the largesse of the society in which man lives. It is the consciousness of free will which informs man that the steps he takes to grasp the objects of desire placed before him are his own steps, deliberately placed and deliberately planned.[7] As the circle is the perfect mathematical figure, so too man perfects his stature when he enscribes the circle that begins from God and ends with God.

Freedom immediately implies responsibility and morality. For Aquinas morality was a necessary consequence of humanity based on the fact that we can mould our lives and carve out our eternal destiny by our actions. There can be no question then of relativism in morals, for humanity is not something we can accept or reject. The only foundation for moral actions is the

The Thomistic Concept of Education

God who made human nature. The freedom which underlies morality is not an end but a means to an end. To be properly exercised it must place itself under the authority of reason. This authority is precisely the stumbling block for contemporary educators. In refusing to accept it they refuse the demands of the nature that is theirs. The First Cause of all reality put it into the nature of snow to melt in the presence of fire, and into the natures of hydrogen and oxygen to form water when chemically combined; so too He put it into the nature of man to be guided by reason even as animals are led on by instinct. Laws that govern the physical, plant and animal worlds are called natural laws. The law by which man follows his natural inclinations under the guiding light of reason, acting as an X-ray bringing into relief the goal of life or happiness, is called the natural moral law. To will the execution of those inclinations which reason reveals as leading us to happiness is to act morally; to will otherwise is to act immorally. St. Thomas could never have any antipathy to laws because he realized they were not restraints on our freedom but directive guides helping us to be human.[8]

This consideration of human nature leaves a gap that reason cannot fill. Man was made for life, for truth, for love, but is always finding death, error, and hatred to thwart his happiness. It is here that revelation bridges the gap; for God has spoken and told us that our natures have been elevated to a supernatural state, with eternal happiness and not a mere earthly bliss as our goal. The yearning towards a higher life is made possible by grace. The Catholic picture of Adam, the first man, is a denial of all mental evolutionism, for wealth of intellectual gifts and splendour of will were his; the decline began with sin.[9] Yet God through Redemption remade man. This has been done without yielding that justice which was due both to God and to sinful man; infinite mercy has been given, infinite love has been outpoured and infinite justice has been satisfied. Redemption raised man once more to the supernatural state and eternal happiness is again possible of attainment. In making man one with Christ, a member of that body of which He is the Head, man now has the life which flows through that body from the Head.[10] Because men are branches united to the vine they know that peace and harmony can exist in the world; that nations can link themselves together for the progress of humanity; that individuals can advance in knowledge and wisdom—but the grace of God is the condition. Because men reject His grace, jealousy, war, race-hatred, and the host of things which disintegrate man are the order of the day.

This then is the Christian picture of man which St. Thomas Aquinas accepts as the material cause of education. His philosophy of education insists on supernatural integration as the complement and perfection of natural integration. It was precisely because he was a theologian and not merely a philosopher that Aquinas could present a true and integral theory of education. If education is the development of the potentialities of the student in relation to the whole meaning of life, how can educators neglect the nature of man as constituted by the Creator, and still claim the right to present theories of education! Their attempts, no matter how honest, can be nothing but feeble understatements; their so-called facts are out of tune with reality; their conclusions nothing but hypotheses whose validity has been challenged by God Himself. Spiritual natures which should be developed in classrooms of the nation have been forgotten while educators have been rooting in the soil of materialism for the husks they may find.

IV. THE FORMAL CAUSE OF EDUCATION

A. The First Essential Element for an Educated Man— Objective Truth

Thomistic education comprises two essential elements, the metaphysical and the psychological; or, in simpler language, education is concerned with objective truth and subjective development. Man in attaining this objective truth must be prepared not only for *learning* but also for *living*. The end of learning is the attainment of the intellectual habits or virtues; development for living demands the building in of the moral habits. The truly educated man will possess both objective truth and the twofold subjective development. To separate them, or to stress education for living while ignoring the intellectual virtues required for learning, has resulted in much of our present-day educational quackery. A mere knowledge of facts and things offers no genuine contribution to learning, to living, or to the attitude towards life as a whole which education should impart. Even vocational education, to be really considered education, should help integrate the student's life so as to enable him to see his work in relation to other types of work and to life. The more vicious error is that which insists on scholarship as an end in itself. Scholarship is good only for a mind that seeks to know the totality of all things.

The horizon of education is limited only by the plasticity of the mind of man to attain being. If one would be a lover of wisdom, which is the end of education, the entire range of being is the field of his work. Moreover, since order is necessary for a proper knowledge of things, a hierarchy must be established which sets forth the relation of one known thing to another. Into this hierarchy must be incorporated scientific observations and individual facts. It is when facts become unified in a body of truth that they have significance in respect to the whole. The essential order demanded by wisdom is unity in multiplicity, for partial knowledge is not true knowledge either of the whole or of the part. For Thomas Aquinas certain definite truths, whose broad outlines embrace the totality of being, constitute the first essential element in the philosophy of education. These truths are:

1. *Objectivity of human thought.* The intelligible species, the subjective impressions and determinations of our intellect, are not the direct objects of thought. They are the means by which the mind is led to a direct knowledge of objective reality. What we know first of all is the external object of which the species is a mental sign.[11] In the relation of the content of our act of thought to reality consists the truth of our knowledge. This character of truth does not presuppose a mechanical similarity between the manner of knowing and the manner of being of the object.[12] While knowledge is derived from experience, the intellect knows things according to its own nature.[13]

2. *The meaning of being.* That which our intellect attains primarily and into which it resolves all its concepts is being. It is necessary that we acquire all other concepts by addition to being. While knowledge is a science of things, intellectual knowledge penetrates the essence of things and implies a grasp of the very reason of being in things.[14] Being would not be attained by knowing if knowing did not already belong to being. Therefore the most perfect and intimate way of possessing a thing is by knowing it.[15]

3. *The Source of being.* Since created things partake of being they have their source in that Being whose essence is His existence.[16] Human thought is led as by a magnet toward Supreme Being, for God is the First Mover in the order of knowledge just as He is the First Cause in the order of being.[17] The object of knowledge is to arrange the parts of the world in perfect unity, estimate their relative values and unite them to Absolute Being. If there are things for the mind to know, it is in virtue of the conformity of beings with the Divine Intellect.[18] In other words, created truth is ordered towards Being, which is its End and Source, since by Being alone it exists and is perfected.

4. *The reality of supernatural truth.* Things are because God is. Knowing this from reason, there is yet a desire to penetrate into the inner life of God, and here philosophy is brought to a standstill. God's promise, however, is that our truth will be perfected by His Truth. In the philosophy of St. Thomas there is ample room left for the insertion of a divine gift which brings the intellect to the highest perfection of which it is capable.[19] Since the intellect is capable, in a finite way, of total intelligibility if God bestows this gift, Aquinas opens the door leading to the wide reaches of the supernatural. Curiosity and presumption are tempered by Revelation which likewise modifies the life of the educated man so that his mind will bring into focus the whole range of being.[20] Our extension in being is measured not

by the narrow limits of our person but by the vision of eternal truths. Whereas the intellect of God is a measure and not a thing measured, the human intellect is a thing measured, measured first of all by God who gives it the first principles of the speculative and practical order; and secondly by things, for the intellect does not give truth and goodness to things.[21]

5. *Self-evident first principles.* In the interpretation of life and the universe as a totality, in the harmonizing of individual facts, in the unification of knowledge, the process of education demands the constant application and flowering of metaphysical principles. These principles must not only be known in a vague impractical way but must be accepted and lived. There pre-exist in us certain seeds of knowledge, first principles, which one immediately knows, once the intellect contacts reality.[22] St. Thomas enumerates, besides the primary notion of being, the principles of contradiction, identity, sufficient reason and causality.

a) Intellectual grasp of being is included in every thought. From this grasp of being may be formulated the first indemonstrable principle, that one cannot at once both affirm and deny the same thing. This principle rests on the concept of being and non-being and metaphysically is the primary basis of all other principles.[23] Since our primary intellectual cognition is of being, in knowing it we know its identity with itself and the impossibility of its being the contradictory. This principle establishes an anchor of truth assuring us of the truth or falsity of any proposition by analyzing the connection of the proposition with the first principles which immediately express the notion of being. Such an analysis or analytic resolution into the primary principles must be the test of the truth of any judgment.

b) Since, apart from being, nothing is knowable or intelligible, the first judgment in the ontological order must be an affirmation of the principle of identity. Because there cannot be an infinite regress in a series of concepts, therefore the first most simple and universal judgment must have being for its subject and that which primarily belongs to being for its predicate.[24] The principle of permanence or substance directly follows upon this principle of identity. Beneath all forms of change or movement there is a permanent and immobile element. It is this element which is being properly speaking because it *is*; for being is predicated of substance primarily and absolutely. From multiplicity the mind passes to unity; the changing and passing are only understood in terms of the permanent and lasting.

c) Everything must have a sufficient reason for its existence and essence either in itself or in another: in itself, if what belongs to it is of its own intrinsic constitution; in another, if what belongs to it does not pertain to its essential constitution. Contingent, caused beings must then have the sufficient reason of their being in something outside of themselves.[25]

d) This principle of sufficient reason is the basis for efficient and final causality. Efficient causality is directly perceived by the intelligence upon the presentation of an object. Since the end is the reason of being of the means, the principle of finality likewise has its basis in that of sufficient reason. That every agent acts for an end is shown by St. Thomas from his observation that otherwise one thing would not follow from the action of an agent more than another, unless it were by chance.[26] The acceptance of these principles is a necessary condition for the discovery of truth. If they are ignored nothing can be known and the entire purpose of education is frustrated. In Thomistic pedagogy, knowledge is acquired when the mind is led from things to principles and back to things again.[27] These principles are not the homespun inventions of an armchair philosopher but postulates of reality formulated by the intellect because it is constituted to know reality. The human intellect must be measured by the standard of reality for it is not the source of truth. Only by rigid adherence to things as they are can the mind possess truth. In the integration of his knowledge, the philosopher, the wise man, obeys the demands of order. He perceives that the objective order imposed on man is in a general way the order of the nature of things with their respective laws, the order of truth, and the order of the supernatural life. This order flows from the Wisdom of the Maker of all things. It is proposed as a demand of his nature by being expressed in his reason. When objective truth brings the intellect of man to a contemplation of things in relation to the First Cause and Last End of all reality, then that man is being educated. In other words, when a man contemplates the highest causes of things, when all particular knowledge is assimilated in this light, when the consideration of truth is recognized as the chief occupation of a learned person, then in Thomistic philosophy is fulfilled the first essential requirement for an educated man. As Thomas Aquinas expressed it: Love of knowledge is the penetration of truth, not of any truth, but of that truth which is the Source of all truth, of that which relates to the First Being of all things; wherefore Its Truth is the First Principle of all truth, since the disposition of things is the same truth as in being.[28]

B. The Second Essential Element for an Educated Man— Subjective Development

1. *Subjective development for learning:* The wisdom which is the truth of contemplating objective reality as springing from the Source of all being cannot be poured into the human mind. God gives man potentialities which must be developed by self-activity. This activity can be either by way of discovery and penetration or by way of instruction. St. Thomas has four

statements to support this conclusion: (1) A being that can form a habit through its own agency is self-active. (2) A being that has a potentiality to be actualized is plastic. (3) A being that can retain its self-acquired habits can form a character. (4) A being that can integrate its character with reality is educable.[29] By polishing, rust is removed and the brightness of the metal made manifest; education is *not* such a process whereby knowledge is drawn from a hidden state into consciousness. Self-activity, for Aquinas, is the abstraction of meanings from things; the potentiality to learn pre-exists as a natural tendency but is brought to maturity by the activity of the agent. The mind feeding on being leads to learning. Knowledge, then, is conditioned by the subject conceiving it; and while it has objective antecedents and is itself objective, it is equally subjective, understood in this Thomistic sense of self-activity. The extremes of idealism and subjectivism were avoided by Aquinas who maintained that the subject or a modification of the subject is not everything; for knowledge implies objective data becoming subjective in the sense that subject and object, in the act of knowing, form a synthesis. There is between them a relationship in being, for it is universally true that knowledge is the return of being on itself.[30]

The process of education, from the viewpoint of subjective development, means that the student develops habits consistent with his rational nature. These will be the intellectual and moral virtues. The reason for this building in of habits should be clear. All action is directed to the attainment of perfection, and the progress of this perfection must be in accordance with human nature—it must follow reason.[31] In order to make reasonable activity enjoy the air of ease and freedom, reason develops certain habits which are determinants of the faculty and aid the faculty to operate with ease and facility.[32] As a determination or modification of man, informing the powers of his nature, habit is not a passing quality but one difficult to uproot; it becomes second nature by deliberate, conscious and repeated effort. In developing habits, pre-existing forces are harnessed and perfected; they are not created.[33] Inborn capacities have been given with the nature; reason organizes them into a definite pattern and makes man master in his own house. This influence of reason ought to be extended to the entire domain of human life. It follows, then, that there ought to be as many habits as there are functions in man, because habit is the stamp of reason on human activities.[34] The truly educated man will be the one with the most fully developed habits, not only because man's human faculties are perfected in proportion to the possession of habitual principles of operation, but also because he is then guided by reason with efficiency and consistency.[35]

The habits of intellect are the intellectual virtues. Reason, perfected by these virtues, is distinguished by Aquinas into speculative and practical.[36] The method of operation here is the same; but the starting point of speculative reason is the form or essence of a thing, whereas practical reason has its beginning from the end intended. The difference is a difference of object. The speculative intellect is concerned with the truth of things; the practical intellect not only knows things but causes them. The habits perfecting the speculative intellect are understanding, science and wisdom; those perfecting the practical intellect are art and prudence.[37] When reason sets its stamp on human nature it disciplines the intuitive (understanding), analytic (knowledge), and synthetic (wisdom) functions of the mind.

a) *Understanding.* This habit perfects the speculative intellect in its grasp of first principles. It assures that relationship between the intellect and the whole of reality which constitutes a necessary element in educability. St. Thomas classifies this habit among those natural habits possessed by man which owe their existence, partly to nature and partly to some extrinsic principle. It is because of the nature of his intellectual soul that man, having once grasped what is a whole and what is a part, perceives immediately that every whole is larger than its part. Yet what is a whole and what is a part cannot be known except through the intelligible species which is received from phantasms. In respect to the individual nature this habit is natural as to its beginning, and one man from the disposition of his organs of sense may be more apt to understand than another. This habit enables man to penetrate to the meaning of first principles, an elementary step if later he would apply these principles.[38]

b) *Knowledge.* Though man possesses the power of grasping some truths immediately, his proper operation is reasoning—the movement from known to unknown truth. The reasoning process begins with an act of intellection, the immediate grasp of a principle, and ends with another simple act, an analysis by which the nature of the object is known. The habit which perfects the intellect in its conclusions is the intellectual virtue of science or knowledge. Like all the intellectual virtues it has truth for its object. The truth it seeks is that which can be deduced from principles furnished by the virtue of understanding. It is a detailed knowledge which enables each section of a scientific field to be investigated. Progress in this habit is attained by the application of principles to deeper levels of reality. This habit operates along particular lines and results in the various sciences, the science of chemistry, of astronomy, the social sciences, etc.[39]

c) *Wisdom.* Knowledge, like facts, can be disorderly. The work of the habit of wisdom is to supply order and harmony. It never rests with immediate truth as knowledge does, but always seeks the ultimate, the last truth. If being is the beginning of man's speculation it is also the end. The synthetic, comprehensive vision of the whole of reality is made possible by wisdom. It completes knowledge and understanding. It contemplates the First Cause, for it is never satisfied to take a principle from some other science. From its vantage point it sees the relation of one truth to another and the relation of all truths, of all the sciences to the last truth. When this wisdom treats primarily of divine things it is called theology; when it deals with human truths it is called first philosophy or metaphysics. In either case it is the supreme speculative virtue perfecting human life in its quest for truth. All the fundamental questions tugging at the mind of man as to his origin, nature and purpose; all the puzzles presented by the universe in which we live; all the hopes and ideals of men and women of this universe receive their answer and fruition in this virtue. The desire for God, for happiness, for peace is explained by wisdom. With its keen vision it guards the hierarchy of values, for it is interested in the truth of things and not in mere things.[40] In education it imparts formation as well as information; or viewed in another way, it is the fruit of good education and by its fruit education may be judged.

Thomistic education demands the presence of intellectual virtues not only for speculation but also for the perfection of activity. The operations of man that have to do with things to be made (*factibilia*) differ from those that concern things to be done (*agibilia*); and so two habits are necessary to perfect these different acts, art perfecting man as a maker, prudence giving direction to his human actions.

d) *Art* is the determination of reason by which external actions attain a due end through determined means. It is concerned with products distinct from the agent who makes them. As contributing to the perfection of the *whole* man in relation to totality, art is the imprinting of an artist not only on the masterpiece of his own life but also on the canvas of the world. Since its true sphere is the discovery of means to attain its own end, art produces the things necessary for man's perfection.[41] If the artist, either in the useful or fine arts, fails in his ordination of means to an end then he does not possess the habit of art. This statement has profound significance in the field of education wherein the arts contribute greatly to the perfection of the educable.

e) *Prudence.* Art has its social and individual values. It has, however, nothing to do with making man good, for man is truly good only when he is morally good. Morality is in the domain of reason which is directed in the attainment of moral perfection by the habit of prudence. Education, to fulfill its purpose, must perfect man. But man is perfected when the life of virtue is in full bloom and made operative by the habit of prudence. There can be no moral virtues without prudence nor prudence without moral virtues.[42]

The Thomistic Concept of Education

The explanation of this important Thomistic doctrine will likewise be the explanation of the subjective development of the educated, the perfect man. The relation of prudence to good living is the nexus between the subjective development of man for learning and the same development for living the good life. Theoretically, the other four intellectual virtues may be had by one who fails to look upon the true goals of education, but for the proper attainment of the real end of education, prudence is of absolute necessity. Metaphysics, first philosophy or wisdom is architectonic in the speculative order; prudence in the practical order.

2. *Subjective development for living:* Thomistic philosophy of education is not satisfied with imparting intellectual culture or scholarship. It insists on something more—the inculcating of sound and solid principles of morality. In a rightly ordered system of knowledge, moral factors can never be neglected, much less ignored. Every phase of human life, precisely because it is human, has moral issues intimately linked to it. The field of education is no exception, for the true atmosphere of knowledge must be a unity based on the nature and destiny of the educable. Schooling is essential in the practice of moral virtues as well as in the exercise of the principles of knowledge. Intellectual achievements and scientific accomplishments alone can never integrate the whole man. In the teaching of Aquinas the student must be prepared for living and consequently the intellectual virtues are inadequate. Reason is the first principle of human action, yet its command is not tyrannical but political. Rebellion is always a possibility and that is why the appetites of man need habits by which they are subjected to the rule of reason. The orientation of the educable to the right goal is the work of these moral virtues. Yet the knowledge that the will and lower appetites must be kept within bounds is not sufficient to guarantee the exercise of the life of virtue. A man may know that the moral virtues must not exceed the mean or rule of reason, but it is not always easy to determine the boundary line of excess or defect. This is the work of the counsel, judgment and command of prudence.[43] Balance and sanity are given to life by the acts of counsel: remembrance of the past, courage for the present, shrewdness in estimating future events, comparison of data received, and docility to the opinion of others, particularly the great teachers of tradition. When this process has been accomplished, reason makes a final judgment on the suitability of a definite series of means which are chosen by the will. The final and principal act is the command of prudence which marshalls all the faculties of man for the performance of an act. As an act of the intellect it intimates to each faculty its particular duty and ordains each to the end of operation. Whereas prudence is a requirement for learning, it is evident how necessary it is for living, with the moral virtues as necessary complements.

The right intention as regards the end is the definite work of these moral virtues; the right attitude towards the means is the concern of prudence. For the *whole* man (the subject of education) to function smoothly, abilities and energies must be harmoniously balanced. This is the keynote of integration—subordination of sense life to reason and reason to God. This balance was once man's gift from his Creator; it must be effected now by the moral virtues with prudence as a lever, for there can be no prudence if the appetitive faculties are bent on obtaining an irrational end; but the appetitive faculties cannot attain their rational end without prudence.[44]

For the sake of brevity we must limit our treatment of these moral virtues to the root habits to which the others may be reduced. Aquinas made a distinct contribution to the philosophy of education in remarking that while the intellectual virtues are incomplete (because they perfect only a faculty of man), the moral virtues are committed to the task of making the whole man good. In the intellectual appetite they balance and regulate the actions of man by the rule of reason; in the sensitive appetite they conform the passions to the rule of reason.

Education for living consists in conforming the whole man to the order of reason. Order can exist in reason itself (the habit of prudence); or it is imposed on actions (the habit of justice); or it regulates the passions either because they impel a man to things contrary to reason (temperance) or withdraw him from what reason dictates (fortitude). There is then a fourfold subject of the moral virtues: the reason for prudence, the will for justice, the concupiscible appetite for temperance and the irascible appetite for fortitude.[45] When the sources of human activity are perfected then the whole man is integrated; personality is integrated in proportion as the educable grows in virtue. Disintegration is caused by the free play of appetites and represents a conflict with the fundamental ordinations of the rational appetite. But once this conflict of reason and appetite is placed under the constant extension and strengthening of the command of reason, education is taking place.

It can be readily seen that the philosophy of education of Thomas Aquinas deals with fundamentals. It insists that truth can be had only by the constant, persistent labor of the human mind making an objective trek into the world of reality. Only then can the intellect hope to penetrate into the heart of things that are proposed to it (understanding), acquire an accurate judgment about creatures (knowledge), and avoid making mistakes about the vital purposes of human living by synthesizing every created reality in the light of the Universal Cause (wisdom). These habits, with wisdom as their crown, are the safeguards of education protecting not only students but teachers also from laziness, stupidity and ignorance. But this is not enough!

Mere intellectual perspicacity can stifle human life and carry with it the danger of lopsidedness. Good mathematicians, good philosophers, good engineers need also to be good men. True learning must be carried over to the more important field of good living, and education must deal with both. The end product in the life of the educated man is, in the language of Aquinas, peace, the tranquillity of order. This demands that the whole life of man be brought under the sway of reason and that the whole of reality be classified and ordered in relation to the First Cause. It is this type of wisdom which makes for peace and removes the causes of civil war within man. Dissension, either in the appetites or between the appetites and reality results in a discordant clash destroying peace and making education impossible. The great educational sin of contemporary civilization is the blindness of positivism which refuses to consider imponderables because they defy the slide-rule and the alembic.

V. THE FINAL CAUSE OF EDUCATION

All of this natural consideration of education will never integrate man as created by God; for, since man has been raised to the supernatural life with a supernatural goal, Catholic philosophy of education must insist on supernatural integration. That is why St. Thomas, in his science of education, placed the intellectual and moral virtues as basic virtues which must be crowned by the infused moral and theological virtues. These latter are not within the competence of the philosopher but it was because Aquinas was a theologian as well as a philosopher that he gave us a true and integral theory of education that neither denies anything to man nor assumes too much for him. A thing is perfect when it returns to its source; so all creatures must find their way back to God, the Source of their supernatural life.[46]

We can now view the entire structure of educational integration as outlined by St. Thomas. Objective reality and the possibility of the mind attaining it, plus the nature and destiny of the educable, are presuppositions to education. Learning in relation to the intellect viewed in its theoretic function demands the acquisition of the habits of understanding, knowledge and wisdom; in its practical working it needs the habits of art and prudence. Education for living requires prudence in the reason and justice perfecting the will. The appetites need the steadying influence of temperance and fortitude with the auxiliary habits of generosity, magnanimity, honor, meekness, docility, eagerness for truth, assiduous application and recreation. This last provides not only for physical well being but also for emotional stability. Finally, the infused moral virtues conform man to his divine model and supernatural integration brings faith to the intellect, hope and charity to the will. Thus is man made capable of his high destiny. This is the Thomistic notion of the modern phrase "integration of personality." Only when that last destiny has been forever determined will man be fully educated; for the process is something limited not merely to the classroom but lasts as long as life. In simple language, sanctity is the final cause in education.

VI. THE EFFICIENT CAUSE OF EDUCATION

1. The teacher, in the rôle of instrumental efficient cause, ministers to the process of learning as self-activity by supplying the material and tools which aid the student in passing from potentiality to actuality. The student cannot spin knowledge out of his own head, for the price paid for plasticity of mind is that one cannot teach himself but one can learn. In the eleventh question of his *De Veritate*, St. Thomas admits a twofold development of this potentiality when he distinguishes between active and passive potentiality. In active potentiality the intrinsic principle is capable of arriving at perfect actuality and the extrinsic agent assists as an instrument by offering aids and helps; in passive potentiality the extrinsic agent does the principal work. In applying this to the acquisition of knowledge Aquinas notes that there pre-exist in the student potentialities of knowledge, namely, the first concepts of the intellect which are generated immediately, once the light of the active intellect has abstracted its intelligible species from sense presentations. From these universal principles all principles follow as from germinal capacities. When one is led to know particular things in actuality which heretofore were known potentially, then one acquires knowledge. Knowledge therefore is in the learner not in purely passive potentiality but in active potentiality, for otherwise man by himself could never achieve knowledge. The analogy of healing in sickness is applied to the theory of education in the following manner. Just as a person may be cured through the operation of nature alone or through nature with the aid of medicine, so there is a twofold manner of acquiring knowledge: (1) when the natural reason of itself comes to a knowledge of the unknown, and this is called *discovery*; (2) when someone extrinsically supplies aid to the natural reason, and this is called *instruction*. Pertinent advice is given to the teacher in these words of Aquinas: "In those things which are done by nature and art, art works in the same way and by the same means as nature does; for just as nature in one suffering from a cold induces health by warming him, so does the doctor."[47] In education this means that the teacher leads the student to knowledge of the unknown in the same way as the student would lead himself to a knowledge of the unknown by discovery. In discovery there must be the application of general, self-evident principles to definite matters and proceeding thence to particular conclusions. The teacher then can instruct when he proposes to the student, by means of symbols, the discursive process

which he himself goes through by natural reason; and thus the reason of the student comes to a knowledge of the unknown through the aid of what is proposed to him.

Psychologically the teacher must stimulate the student by presenting problems in such a way as to arouse the interest of the beginner. This is merely the approach to teaching, for the real art is expressed by the organization and integration of the concepts presented. This integration will reflect the teacher's philosophy of life. In Catholic education there is complete unity between theory and practice by reason of the unity of Catholic philosophy of life. The method then is of utmost importance and for all practical purposes this means for the teacher: (1) perfection of his own knowledge and virtue, natural and supernatural; (2) presentation of the problems of the various disciplines in hierarchical order and their relation to God for the twofold purpose of arousing psychological interest and of transmitting scientific and philosophical content; (3) integration of knowledge in each subject, which means placing each intellectual perfection in its objective category and showing its rôle in the Catholic philosophy of life; (4) cultivation of true freedom by protecting the student from contrary influences and insisting on the truths of reason and revelation which make men free.

2. The *student* as the principal efficient cause in education (under God who is the principal cause in the primary order of all things) depends on things outside himself—the orderly universe, the great books of all ages, divine revelation, and the instruction of mentors. The student has the right and duty to perfect all his faculties both in the natural and supernatural order. It is his task to develop himself not only as an individual but as a member of society. As an individual he must perfect the potentialities of his soul and of his body. The potentialities of his intellect must be trained for the investigation and possession of truth, for the direction of human activity in the moral order, and for the production of human works by developing the practical habit of art which produces skill and appreciation in both the useful and fine arts. The will must be stimulated in its operations to act in conformity with the hierarchy of values. The body must be trained not as a thing in itself but as giving perfection to the whole man. This is accomplished by the discipline of sports, recreation, refinement of the senses by exercise of the powers of observation, memory and imagination, and by the perfection of the sensitive appetites by their moderation. As a citizen the student benefits from society by the opportunities of peace and protection as well as by the direction which society gives him. He must contribute to society by inculcating a regard for his fellowmen, respect, honor, and obedience for his parents, his country, his superiors. This can be done when he

has made himself, through discipline, prudent, just, self-controlled and courageous.

VII. RÉSUMÉ

It can be readily seen that Christian education takes in the whole aggregate of human life—physical and spiritual, intellectual and moral, individual and social—not with a view of reducing it, as St. Thomas says, but in order to elevate, regulate and perfect it. The great encyclical letter of Pope Pius XI on *The Christian Education of Youth* sums up these teachings of Aquinas when it says: "The true Christian product of education is the supernatural man who thinks, judges, and acts constantly and consistently in accordance with right reason illumined by the supernatural light of the example and teaching of Christ; in other words, to use the current term, the true and finished man of character. For, it is not every kind of firmness and consistency of conduct based on subjective principles that makes true character, but only constancy in following the eternal principles of justice. The scope and aim of Christian education, as here described, appears to the worldly as an abstraction, or rather as something that cannot be attained without the suppression of dwarfing of the natural faculties and without a renunciation of the activities of the present life, and hence inimical to social life and temporal prosperity, and contrary to all progress in letters, arts and sciences, and all the other elements of civilization. . . . The true Christian does not renounce the activities of this life, he does not stunt his natural faculties; but he develops them and perfects them, by co-ordinating them with the supernatural. He thus ennobles what is merely natural in life and secures for it new strength in the material and temporal order, no less than in the spiritual and eternal."[48]

Positivistic educators by their misuse of education have been leading students steadily and surely toward the pit of spiritual and cultural dissolution. When students become indifferent to the real dignity of being men they begin to think that saving their physical existence means saving their humanity. When they grow indifferent to truth they are open targets for the shattering gunfire of propaganda and emotionalism. When spiritual values are rejected because they do not have pragmatic validity then life becomes a mad scramble to worship lesser man-made gods. When the final goal of life ceases to be the center around which hopes and desires revolve, people grow weary of being human and think they can shake off their humanity. The cult of self-made man, the debasing teachings of naturalism, the tragic rejection of man's submission to God, the false humanism closing the avenues leading to the joy of human living, the glorification of method to content, the premium placed on research at the expense of the sparkling vitality of teaching, the neglect of philosophy and theology—these are but natural consequences of any philosophy of life that has forgotten the real nature of man. If education is the progressive development of the potentialities of man in relation to the whole meaning of life, how can teachers ignore the things that really matter and still lay claim to teaching! Sociology divorced from ethics, psychology from the spiritual soul of man, science from the Supreme Cause of all reality, economics from morals, politics from human nature—these and other similar divorces are disintegrating that creature of God called man.

The field of Thomistic education is much wider than any classroom. It reaches out to the home, to the Church, to occupational groups, to any and every agency which influences men and women. It can never be restricted to any particular period of a person's life but encompasses the whole of life. It is the work not merely of the professional teacher but also of the preacher, the lecturer, parents, employers and all those who have guidance over others. In formal education the great responsibility is on the teachers. Only when the pulsating throbs of Christian Thomistic truths and objectives motivate their work can they be said to fulfill their task as educators. When educational institutions not only reaffirm their devotion to truth but also reorganize their curricula so as to impart truth, they will be the strongest bulwark of a nation dedicated to the rights of all to "life, liberty and the pursuit of happiness."

Fifteenth Essay

THE PERENNIAL THEME OF
BEAUTY AND ART

by

Emmanuel Chapman

The Perennial Theme of Beauty and Art

S T THOMAS, fortunately, did not leave any special treatises on aesthetics. These were to come much later as a kind of dessert to top the supposedly all-inclusive philosophical systems from which beauty had somehow escaped; or as psychological or even experimental *pièces de résistance* which were to serve as substitutes after such fare had spoiled men's philosophical appetite. It would have been surprising had St. Thomas dealt specially with the beautiful, which for him was not a special category restricted to the fine arts or any other, but a transcendental common to every being, as common as unity, truth, good and the other transcendentals, and like them to be found everywhere in all its analogical realizations, if one knows how to discover it by penetrating into the deepest ontological secrets of a being.[1]

No wonder, then, that St. Thomas did not confine his treatment to a separate work, but freely expressed his superabundant reflections on beauty and art in his theological writings, in his philosophical demonstrations of how the beautiful differs from the true and the good and yet is related to them, in his analysis of the psychological functioning of the firm and perfect disposition of the power or *habitus* of art, its logical status, its relations to morality, the contemplative life, etc.[2]

Far from regretting the absence of a special, separate treatise on beauty and art, the Thomist philosopher is challenged to develop further St. Thomas' fecund insights and to give them a more fully elaborated expression in a philosophical body with its own rhythm of growth and way of putting questions, really distinct from the theological matrix in which these truths were unfolded, like so much of his other philosophy, at the much swifter pace of theology. In thus seeking no longer to be carried in the arms of theology, but to walk on its own philosophical legs, Thomist philosophy will be repaying in small part its debt to St. Thomas, who liberated philosophy by keeping distinct but not separate the powers of faith and reason which had sought to devour one another imperialistically before his genius taught them to live together as good neighbors in mutual harmony and benefit, so that both theology and philosophy thus polarized in a creative tension could develop to their fullest scope.

The lasting philosophical truths on the nature of beauty and art abounding in St. Thomas' writings are delivered much too rapidly, as is to be expected from the theological setting in which they make their appearance, for the theologian glances swiftly at the things to which he descends from the heights of God and in the light of which he looks at them. The philosopher pays a different kind of attention to things which are his starting point: he lingers much longer with them, puts other questions to them, listens attentively to all their creaturely articulations and patiently explores them in their own light and in the light of his senses and reason by which he slowly ascends to the Divine heights. The truths of things demand a much slower expression and a different order of presentation in a distinctly philosophical work properly conscious of itself and its method.

The philosophical truth uttered so cryptically by St. Thomas in his theological *Commentary on Divine Names*, ". . . and thus movement and repose are reduced to the causality of the beautiful," along with the other truths in the same highly condensed sentence about the forms of things pertaining to splendor and their order to their end and harmony, are not made to yield all their philosophical consequences in this context, but are touched upon instrumentally, as is proper in a theological work, in describing the self-same, unfailing Divine Beauty, the cause of all that exists, and the beauty of all the participated likenesses made by Him.[3]

In its own philosophical body, the beauty of God would not be a starting-point, but rather a terminus, in establishing the dialectical conception of how the operative power of beauty dynamically resolves the contraries of all movement and repose, as well as other more fundamental ones. Nor would the point of departure be the beauty of works of art only, to which so many of the system-builders of aesthetics have arbitrarily restricted themselves. Neither does the philosopher have to start with the special data obtained through the measuring techniques of empirical aesthetics and psychology, interesting as they sometimes may be, and valuable in their own spheres of investigating empiriologically the metrical aspects of the phenomena in question. These findings at best could only provide illustrations, less significant in the field of aesthetics than those provided by artists themselves sufficiently conscious of their own activity and its products.

An unprejudiced philosopher, like the Thomist, critical enough to be open to all of reality, notwithstanding that such openness has been looked down upon by some of his more sophisticated colleagues as naïve and rating the I.Q. of a twelve-year-old mentality, can start with any movement-repose polarity whatsoever. The point of departure can be any movement and repose in nature or art, within man or outside himself, of light on water, a bird in the air, or the myriad others in nature, of his own cognitive and appetitive powers and their accompanying emotions, or, analogically, that of lines, planes, masses, tones, in the visual and audible arts presenting themselves in space and time. By starting from movement and repose, a most common and obvious fact, yet so difficult to explain philosophically, an understanding can be arrived at of how the beautiful resolves in its own unique way this tension as well as other more basic ones underlying it.

A choice presents itself at this point between two approaches which cannot be simultaneously presented though they are closely interwoven: should an ontological analysis first be given of what essentially constitutes the movement-repose polarity in itself, or should the psychological aspects be considered first? Since being is prior to being known, the ontological approach which is prior by right will be taken for a short way only, before the psychological which is nearer to man and more open to direct introspection.

It might be of interest here to recall St. Thomas' deepened use of the Aristotelian analysis of the motion-rest correlate, to show also how movement and repose necessarily imply each other, and that within each mobile being there is a relative unmoved mover or center of repose, but these will have to be passed over for the sake of more relevant ontological considerations which penetrate still deeper. Unruly movements are temporarily brought into dynamic repose by their proper forms. The insatiable craving, so to speak, of ever restless matter in potency to all forms, can be quieted only by actuality-giving form. Form not only communicates actuality to the matter which it organizes from within by making it to be the kind it is, but acts in other important ways. Form also energizes the tendencies it communicates to a being thus finalized by it whereby the being tends to achieve its good and other perfections by realizing itself more fully in existence, acting upon and along with other beings. The realization of form is often obstructed in nature by the opacity and resistance of matter with its unregulated craving for other forms. Yet to the degree that the proper forms have realized themselves in their matter, or insofar as they have actualized their potentialities, or to the extent that the essences of material beings have realized themselves in existence, these natures have a corresponding degree of beauty.[4] They also have a relative ugliness to the degree that they have not achieved the form or actuality which their natures require. Here, too, as with the transcendentals which are realized analogically in being, that is, proportionately to the subjects in which they are found, a metaphysical drama presents itself. These bifurcated material beings seek to overcome within themselves the gap between their essence and existence, potentiality and actuality, matter and form. They struggle to realize themselves more fully in existence, to achieve more unity, truth, goodness and beauty, while at the same time resisting the pull towards non-being, multiplicity, falsity, evil and ugliness. But even at the successful conclusion of this drama, when these doubly composed actors have achieved all their capacities, the gap will not be completely overcome, and they will still carry, as do the singly composed immaterial beings, this metaphysical brand of the creature which points to the Being whose essence is existence, self-subsisting actuality, indivisible unity, absolute truth, goodness, beauty and all else that He is infinitely.[5]

The foregoing illustrates the danger warned against at the beginning of going much too swiftly, at a theological rather than at a philosophical pace. This will be remedied somewhat in the following unfolding of some of the philosophical themes blended into St. Thomas' staccato but gem-like phrasing of the threefold requirements of the beautiful: *integritas sive perfectio, debita proportio sive consonantia, et iterum claritas.*[6] Integrity or perfection is to be understood not in a moral sense, but in its primary ontological meaning. For St. Thomas, as indeed for any philosopher gifted with a metaphysical intuition of being, the highest perfection of a being is actual existence—the dynamic act exercised inviolably by an essence whereby it stands outside of its causes, infinitely opposed to nothingness. The perfection of existence is likewise the highest integrity a being can have.[7] As the perfection or integrity of existence is expressed proportionately to the subjects which it actualizes, everything will have its proportionate kind of perfection or integrity of existence. If *integritas* is translated as wholeness or completeness, or if its meaning is extended to include unity, then these, too, as well as all the co-transcendentals united in beauty, should be rendered ontologically in their various analogical realizations. A particular torso of Venus, for example, though a fragment, may have the unity, wholeness, completeness, perfection or integrity proper to the nature of a torso, and hence be beautiful to the degree that it possesses these as well as the other co-ingredients of beauty.

To take another example from nature, in order to illustrate further how all the transcendentals distinguished formally by reason but coalescing in a being are realized analogically in the different kinds of subjects in which they are found. The unity or undividedness of a being, for instance—and any of the other transcendentals could serve equally as an illustration—is expressed differently in a human being than in an animal, plant, or mineral being. As this is proportioned to these different kinds of natures, the unity of a human being would be greater than that of the others, as man's nature holds together in unity or undividedly, to illustrate it physically, not only the physico-chemical energies of the mineral, but also those informed by the life of the plant and the sentiency of the animal—all of these energies being interpenetrated in a radically different way with rationality and all that goes with it. Though undivided or one, composite beings are not indivisible, and throughout their existence they must resist the pull toward multiplicity and division. Through his rational form which has a kind of indivisibility, man can acquire an analogical knowledge of the highest kind of unity or undividedness which is absolutely indivisible. Besides these various kinds of substantial unity proportioned to the nature of a being, there are also the different kinds of accidental unity, very real in their own order, the various kinds of moral unity of persons united for different common goods, and also by beauty as St. Thomas points out,[8] the minimal unity of aggregates, and the artificial unity of artifacts made by man's art. How beauty in different ways unites persons, things, and also persons and things, if understood analogically, would avoid the errors of univocal merging with beauty or the other extreme of an equivocal separateness, but the kind of union which should exist between the beholder and the beautiful will be taken up later in its psychological context. These illustrations were introduced simply to bring out the fact that the perfection, integrity, wholeness, completeness, and, by extension, the unity or undividedness of a being, like truth, goodness, beauty and the other transcendental aspects of being, are realized in radically different ways in nature and in art.

Let us proceed with the other pairs of the threefold root of the beautiful which digs so deeply and pushes upward many clusters of meanings. Proportion or harmony are far removed from the superficial meanings usually associated with them of symmetry, assonance and the like. Each being has its due proportion or harmony in so far as its confluent parts are arranged in accordance with its intrinsic end determined by its form. This may require asymmetry or dissonance as well as the more accepted kinds of proportion and harmony. The work of art also has its own end, determined by the art-form which the artist gives its intelligible or sensible matter, and it is important to consider first how the work of art conforms to its own end rather than to that of the beholder. The confluent arrangement of parts in accordance with an end is in a deeper sense the ontological order or good of a thing, for each being realizes its good in so far as it conforms to its intrinsic end or purpose, as well as to the ends or purposes of others. In thus seeking to achieve its end, which is also to achieve its form, each being seeks its good. To the degree that each being is good, that is, desirable, suitable or agreeable to its own nature or essence, conforming to the purpose or end determined by its form, it has its due proportion or harmony.[9]

Claritas, more broadly, is the shining out of all the transcendentals united in the beautiful. More specifically, *claritas* is the intelligible radiance permeating the whole of a being, the splendor of form irradiating it from within, the light of ontological truth, the knowable, adequating it to an intellect.[10] So dazzling in itself as to be blinding to human eyes, *claritas* illuminates the darkness of matter so that material beings may enlighten man's intellect through his senses. If the senses, which are a kind of measure and proportion, know delight in the likeness they find between themselves and the right proportions of beautiful things, how much more does the intellect, which in its conscious assimilation of the likeness of beautiful things intentionally becomes them, identifies itself with their forms which exist in quite a different way in the life of the intellect.[11] The beauty of the splendor of form lighting up the integrity, perfection, proportion, harmony, and their equivalents, of a material being can be enjoyed without abstraction and without the elaboration of concepts, though the latter may be germinally present, by means of a sensible intuition which puts the intelligence, through the senses, in direct contact with it.[12]

That the lapidary *integritas*, *consonantia* and *claritas* articulated so incisively by St. Thomas are not of too high a degree of generality for a creative understanding of beauty may be seen from the influence it has exerted—and is this not a sign of its vitality?—more on artists than on professors of philosophy. Though there are certain crucial differences between a genuinely Thomistic interpretation and the one presented by James Joyce in his novel *A Portrait of the Artist as a Young Man*, what he says there can provide the kind of objections which will help to bring out the truth more sharply.[13] Joyce's depth as an artist made him aware of certain aspects of St. Thomas' aesthetics missed by some of the philosophers, but unfortunately the truths which Joyce the artist saw were often marred by the distortions introduced by Joyce the man, who was often in tragic conflict with the artist in him. (Poor Joyce, who in turning against the Word, spent himself multiplying words demoniacally to recapture the unity he lost, telling and re-telling of the perpetual search of the son for the father!)

In interpreting St. Thomas's three requisites of the beautiful, Stephen Dedalus, who images so perfectly Joyce, his artificer, glimpses certain truths which he obscures and combines in the wrong way. It is not surprising that the existential meanings of the requirements of the beautiful are missed altogether. Nor is there any fundamental objection to Stephen extending the meaning of *integritas*, which he translates as wholeness, to unity: "You apprehended it as one thing. You see it as one whole. You apprehend its wholeness. That is integritas." In explaining this one thing as self-bound and self-contained, as distinct from other things, though he may not have been aware of it, Joyce is really touching upon the transcendental *aliquid* rather than *unum*, but this could hardly be avoided as a being presents the concrescence of all the transcendentals formally distinguished by reason.

The truth is glimpsed that *consonantia* flows from the form, but Joyce does not see that it is the ontological good of a thing and confuses it with other things. "You apprehend it as complex, multiple, divisible, separable, made up of its parts, the result of its parts and their sum, harmonious. That is consonantia." *Consonantia* is qualitatively more than the sum of its parts, but more serious is the failure to recognize that it is the ontological good of a thing. As will be shown later, this disbalances one of the pivotal relations between the beautiful, the good and the true.

Claritas, as might be expected, is given the best interpretation by Joyce: "It would lead you to believe that he (*St. Thomas*) had in mind symbolism or idealism, the supreme quality of beauty being a light from some other world, the idea of which the matter is but the symbol. I thought he might mean that claritas was the artistic discovery and the representation of the divine purpose in anything or a force of generalization which would make the esthetic image a universal one, make it outshine its proper conditions. But that is literary talk. I understand it so. When you have apprehended that basket as one thing and have then analyzed it according to its form and apprehended it as a thing, you make the only synthesis which is logically and esthetically permissible. You see that it is that thing which it is and no other thing. The radiance of which he speaks is the scholastic quidditas, the whatness of a thing."

Joyce was right in rejecting an idealist and symbolist interpretation and insisting that radiance refers to the *quidditas* or whatness of a thing. He, too, might have been surprised by the realist emphasis given by St. Thomas that not only form but matter is an integral part of the essence of material things, and enters into its very definition. In a way hardly suspected by Joyce and others, which brings out even more sharply the radiance of each being's own form, St. Thomas spoke of *claritas* as a resplendent ray of light irradiating a being from within and belonging to it by its very nature, the "beautifying" givenness making things beautiful, really given to these participated likenesses by the Source of all light.[14]

Tragically mistaken about the Source of light, Joyce was still able to see by the light of things to which he was especially sensitive but not enough so to recognize its derivative nature, what Stephen expresses in his own literary talk: "The instant wherein that supreme quality of beauty, a clear radiance of the esthetic image is apprehended luminously by the mind which has been arrested by its wholeness and fascinated by its harmony is the luminous silent stasis of esthetic pleasure . . ."

Though the question of what constitutes the aesthetic emotion has certainly been given too much attention at the expense of eclipsing more important aspects—indeed, anyone who is honest with himself will admit that the amount of pleasure one gets from art has been greatly exaggerated (does not a cup of tea at the Metropolitan Museum of Art often give more pleasure than looking at some of the masterpieces?)—a few of the distinguishing characteristics of the aesthetic emotion should be pointed out. This will be done more rapidly by bringing forward again another of Joyce's declarations which may serve as an objection and help to bring out the proper solution: "Desire urges us to possess, to go to something; loathing urges us to abandon, to go from something . . . The esthetic emotion (I use the general term) is therefore static. The mind is arrested and raised above desire and loathing . . . The desire and loathing excited by improper esthetic means are really not esthetic emotions not only because they are kinetic in character but also because they are not more than physical . . . Beauty expressed by the artist cannot awaken in us an emotion which is kinetic or a sensation which is purely physical. It awakens, or ought to awaken, or induces, or ought to induce, an aesthetic stasis, an ideal pity or an ideal terror, a stasis called forth, prolonged and at last dissolved by what I call the rhythm of beauty."

One may object to the static emphasis, and certain Platonic overtones in the statement that "the mind is arrested and raised above desire and loathing." It would be more accurate to say that the mind is brought into dynamic repose by a proper resolution of these as well as other contrary emotions. The more serious objection is the failure here as elsewhere in the field of aesthetics of explaining rightly how the beautiful, differently than the true and good, brings into repose the movements of man's rational and sense cognitive and appetitive powers, and their accompanying emotions towards and away from things. It is highly regrettable that the profound hints given by St. Thomas long before Freud and others dared to descend into these infra-rational realms and to explore by the light of reason such explosive material as the emotions concerning the single contraries of the concupiscible emotions of desire and aversion, love and hate, joy and sadness, and the irascible emotions with their double contrariety of fear and courage, hope and despair, and anger,[15] have not been more fully developed by Thomist psychologists, and that no one as yet has attempted to transpose some of these insights with all the necessary modifications into the field of aesthetics. Such studies which should certainly bring out, among other things, how man's reason can penetrate and humanize those emotions, which follow rather than precede its activity in relationship to the aesthetic object, can be dispensed with in the present inquiry. Here the primary concern is not with the emotions, which are resonances in the mind of the movements of the sensible appetite in regard to what is good or bad, but with the way the beautiful, differently than the good and the true, resolves these movements, as also those of man's rational appetite or will, and cognitive powers.

Broadly speaking, those things are called beautiful the vision or apprehension of which placate.[16] Charged with implications, this saying strikes the two inter-blending notes which will help to explain how man's cognitive and appetitive movements are brought into repose by the beautiful, differently than by the true and the good. The beautiful, it says, refers essentially to vision or apprehension, and it also pertains to the nature of the beautiful that its very vision or apprehension placate appetition.[17] Vision not only signifies the act of the sense of sight, but by reason of its worth and certainty is applied to the cognition of all the other senses, and also further to intellectual cognition.[18]

Any cognition in the practical or speculative order may bring some kind of satisfaction,[19] but the cognition of the beautiful brings its own special kind of satisfaction. To get to know in what this consists, it is important to ascertain how aesthetic apprehension differs noetically from other fundamental ways of knowing and their attendant satisfactions, the scientific, philosophical, theological and mystical. Here only a few general and quite superficial characteristics will be mentioned regarding these different modes of cognition and their respective ways of abstracting and expressing their truths.

A truth of the empirical sciences, good as far as it goes, is always of partial aspects of correlated phenomena abstracted or disengaged from a whole thing, and its symbolic notation varies according to the different shorthands used in the various sciences. This only partially satisfies the intellect which seeks to penetrate still further, in its more perfect mode of operating in philosophy, to the essences of whole things abstracted or considered apart from the material things in which they are realized. Philosophical truth gives greater satisfaction to the intellect, desiring it as its good, but although the power of reason is more appeased, the appetitive powers may be left unappeased. While more perfect than philosophy in its content but not in its mode of knowing because it cannot be demonstrated, the theological knowledge of supernatural truths accepted on Faith leaves the intellect still desiring to see God, not darkly and as in a glass through His revelation but as He is in Himself. The mystical experience properly understood as the experiential awareness of God as He is in Himself, which can be had only through the infused gift of Wisdom and through the connaturality of love, fulfills the whole man most completely. This mystical contemplation offers, analogically of course, with all due proportions regarded, and in a radically different way, certain resemblances to the aesthetic experience.[20] An aesthetic truth is not abstracted or disengaged or considered apart from the thing in which it is realized, but is seen or apprehended in the whole thing in which it presents itself, and satisfies man in his cognitive and appetitive powers and their accompanying emotions. This does not imply that the artist, in the manner proper to the arts, does not abstract from larger wholes in nature those aspects expressed by him through the appropriate kind of aesthetic symbols; but this should be discussed in connection with the meaning of art. It is important to explore more specifically how the self is integrated by the different kinds of whole objects presented in different degrees and known accordingly. Concerning this, only one observation will be given here. What is known aesthetically has its own kind of universality different from that of philosophy and the sciences and does not primarily lead outward to further knowledge of the connections between the truths of things. Aesthetic knowing is concretized in the subject, through the object, and leads inwards to a further knowledge of certain truths of the self and other selves, and the relations between selves and things. More generally, any truth is the conformity of intellect and things, but an aesthetic truth is a desirable conformity which visibly delights, in which not only the intellect of man but the whole self is involved, in which his cognitive and appetitive powers and their accompanying emotions are integrated. The true is any adequation of intellect and thing, but the truth of a beautiful thing is an agreeable, satisfying, gratifying, joyful, lovable, reposeful, peaceful, tranquil adequation. Truth, or that in things which can be known, is seen. Beauty, or that in things which makes us enjoy knowing them, is seen and loved.[21]

Like the true, the beautiful is a visible good of cognition,[22] but it differs not only from the true but also from the good. In that the beautiful placates upon being seen or apprehended it is a good, for anything is a good simply speaking that quiets appetition, which is a kind of movement towards a thing.[23] But although the beautiful is akin to the good in quieting appetition,[24] and also because it shares the same metaphysical foundation in that both flow from the form of a thing, the beautiful is not to be confused with the good from which it differs.[25] The good placates the appetite, stirred by it as a final cause, when it is partaken of through direct acquisition and possession. The beautiful, operating as a formal cause, placates by being seen, apprehended, cognized or contemplated. The good as such is anything that is desirable, lovable, delectable in itself and to others. The beautiful is only the desirableness, lovableness and delectability of apprehensible being, which it is enough just to behold in itself and to contemplate for its own sake. In relationship to the good, one is a direct participator, a consumer, even of those goods which are inconsumable. In relationship to the beautiful, one is a knower, a contemplator. In satisfying appetition the good gladdens. The beautiful gladdens by illuminating cognition.

The Perennial Theme of Beauty and Art

Properly understood, the more psychological characterization of the beautiful, gnomically expressed by St. Thomas, coincides with his more ontological description of its threefold requirements. Yet these two converging descriptions, which say so much about what the beautiful is, do not strictly speaking define it, by delimiting it within the barriers of a genus and the addition of a specific difference. This cannot be done, for the addition of any specific difference would itself have to be beautiful, and the transcendental dimensions of the beautiful cannot be narrowed into a genus. Beauty cannot be restricted to a special category because it is as wide and deep as being itself and all its co-extensive transcendentals. Like them, beauty is indefinable, but presents its own evidence so superabundantly that it spills over all its conceptualizations in analogical profusion. That beauty lights up the other transcendentals in no way diminishes or subordinates its own distinctive light, but enhances its intrinsic importance, known and loved for its own sake in its fugitive or lasting expressions wherever it shines out analogically, whether in the lowest degree of being or the highest, and calling for appropriate responses.

Having considered how the beautiful resolves the movements and reposes which terminate in nature and in acts of cognition and appetition and their accompanying emotion, there remains to show briefly how this is done when they terminate in things made by man's art. The specious distinction between the fine arts and the others, which has had such disastrous effects upon the arts themselves, artists and the public, should bring out all the more sharply that art is concerned not only with this special kind of making, but with every category of making, all making. Art as such is the right specification of the *makable* (recta ratio factibilium), primarily in the intellect of the maker, always in reference to or along with making, and also in a different way in the work of art made. This right design or essential pattern of the *makable*, living in the artist's intellect, nourished by his sensibility, imagination and all the other sensory powers conscious and unconscious, has nothing in common with academic rules, for each work has its own intrinsic regulation and its infallible rightness. A lack in the material conditions of art does not necessarily affect its form. In a work of art the form may shine out even more conspicuously through poor material means, as may be witnessed in certain types of Egyptian, primitive African, pre-fifth century Greek and Gothic sculpture, and other high peaks of expression up to the present. As previously suggested, art or making does not copy nature, but may be said to imitate nature in the sense that like nature art also seeks in its own way to realize art-forms in its own sensible and intelligible matter. The other ways in which the different arts are said to imitate nature cannot be entered upon here. In this realm, too, however great the work of art, the

[345]

form-matter hiatus which is a condition of all things human and material will never be completely overcome. To the degree that the right art-form is made to shine out through its appropriate matter, actualizing its potentialities, realizing its essence, integrating, perfecting, completing, unifying, proportioning and harmonizing its existence, the object made will have its own kind of truth, goodness and beauty. To the degree that these do not shine out as fully as the nature of the thing made requires, the work of art will be relatively false, bad and ugly.

Strictly specified by its object, which is the making of a work as true, good and beautiful as its nature demands, the irreducible power of art has its own autonomy and is not subordinate in its own sphere to the moral virtues. The firm disposition of the power of art, considered not in the abstract, but as exercised in a subject under certain concrete conditions of existence, may give rise to a conflict in man between his good as a subject and the good of the object made. In such conflicts the good of the subject man, the attainment of his true end and happiness, takes precedence naturally over the good of the work. In a subject enjoying the radically changed conditions of existence effected gratuitously by the life of grace and its infused intellectual and moral virtues and gifts, the exercise of the power of art may benefit greatly from the vital synergy between these various powers established in the subject. The intrinsic purity and autonomy of the nature of art and its object, far from suffering any diminution from such an interchange, could come into their own more richly. However, to explore from a Thomist perspective the meaning of Christian art, as well as the relations between art and morality, and art and society, would require another essay.

It should be pointed out that the contemporary discussions of the various kinds of aesthetic images, metaphors, signs and symbols made by the different arts and expressed in their respective form-languages could be illuminated by the Thomist doctrine of the different kinds of analogy, as well as its analysis of the various kinds of signs and symbols. These have hardly been applied as yet to the field of aesthetics, though some creative hints have been suggested. Besides other important solutions, Thomism can also resolve the fierce conflict at the core of much that is significant in modern art between the transcendental demands of beauty and the categorical claims of art.

EPILOGUE

by

Herbert Thomas Schwartz, T. O. P.

"I am black but beautiful, O ye daughters of Jerusalem, as the tents of Cedar, as the curtains of Solomon. Do not consider me that I am brown, because the sun hath altered my color: the sons of my mother have fought against me, they have made me the keeper in the vineyards: my vineyard I have not kept."—*Canticle of Canticles* 1, 4-5

There is the knowing 24
Which has its beginning and its end
In human knowing;
There is the knowing
Which has its beginning only
In human knowing,
Whose end is not in knowing,
But in wonder and in love.

These are both natural knowings,
The knowing which is science,
The mode of Aristotle,
The knowing which is wisdom,
The mode of Plato,
Whose dialectic imitates the playfulness of Wisdom herself.

This mode of wisdom
Aristotle knew,
Of it he did not speak,
Striving to keep it undefiled,
Distinguishing it from false science:
This was the work of Aristotle, faithful disciple,
Defending the higher doctrine through the lower,
As from afar imitating the sacrifice of Abraham
On the altar which is Wisdom.

These two knowings,
Two which are one
And likeness, therefore, of acceptable sacrifice.
These the order of Christ transformed,
The order which was in the Beginning:
In this order is the knowing
Beginning in revelation,
Ending in human knowing,
Beginning in revelation,
And never ending,
Both supernatural knowings:
Theology which is science,
The mode of St. Thomas,
Theology which is wisdom,
The mode of St. Augustine and of St. Thomas,
Theology which is the love of the Saints,
The wisdom of the Doctors,
Whose wisdom is the movement of love,
A fire which burns human knowing
For an odor of sweetness,
Bearing testimony to Him that made all things
That His making was not in vain,
As the water fallen from the heavens,
Drawn back to its source
By the fire which is the sun.

Likewise these two knowings are one,
For the term, which is without end,
Is one;
Likewise faithful disciple,
Distinguishing higher doctrine,
Perfecting the lower,
Bringing his fruits to the altar of Christ.

From this same One
Are likewise two arts:
The art beginning in imitation,
Ending in human delectation,
The art beginning in imitation,
Ending in wonder and in love,
Bringing sacrifice of delectation

Epilogue

In natural piety,
The delectation which is in an imitation,
In the knowability of the individual
Under the form of imitation,
Not as he is in himself,
Changing and unknowable,
Not as he is in God,
Perfectly known,
But known through art,
Conformed by art
To human intelligence;
Delectation in such an object
The art of natural piety sacrifices,
Unwilling to rest in the plaything of imitation,
Making of imitation itself an instrument,
Delighting not in the thing understood,
But in the humiliation of the understanding.

These are both natural arts:
The art which imitates nature,
The mode of Sophocles,
The art which imitates Wisdom,
The mode of Plato,
Transforming delectation through dialectic,
Imitating the humility of Wisdom herself.

Likewise two supernatural arts:
Sacred art,
Through Christ bringing man to God,
Fulfilling in art
Imperfect sacrifice of natural piety,
As St. Augustine fulfilled
The wisdom of dialectic in Christ;
Second, a lesser supernatural art,
An art of delectation,
Making things intelligible
Under the supernatural light,
Terminating in human delectation,
Delectation in the intelligibility of things,
In the darkness of Faith,
Under the light of Mysteries.

[351]

There is the form which is seen,
The form embodied in the matter,
There is the movement of the soul,
Through that which is seen,
To that which is loved,
Which cannot be embodied in matter,
Because it is loved for itself.

There is the science of the term,
And the wisdom of the term,
There is the wisdom of the not-term,
Term beginning, not-term ending,
And this, from term to not-term,
Is best of natural wisdoms,
For which the rest are but means.

There is the art of the term,
And the art of the not-term,
Both natural arts,
As there is a natural science
And a natural wisdom.

There is a supernatural science of the term,
Not-term beginning,
Term ending,
There is a wisdom of the Saints,
Not-term beginning, not-term ending,
And this is best of all wisdoms
Among the children of men,
The children of her
Who is best of all created wisdoms,
Wisdom herself, herself beginning,
Of all things the beginning,
In whom unending
The chosen have life unending,
Whose soul, therefore,
Doth magnify the Lord.

To this Wisdom
Sacred art is handmaid,
As she to the Lord,

Epilogue

As the harp to David,
(The harp which is mystically
The voice of Mary,
As David's voice is the voice of Christ)
As the body to the soul,
Elevated in the Resurrection
Which is Christ:
For the humility of wisdom is the dust of the body,
And the Lord has made the temple worthy of Himself.

For in the likeness of Mary, who is Wisdom,
God created heaven and earth,
She from whom God Himself proceeded,
She who is therefore heaven itself, the City of Jerusalem,
In whom are all the Saints,
A created heaven,
For "In the beginning God created heaven and earth,"
And the earth is the image of her
Who is the fulfillment of earth,
Being heaven and earth;
And the spirit of God
Moved over the waters of her womb,
For she was sanctified in the beginning.
For her the waters of the earth bring nurture to the trees,
The darkness on the face of the deep
Is in the likeness of her humility,
Who is dark but beautiful,
For her the Lord has made the temple
Worthy of Himself.

She it is who is comely to behold,
By whose voice the Lord of all things is constrained,
Whose touch inebriates Him,
In her the senses,
Which are the matter of the arts,
Find their fulfillment
In the plenitude of forms,
In the beauty that is dark
Because it is full,
As she was made dark
By the Sun which is subsistent Beauty.

She is the perfection of delectation,
Of created delectation
In whom the Uncreated delights,
The intelligibility of the singular
Who is imitated by the arts,
Herself an image of Him alone,
To whom the arts, even in their perversity,
Perversely aspire,
While her children for whom she weeps, telling them:
"My own vineyard I have not kept,"
Rest in an art made in their own image,
Sing hymns of self-love in her temple;
They are struck dumb by the perversity of their enemies,
Unable to understand it,
Being themselves perverse,
Having forsaken her who is the measure.

We are in a strange land:
Here is wisdom of Satan,
Of him who first tempted,
Offering the fruits of the Tree of Wisdom
In defiance of the Lord,
Offering of her fruit who said:
"Be it done unto me according to thy word,"
For disobedience;
Here is the wisdom of those in his image,
Who would have the reward of God,
Denying his Son,
Mocking his Daughter,
Who would have the beatitude they despise,
Whose burden is too great
Because they would carry it alone.
We are among men who hate science
Because it is less than God,
Who have turned from God
Because He is more than they.
They deny the finitude of science,
As if loving wisdom,
Intoxicated with a selfish love of the Virgin,
As our first parents,
Eating of the fruit which is for her children,

Epilogue

Her children who will not eat,
Who do not admire the gift which others steal.

These are the unlawful inheritors,
Perverting not only Wisdom herself,
But her imitation,
Wisdom of the Greeks,
Of Plato distinguishing fable from truth,
Loving the truth of fable,
As if knowing the truth which is Mary
In the fable of Athena.
To the unending ladder of Plato's dialectic
They have added a last rung,
The rung of achievement and of power
Which Plato, hater of idolatries,
Hated worst of all idolatries.
They have stolen the instrument for its power,
Denying its Source,
They have distorted the instrument,
Persuading men, through the movement which is of love,
That He who is loved does not exist,
Desecrating the Virgin,
Making her into the likeness of Satan.

The merging of forms in their actuality,
The unreal identity of distinct things,
Which was the imitative instrument of Plato,
Which is fruitful because it imitates
The eminent actuality of all act in Pure Act,
They pervert to deny reality of act.
Hating humility, they deny a limit
Of human objectivity,
The limit which is the principle of the genus,
The artefact through which man
Imitates the eternity of Divine science.
Following the abomination of Hegel,
They have made limit and limited one,
Not-being being,
Finite infinite,
The discrete is the continuous,
The continuous is the discrete,

[355]

The function is its limit,
The brute is man,
Society is an organism,
Spiritual love is sexual.
They have lost the playfulness of the imitation,
Saying what works is true
Because they would deny Truth,
The very Truth that is the source of their fruitfulness,
The achievement which Satan promised on the mountain top.

They are indeed right in their saying,
But they see not the Truth in the working:
They do not see that it is true
Because the likeness of Him who made nature
Is in the nature which He made,
That the likeness is to bring men to Him,
But their denial is martyrdom to Satan,
They have proved themselves by the works
Which Satan promises to those who adore him:
Now with those works they destroy each man his neighbor,
Denier denying denier
In imitation of him who denies,
Of him in whom there is no love.

For it is he, the evil one,
Who first denied,
And it is his children who have always denied,
First the things of heaven,
Calling this denial nature,
Then the things of nature,
Calling this denial wisdom.
Imitating the mode of wisdom,
Perversely they deny the natural,
Not for God,
Not in his Christ,
Not in the darkness of ignorance loving light,
Not in the light of faith,
Loving the Father through the Son,
Loving the Son through the Daughter;
But as a perverse generation
Seeking its own destruction.

Epilogue

In ignorance they deny science
Because there is something better than science;
But their denial is a sign,
The denial of the nature which God created,
Which God said was good,
A sign that they do not move from the things that are seen
To the invisible things,
That they do not move to the uncreated Good
In whom no good is denied.

But we who follow the created good of science,
Created image of creation,
We who should know
That science imitates only the eternity of God,
His changelessness,
Are become as blind
To the Procession within God,
Therefore forsaking the movement of the mind
That is better than science
Because it contains science
In imitation of the Divine Eminence.
We are become as enamoured of multiplicity,
Science has become for us a term in which we rest,
We, for whom everything except God is darkness,
Rest in the light of a science
Which has become dark for our enemies.
Our science is without power,
Because it no longer proceeds
From that which is greater than science;
Therefore it no longer comprehends the science
Of those who are without faith,
Of those who have been taught by Satan, perverting truth,
The truth we no longer follow in God's teaching.
We are become enamoured of multiplicity
Whilst our enemies destroy us,
Perverting the oneness of things,
Destroying themselves because they pervert it,
Destroying us because we no longer seek it,
Because we cannot love them,
And the truth that is in them,
Having made an idol of science and of a saint.

This is not the sorrow of Egypt:
We have not accepted the idol of our enemy:
We have made our own,
An idol mocked by the power of the enemy.
For we say with our tongues that God is pure act,
But the acts of our enemies we do not understand,
Not the evil of those acts,
But the truth perverted in the evil;
Because we do not see our own evil:
That the children of Satan bring, defiled, to Satan,
That which we should bring to the Father,
Sanctified in the Son.

For the science and the art
Of those who are not in Christ
Is the manifestation of power in darkness,
The fruit of the evil one
Exploiting the truth which is above reason;
And we are powerless before the power of an angel
Because we are faithless to the power of God.

Our science is become dry,
It no longer bears fruit,
Because it brings no sacrifice to Him Who Is,
Our theologians are as Pharisees
Who know the letter of the law, not the spirit.
To his own our Lord said:
"I am not come to destroy, but to fulfill,"
Because the Spirit is the fulfillment of the law.

But our science has made us hostile to the Spirit,
And therefore, like the Pharisees,
We no longer understand
Even the letter.
For the letter contains mystery,
As the tree, straight and measurable,
It is nourished by the running of waters,
The waters of grace flowing from the womb of Wisdom
Playing before God.

Therefore we do not understand
Even the tree,

Epilogue

Spreading its branches upward,
Returning in gentle stirrings of praise
The grace of the waters
Running from the high mountains,
Sensitive, as the waters,
To the Breath which moves them.

We do not understand the moderns,
Not because they are worse than we,
But because they are better;
Our failure is not because their science adores Satan,
(This too we could understand,
Understanding the Master of Satan)
We do not understand
Because our science
No longer is the child of adoration.

We say "pure act"
Unmindful in the saying
That it is denied in the saying,
Because the saying moves,
We say "God is one,"
But in our mind we do not seek
The One that is God,
Satisfied with the one of our saying.
And because we love the many,
Not in the One,
We fear the moderns seeking diversity of fact,
Bringing adoration of denial
To him who denies;
Because we are become as they, deniers.
For they bring denial to the denier, through denial,
But we do not bring being to Him Who Is,
Through denial, through Him.

As Wisdom begets love of Wisdom,
Love of Wisdom begets science,
When the traces of that movement
Which is love of Wisdom
Are fixed in imitation
Of uncreated Wisdom,
When the Chant overflows into silence,

[359]

As Plato's love of wisdom
Begot the science of Aristotle,
As the Fathers' love of Wisdom
Begot the science of St. Thomas.

But we glory in the fruit,
We acknowledge wisdom for the sake of science,
We patronize St. Augustine,
And of Plato we have made a symbol of error;
We are as rich men disdainful of the poor,
Gathering wealth into barns,
Having lost our poverty,
And therefore unnourished by our wealth.

Modern art we cannot understand,
Because we do not understand sacred art,
The art of sacrifice,
For modern art is the art of sacrifice to Satan,
Its history the history of denial,
In its beginning denying the things of God,
Affirming nature:
Death which is called re-birth;
Then denial of nature:
(For man, after Christ, cannot rest in nature)
Self-love become manifest in self-hatred,
Not the holy hatred of self
Which our Lord asks,
Not hatred of self in love of God,
But hatred of self in hatred of God.

The renaissance splendour of form,
Hiding denial of God,
Now is unmasked,
First in romantic denial of form,
Wedded to self-love,
Now the perfect image of its archetype,
Hatred and denial,
Its doctrine blasphemous as its art.

For to those who deny,
What denies, pleases,

Epilogue

And denial of God is assertion of self:
Therefore the doctrine, self-expression,
Not the form, for this does not please
Those who deny the Plenitude and Eminence of forms,
Only the form of expression,
Having its beginning and its end
In man, made in the image of Satan,
Arrogating to himself, even as his model,
The perfect immanence of expression
Which is the Blessed Trinity;
Denying form, denying end,
Asserting only expression and change:
The expression which asserts man,
The change which denies God.

Bibliography

In citing the works of Aristotle, the divisions of the Berlin Academy edition have been used.

The following abbreviations of bibliographical sources should be carefully noted:

S.T.	*Summa Theologica* of Aquinas
C.G.	*Contra Gentiles* of Aquinas
Q.D.	*Quaestiones Disputatae* of Aquinas
in	commentary on
a.	article
b.	book
c.	chapter
d.	distinction
l.	lecture
lin.	line
n.	number
p. I	part one of the *Summa Theologica*
p. I-II	first part of part two of the *Summa Theologica*
p. II-II	second part of part two of the *Summa Theologica*
p. III	part three of the *Summa Theologica*
vol.	volume

First Essay

TROUBADOUR OF TRUTH

1. Tocco, in J. Bollandus, *Acta Sanctorum*: c. 7, n. 39, p. 670.

2. Tocco, *op. cit.*, c. 6, n. 37, p. 669.

3. *Cambridge Modern History*: New York, Macmillan, 1903, vol. I, p. v.

4. M. C. D'Arcy, *Thomas Aquinas*: Boston, Little, Brown, 1930, p. vii.

5. M. J. Adler, *What Man Had Made of Man*: New York, Longmans, 1937, Introduction, p. xvi.

6. R. J. Hoffman, *Tradition and Progress*: Milwaukee, Bruce, 1938, pp. 22-23.

7. H. O. Taylor, *Independence, Convergence and Borrowing*: Cambridge, Harvard Tercentenary Publications, 1937, p. 166.

8. *Q. D. de Veritate*: q. 2, a. 2.

9. *In Meteorologicorum*: b. III, l. 2.

10. *In de Coelo et Mundo*: b. II, l. 17.

11. J. Maritain, *The Angelic Doctor*: New York, Dial Press, 1931, p. 165, footnote.

12. *Revue Néo-scolastique*: 1912, vol. 19, pp. 157-76, *passim*.

13. "The Influence of Mediaeval Philosophy on the Intellectual Life of Today," *The New Scholasticism*: 1929, vol. 3, p. 32.

14. Thus Albert writes of "certain ignorant persons (even among the Friars Preachers where no one opposes them) who fight against the study of philosophy by every means in their power." Cf. M. Grabmann, *Die Kulturphilosophie des hl. Thomas von Aquin*: Augsburg, Filser, 1925, p. 122.

15. Quoted in Schoepfer's *Thomas von Aquin*: Innsbruck, Verlagsanstalt Tyrolia, 1925, p. 26.

16. Cf. A. Masnovo, *La Novità di S. Tom-maso d'Aquino*: Milan, Sesto Centenario della Canonizzazione, 1923, pp. 41-50.

17. Petrus Calo, died 1310. Cf. M. Grabmann, *Introduction to the Theological Summa of St. Thomas*: St. Louis, Herder, 1930, p. 68.

18. It may interest readers to know something of the aims of the Angelic Doctor in writing his *Summa Theologica*. Thus, the preface tells us that his first ambition was to avoid needless questions, articles and arguments. In achieving this result, he was able to show a greater conciseness and unity of treatment than any previous text on theology could claim. His second aim was to avoid excessive complexities in the arrangement of his materials. Every treatise and every question is preceded by a clear statement of its division, so that no forward step is taken until it has been linked up with what precedes. The third and final goal of Aquinas was to avoid repetitions. Hence, there is always new subject matter as the text develops; or, in the instances where things already treated re-appear, there is always a new way of presenting them, a new context in which they are included, or a new purpose in bringing them into the discussion.

19. A detailed account of the immediate opposition to Aquinas and the resultant controversies is given by M. Grabmann in his *Thomas Aquinas* (trans. by Virgil Michel): New York, Longmans, Green, 1928, pp. 57-65.

20. Cf. the excellent article of Duhem on "Physics" in the *Catholic Encyclopedia*: vol. 12, pp. 47-67.

21. Cf. M. Grabmann, "The Influence of

Mediaeval Philosophy on the Intellectual Life of Today," *The New Scholasticism*: 1929, vol. 3, pp. 36-37; and E. Gilson, *The Unity of Philosophical Experience*: New York, Scribner's, 1937, pp. 119-20.

22. Cf. article cited in footnote 20: p. 45.

23. *The Angelic Doctor*: New York, Dial Press, 1931, p. 70.

24. Cf. H. Rashdall, *The Universities of Europe in the Middle Ages*: Oxford, Clarendon Press, 1936, revised edition, vol. I, pp. 368-69.

25. Cf. A. E. Taylor, *Philosophical Studies*: London, Macmillan, 1934, pp. 225-26.

26. Cf. B. W. Switalski, "The Spirit of the New Scholasticism," in Zybura's *Presentday Thinkers*: St. Louis, Herder, 1926, pp. 177-84.

27. Cf. the author's "The Thomist Revival," *Ecclesiastical Review*, 1941, vol. 104, n. 1, pp. 12-25.

Second Essay

REFLECTIONS ON NECESSITY AND CONTINGENCY

1. At least as regards creatures. *In God* there is *freedom* without contingency; in other words all contingency is found in the *created* object willed or not willed by God, and the divine *act*, which is free in regard to such-and-such an object, is *necessary* in itself, insofar as it is identical with the divine essence.

2. *In Perihermenias*: b. I, l. 14: dicatur illud necessarium, etc.

3. Cf. *In Perihermenias*: b. I, l. 13.

4. Cf. *Q. D. de Veritate*: q. 5, a. 2.

5. In this case events of will are conjoined to events of nature along with the antecedents of these. For instance: "The careful attention of the physician cured this disease; Napoleon was victorious at Jena." And even in the examples cited in the text, man may have interfered to plant the hazel tree, or the tree in which the nest was built, and to care for and protect the one or the other, etc.

6. We take the liberty of proposing this expression as a development from the foregoing considerations. Such terminology, to be sure, is not found in the vocabulary of the ancients, who, because of erroneous concepts regarding cosmology and astronomy, considered the events in questions as necessary by right (*de droit*).

7. "Contingens ad utrumlibet," as Aquinas puts it. Cf. reference in footnote 2.

8. The free act (election) is hypothetically necessary (*in sensu composito*) in relation to the last practical judgment, but the very placing of this determining condition depends on free will.

9. The question here, by hypothesis, is only

of natural agents, operating without intervention of free agents, such as a man planting and cultivating trees in his garden.

10. Cf. *Q. D. de Veritate*: q. 2, a. 14, reply to obj. 3.

11. Cf. *Q. D. de Veritate*: q. 12, a. 3.

12. *Ibid.*: q. 5, a. 2.

13. Cf. *Q. D. de Veritate*: q. 8, a. 12.

14. The infinite intelligence of God knows all future contingents with absolute certitude in the multitude of all the factors of the universe. Yet, properly speaking, God sees rather than foresees such events.

15. *Q. D. de Veritate*: p. 12, a. 2.

16. The word "chance" could be applied to this regular meeting of two independent causal series if, as Saint Thomas and Aristotle point out, it were not reserved to designate either particularly happy meetings (such as the accidental fall of a tripod on its three legs) or particularly unhappy meetings. It is purely a matter of accident that in going to give a class at eight o'clock in the morning I should meet every day a certain laborer going to his work at the same hour. Such an accidental meeting would be called a chance meeting, if I had a special need either of meeting the laborer in question or of avoiding him. Apropos of the finality involved in chance occurrences, Aristotle says it is accidental that one meet a certain unknown person along the way; but it is by chance that we run into a debtor who hands us some money at the very moment that we have need of it.

We see that all these considerations are related to the problem of finality and also the

Bibliography

question of human interests, all of which are beyond the scope of the present essay.

17. *Q. D. de Veritate:* q. 5, a. 10, reply to obj. 7.

Third Essay

INTELLECTUAL COGNITION

1. *S. T.:* p. I, q. 76, a. 1. Cf. P. Rousselot, *The Intellectualism of St. Thomas* (trans. by J. E. O'Mahoney): New York, Sheed and Ward, 1935.

2. *S. T.:* p. I, q. 84, a. 6; q. 85, a. 1. Also, *Q. D. de Veritate:* q. 10, a. 6.

3. *S. T.:* p. I, q. 79, a. 2; p. I-II, q. 51, a. 1. Also, *Q. D. de Veritate:* q. 10, a. 6, reply to obj. 12. Also, *Q. D. de Anima:* a. 7.

4. *S. T.:* p. I, q. 84, a. 3. Also, *Compendium Theologiae:* c. 82.

5. On sense reactions in general, v. *S. T.:* p. I, q. 75, a. 3, corp. and reply to obj. 3. Also, *Q. D. de Veritate:* q. 26, a. 6; also, *In Libros Sententiarum:* b. I, d. 40, q. 1, a. 1, reply to obj. 1. On the passivity of the senses, v. *S. T.:* p. I, q. 78, a. 3.

6. *S. T.:* p. I, q. 13, a. 1. Also, *In Perihermenias:* b. I, l, 1. Cf. Augustine, *De Trinitate:* b. XV, c. 12: "Verbum simillimum rei notae . . . et imago ejus."

7. The notion of such *eidola* is expressly repudiated by Aquinas, *S. T.:* p. I, q. 84, a. 6.

8. Cf. O. F. Knapke, *The Scholastic Theory of the Species Sensibilis:* Washington, D. C., Catholic University of America Press, 1915.

9. Anselm, *Dialogus de Veritate:* c. VI; Migne's *P. L.:* vol. 158, p. 474.

10. Cf. *S. T.:* p. I, q. 84, a. 7. Also, *Q. D. de Veritate:* q. 10, a. 6. For a detailed report, v. R. E. Brennan, *A Theory of Abnormal Cognitive Processes:* Washington, D. C., Catholic University of America Press, 1925.

11. On the general psychology of sensory functions, v. Domet de Vorges, *La Perception et la Psychologie Thomiste:* Paris, 1892. Also, J. K. Ledvina, *The Psychology and Philosophy of Sensation according to St. Thomas Aquinas:* Washington, D. C., Catholic University of America Press, 1941.

12. When thinking of incorporeal substances, the human intellect also makes use of phantasms, although the phantasms, in such a case, do not correspond to the sub-

stances. Cf. *S. T.:* p. I, q. 84, a. 7, reply to obj. 3.

13. Imagination is frequently referred to by Aquinas as a *thesaurus* or treasure house. Cf. *S. T.:* p. I, q. 78, a. 4. *Q. D. de Anima:* a. 13.

14. T. V. Moore, *Cognitive Psychology:* Philadelphia, Lippincott, 1939, p. 237 ff.

15. Cf. *In de Sensu et Sensato:* l. 17.

16. A. Galli, "Sopra la percezione di movimenti apparenti prodotti con stimoli sensoriali diversi," *Arch. di Sci. Biol.:* 1931, n. 5, pp. 79-122.

17. *Q. D. de Spiritualibus Creaturis:* a. 2.

18. *S. T.:* p. I, q. 78, a. 3 and reply to obj. 3, of a. 4; q. 87, a. 3, reply to obj. 3; p. I-II, q. 47, a. 3, reply to obj. 3. Also *C. G.:* b. I, c. 61. Also, *Quodlibetum Primum:* q. 7, a. 2, reply to obj. 1.

19. *S. T.:* p. I, q. 78, a. 4, reply to obj. 1. Also, *In de Anima:* b. III, l. 3.

20. For a more detailed discussion of the problems pertaining to the *vis aestimativa* or the *vis cogitativa,* v. the author's "Evaluation and the Vis Cogitativa," *The New Scholasticism:* 1941, vol. 15, n. 3, p. 195.

21. Even the *vis aestimativa* of animals is said "to come close to reason": attingere rationem. Cf. *In Libros Sententiarum:* b. III, d. 26, q. 1, a. 2.

22. Cf. G. P. Klubertanz, "The Internal Senses in the Process of Cognition," *The Modern Schoolman:* 1941, vol. 18, n. 1, p. 29.

23. Cf. author's article refered to in footnote 20.

24. The senses apprehend their objects "materially though without matter." Cf. *Q. D. de Veritate:* q. 2, a. 5, reply to objections 1 and 2.

25. *S. T.:* p. I, q. 78, a. 3. The notion of *inexistentia mentalis objecti* became very influential in certain schools of psychology. It was reintroduced by Franz Brentano, *Psychologie vom empirischen Standpunkt:* second edition, Leipzig, F. Meiner, 1924, vol. I, p. 124.

26. W. Jaeger, *Studien zur Entstehungs-*

geschichte der Metaphysik des Aristoteles: Berlin, 1912; also, *Aristotle: Fundamentals of the History of his Development*, (trans. by R. Robinson): Oxford, Clarendon Press, 1934. Also, A. Mansion, "La genèse de l'oeuvre d'Aristote d'après les travaux récents," *Revue Néo-Scolastiques*: 1927, vol. 29, pp. 307, 423. Also, F. J. C. J. Nuyens, *Ontwikkelingsmomenten in de Zielkunde van Aristoteles*: Nijmegen, Dekker and van de Vegt, 1939.

27. *Q. D. de Veritate*: q. 15, a. 1; Also, *Q. D. de Anima*: a. 14.

28. "Abstraction does not require the presence of the many, and may be legitimately performed on a single thing or phenomenon." J. T. Casey, *The Primacy of Metaphysics*: Washington, D. C., Catholic University of America Press, 1935, p. 65.

29. Augustine, *De Doctrina Christiana*: b. I; also, *De Trinitate*: b. V, c. 1; b. XV, cc. 10, 11, 12.

Aquinas: "Cogitamus enim omnia quod dicimus, etiam interiori illo verba quod ad nullius gentis pertinet lingua." Cf. *S. T.*: p. I, q. 93, a. 7, reply to obj. 3. Similar statements occur in many treatises. E. g. William of Ockham, *Summa Totius Logice*: Venetiis, 1508, b. I, c. 1. By a curious misunderstanding Ockham has been credited with the "discovery" of pre-verbal language by many students of linguistics and the psychology of language. They evidently relied on some secondhand information, probably in Prandtl's *Geschichte der Logik des Abendlandes*, and overlooked that the *venerabilis inceptor* himself refers to Augustine.

30. J. B. Watson, *Psychology from the Standpoint of a Behaviorist*: Philadelphia, Lippincott, 1919, p. 14 ff.; also, "The Place of Kinaesthetic Organization in Thinking," *Psychological Review*: 1924, vol. 31, p. 34 ff. Also, J. F. Dashiell, "A Physiological-Behavioristic Description of Thinking," *Psychological Review*: 1925, vol. 32, p. 54 ff.

31. These problems and others related to them have been analyzed to some extent by the present writer in an article, "The Intellectual Cognition of Particulars," *The Thomist*: 1941, vol. 3, p. 95 ff. The reader is referred to this article for a review of most of the modern and older literature dealing with this matter.

32. V. J. Wébert, "Reflexio, Etude sur les opérations réflexes dans la psychologie de St. Thomas," *Mélanges Mandonnet*: Paris, 1930,

vol. 1, p. 285 ff. Also, the present writer's article cited in footnote 31.

33. The reflection of the intellect on itself and its operation is secondary to the operation in any case. The intellect cannot reflect on itself independently of the acts that it performs or has performed. The addition of *"nisi intellectus ipse"* to the *intellectus-sensus* axiom is therefore incompatible with the principles of Thomistic psychology. On the secondary nature of reflection, cf. *Q. D. de Veritate*: q. 10, a. 8.

34. *S. T.*: p. I, q. 91, a. 3, reply to obj. 3; p. I-II, q. 50, a. 4, reply to obj. 4. Also, *C. G.*: b. II, c. 60; also, *Q. D. de Veritate*: p. 18, a. 8.

35. On the role of the phantasm, cf. J. Barron, *Die Bedeutung des Phantasma für die Entstehung der Begriffe bei Thomas von Aquin* (doctoral thesis): Münster, 1902. Also, T. V. Moore, "The Scholastic Theory of Perception," *The New Scholasticism*: 1933, vol. 7, p. 222 ff. Also, M. A. Coady, *The Phantasm according to the Teaching of St. Thomas Aquinas*: Washington, D. C., Catholic University of America Press, 1932. Also, F. A. Walsh, "Phantasm and Phantasy," *The New Scholasticism*: 1935, vol. 9, p. 116 ff.

36. *S. T.*: p. I, q. 5, a. 2. Also, *Q. D. de Veritate*: q. 1, a. 1.

37. The senses imitate the intellect, as it were. Cf. *In Librum Boethii de Trinitate*: q. 5, a. 3.

38. For a complete statement of the faculty theory in the Thomistic philosophy, v. C. A. Hart, *The Thomistic Theory of Mental Faculties*: Washington, D. C., Catholic University of America Press, 1930. A remarkably sensible viewpoint is advocated by R. S. Woodworth when he says: "If we substitute for 'faculty' a more modern-sounding word such as 'function' there is nothing repugnant or absurd about this theory." *Experimental Psychology*: New York, Holt, 1939, p. 178.

39. Willwoll, *Über Begriffsbildung*: Leipzig, S. Hirzel, 1927. Cf. also, J. Lindworsky, *Das Schlussfolgernde Denken*: Freiburg, Herder, 1916. Also, M. F. Dunn, "The Psychology of Reasoning," *Studies in Psychology and Psychiatry*: 1926, vol. 1, p. 141 ff. Also, T. V. Moore, *Cognitive Psychology*: Philadelphia, Lippincott, 1938, pp. 382-87.

40. K. Bühler, "Über Gedanken," *Arch. f. d. ges. Psychol.*: 1907, vol. 9, p. 357 ff. Also, R. S. Woodworth, "Imageless Thought,"

Bibliography

Journal of Philosophy: 1906, vol. 3, p. 70 ff. For further references, v. the present writer's article referred to in footnote 31, especially pp. 118-27.

41. Aquinas also points out that the objects of the active and passive intellects are formally different. Cf. *S. T.*: p. I, q. 97, a. 7. Also,

Q. D. de Veritate: q. 15, a. 2 and reply to objections 12 and 13.

42. *S. T.*: p. I, q. 79, a. 6. Also, *C. G.*: b II, c. 74. Also, *Q. D. de Veritate*: q. 10, a. 2.

43. H. Bergson, *Matter and Memory* (trans. by N. M. and P. W. Scott): London, Allen & Co., 1911.

Fourth Essay

THE PROBLEM OF TRUTH

1. Cf. Harold Joachim, *The Nature of Truth*: Oxford University Press, 1907, pp. 66-68.

2. William James, *Pragmatism*: New York, Longmans, Green, 1910, p. 222.

3. Cf. *S. T.*: p. I, qq. 16-17; *Q. D. de Veritate*: q. 1; *C. G.*: b. I, cc. 59-62. The writer has found Father Leslie J. Walker's *Theories of Knowledge*: New York, Longmans, Green, 1910, particularly helpful both for the Thomistic doctrine and modern theories of truth.

4. *S. T.*: p. I, q. 16, a. 5.

5. Cf. *Q. D. de Veritate*: q. 1, a. 11.

6. For a simple but vivid illustration of these three kinds of truth cf. de Maupassant's famous short story *La Parure*.

7. "The 'absolutely' true, meaning what no farther experience will ever alter, is that ideal vanishing-point towards which we imagine that all our temporary truths will some day converge. It runs on all fours with the perfectly wise man, and with the absolutely complete experience; and, if these ideals are ever realized, they will all be realized together. Meanwhile we have to live to-day by what

truth we can get to-day, and be ready to-morrow to call it falsehood. Ptolemaic astronomy, euclidean space, aristotelian logic, scholastic metaphysics, were expedient for centuries, but human experience has boiled over those limits, and we now call these things only relatively true, or true within those borders of experience. 'Absolutely' they are false; for we know that those limits were casual, and might have been transcended by past theorists just as they are by present thinkers." William James, *op. cit.*: pp. 222-23.

8. Cf. the writer's "Concerning a Matter of Method," *The New Scholasticism*: October, 1934, vol. 8, n. 4.

9. Cf. *Q. D. de Veritate*: q. 1, a. 1; q. 11 a. 1. *S. T.*: p. I, q. 117, a. 1. *In Metaphysica, passim.*

10. *S. T.*: p. I, q. 1, a. 8, ad 2.

11. *The Republic*: b. II, 382 a. (Jowett translation).

12. *Hamlet*: Act IV, Scene 4.

13. *S. T.*: p. I, q. 11, a. 3.

14. *Pensées*: (translated by Wm. F. Trotter) Everyman's Library edition, p. 45.

15. *S. T.*: p. I, q. 1, a. 1.

Fifth Essay

THE ONTOLOGICAL ROOTS OF THOMISM

1. *Introduction to Philosophy*: p. 42.

2. *The Degrees of Knowledge*: p. 5.

3. The transcendental distinctions in "being" are not divisions of "being." They are purely rational distinctions.

4. *S. T.*: p. I, q. 5, a. 1.

5. The meaning and importance of this key-

word will be discussed later. See page 92 ff.

6. *Q. D. de Potentia Dei*: q. 7, a. 3.

7. *C. G.*: b. I, c. 26.

8. "(Deus) non habet quidditatem nisi suum esse. . . . Deus non habet essentiam quae non sit suum esse." *C. G.*: b. I, cc. 22, 25.

Sixth Essay

THE ROLE OF HABITUS IN THE THOMISTIC METAPHYSICS OF POTENCY AND ACT

1. "Nomen potentiae primo impositum fuit ad significandum potestatem hominis, prout dicimus aliquos homines esse potentes, ut Avicenna dicit, tract. IV *Metaph.*, c. II, et deinde etiam translatum fuit ad res naturales." *In Libros Sententiarum:* b. I, d. 42, q. 1, a. 1; ed. Mandonnet, I, 983.

In the Latin translation of Avicenna, the text cited reads in part: "Quod intelligitur de hoc nomine potentia: primum imposuerunt intentioni quae est in animalibus. . . . Deinde transtulerunt ab hoc ad intentionem quae est potentia difficile faciendi et facile faciendi: . . ." *Metaphysica Avicenne sive ejus prima philosophia:* Venetiis, 1495; (this is the first printing of the translation attributed to Gundisalvi; it is without pagination or folio numeration but the internal reference given in the text of St. Thomas is correct.)

2. "Ad hujus quaestionis evidentiam sciendum, quod potentia dicitur ab actu: actus enim est duplex: scilicet primus, qui est forma; et secundus, qui est operatio: et sicut videtur ex communi hominum intellecto, nomen actus primo fuit attributum operationi: sic enim quasi omnes intelligunt actum: secundo autem exinde fuit translatum ad formam, in quantum forma est principium operationis et finis; unde et similiter duplex est potentia; una activa cui respondet actus, qui est operatio; et huic primo nomen potentiae videtur fuisse attributum: alia est potentia passiva, cui respondet actus primus, qui est forma, ad quam similiter videtur secundario nomen potentiae devolutum." *Q. D. de Potentia Dei:* q. 1, a. 1; Taurini-Romae (Marietti) 1931, I, 2.

3. "Duplex sit potentia, scilicet potentia ad esse, et potentia ad agere." *S. T.:* p. I-II, q. 55, a. 2; ed. Leon. VI, 351. Cf. *In Libros Metaphysicorum:* b. IX, l. 5; ed. Cathala, p. 529, nn. 1823-1825.

4. "Inter alios autem actus, maxime est nobis notus et apparens motus, qui sensibiliter a nobis videtur." *In Libros Metaphysicorum:* b. IX, l. 3; 523, n. 1805.

5. *Metaphysics:* 1046 a 10-14.

6. "Et hoc est principium activum, quod est principium transmutationis in alio inquantum est aliud. Et hoc dicit, quia possibile est quod principium activum simul sit in ipso mobili vel passo, sicut cum aliquid movet seipsum; non tamen secundum idem est movens et motum, agens et patiens. Et ideo dicitur quod principium quod dicitur potentia activa, est principium transmutationis in alio inquantum est aliud; quia etsi contingat principium activum esse in eodem cum passo, non tamen secundum quod est idem, sed secundum quod est aliud." *In Libros Metaphysicorum:* b. IX, l. 1; 516, n. 1776.

7. "Est enim aliqua potentia tantum agens; aliqua tantum acta vel mota; alia vero agens et acta. Potentia igitur quae est tantum agens, non indiget, ad hoc quod sit principium actus, aliquo inducto; unde virtus talis potentiae nihil est aliud quam ipsa potentia. Talis autem potentia est divina, intellectus agens, et potentiae naturales; unde harum potentiarum virtutes non sunt aliqui habitus, sed ipsae potentiae in seipsis completae. Illae vero potentiae sunt tantum actae quae non agunt nisi ab aliis motae; nec est in eis agere vel non agere, sed secundum impetum virtutis moventis agunt; et tales sunt vires sensitivae secundum se consideratae; unde in III *Ethic.* (com. 8, circa fin.) dicitur, quod sensus nullius actus est principium; et haec potentiae perficiuntur ad suos actus per aliquid superinductum; quod tamen non inest eis sicut aliqua forma manens in subjecto, sed solum per modum passionis, sicut species in pupilla. Unde nec harum potentiarum virtutes sunt habitus, sed magis ipsae potentiae, secundum quod sunt actu passae a suis activis. Potentiae vero illae sunt agentes et actae quae ita moventur a suis activis, quod tamen per eas non determinantur ad unum; sed in eis est agere, sicut vires aliquo modo rationales; et haec potentiae complentur ad agendum per aliquod superinductum, quod non est in eis per modum passionum tantum, sed per modum formae quiescentis, et manentis in subjecto; ita tamen quod per eas non de

Bibliography

necessitate potentia ad unum cogatur; quia sic potentia non esset domina sui actus. Harum potentiarum virtutes non sunt ipsae potentiae; neque passiones, sicut est in sensitivis potentiis; neque qualitates de necessitate agentes, sicut sunt qualitates rerum naturalium; sed sunt habitus, secundum quos potest quis agere cum voluerit, ut dicit Commentator in III de Anima (com 18). Et Augustinus in lib. de Bono Conjugali (cap. xxi) dicit, quod habitus est quo quis agit, cum tempus affuerit." Q. D. de Virtutibus in Communi: a. 1; (Marietti) II, 486-87.

8. "Virtus alicujus rei attenditur secundum ultimum quod potest, puta in eo, quod potest ferre centum libras, virtus ejus determinatur non ex hoc quod fert quinquaginta, sed ex hoc quod centum, ut dicitur primo Caeli." In Ethica Nicomachea: b. II, l. 6; ed. Pirotta, Taurini (Marietti) 1934, p. 105, n. 308.
"Virtus nominat quamdam potentiae perfectionem." S. T.: p. I-II, q. 55, a. 1; ed. Leon. VI, 349.
The source of this precision in terminology, and the example, are to be found in Aristotle's De Caelo: 281 a 7.

9. Aristotle's fourfold division of qualities provides the basis for the differentiation of habitus and passion. Habitus belongs to the first species; passion to the third. V. Categoriae: 8 b 25-10 a 25.

10. If the doctrine of this text from Q. D. de Virtutibus in Communi: a. 1, be compared with the parallel passages in the Scriptum super Libros Sententiarum: b. II, d. 27, q. 1, a. 1, reply to objections 1, 2 and 3; ed. Mandonnet, II, 695-97; and S. T.: p. I-II, q. 55, aa. 1 and 2; VI, 349-51, the Q. D. de Virtutibus in Communi will be found to be most complete and explanatory. There is a chronological spread of some fifteen years between the Script. in II Sent. (1254-55) and the S. T. and the Q. D. de Virtutibus in Communi, but the precise relations of the last two works are difficult to determine. Most authorities, however, regard the Q. D. de Virtutibus in Communi as posterior to the Prima Secundae; see the survey of this chronological problem, with references to Mandonnet, Birkenmajer, Koch and Synave, in: M. Grabmann, Die Werke des hl. Thomas von Aquin: BGPM XXII, 1-2; Münster i W., 1931, pp. 275-81.

11. "Virtus est bona qualitas mentis, qua recte vivitur, qua nullus male utitur, quam Deus in nobis sine nobis operatur." This definition is gathered from the De Libero Arbitrio: b. II, cc. 19-20; PL: vol. 32, col. 1267-70. In this form it was known in the thirteenth century through the text of Peter Lombard, Liber II Sent.: d. 27; it may be read in connection with the commentary of St. Thomas, In Libros Sententiarum: b. II; Mandonnet, II, 688.
That Augustine knew that such a qualitas was a habitus, is clear from the passage cited by St. Thomas; ("Ipse est enim habitus, quo aliquid agitur, cum opus est." This is the original form of the Augustinian definition, De Bono Conjugali: cc. 21, 25; PL.: vol. 40, col. 590.)

12. "Nam virtus est animi habitus naturae modo atque ratione consentaneus." Rhetoricae Libri Duo (Qui sunt de Inventione Rhetorica): ed. W. Friedrich, Leipzig, 1908, II, 53; p. 230, line 2.

13. This date is obtained from a MS in the Biblioteca Marciana, Cod. lat. class. 10, n. 20; v. A. Mansion, "Pour l'histoire du Commentaire de s. Thomas sur la Métaphysique d'Aristote," Rev. Néo-scolastique, 1925, vol. 26, pp. 274-78; M. De Corte, "Themistius et s. Thomas d'Aquin," Archives d'hist. doct. et lit. du moyen âge: 1932, vol. 7, p. 52; and M. Grabmann, "Forschungen über die lateinischen Aristoteles Uebersetzungen des XIII Jahrhunderts," BGPM XVII, 5-6, pp. 147-48.

14. 1022 b 1.

15. αὐτίκα τὴν διάθεσιν λέγεσθαι μέν φησιν τοῦ ἔχοντος μέρη τάξιν τὴν κατὰ τόπον ἢ κατὰ δύναμιν ἢ κατ' εἶδος. In Aristotelis Categorias Commentaria: c. 8; ed. Kalbfleisch, Berlin, 1907, p. 240, line 27. (Almost the same words are found in Aristotle's Metaphysics: loc. cit.)

16. "Dispositio quidem semper importat ordinem alicujus habentis partes; sed hoc contingit tripliciter, ut statim ibidem Philosophus subdit; scilicet aut secundum locum, aut secundum potentiam, aut secundum speciem; in quo, ut Simplicius dicit, comprehendit omnes dispositiones; corporales quidem in eo quod dicit secundum locum; et hoc pertinet ad praedicamentum situs, qui est ordo partium in loco; quod autem dicit secundum potentiam, includit illas dispositiones quae sunt in praeparatione et idoneitate nondum perfecte, sicut scientiae et virtus inchoata; quod autem dicit secundum speciem, includit perfectas dispositiones, quae dicuntur habitus, sicut scientia et

virtus complete." *S. T.:* p. I-II, q. 49, a. I, reply to obj. 3; ed. Leon., VI, 310.

17. "Ad hoc quod aliquid indigeat disponi ad alterum, tria requiruntur: primo quidem ut id quod disponitur sit alterum ab eo quod disponitur, et sic se habeat ad ipsum ut potentia ad actum." (This condition of being in potency in relation to some act is the necessary prerequisite of any disposition or habitus.) "Secundo requiritur quod id quod est in potentia ad alterum, possit pluribus modis determinari, et ad diversa." (And this condition distinguishes these potencies from all those which are *determinatae ad unum.*) "Tertio requiritur quod plura concurrant ad disponendum subjectum ad unum eorum ad quae est in potentia, quae diversis modis commensurari possunt; ut sic disponatur bene vel male ad formam vel ad operationem." *S. T.:* p. I-II, q. 49, a. 4; ed. Leon. VI, 315.

18. St. Augustine, incidentally, through whom a good deal of diluted Stoicism has come into Christian mediaeval thought, knew that σχῆμα was related in meaning to ἕξις. He pointed out that ἕξις was used by the Greeks for that sort of *habitus* which is not a species of quality but a separate category, the state of being dressed or armed. "Sed illum habitum, qui est in perceptione sapientiae et disciplinae, Graeci ἕξιν vocant: hunc autem, secundum quem dicimus vestitum vel armatum, σχῆμα potius vocant." *De Diversis Quaestionibus* LXXXIII, q. 73; *PL.:* vol. 40, col. 84-85.

19. The outline of the Arabian doctrines, given above, is a conscious generalization of a movement covering at least three centuries. Important individual differences distinguish the theories of Al Kindi, Al Farabi, Ibn Sina, and Ibn Rushd. Taking for example a text from the mediaeval Latin translation (since that is the form in which it influenced Christian thought in the 13th century), we find him saying: "Intellectus est secundum quatuor species, prima est intellectus qui semper est in actu. secunda est intellectus qui in potentia est in anima. tertia est intellectus qui cum exit in anima de potentia ad effectum. quarta est intellectus, quem vocamus demonstrativum." *Liber Alkindi de intellectu (et intellecto),* in: A. Nagy, *Die philosophischen Abhandlungen des Ja'qûb, Ben Ishâq Al-Kindi,* BGPM II, 5, p. I, col. 2, lines 11-19.

Alexander of Aphrodisias' interpretation of Aristotle's distinction between the intellect which "becomes all things" and the intellect "which makes all things" is, of course, an important antecedent of the Arabic development, as De Boer has noted ("Zu Kindi und seiner Schule," *Archiv für Geschichte der Philos.:* 1900, vol. 13, p. 172) but, so far as I know, St. Thomas did not know Alexander at first hand but only through such reports as are found in Simplicius and the Arabs.

20. "Sed sunt habitus, secundum quos potest quis agere cum voluerit, ut dicit Commentator in III de Anima." *Q. D. de Virtutibus in Communi:* a. 1, ad. fin.; II, 487. See also, the quotation of Averroës's definition, again juxtaposed with the dynamic definition of St. Augustine, in the *Sed contra* of *S. T.:* p. I-II, q. 49, a. 3; ed. Leon. VI, 312. Averroës' original definition, with its contextual relation to the perfecting of the *intellectus materialis,* i.e., the possible intellect in its purely potential condition, is found in the following text: "Et hoc pronomen, ipsum, potest referri ad intellectum materialem, sicut diximus: et potest referri ad hominem intelligentem. Et oportet addere in sermone secundum quod facit ipsum intelligere omne ex se, et quando voluerit; haec enim est definitio hujus habitus, scilicet ut habens habitum intelligat per ipsum illud, quod est sibi proprium ex se, et quando voluerit, absque eo quod indigeat in hoc aliquo extrinseco." Averrois Cordubensis, *Commentarium in Aristotelis de Anima:* III, 3; in Aristotelis, *Opera:* Venetiis apud Juntas, 1550; t. VI, fol. 169 v. line 22.

21. *S. T.:* p. I-II, q. 71, a. 3; ed. Leon. VII, 6. *Q. D. de Veritate:* q. 10, a. 2, reply to obj. 4; (Marietti) III, 229. *C. G.:* b. I, c. 56; ed. Leon. XIII, 161-62; I, 92; XIII, 251-52; II, 74; XIII, 470. *In de Anima:* b. II, l. 11; ed. Pirotta, p. 128, n. 361. *In de Anima:* b. III, l. 8, p. 232, n. 703. *In de Memoria et Reminiscentia:* l. 2; ed. Pirotta, n. 316. Frequently reiterated throughout the *S. T.:* for instance p. I, q. 79, a. 6, reply to obj. 3; V, 271; q. 87, a. 2; V, 360; p. I-II, q. 50, a. 4, reply to obj. 2; VI, 321; p. III, q. 11, a. 5; X, 163.

22. "Habitus est actus quidam, inquantum est qualitas; et secundum hoc potest esse principium operationis; sed est in potentia per respectum ad operationem: unde habitus dicitur actus primus, et operatio actus secundus." *S. T.:* p. I-II, q. 49, a. 3, reply to obj. 1; ed.

Bibliography

Leon. VI, 312. Cf. *In de Anima*: b. II, lect. 11, ed. Pirotta, p. 128, nn. 360-61, where, after describing the three states of possible intellect, St. Thomas says: "Horum igitur trium, ultimus est in actu tantum: primus in potentia tantum; secundus autem in actu respectu primi, et in potentia respectu secundi."

23. The expression, *habitus entitativus*, is not used by St. Thomas but by later Latin commentators, such as Suarez. Sylvester of Ferrara speaks of *habitus ad essendum*.

24. Aristotle first says that heat, cold, disease and health are dispositions distinguished from habitus by their susceptibility to change, but where such conditions become rather permanent they would be called habitus. *Categoriae*: 8b35-9a3.

25. "Et hoc modo sanitas et pulchritudo, et hujusmodi, habituales dispositiones dicuntur; non tamen perfecte habent rationem habituum, quia causae eorum ex sua natura de facili transmutabiles sunt." *S. T.*: p. I-II, q. 50, a. 1; ed. Leon. VI, 317.

26. "Si ergo accipiatur habitus secundum quod habet ordinem ad naturam, sic non potest esse in anima, si tamen de natura humana loquamur; quia ipsa anima est forma completiva humanae naturae." *S. T.*: p. I-II, q. 50, a. 2; VI, 318.

27. "Sed si loquamur de aliqua superiori naturae, cujus homo potest esse particeps, secundum illud II Pet. 1, 4: *Ut simus consortes naturae divinae*, sic nihil prohibet in anima secundum suam essentiam esse aliquem habitum, scilicet gratiam, ut infra dicetur (quaest. CX, art. 4)." *Ibid.*

28. In this connection, see the brief but excellent discussion of grace as a habitus, in: P. De Roton, *Les Habitus, Leur caractère spirituel*: Paris, 1934, pp. 149-51.

29. "αι ουν εν αυτοις ειρημέναι ἕξεις αυτουσι-ωμέναι εισίν, ου μὴν ὡς συμβεβηκὸς ἐν ὑποκει-μένῳ δια τὸ ἄϋλον." S. Maximi, *Scholia in Lib. De Coelesti Hierarchia*: In cap. vii; *PG*: vol. 4, col. 65.

30. "Sed quia intellectus angelicus non pertingit ad perfectionem Dei, sed in infinitum distat; propter hoc, ad attingendum ad ipsum Deum per intellectum et voluntatem, indigent aliquibus habitibus, tamquam in potentia existentes respectu illius actus puri." *S. T.*: p. I-II, q. 50, a. 6; ed. Leon. VI, 323.

31. *Q. D. de Veritate*: q. 20, a. 2; Taurini-Romae (Marietti) 1931, IV, 103-4. The text is too long to quote here, but my English analysis follows the Latin almost literally.

32. These are the famous and much quoted lines on the psychological effects of habitus: "Inde est etiam quod operationes ex habitu procedentes delectabiles sunt, et in promptu habentur, et faciliter exercentur, quia sunt quasi connaturales effectae." *Ibid.*: p. 104, col. 1, med.

They may be compared with a longer explanation, in which the significant passages are the following: "Ex his etiam potest patere quod habitibus virtutum ad tria indigemus. Primo ut sit uniformitas in sua operatione; ea enim quae ex sola operatione dependent, facile immutantur, nisi secundum aliquam inclinationem habitualem fuerint stabilita. Secundo ut operatio perfecta in promptu habeatur; . . . Tertio, ut delectabiliter perfecta operatio compleatur; quod quidem fit per habitum." *Q. D. de Virtutibus in Communi*: a. 1; II, 487.

33. "Ex utraque autem praedictarum rationum oportet in anima Christi ponere aliquid superadditum." *Q. D. de Veritate*: ad loc. cit.

34. "In Christo autem fuit ut habitus ipsam animam Christi beatificans a principio suae creationis." *Ibid.*

35. "Sic igitur est dicendum, quod anima Christi in cognitione qua Verbum videbat, indiguit habitu, quod est lumen, non ut per quod fieret aliquid intelligibile actu, sicut est in nobis lumen intellectus agentis; sed ut per quod elevaretur intellectus creatus in id quod est supra se. Quantum vero ad cognitionem aliarum creaturarum habuit habitum, qui est collectio specierum ordinatarum ad cognoscendum." *Ibid.*: ad fin. resp. Cf. *S. T.*: p. III, q. 11, a. 6, corpus, and reply to obj. 3; ed. Leon. XI, 164.

Seventh Essay

THE NATURE OF THE ANGELS

1. *Proemium:* (p. 70.) The edition used in the preparation of this paper is that of Mandonnet in the *Opuscula Omnia* of St. Thomas: Paris, Lethielleux, 1927, vol. I, pp. 70-144. The page references in parentheses are to this edition.

2. "Die Werke des hl. Thomas von Aquin," *Beitrage zur Geschichte der Philosophie und Theologie des Mittelalters:* 1931, vol. 22, p. 292.

3. In the introduction to the *Opuscula Omnia:* vol. I, p. lii.

4. At Rome the Leonine Sacramentary (sixth century) lists the "Natale Basilicae Angeli via Salaria," September 30, and assigns five proper collects and prefaces to the feast. The Gelasian Sacramentary (seventh century) gives the feast "S. Michaelis Archangeli," and the Gregorian Sacramentary (eighth century), "Dedicatio Basilionis S. Angeli Michaelis," September 29. The feast of the guardian angels, October 2, is a modern feast.

5. It seems to be unfinished. At the beginning of chapter 16 (p. 128) St. Thomas promises to discuss four topics from the point of view of the Christian religion. Chapter 18 ends with the third topic unfinished, and the fourth topic still untouched. Cf. footnote 114.

6. *Metaphysics:* 983b6-984a16. A somewhat similar enumeration is in St. Augustine, *De Civitate Dei:* b. VIII, c. 2; *PL.:* vol. 41, pp. 225-26.

7. Cf. *Q. D. de Spiritualibus Creaturis:* a. 5, (p. 65), where they are not called Epicureans, but "*Anthropomorphitae.*" The page reference in parentheses is to the edition of L. Keeler (Rome: Pontificia Universitas Gregoriana, 1937), who cites in this connection St. Augustine, Epistola CXLVIII, c. 4; *PL.:* vol. 30, p. 628.

8. Cf. *Acts:* c. XXIII, v. 8. St. Thomas, *S. T.:* p. I, q. 50, a. 1, attributes the same opinion to the Sadducees.

9. *De Substantiis Separatis* (opusculum): c. 1, (pp. 71-74). Cf. also, *Q. D. de Spiritua-*

libus Creaturis: a. 5 (pp. 65-66); *Q. D. de Potentia Dei:* q. 6, a. 6.

10. Cf. Aristotle, *Metaphysics:* 989a 30-989b 21.

11. *Ibid.:* 987a 29-988b 16.

12. There is some similarity to *De Anima:* 406b 25-407b 26, where reference is made to the *Timaeus* (beginning at 33a; cf. esp. 39e-40b.) Cf. F. M. Cornford, *Plato's Cosmology:* New York, Harcourt, Brace and Co., 1937, p. 117 ff.

13. Cf. in this order prop. 12, 13, 113, 119, 116, 20, 121, 190, 184, 189, 196. The edition used for this paper was that of E. R. Dodds, Oxford, Clarendon Press, 1933. St. Thomas refers to the *Elements* in the *De Substantiis Separatis:* c. 18, once without naming it (p. 144) and once under the title of *Liber Divinarum Coelementationum,* and he says at the end of c. 3 (p. 82) that he has gathered the opinions of Plato and Aristotle "ex diversis scripturis." He has a similar treatment of the Platonic hierarchies in his *Expositio super Librum de Causis:* l. 3 (Mandonnet, *Opuscula Omnia:* vol. I, pp. 206-207), and in l. 1 (p. 196) he refers to the *Elements* under the title of *Elevatio Theologica.* It is noteworthy that he makes no mention of the hierarchies in his discussion of the Platonic doctrine in his *Q. D. de Spiritualibus Creaturis:* a. 5, (p. 65).

14. Cf. Proclus, *Elements of Theology:* prop. 20 and 119 for this identification of the idea of the one-and-good with God.

15. This identification of Proclus's lesser gods with Plato's ideas seems to be, not Proclus's, but St. Thomas's own interpretation. *Expositio super Librum de Causis:* l. 3, (p. 206): "Ideo omnes hujusmodi formas subsistentes deos vocabat. Nam hoc nomen Deus universalem quamdam providentiam et causalitatem importat."

16. On the subject of the celestial intelligences cf. Al. Schmid, "Die peripatetisch-scholastische Lehre von den Gestirngeistern," *Athenaeum:* München, J. von Froschammer, 1862, vol. 1, pp. 549-89; Cl. Baeumker, "Wi-

Bibliography

telo, ein Philosoph und Naturforscher des XIII Jahrhunderts," *Beiträge zur Geschichte der Philosophie des Mittelalters*: 1908, vol. 3, Teil 2, "Die Intelligenzen und die Intelligenzenlehre der Schrift, *De Intelligentiis*."

17. Demons are not explicitly mentioned by Proclus in the *Elements of Theology*, but he does speak of souls with special bodies (prop. 196). St. Thomas's source for his discussion of demons is probably St. Augustine, *De Civitate Dei*: b. IX; *PL.*: vol. 41, pp. 255-76, which is the reference he gives in *De Substantiis Separatis*: c. 18, (p. 141). Cf. also *De Civitate Dei*: b. VIII, cc. 14-22; *PL.*: vol. 41, pp. 238-47. On the demons in neo-Platonic literature cf. E. R. Dodds, *Proclus, The Elements of Theology*: pp. 294-96, 313-21. St. Thomas holds that there are demons (fallen angels), but not that they have aërial bodies. Cf. *De Substantiis Separatis*: c. 18, (pp. 137-44); *Q. D. de Spiritualibus Creaturis*: a. 7, (pp. 83-86); *Q. D. de Potentia Dei*: q. 6, a. 6.

18. *Enchiridion de Fide, Spe et Charitate*: c. 58. *PL.*: vol. 40, pp. 259-60. In the *De Substantiis Separatis*: c. 17, (p. 135), and in the *Q. D. de Spiritualibus Creaturis*: a. 6, (p. 76), St. Thomas refers also to St. Augustine's *De Genesi ad Litteram*: b. II, c. 18, n. 38. *PL.*: vol. 34, pp. 279-80. In both places St. Thomas restates St. Augustine's doubt as to whether the heavenly bodies are animate or not.

19. *Matthew*: c. XXV, v. 41.

20. *Metaphysics*: 1076a 8-1080a 11.

21. This discussion follows the order of *Physics*: 256a 4-267b 26.

22. This discussion follows *Metaphysics*: 1072a 19-1074a 31.

23. That is, forty-seven or fifty-five. St. Thomas adds that Avicenna, whom he characterizes as a follower of Aristotle, says that the number of the intelligences is equal to the number of the heavenly bodies and not to the number of their motions. Cf. Avicenna, *Metaphysics*: tr. IX, c. 3, (fol. 104 rb, lin. 49-63). The folio reference is to the Venice, 1508, edition of the Latin translation of Avicenna's philosophical works. The passage, however, does not conclusively reveal Avicenna's own opinion. Avicenna states the two alternatives, and St. Thomas chooses the first as Avicenna's. On the other hand, Giles of Rome, *Errores Philosophorum*: c. 6, err. 15, chooses the second, namely that Avicenna was of the opinion that the number of intelligences is

equal to the number of the motions, that is, "about forty." I am indebted to Prof. Joseph Koch of the University of Breslau for this variant reading from Mandonnet's edition in *Siger de Brabant et l'averroisme latin au XIIIme siècle*: 2e édition, Louvain, Institut Supérieur de Philosophie, 1911, vol. II, p. 13.

24. St. Thomas's proof of this statement seems to be made from *De Anima*: 411a7-22; 413b4-10.

25. In *De Substantiis Separatis*: c. 18, (p. 138) St. Thomas gives St. Augustine, *De Civitate Dei*: b. X, c. 11; *PL.*: vol. 41, pp. 288-91, as his source of information concerning Porphyry's *Epistola ad Anebontem*.

26. Cf. *Metaphysics*: 1074a 16-17. The reference to Avicenna which St. Thomas makes in the course of this argument is from *Metaphysics*: tr. IX, c. 3, (fol. 104 rb, lin. 27-41).

27. a. 5, (p. 66). The three proofs of St. Thomas, "ex perfectione universi," "ex ordine rerum" and "ex proprietate intellectus" follow immediately.

28. c. 2, init. (p. 74).

29. c. 2, med. (pp. 76-77).

30. c. 2, ad. init. (p. 75); med. (p. 76).

31. c. 2, fin. (p. 79).

32. c. 2, ad fin. (p. 78).

33. c. 2, med. (p. 76).

34. c. 2, ad fin. (pp. 78-79).

35. Cf. esp. *Q. D. de Spiritualibus Creaturis*: a. 6, (pp. 71-83, esp. p. 79).

36. *Ibid.*: (p. 78).

37. Proclus, *Elements of Theology*: prop. 12, 13.

38. *S. T.*: p. I, q. 2, a. 3.

39. *Metaphysics*: 993b 24-31.

40. *Ibid.*

41. Proclus, *Elements of Theology*: prop. 3, 4, 8.

42. Cf. *Metaphysics*: 1072a 24-28.

43. Proclus, *Elements of Theology*: prop. 122, 141, 145, 204.

44. St. Augustine, *De Civitate Dei*: b. VIII, c. 14; *PL.*: vol. 41, p. 238. Cf. footnote 17.

45. *Metaphysics*: 1075a 11-25. On providence in Aristotle, cf. É. Gilson, *The Spirit of Mediaeval Philosophy*: New York, Scribner's, 1940, pp. 148-67, 457-58; J. Maritain, *La philosophie bergsonienne*: 2e édition, Paris, Marcel Rivière, 1930, pp. 420-26.

46. St. Augustine, *De Civitate Dei*: b. IX, c. 2; *PL.*: vol. 41, p. 257.

47. Cf. footnote 15.

48. Aristotle says that the first mover unmoved is an intelligence which has itself for its object: a thinking of thinking. *Metaphysics*: 1074b 33-35.

49. The fifty-five or forty-seven prime movers. Cf. *Metaphysics*: 1074a 10-16.

50. Aristotle says merely that a divine being must think of that which is *"most* divine and precious, and it does not change." *Metaphysics*: 1074b 25-26.

51. Aristotle, *Metaphysics*: 1074b 35-1075a 5, uses the terms, "thought" and "the object of thought." He points out that in some cases the knowledge is the object, as for example in the speculative sciences the definition or the act of thinking is the object of thought. He says that this is the case in "things which contain no matter." And this is the kind of activity which is proper to the divine beings.

52. Here the text in the Vivès edition of the *Opera Omnia* is followed. There is a lacuna in the text of Mandonnet.

53. *De Substantiis Separatis*: c. 3, (pp. 79-80); c. 15, (p. 126); c. 16, (p. 128).

54. Avicebron is the name by which the Jewish philosopher Ibn Gabirol (1021-1058/70) was known in the Latin West. His *Fons Vitae* was translated from the original Arabic into Latin in the middle of the twelfth century by Dominicus Gundissalinus of Toledo and the convert Jew, John of Seville (Ibn-Daoud, Ben David, Avendeath, Joannes Hispalensis, etc.). Cl. Baeumker has edited this translation in the *Beiträge zur Geschichte der Philosophie des Mittelalters*: 1892-95, vol. 1, nn. 2-4, pp. 558, to which reference will be made in parentheses. Cf. also M. Wittmann, "Die Stellung des hl. Thomas von Aquin zu Avencebrol," *Beiträge zur Geschichte der Philosophie des Mittelalters*: 1901, vol. 3, n. 3, pp. 79.

55. *Fons Vitae*: tr. IV, c. 7, (p. 226).

56. *Ibid.*: tr. I, c. 14, (p. 17).

57. *Ibid.*: (p. 18).

58. *Ibid.*: tr. I, c. 15, (p. 19).

59. *Ibid.*: tr. I, cc. 16-17, (pp. 19-21).

60. The existence of separate substances is proved in tr. III.

61. Cf. *ibid.*: tr. I, c. 9, (p. 12).

62. *Ibid.*: tr. IV, c. 1, (pp. 212-13).

63. *Ibid.*: tr. IV, c. 2, (pp. 213-14).

64. *Ibid.*: tr. IV, c. 4, (p. 217).

65. *Ibid.*: tr. IV, c. 6, (p. 222).

66. *Ibid.*: (pp. 223-24).

67. c. 4, (p. 30). The page reference is to the text of Roland-Gosselin in *Bibliothèque Thomiste*: 1926, t. VIII.

68. a. 1, reply to objections 9 and 25, (pp. 16, 19).

69. In *Libros Sententiarum*: b. II, d. 3, q. 1, a. 1.

70. Prop. 72, 80, 81. Cf. Mandonnet, *Siger de Brabant et l'averroisme latin au XIIIme siècle*: vol. II, p. 179, items 40, 41, 43. The propositions in their original order are given in H. Denifle et E. Chatelain, *Chartularium Universitatis Parisiensis*: Paris, Delalain, 1889, vol. I, p. 543 ff. On the condemnation of 1270 cf. footnote 120.

71. J. D'Albi, *Saint Bonaventure et les luttes doctrinales de 1267-77*: Tamines, Belgique, Duculot-Roulin, 1922, pp. 93-94, names Alexander of Hales, St. Bonaventure, and "tous les docteurs de la Sorbonne" as St. Thomas's opponents. Cf. also Roland-Gosselin's list of the representatives of mediaeval augustinism on the point in "Le 'De ente et essentia' de St. Thomas d'Aquin:" p. 30, nn. 2-4.

72. cc. 5-6, (pp. 85-98).

73. Prop. 46 of the condemnation of 1277 seems to be involved here. Prop. 45 and 70, however, have in the notion of conservation the possible implication of a higher kind of becoming than that by way of change or motion, and this implication may also be reflected in prop. 46. Cf. Mandonnet, *Siger de Brabant et l'averroisme latin au XIIIme siècle*: vol. II, pp. 179, 184, items 37, 38, 108. Siger de Brabant, *De Necessitate et Contingentia Causarum*: ad. init., says explicitly that the first cause is the eternal cause of the separate intelligences, but not of all immediately. *Ibid.*: vol. II, p. 112.

74. Prop. 80, (p. 179, item 40).

75. There seems to be no corresponding proposition in the condemnation.

76. Prop. 72, 80, (p. 179, items 41, 40). Siger de Brabant, *Quaestiones de Anima Intellectiva*: q. 5, appeals to the authority of Aristotle that nothing prevents an eternal and necessary being from having a cause of its eternity and necessity. Cf. Mandonnet, *Siger de Brabant et l'averroisme latin au XIIIme siècle*: vol. II, p. 159.

77. *Metaphysics*: tr. IX, c. 4, (fol. 104 vb. lin. 49,—105ra, lin. 13). Cf. A. Forest, *La structure métaphysique du concret selon Saint*

Bibliography

Thomas d'Aquin: Paris, J. Vrin, 1931, pp. 331-60, for a list of references to Avicenna in St. Thomas's works. Siger de Brabant, *De Necessitate et Contingentia Causarum*: vol. II, p. 112 ad init., also subscribes to the doctrine of cascade creation.

78. n. 1, (pp. 163-64). The page reference is to the edition of O. Bardenhewer, *Die pseudo-aristotelische Schrift über das reine Gute, bekannt unter dem Namen Liber de causis*: Freiburg i. B., 1882. Cf. also Proclus, *Elements of Theology*: prop. 55, 56, 70. St. Thomas, *Expositio super Librum de Causis*: l. 1, (p. 196), observes that the *Elements of Theology* exists in Greek, while the *Liber de Causis* exists in Arabic but seemingly not in Greek. He hazards the guess that some one of the Arabian philosophers made the *Liber de Causis* by taking excerpts from Proclus's *Elements*, since what is found in the former is contained more fully in the latter. Today Alkindi is thought to be the compiler of the *Liber de Causis*, although Alfarabi's name frequently occurs in the manuscripts.

79. *De Substantiis Separatis:* c. 8, ad init. (p. 104).

80. In the *Liber de Causis*, the example used is man.

81. The example is used frequently. Cf. *Metaphysics:* 1040a 8-29.

82. c. 7, init. (p. 99).

83. c. 15, init. (pp. 125-26).

84. It is significant that he attended at Alexandria the lectures of Ammonius Saccas, founder of neo-platonism and teacher of Plotinus.

85. tr. I, c. 8. Cf. also tr. II, c. 9. The Latin translation of Rufinus, which takes such liberties with the original that St. Jerome made a new translation, is the only complete version extant. It is included in the *Opera Omnia* of Origen; *PG.*: vols. 11-17. The edition used for this paper is the Latin translation of the *Opera Omnia*: Paris, Joannes Parvus and Jodocus Badius Ascensius, 1512-19, vol. 4, fol. 122 rb, 133 rb.

86. Cf. Mandonnet, *Siger de Brabant et l'averroisme latin au XIIIme siècle*: vol. I, p. 111, n. 1. The document is also given in Denifle et Chatelain, *Chartularium Universitatis Parisiensis*: vol. I, pp. 486-87.

87. Cf. footnote 70.

88. *De Substantiis Separatis:* c. 11, ad init. (p. 114): "Posuerunt Deum, et alias substantias

immateriales singularium cognitionem non habere, nec inferiorum, et praecipue humanorum actuum providentiam gerere." The condemned propositions read as follows:

"10. Quod Deus non cognoscit singularia.
11. Quod Deus non cognoscit alia a se.
12. Quod humani actus non reguntur providentia Dei."

89. For a discussion of the Averroist doctrine of angels, cf. A. Vacant, "Angelologie parmi les averroistes latins," *Dictionnaire de théologie catholique*: Paris, 1902, vol. I, pp. 1260-64, esp. p. 1262 where St. Thomas's treatment of Averroism in the *De Substantiis Separatis* is discussed.

90. This reasoning is like that of the second argument in prop. 42 (Mandonnet, vol. II, p. 177, n. 15) of the condemnations of 1277.

91. Cf. footnote 88. Cf. also prop. 3 (Mandonnet, vol. II, p. 177, n. 13) of the condemnations of 1277.

92. Cf. the third argument in prop. 42 of the condemnations of 1277.

93. *Metaphysics:* 1027a 29-1027b 16. Aristotle argues that accidental things have accidental causes, and necessary things necessary causes. This text from the sixth book of the *Metaphysics* is essentially the basis for Siger de Brabant's discussion in the *De Necessitate et Contingentia Causarum*: vol. II, p. 111, init.

94. Cf. prop. 21 (Mandonnet, vol. II, p. 183, n. 102) of the condemnations of 1277, in which it is asserted that nothing happens by chance, but that all things take place by necessity.

95. This doctrine is not in the condemnations of 1277. St. Thomas mentions it in the *S. T.*: p. I, q. 22, a. 2. He adds that Rabbi Moses (Maimonides) has a variation of it in that he excepts men from the group of corruptibles because of the splendor of their intellect, but insists that all other individuals among corruptible things are outside the divine providence. The reference in Maimonides is to the *Dux Neutrorum sive Dubiorum*: tr. III, c. 18, (fol. 81v) according to the edition of Augustinus Iustinianus (Paris, 1520).

96. c. 12, ad init. (p. 116).

97. This is established in c. 9, (pp. 108-10).

98. *Metaphysics:* 1072b 26-30.

99. In both places the doctrine is a reduction of Empedocles's views to the absurd conclusion

[377]

that God knows less things than any other being. Cf. *De Anima*: 410b 4-7; *Metaphysics*: 1000b 4-6.

100. Esp. *Metaphysics*: 1074b 15-1075a 10, in which Aristotle discusses "certain problems" which ".the nature of divine thought involves."

101. c. 12, ad fin. (p. 119).

102. Cf. footnote 98.

103. *De Natura Boni contra Manichaeos*: c. 41; *PL*.: vol. 42, p. 563-64. Cf. also *Confessionum*: b. V, c. 10, n. 20, *PL*: vol. 32, p. 715.

104. *De Natura Boni contra Manichaeos*: c. 42; *PL*.: vol. 42, p. 565.

105. *Ibid.; PL*.: vol. 42, p. 566, where the Manichaean doctrine that good things are subservient to the light, and evil things to the darkness, is criticized.

106. *De Anima*: 429a 18-25.

107. The text to which reference is made in this paper is that of John Scotus Eriugena, *PL*.: vol. 122, pp. 1035-70; pp. 1111-76, though it is not exactly like that which St. Thomas quotes. In fact, St. Thomas uses two translations, as is evident from his reference to an "alia littera" (p. 135). His quotations have also been checked against the version of Abbot Thomas Gallus Vercellensis and that of John Sarrasin, as contained in Dionysius the Carthusian's commentaries on Dionysius the Areopagite (Cologne, 1556), and have been found to have great similarity to that of John Sarrasin. The translation of Abbot Hilduin and, in part, that of Robert Grosseteste have also been checked. The former was edited by G. Théry, *Études dionysiennes. II, Hilduin, traducteur de Denys. Édition de sa traduction:* Paris, Vrin, 1937, and both are included, in part, in *Dionysiaca*, edited by Philippe Chevallier, vol. I: Bruges, Desclée de Brouwer et Cte, 1937.

108. Matthew: c. XIX, v. 17; *Exodus*: c. III, v. 14; *Deuteronomy*: c. XXX, v. 20.

109. Cf. Pseudo-Dionysius, *De Divinis Nominibus*: c. 5; *PL*.: vol. 122, p. 1147.

110. I.e., as St. Thomas explains in the following chapter, (p. 136), "in a spiritual manner, through some contact of power; not

in a bodily manner, through contact of dimensive quantity."

111. *Psalm* CII, v. 20; Matthew: c. XXIV, v. 29.

112. *De Coelesti Hierarchia*: c. 1; *PL*.: vol. 122, pp. 1037-38.

113. St. Thomas refers to Aristotle here. Cf. *De Anima*: 429a 22-25.

114. The chapter is incomplete. St. Thomas says in the beginning of it, *"primum considerandum occurrit de differentia bonorum et malorum."* Moreover, certain objections are not answered. Cf. footnote 5.

115. *De Divinis Nominibus*: c. 4; *PL*.: vol. 122, pp. 1142-43.

116. St. Thomas's source is, as he himself says, St. Augustine's *De Civitate Dei*: b. X, c. 11; *PL*.: vol. 41, p. 289. Cf. *C. G.*: b. II, c. 107.

117. *De Civitate Dei*: b. VIII, c. 17; *PL*.: vol. 41, p. 241. The reference which St. Thomas makes to Apuleius, *De Deo Socratis*, is from *ibid.*: b. IX, c. 8; *PL*.: vol. 41, p. 263.

118. *De Divinis Nominibus*: c. 4; *PL*.: vol. 122, p. 1142 c.

119. Three of the four difficulties are answered in the *C. G.*: b. III, c. 110.

120. Cf. Mandonnet, *Siger de Brabant et l'averroisme latin au XIIIme siècle*: vol. I, pp. 105-8; vol. II, pp. 29-30, 51-52. In a letter which Giles (of Lessines) sent to his former teacher, St. Albert, we learn of the other two propositions which Bishop Tempier intended to have condemned. One is the doctrine of the unity of the substantial form, carefully hidden in a theological question; and the other, the doctrine of the simplicity of the angels and the soul. St. Albert wrote his *De Quindecim Problematibus* in answer to Giles's request for information. Mandonnet has published both, *op cit.*, vol. II, pp. 29-52. Cf. also St. Thomas *Quaestiones Quodlibetales*: quod. II, a. 1; quod III, a. 4; quod IV, a. 8.

121. Mandonnet, *Siger de Brabant et l'averroisme latin au XIIIme Siècle*: vol. II, p. 175.

Bibliography

Eighth Essay

THE DILEMMA OF BEING AND UNITY

1. E. Gilson, "Franz Brentano's Interpretation of Mediaeval Philosophy," *Mediaeval Studies*: 1939, vol. 1, p. 8.
For the sake of clearness I should like to indicate here that I have elsewhere expressed some of the ideas of this paper. Cf. *St. Thomas and the Greeks*: Milwaukee, Marquette U. Press, 1939; "Necessity and Liberty: an Historical Note on St. Thomas Aquinas," *The New-Scholasticism*: 1941, vol. 15, n. 1, pp. 18-45. In this paper, however, I am not concerned with the conflict itself between necessitarianism and creationism, even though this same conflict dominates the present discussion; I am rather concerned with the antinomy between intelligibility and unity in Platonism as the ultimate philosophical source of the nominalism of Ockham. The development of this point exceeds the limits of a single essay, and therefore I have limited myself to indicating how the Platonic theory of Forms contains within itself not only what is called a realism of essences, but also (if I may use the expression) a realism of non-being, i.e., a realism of the unintelligible and the indeterminate; and how out of this second realism there can arise the Ockhamist doctrines of singularity in things and liberty in God. My contention is that these doctrines are latent possibilities within Platonic realism, and that one has only to explore the implications of Platonic non-being for the nature of unity in order to discover them.—For an introduction to the question of the historical location of Ockhamism, cf. the rapid article of Jean Paulus, "Sur les origines du nominalisme," *Revue de philosophie*: 1937, vol. 37, n. 4, pp. 313-30.

2. It is in the direction of this realism of the unintelligible that we must seek the first principle of Ockhamism. We cannot deny that the philosophy of Ockham is the philosophy of a believer, as L. Baudry has rightly insisted (cf. *Le tractatus de principiis theologiae attribué à G. d'Occam*: Paris, J. Vrin, 1936, pp. 30-35). But to argue from this that the dogma of the divine omnipotence can lead Ockham into all the conclusions of his nominalism (*op. cit.*: pp. 35-40) is to raise the question as to why that dogma, which was also accepted by a St. Thomas Aquinas, did not, and could not possibly, lead to the same result in his thought (cf. the just observations of J. Paulus, "Les origines du nominalisme," p. 329). That which appears to command *both* the doctrine of omnipotence stressed by L. Baudry *and* the radical indivisibility of beings stressed by J. Paulus, following the work of P. Vignaux (cf. *fn. 3*), is the notion of being, whether it be creatures or the will of God, as consisting in the exhaustion point of the elimination of plurality —*but in the line of intelligibility itself*. This is as Platonic a conclusion as it can possibly be, for it is a theory of *singularity as indistinction* which is the strict parallel of the *radical indetermination* of the Platonic and Plotinian One.

3. P. Vignaux, "Nominalisme," *Dictionnaire de théologie catholique*: 1931, vol. xi, n. 1, col. 734.

4. E. Hochstetter, *Studien zur Metaphysik und Erkenntnislehre Wilhelms von Ockham*: Berlin, W. de Gruyter, 1927, p. 25, note.

5. N. Abbagnano, *Guglielmo di Ockham*: Lanciano, G. Carabba, 1931, p. 56.—For the doctrine of intuitive and abstractive knowledge in Ockham, it is now possible to consult the text edited recently by Philotheus Boehner, *Guillelmi Ockham Quaestio prima principalis Prologi in primum librum Sententiarum, cum interpretatione Gabrielis Biel*: Paderborn, F. Schoeningh, 1939.—I may indicate here that Father Boehner accepts my interpretation of Ockham's critique of St. Thomas (cf. "Necessity and Liberty," pp. 22-32), but not my estimate. I am quite willing to leave the matter rest there, for what Father Boehner is saying is that I find nominalism unacceptable: *concedo*. Cf. Ph. Boehner, "Ockham's Tractatus de Praedestinatione et de Praescientia Dei et de Futuris Contingentibus and its Main Problems," *Proceedings of the American Catholic*

Philosophical Association: 1940, vol. 16, p. 182, note 14. In sharing the opinion of L. Baudry on Ockham as a defender of the Faith, Father Boehner accepts also, it would seem, the conclusions to which Baudry has come on the notion of the divine omnipotence in Ockham. Now this is certainly to be contested, for the obvious reason which has been raised by Paulus. Cf. footnote 2 above. Father Boehner will, therefore, not be surprised if I disagree quite definitely with his conception of the three steps by which Christian thought liberated itself from Greek and Arabian necessitarianism (cf. *art. cit.*: p. 183). It is one thing to avoid this necessitarianism, and quite another to suppose that only the destruction of created natures is the passport to the defense of liberty.

6. E. Gilson, *God and Philosophy*: New Haven, Yale U. Press, 1941, p. 110.

7. *Op. cit.*: p. 67.

8. *Ibid.*

9. *Op. cit.*: pp. ix-xvi.

10. F. Ehrle, *Der Sentenzenkommentar Peters von Candia*: Münster, Aschendorff, 1925, p. 263.

11. F. Gilson, *L'Ésprit de la philosophie médiévale*: 2 vols., Paris, J. Vrin, 1932.

12. Plato, *Sophistes*: pp. 252E-253B.

13. *Op. cit.*: pp. 243D-245, 250BC, 257A, 258BC, 259A-E.

14. *Theatetus*: pp. 180C-181B.—For a metaphysical interpretation of Plato along Neoplatonic lines, which is marred only by its somewhat lame conclusion, cf. the work of W. F. R. Hardie, *A Study in Plato*: Oxford, Clarendon Press, 1936.

15. On the Plotinian One, cf. the recent discussion of A. H. Armstrong, *The Architecture of the Intelligible World in the Philosophy of Plotinus*: Cambridge University Press, 1940, pp. 1-47.—For some reservations on this book, cf. *Thought*: 1941, vol. 16, pp. 191-92.

16. Cf. René Arnou, *Le désir de dieu dans la philosophie de Plotin*: Paris, F. Alcan, 1921, pp. 191-282; Maurice Burque, "Un problem plotinien: l'identification de l'ame avec l'Un dans la contemplation" (Offprint of the *Revue de l'Université d'Ottawa*, 1940).

17. Cf. Plotinus, *Enneads*: VI, 9, 1-2.

18. For Augustine, cf. the important text of *De Moribus Manichaeorum*: b. II, c. 6, 8, and especially the following: "Haec vero quae tendunt esse ad ordinem tendunt, quem cum fuerint consecuta ipsum esse consequuntur, quantum id creatura consequi potest. Ordo enim ad convenientiam quamdam quod ordinat redigit. Nihil est autem esse quam unum esse. Itaque inquantum quidque unitatem adipiscitur, intantum est. Unitatis est enim operatio convenientia et concordia, qua sunt inquantum sunt ea quae composita sunt. Nam simplicia per se sunt, quae una sunt: quae autem non sunt simplicia, concordia partium imitantur unitatem, et intantum sunt inquantum assequuntur."—This "essentialism" of St. Augustine has been diagnosed briefly but critically by E. Gilson, *God and Philosophy*: pp. 48-62.

For Boethius, cf. *De Trinitate*: II, IV.—It is the relation of things to *determination*, not existence, which commands Boethius's discussion of being. The "essentialism" of Boethius, whose *De Hebdomadibus* contains formulas which will become classic in mediaeval discussions on the nature of being, has been well brought out by H. J. Brosch, *Der Seinsbegriff bei Boethius*: Innsbruck, F. Rauch, 1931.

19. *Liber de Diversis Quaestionibus LXXXIII*: q. 46.—For an historical introduction to this text, cf. M. Grabmann, "Des hl. Augustinus quaestio de ideis (de diversis quaestionibus LXXXIII, q. 46) in ihrer inhaltlichen und geschichtlichen Bedeutung," *Philosophisches Jahrbuch*: 1930, vol. 43, n. 3, pp. 297-307.

20. Gabriel Biel, *In I Sent.*: d. XXXV, q. 5C; ed. Tubingen, 1501, fol. 113 rb (unnumbered).

21. *In I Sent.*: d. 2, q. 7A; ed. Lyons, 1495, fol. 102 rb (unnumbered).

22. *Op. cit.*: d. 2, q. 7B; fol. 102 rb.

23. *Op. cit.*: d. 2, q. 7F; fol. 102 va.—The identification of Ockham's opponents is rather hazardous, and historians are not agreed. Cf. P. Vignaux, "Nominalisme," coll. 734-35; N. Abbagnano, *Guglielmo di Ockham*: pp. 75-88.

24. *In I Sent.*: d. 2, q. 7A; fol. 102 rb.

25. Cf. P. Vignaux, "Occam," *Dictionnaire de théologie catholique*: 1931, vol. xi, n. 1, coll. 877-78.

26. *In I Sent.*: d. 2, q. 4B; fol. 88 va.

27. *Op. cit.*: d. 2, q. 4D; fol. 89 rb.

28. *Op. cit.*: d. 2, q. 4D; fol. 90 va.

29. *Op. cit.*: d. 2, q. 5B; fol. 94 ra.

30. *Op. cit.*: d. 2, q. 5D; fol. 94 ab.

31. *Op. cit.*: d. 2, q. 6A; fol. 94 vb.

32. *Op. cit.*: d. 2, q. 6B; fol. 94 vb.

Bibliography

33. The quotations are verbatim. Cf. *Opus Oxoniense*: II, d. 3, q. 1 and 6; ed. Garcia, vol. II, p. 230 (n. 238), p. 232 (n. 239), pp. 265-66 (n. 286), pp. 269-70 (n. 289).—In locating Scotus *after* Platonic realism, in his sequence of questions on the universals, Ockham finds confirmation in the interpretation of Scotus proposed by Johannes Kraus, *Die Lehre des Johannes Duns Skotus, O. F. M. von der Natura Communis*: Freiburg, Studia Friburgensia, 1927. But if Scotistic formalism did not intend to be a Platonic realism, it is the point of Ockham's critique that it could not maintain itself without doing it. Cf. also the reservations of J. Kraus, *op. cit.*: p. 138.

34. *In I Sent.*: d. 2, q. 6BC; foll. 94 vb-95 va.

35. *Op. cit.*: d. 2, q. 6C; fol. 95 va.

36. *Op. cit.*: d. 2, q. 6A; fol. 94 vb.

37. *Op. cit.*: d. 2, q. 6E; fol. 96 rb.

38. *Op. cit.*: d. 2, q. 6F; fol. 96 vab.

39. *Op. cit.*: d. 2, q. 6PQ; fol. 98 vb.

40. *Expositio Aurea super Artem Veterem*: I, Proemium; ed. Bologna, 1496, fol. 8 va.

41. *Ibid.*: fol. 8 vab.

42. *Ibid.*: fol. 8 vb.

43. The "villainy" of Porphyry is one of the essential themes of Ernest A. Moody's book, *The Logic of William of Ockham*: New York, Sheed and Ward, 1935. Cf. especially pp. 18, 66-117. However, the work of Jean Paulus (cf. footnote 48) makes it increasingly evident that Ockham's difficulties are *in* metaphysics and that, instead of the Porphyrian problem of genera and species, he was much more concerned with the Avicennian problem of the absolute nature.

44. *Summa Logicae*: I, 16; ed. Paris, 1488, fol. 8 vb.—This opinion of Scotus is not only false, but also against the intention of Aristotle, *op. cit.*: I, 7; fol. 4 ra. And, to complete the picture, Ockham contests to Scotus even the interpretation of Avicenna on the doctrine of absolute natures, *op. cit.*: I, 8; foll. 5 rb-5 va.

45. Cf. especially Paul Vignaux, "Nominalisme"; coll. 754-82.

46. *In I Sent.*: d. 2, q. 2F; fol. 84 va.

47. This is the position of Ph. Boehner, "Ockham's Tractatus": p. 183.

48. *In I Sent.*: d. 35, q. 5; fol. 253 va.— J. Paulus, *Henri de Gand*: Paris, J. Vrin, 1938, p. 87, with note 1, has indicated Henry as the background of this question. The same author insists on many philosophical points of contact between Henry of Ghent and William of Ockham: *op. cit.*: pp. 387-88.

49. *In I Sent.*: d. 35, q. 5; fol. 252 va.

50. Gabriel Biel, *In I Sent.*: d. 17, q. 1, a. 3K; quoted by Paul Vignaux, "Nominalisme": col. 764.

51. I refer especially to the works cited above in notes 3 and 4.

52. J. Paulus, *Henri de Gand*: p. 69.

53. Aristotle, *Posterior Analytics*: 77a.

54. J. Paulus, *op. cit.*: pp. 94-95.

55. *Op. cit.*: pp. 95-96.

56. Cf. E. Bréhier, *La philosophie de Plotin*: Paris, Boivin et Cie, 1928, pp. 23-45.

57. J. Paulus, *op. cit.*: pp. 98-99.—The inclusion of Eriugena within the Augustinian tradition on the doctrine ideas is more than a little surprising: Eriugena holds that the divine ideas are eternal, but *not* co-eternal. Cf. *De Divisione Naturae*, ii, 21; P.L., vol. 122, coll. 561B-562A.

58. Henry of Ghent, *Quodl.*: IX, 2; *Summa*: 68, 5, 7-14; cited by J. Paulus, *op. cit.*: p. 91, note 1.—For St. Albert the Great, cf. *op. cit.*: pp. 101-2, 111-12, 115; Ulrich Dähnert, *Die Erkenntnislehre des Albertus Magnus*: Leipzig, S. Hirzel, 1934, pp. 90 ff.

58a. In some forthcoming articles in *Thought*, I shall try to examine the metaphysical significance of the transition from the Platonic to the Thomistic theory of man and of knowledge. This transition is governed by the Christian doctrine of creation and of divine ideas, and it founds a new conception of the nature and structure of human knowledge.—For an important recent discussion of the existentialism of the Thomistic doctrine of man, cf. Jacques Maritain, "L'Humanisme de saint Thomas d'Aquin," *Mediaeval Studies*: 1942, vol. 3, pp. 174-184.

59. J. Paulus, *op. cit.*: p. 101.

60. *S. T.*: p. I, q. 15, a. 2.

61. St. Augustine, *De Diversis Quaestionibus LXXXIII*: q. 46; PL.: vol. 40, col. 30; quoted by St. Thomas Aquinas, *ibid.*

62. *S. T.*: *ibid.*

63. *Ibid.*

64. *S. T.*: p. I, q. 14, a. 6.

65. *Op. cit.*: p. I, q. 4, aa. 1 and 2; q. 6, a. 3; q. 7, a. 1; q. 9, a. 1; q. 11, aa. 3 and 4; q. 13, a. 11.

66. *Op. cit.*: p. I, q. 14, a. 6.

67. *Ibid.*

68. It is beyond my present purpose to develop this point. In what follows, I am concerned only to indicate, in reference to the *De Substantiis Separatis*, the direction which the exegetical question presented by the Thomistic texts ought to take. For the question itself, cf. E. Gilson, *L'Ésprit de la philosophie médiévale*, vol. I, pp. 240-242; A. C. Pegis, *St. Thomas and the Greeks*, pp. 101-104.

69. *Q. D. de Potentia Dei*: q. 3, a. 5; *S. T.*: p. I, q. 44, a. 2.

70. *De Substantiis Separatis:* c. VII; ed. P. Mandonnet, *Opuscula Omnia*, Paris, P. Lethielleux, 1927, vol. I, pp. 99-100.

71. *Ibid.; ed. cit.*, vol. I, pp. 100-101.

72. *Ibid.; ed. cit.*, vol. I, pp. 98-99.

73. *Ibid.; ed. cit.*, vol. I, p. 100.

74. *Op. cit.;* c. VII; *ed. cit.*, vol. I, p. 104.

75. *Ibid.*

76. *Op. cit.;* c. IX; *ed. cit.*, vol. I, pp. 108-109.

77. *Ibid.; ed. cit.*, vol. I, p. 109.

78. *Ibid.; ed. cit.*, vol. I, p. 110.

Ninth Essay

PRUDENCE, THE INCOMMUNICABLE WISDOM

1. Aristotle, *Nichomachean Ethics*: b. VI, c. 13, 1144 b. 28-30.

2. On Socrates cf. St. Thomas, *Q. D. de Malo*: q. 3, a. 9: "Omnes virtutes nominabat scientias et omnia vitia seu peccata nominabat ignorantias: ex quo sequebatur quod nullus sciens ex infirmitate peccat: quod manifeste contrariatur his quae cotidie experimur."

3. On this point cf. *S. T.*: p. I-II, q. 14, a. 3: "Cognitio autem veritatis in talibus [sc. agibilibus] non habet aliquid magnum ut per se sit appetibilis, sicut cognitio universalium et necessariorum: sed appetitur secundum quod est utilis ad operationem." An excellent exposition of the Thomistic doctrine on the nature and relationship of moral sciences and prudence will be found in Yves Simon's *Critique de la Connaissance Morale*: Paris, 1934.

4. Not the entire solution, of course. For that, one also needs great precision on the nature of election (among other things) into which the present essay does not go. In this connection the study of Gerard Smith, "Intelligence and Liberty," *The New Scholasticism*: 1941, vol. 15, n. 1, pp. 1-17, is very valuable.

5. *Q. D. de Virtutibus Cardinalibus*: a. 3.

6. *Ibid.*: a. 2: "Bonum . . . in actibus humanis invenitur per hoc quod pertingitur ad regulam humanorum actuum; quae quidem est una quasi homogenea et propria homini, scilicet ratio recta, alia autem est sicut prima mensura transcendens, quod est Deus. Ad rationem autem rectam attingit homo per

prudentiam quae est recta ratio agibilium, ut Philosophus dicit in VI Ethic." Cf. *S. T.*: p. I-II, q. 71, a. 6.

7. In answer to the suggestion that the theological virtues be called "cardinal" St. Thomas says: "quod virtutes theologicae sunt supra hominem . . . unde non proprie dicuntur virtutes humanae sed superhumanae vel divinae." *S. T.*: p. I-II, q. 61, a. 1, reply to obj. 2.

8. For example, *Q. D. de Virtutibus in Communi*: a. 5; *S. T.*: p. I-II, q. 71, a. 2. Cf. *Nichomachean Ethics*: b. II, c. 6, 1106 a 16-24.

9. *S. T.*: p. I-II, q. 71, a. 1: "Directe quidem virtus importat dispositionem quamdam alicuius convenienter se habentis secundum modum suae naturae; unde Philos. dicit in 7 Physic. quod 'virtus est dispositio perfecti ad optimum: dico autem perfecti quod est dispositum secundum naturam.'"

10. Cf. *In Libros Sententiarum*: b. II, d. 25, q. 1, a. 2, reply to obj. 7: "Animalia . . . ex determinatione naturae acus suos exercent, non autem ex propria determinatione; unde omnes ejusdem speciei similes operationes faciunt, sicut omnis aranea similem facit telam, quod non esset si ex seipsis quasi per artem operantem sua opera disponerent."

11. *Q. D. de Virtutibus in Communi*: a. 6: "Aliquod bonum apprehensum oportet esse objectum appetitus animalis et rationalis; ubi ergo istud bonum uniformiter se habet potest esse inclinatio naturalis in appetitu et judicium naturale in vi cognitiva. . . . et ex hoc na-

Bibliography

turali judicio et naturali appetitu provenit quod omnis hirundo uniformiter facit nidum et omnis aranea uniformiter facit telam."

12. From the article cited in footnote (11).

13. *Q. D. de Virtutibus in Communi:* a. 6: "Homo autem est multarum operationum et diversarum et hoc propter nobilitatem sui principii activi, scilicet animae, cuius virtus ad infinita quodammodo se extendit: Et ideo non sufficeret homini naturalis appetitus boni nec naturale judicium ad recte agendum nisi amplius determinetur et perficiatur."

14. *Q. D. de Veritate:* q. 22, a. 7: "Differenter est aliquid provisum homini et caeteris animalibus .... ex parte apprehensionis ... aliis animalibus sunt inditae ... quaedam substantiales conceptiones eis necessariae ... sed loco horum homini sunt indita universalia principia naturaliter intellecta per quae in omnia quae sunt ei necessaria procedere protest. Et similter est etiam ex parte appetitus."

15. *Q. D. de Veritate:* q. 22, a. 5. Cf. *S. T.:* p. I, q. 82, a. 1; p. I-II, q. 10, a. 1, corpus and reply to obj. 3: "Semper naturae respondet unum proportionatum naturae."

16. *S. T.:* p. I, q. 82, a. 1. Cf. *Q. D. de Malo:* q. 16, a. 4, reply to obj. 5; *S T.:* p. I-II, q. 10, aa. 1 and 2.

17. This point is discussed once more in the closing section of this essay; see especially footnotes 68-77.

18. *Q. D. de Veritate:* q. 22, a. 7: "Homini inditus est appetitus ultimi finis sui in communi, ut scilicet appetat naturaliter se esse completum in bonitate. Sed in quo ista completio consistat, utrum in virtutibus, vel scientiis, vel delectabilibus, vel hujusmodi aliis non est ei determinatum a natura."

19. *Q. D. de Veritate:* q. 22, a. 5.

20. *Q. D. de Veritate:* q. 16, a. 2.

21. *Q. D. de Veritate:* q. 16, a. 2.

22. *Q. D. de Veritate:* q. 16, a. 1, reply to obj. 12; also, a. 3.

23. *Q. D. de Veritate:* q. 22, a. 10 reply to obj. 4: "Objectum intellectus practici non est bonum sed verum relate ad opus."

24. A catalogue of the precepts of synderesis is a delicate job. Those cited are drawn from *In Libros Sententiarum:* b. II, d. 24, q. 2, a. 3; *Q. D. de Veritate:* q. 16, a. 1 and reply to obj. 2 of a. 2.

25. *In Libros Sententiarum:* b. II, d. 24, q. 2, a. 4.

26. *Q. D. de Veritate:* q. 16, a. 3.

27. Operationes sunt in singularibus. *Q. D. de Veritate:* q. 22, a. 4, reply to obj. 3. St. Thomas often repeats this, e. g. *S. T.:* p. I-II, q. 90, a. 2, reply to obj. 2.

28. *Q. D. de Virtutibus in Communi:* a. 6: "Oportet quod ratio practica perficiatur aliquo habitu ad hoc quod recte dijudicet de bono humano secundum singula agenda. Et haec virtus dicitur prudentia."

29. *S. T.:* p. II-II, q. 47, a. 15: "Prudentia includit cognitionem et universalium et singularium operabilium ad quae prudens universalia principia applicat." This statement is of the utmost importance. There is no more completely misleading conception of prudence than that which makes "means" its *exclusive* concern.

30. V. preceding note and the whole of the text there cited. Cf. also *ibid.:* reply to obj. 3.

31. *S. T.:* p. II-II, q. 47, a. 5: Utrum prudentia sit virtus specialis.

32. *S. T.:* p. I-II, q. 57, a. 5, reply to obj. 3: "Verum intellectus practici aliter accipitur quam verum intellectus speculativi ... nam verum intellectus speculativi accipitur per conformitatem intellectus ad rem ... verum autem intellectus practici accipitur per conformitatem ad appetitum rectum; quae quidem conformitas in necessariis locum non habet quae voluntate humana non fiunt; sed solum in contingentibus quae possunt a nobis fieri, sive sint agibilia interiora sive factibilia exteriora."

33. *S. T.:* p. II-II, q. 47, a. 4: Utrum prudentia sit virtus: "Ad prudentiam ... pertinet ... applicatio rectae rationis ad opus quod non fit sine appetitu recto; et ideo prudentia non solum habet rationem virtutis quam habent aliae virtutes intellectuales; sed etiam habet rationem virtutis quam habent aliae virtutes morales quibus etiam connumeratur." Cf. *Q. D. de Virtutibus in Communi:* a. 7, reply to obj. 1.

34. The act of the speculative intellect is "consideratio veri" and the speculative intellect "finem habet in actu suo proprio." The act of the practical intellect is described as "consideratio de agendis vel faciendis (verum relate ad opus)." The practical intellect is ordered "as to an end to a further exterior act"; it knows "propter agere vel facere." The difference, therefore, does not lie in the "consideratio" but in the "verum."

Notice that the practical intellect is "ordered to good" only by its special relation to the will. This ordination does not make it an appetite. Hence its act can still be called "consideratio veri." Cf. *Q. D. de Virtutibus in Communi*: a. 7, reply to obj. 1.

35. *Job*: c. XXXI, v. 18, cited by Aquinas in *Q. D. de Virtutibus Cardinalibus*: a. 2. Cf. *S. T.*: p. I-II, q. 65, a. 1; also, Aristotle, *Nichomachean Ethics*: b. VI, c. 13 1144 b 8-10.

36. *Q. D. de Virtutibus Cardinalibus*: a. 2: "Sunt enim quaedam virtutes omnino imperfectae quae sine prudentia existunt non attingentes rationem rectam. . . . Hae autem inclinationes non habent rationem virtutis . . . Unde Gregorius dicit . . . quod ceterae virtutes nisi ea quae appetunt, prudenter agant, virtutes esse nequaquam possunt; unde ibi inclinationes quae sunt sine prudentia non habent perfecte rationem virtutis. Secundus autem gradus virtutum est illarum quae attingunt rationem rectam."

37. *Q. D. de Virtutibus in Communi*: a. 13: "Cum homo sit homo per hoc quod rationem habet oportet quod bonum hominis sit secundum rationem esse."

38. *Ibid.*: "Materia virtutum moralium sunt passiones et operationes humanae."

39. *Ibid.*: "Cuiuslibet habentis regulam et mensuram bonum consistit in hoc quod est adequari suae regulae vel mensurae . . . . ita bonum in passionibus et operationibus humanis est quod attingatur modus rationis qui est mensura et regula omnium passionum et operationum humanarum."

40. *Q. D. de Virtutibus in Communi*: a. 13, reply to obj. 8: "Medium competit virtuti non in quantum medium sed in quantum medium rationis quia virtus est bonum hominis quod est secundum rationem esse."

41. *Q. D. de Virtutibus in Communi*: a. 13.

42. *Ibid.*, reply to obj. 5: "Et hoc ipsum quod quaedam attingunt ad maximum pertinet in eis ad rationem medii in quantum maximum attingunt secundum regulam rationis; sicut fortis attingit maxima pericula secundum rationem scilicet quando debet, ut debet, et propter quod debet."

43. *Ibid.*, reply to obj. 6: "Virginitas et paupertas licet sint in extremo rei sunt tamen medio rationis: quia virgo abstinet a venereis omnibus propter quod debet et secundum quod debet; quia propter Deum et delectabiliter."

44. *Q. D. de Virtutibus in Communi*: a. 13: "Sicut igitur virtutes morales consistunt in medio determinato per rationem; ita ad prudentiam quae est virtus intellectualis practica circa moralia pertinet idem medium in quantum ponit ipsum circa moralia pertinet idem medium in quantum ponit ipsum circa actiones et passiones. Et hoc patet per definitionem virtutis moralis quae, ut in II Ethic (cap. vi) dicitur est habitus electivus, in medietate consistens, ut sapiens determinabit. Idem ergo est medium prudentiae et virtutis moralis, sed prudentiae est sicut imprimentis, virtutis moralis sicut impressi."

45. *S. T.*: p. I-II, q. 58, a. 2, reply to obj. 4: "Recta ratio quae est secundum prudentiam ponitur in definitione virtutis moralis, non tamquam pars essentiae ejus, sed sicut quiddam participatum in omnibus virtutibus moralibus."

46. *Q. D. de Virtutibus in Communi*: a. 12, reply to obj. 16: "Ratio recta prudentiae non ponitur in definitione virtutis moralis, quasi aliquid de essentia ejus existens, sed sicut causa quodammodo effectiva ipsius, vel per participationem; nam virtus moralis nihil aliud est quam participatio quaedam rectae rationis in parte appetitiva." Cf. *S. T.*: p. I-II, q. 58, a. 3, reply to obj. 2.

47. *S. T.*: p. II-II, q. 47, a. 7, reply to obj. 2: "Sicut agens naturale facit ut forma sit in materia, non tamen facit ut formae conveniant ea quae per se ei insunt: ita etiam prudentia medium constituit in passionibus et operationibus; non tamen facit quod medium quaerere conveniat virtuti." Cf. also *ibid.* reply to obj. 3: "Virtus moralis per modum naturae intendit pervenire ad medium: sed quia medium, secundum quod medium, non eodem modo invenitur in omnibus, ideo inclinatio naturae quae semper eodem modo operatur, ad hoc non sufficit, sed requiritur ratio prudentiae."

48. *Q. D. de Virtutibus in Communi*: a. 5, reply to obj. 8: "Felicitas contemplativa nihil aliud est quam perfecta contemplatio summae veritatis; felicitas autem activa est actus prudentiae quo homo se et alios gubernat."

49. Cf. *De Regimine Principum*: c. 14.

50. *S. T.*: p. I-II, q. 72, a. 5. Cf. also p. I-II, q. 73, a. 3: "Ratio autem ordinat omnia in agibilibus ex fine;" *ibid.* reply to obj. 3: "omnia objecta humanorum actuum habent ordinem ad invicem: et ideo omnes actus humani quodammodo conveniunt in uno genere secundum quod ordinantur ad ultimum

Bibliography

finem;" also, p. I-II, q. 90, a. 1: "rationis . . . est ordinare ad finem, qui est primum principium in agendis."

On the ultimate end as first principle in the "ordo in moralibus" see my note, "The Unity of the Moral Order," *The New Scholasticism*: 1941, vol. 15, n. 3, pp. 280-83.

51. Cf. *S. T.*: p. I-II, q. 90, a. 2, reply to obj. 3: "Sicut nihil constat firmiter secundum rationem speculativam, nisi per resolutionem ad prima principia indemonstrabilia: ita firmiter nihil constat per rationem practicam nisi per ordinationem ad ultimum finem, qui est bonum commune."

52. *S. T.*: p. I-II, q. 65, a. 1: "Sicut scientia speculativa non potest haberi sine intellectu principiorum; ita nec prudentia sine virtutibus moralibus."

53. *Ibid.*: reply to obj. 3.

54. St. Thomas seems to say it to those who lose themselves in the "circularity of prudence and the moral virtues;" e.g., *S. T.*: p. I-II, q. 58, a. 5, reply to obj. 1: "Appetitus finis praecedit rationem ratiocinantem ad eligendum ea quae sunt ad finem quod pertinet ad prudentiam: sicut etiam in speculativis intellectus principiorum est principium rationis syllogizantis."

55. *S. T.*: p. I-II, q. 66, a. 3, reply to obj. 3. The objection concluded that moral virtue was "nobilior prudentia quae est virtus intellectualis circa moralia."

If we express the analogy which we seem to have in the previous texts we get: intellectus principiorum: scientia:: virtus moralis (appetitus finis): prudentia. But in the text cited here we seem to have: intellectus principiorum: scientia:: prudentia: virtus moralis. I think the mere grouping of these texts makes it clear that moral virtue is not used at all times in the strictest sense (habitus electivus, etc.), but stands for natural knowledge of certain things naturally conducive to the end of man.

56. *S. T.*: p. II-II, q. 47, a. 6: Utrum prudentia praestituat finem virtutibus moralibus. The objection *contra* refers to the *Nichomachean Ethics*: b. VI, c. 12 1144 a 8-9, where Aristotle is giving his own keen solution of the difficulties relative to prudence and the moral virtues.

I should like to remark in passing that the Aristotelian and Thomistic solutions are not the same; but this is not the occasion to discuss

the differences. One may be mentioned by way of example: the rôle of synderesis (cf. reply to obj. 1). There is no synderesis in Aristotle.

57. The corpus of the article cited in footnote 56 concludes thus: "Ad prudentiam non pertinet praestituere finem virtutibus moralibus, sed solum disponere de his quae sunt ad finem."

This is worth citing immediately in order to point out that "disponere de his quae sunt ad finem" is *not* the whole story of the prudential act. Prudence is conciliative, judicative, preceptive. I believe the three are well summed up in ordinative; but the conciliative, judicative, and preceptive, or the ordinative, cannot be confined to means with no *knowledge* of ends. Or whence the order? How conciliative? The most thoroughly misleading misconceptions of prudence arise from misconception of *means*. Means are "ea quae sunt ad finem." The best way to render any relation unintelligible is to deprive it of its term!

58. *S. T.*: p. II-II, q. 47, a. 6: "In ratione speculativa sunt quaedam ut naturaliter nota quorum est intellectus, et quaedam quae per illa innotescunt, scilicet, conclusiones quorum est scientia." The italics in the translation are mine.

59. Cf. footnote 51.

60. Continuation of the text cited in footnote 58: "ita in ratione practica praeexistunt quaedam ut naturaliter nota et huismodi sunt fines virtutum moralium: quia finis se habet in operabilibus sicut principium in speculativis . . . et quaedam sunt in ratione practica conclusiones: et huismodi sunt ea quae sunt ad finem in quae pervenimus ex ipsis finibus et horum est prudentia."

61. *Q. D. de Veritate*: q. 16, a. 2, reply to obj. 5.

62. *S. T.*: p. II-II, q. 47, a. 6, reply to obj. 1.

63. *Q. D. de Veritate*: q. 16, a. 3: "Hoc enim lumen [includes synderesis] est de natura ipsius animae cum per hoc sit intellectualis; de quo lumine dicitur in Pslam. iv, 7: 'Signatum est super nos lumen vultus tui, Domine,' quod scilicet nobis bona ostendit; haec enim erat responsio ad id quod dixerat: 'Quis ostendit nobis bona?' " Cf. *S. T.*: p. I-II, q. 91, a. 2.

64. Thus we return to the text cited in footnote 57. Prudence includes knowledge of the end insofar as it includes synderesis. But its

task as a virtue is not to duplicate what nature supplies but to dispose to ends appointed by nature the variable contingents over which man has dominion.

65. *S. T.:* p. II-II, q. 53, a. 5, reply to obj. 1: "Bonum prudentiae participatur in omnibus virtutis moralibus." See also section II above, pp. 194-196.

66. *S. T.:* p. I-II, q. 71, a. 2: "Id quod est contra ordinem rationis proprie est contra naturam hominis, in quantum est homo: quod autem est secundum rationem est secundum naturam hominis in quantum est homo: bonum autem hominis est secundum rationem esse et malum hominis est praeter rationem esse."

67. *S. T.:* p. II-II, q. 47, a. 6, reply to obj. 3: "Virtutes morales . . . tendunt in finem a ratione naturali praestitutum: ad quod juvantur per prudentiam quae eis viam parat, disponendo ea quae sunt ad finem, unde relinquitur quod prudentia sit nobilior virtutibus moralibus et moveat eas: sed synderesis movet prudentiam sicut intellectus principiorum scientiam." This is, it seems to me, St. Thomas's own answer to the charge of apparent contradiction with p. I-II, q. 66, a. 3 (Utrum virtutes morales praemineant intellectualibus) reply to obj. 3, cited above in footnote 55.

68. Cajetan, *In Summam Theaologicam:* p. I-II, q. 66, a. 3 (ed. Leon. vol. VI, pp. 433-34) p. 434: "Responsio litterae est ad minorem (scil. tertiae objectionis) dicens quod prudentia est eorum quae sunt ad finem et finis." The solution of this "conflict" which I have given agrees on the whole with that of Cajetan. Any reservations to complete agreement would be on the score of the function of synderesis *as such* and, therefore, not appropriate here. Cajetan's explanation of the rôle of synderesis in prudence is, so far as I can see, St. Thomas's own explanation, v. footnote 67.

69. This and the preceding text are translated from *S. T.:* p. I-II, q. 94, a. 2. It may be useful to note that the very nature of the practical intellect makes all of its judgments preceptive. Any other view of its nature arises from a fundamental misunderstanding of its nature. This is not to say, of course, that every practical precept is the prudential precept which is discussed below.

70. *S. T.:* p. I-II, q. 94, a. 2, corpus and reply to objections 1 and 2.

71. See footnote 69 above.

72. The procedure is from the principles of synderesis to the prudential conclusion and moral election. (In what sense these last *coincide* is explained in *S. T.:* p. I-II, q. 13, a. 1.) I know of no place where St. Thomas sets down *finis est prosequendus* as a judgment of synderesis (Cajetan, however, does *loc. cit.* footnote 68). There are, I think, some very good reasons for this. Perhaps the chief is that this expression connotes a definite and delimited good, a fixed term of activity; and nature supplies no such definite knowledge. Cf. *Q. D. de Veritate:* q. 22, a. 7. However, the good is not done unless the end is achieved and we may, therefore, join Cajetan in the use of the expression. We cannot become more precise about it without entering into the question of infused and acquired prudence which is not included in the intention of the present essay.

These remarks bear only on the expression itself; that *finis est prosequendus* is indeed a first principle of practical knowledge is established from the texts cited just below.

73. *S. T.:* p. I-II, q. 91, a. 2, reply to obj. 2. On "joint action" cf. p. I-II, q. 58, a. 5, reply to obj. 1: "Ratio secundum quod est apprehensiva finis praecedit appetitum finis: sed appetitus finis praecedit rationem ratiocinantem ad eligendum ea quae sunt ad finem quod pertinet ad prudentiam." The prior apprehension includes more than end in an absolute sense and, therefore, the prior appetite also does; cf. p. I-II, q. 10, a. 2. reply to obj. 3: "Finis ultimus ex necessitate movet voluntatem . . . et similiter illa quae ordinantur ad hunc finem sine quibus finis haberi non potest; sicut esse, et vivere et huiusmodi: alia vero sine quibus finis haberi potest non ex necessitate vult qui vult finem: sicut conclusiones sine quibus principia possunt esse vera non ex necessitate credit qui credit principia."

74. *Q. D. de Veritate:* q. 16, a. 2, reply to obj. 1: "In ipsa applicatione universalis principii ad aliquod particulare potest accidere error, propter imperfectam vel falsam deductionem vel alicuius falsi assumptionem;" and in reply to obj. 6: "sicut in speculativis ratio falsa, quamvis originem sumat a principiis non tamen a principiis primis falsitatem habet, sed ex malo usu principiorum, ita etiam in operativis accidit."

75. *S. T.:* p. I-II, q .58, a. 4: "Ad hoc autem quod electio sit bona duo requirantur: primo ut sit debita intentio finis . . . se-

Bibliography

cundo ut homo recte accipiat ea quae sunt ad finem: et hoc non potest esse nisi per rationem recte consiliantem, judicantem, et praecipientem quod pertinet ad prudentiam ad et virtutes sibi annexas." The related virtues are *eubulia, synesis* and *gnome* to which p. II-II, q. 51 is devoted. The relation is, I think, well and summarily expressed in p. II-II, q. 51, a. 2, corpus and reply to obj. 2.

76. *Nichomachean Ethics:* b. VI, c. 5 1140a pp. 25-28 (the italics of the English text are added). Cf. St. Thomas's *In Ethica Nichomachea:* b. VI, l. 4.

77. *S. T.:* p. II-II, q. 51, a. 1, reply to obj. 1: "Non est bonum consilium sive aliquis malum finem in consiliando praestituat, sive etiam ad bonum finem malas vias adinveniat." In p. II-II, q. 55, a. 1, "prudentia carnis" is said to be sinful because through it "homo deordinatur circa ultimum finem qui non consistit in bonis corporis." On some false goods which can be substituted for the summum bonum, cf. p. II-II, q. 45, a. 1, reply to obj. 1.

78. *S. T.:* p. I-II, q. 57, a. 4, reply to obj. 3; also, p. II-II, q. 51, a. 2, reply to obj. 2; also, p. II-II, q. 47, a. 2, reply to obj. 1: "Consideratio causae altissimae in quolibet genere pertinet ad sapientiam in illo genera: in genere autem actuum humanorum causa altissima est finis communis toti vitae humanae; et hunc finem intendit prudentia . . . unde manifestum est quod prudentia est sapientia in rebus humanis."

79. *S. T.:* p. II-II, q. 51, a. 3, reply to obj. 1: "Rectum judicium in hoc consistit quod vis cognoscitiva apprehendat rem aliquam secundum quod in se est . . . quod autem virtus cognoscitiva sit bene disposita ad recipiendum res secundum quod sunt contingit quidem radicaliter ex natura, consummative autem ex exercito vel ex munere gratiae: et hoc dupliciter: uno modo directe . . . alio modo indirecte ex bona dispositione appetitivae virtutis." Cf. also, p. II-II, q. 47, a. 15: "Talis cognitio (scil. circa ea quae sunt ad finem) non potest inesse homini naturaliter; licet ex

naturali dispositione unus sit aptior ad hujusmodi discernenda quam alius."

80. *S. T.:* p. II-II, q. 47, a. 13. (Utrum prudentia possit esse in peccatoribus): "Prudentia est et vera et perfecta quae ad bonum finem totius vitae recte consiliatur, judicat, et praecipit;" and reply to obj. 3: "non est in eis (scil. peccatoribus) prudentia quae se habet solum ad bonum; sed . . . est in talibus dinotica, id est naturalis industria quae se habet ad bonum et malum; vel astutia, quae se habet solum ad malum."

81. *S. T.:* p. II-II, q. 47, a. 8 (Utrum praecipere sit principalis actus prudentiae): "Et est tertius actus eius praecipere; qui quidem actus consistit in applicatione consiliatorum, et judicatorum ad operandum: et quia iste actus est propinquior fini rationis practicae inde est quod iste est principalis actus rationis practicae et per consequens prudentia." Cf. p. I-II, q. 57, a. 6; also, *Q. D. de Virtutibus Cardinalibus:* a. 1.

82. *S. T.:* p. I-II, q. 14, a. 1, reply to obj. 1: "Ex hoc quod homo vult finem movetur ad consiliandum de his quae sunt ad finem;" also, p. I-II, q. 13, a. 1: "et ideo electio substantialiter non est actus rationis, sed voluntatis: perficitur enim electio in motu quodam animae ad bonum quod eligitur;" and a. 3: "electio consequitur sententiam vel judicium quod est sicut conclusio syllogismi operativi."

83. *S. T.:* p. II-II, q. 51, a. 2, reply to obj. 2: "Ad unum finem ultimum quod est bene vivere totum ordinantur diversi actus secundum quemdam ordinem: nam praecedit consilium, sequitur judicium, et ultimum est praeceptum quod immediate se habet ad finem ultimum: alii duo actus remote se habent."

84. *S. T.:* p. II-II, q. 50, a. 2: "Homines servi vel quicumque subditi ita aguntur ab aliis per praeceptum quod tamen agunt seipsos per liberum arbitrium." On person and the prudential precept cf. Gerald B. Phelan, "Person and Liberty," *Proceedings of the American Catholic Philosophical Association:* 1941, vol. 16, pp. 53-69.

Essays in Thomism

Tenth Essay

A QUESTION ABOUT LAW

1. In documenting misunderstandings of natural law and the growth of legal positivism in the last three hundred years, I shall cite only works in the tradition of Anglo-American jurisprudence; Hobbes, *A Dialogue on the Common Law*; Blackstone, *A Commentary on the Laws of England*: Introduction; Bentham, *A Comment on the Commentaries*; Austin, *Lectures on Jurisprudence*; Dicey, *Law and Opinion in England*; Carter, *Law: Its Origin, Growth and Function*; Gray, *The Nature and Sources of the Law*; Pollock, *Essays in Law; Essays in Jurisprudence and Ethics*; Allen, *Law in the Making*; Cardozo, *Growth of the Law*; Haines, *The Revival of Natural Law Concepts*; Frank, *Law and the Modern Mind*; Pound, *Introduction to the Philosophy of Law*; M. Cohen, *Law and the Social Order*; F. Cohen, *Ethical Systems and Legal Ideals*; Llewellyn, "Realistic Jurisprudence," *Columbia Law Review*: vol. 30, p. 431; Bingham, "What is the Law," *Michigan Law Review*: vol. 11, pp. 1-25, 109-21; Cook, "Scientific Method and the Law," *American Bar Association Journal*: vol. 13, pp. 303-9; Dewey, "Logical Method and the Law," *Cornell Law Quarterly*: vol. 10, pp. 17-27; Patterson, "Can Law be Scientific," *Illinois Law Review*: vol. 25, pp. 121-47; Dickinson, "The Law Behind Law," *Columbia Law Review*: vol. 29, pp. 113-46, 285-319; Vinogradoff, "Crises of Modern Jurisprudence," *Yale Law Journal*: vol. 29, p. 312; M. Cohen, "Jus Naturale Redivivum," *Philosophical Review*: vol. 25, p. 761; M. Cohen, "Positivism and the Limits of Legal Idealism," *Columbia Law Review*: vol. 27, pp. 237-50; M. Cohen, "Real and Ideal Force in Civil Law," *International Journal of Ethics*: vol. 26, pp. 469-93; M. Cohen, "Mr. Justice Holmes and the Nature of Law," *Columbia Law Review*: vol. 31, p. 352; Llewellyn, Adler, Cook, "Law and the Modern Mind—a Symposium," *Columbia Law Review*: vol. 31, p. 82 ff.

The most recent contributions to this controversial literature are: L. L. Fuller, *The Law in Quest of Itself*, Chicago, 1940; and M. S. McDougall, "Fuller vs. the American Legal Realists: An Intervention," *Yale Law Review*: vol. 50, pp. 827-840. I take pleasure in citing Prof. McDougall's article because it is, among other things, an attack on me, and shows why a Thomist must explain himself more fully if he wishes to be understood by contemporary positivists. I must add that I do not expect Prof. McDougall and the others to understand this article. It is written for Thomists and not for positivists. Nevertheless, I believe that the analysis which this article tries to present would go a long way toward eliminating much controversy in contemporary jurisprudence by removing false or unreal issues between "naturalists" and "positivists." I even naively hope that it may be possible some day to communicate to others what is here offered as intelligible only to Thomists. But my reason for undertaking this analysis will not be intelligible to Thomists unless they acquaint themselves with contemporary discussion. The bibliography here given is recommended reading.

1a. As a matter of fact, the apparent simplicity is deceptive. In the judgment of such scholars as Father Walter Farrell, intensive study of this Treatise reveals it to be one of the more obscure sections of the *Summa Theologica*, greatly in need of expansion and explication.

2. There are eleven questions on Divine (positive) law, one each on Eternal Law and natural law, and three on human (positive) law.

3. The same point can be made about the philosophy of nature, as about the philosophy of law. There is no adequate statement of the principles, evidences, and conclusions of the philosophy of nature in the *Summa Theologica*. For this one must turn to St. Thomas's commentaries on Aristotle's physical treatises, and to such opuscula as the *De Principiis Naturae*. Unfortunately, there is nothing similar to these commentaries and opuscula in the case of the philosophy of law, except, perhaps, for the commentary on the fifth book of Aristotle's *Nichomachean Ethics*.

4. It may be thought that, in the context

Bibliography

of theological discussion, this point about the ambiguity of law ceases to be important. That, however, is not the case, as is shown by the comparison of Eternal Law with Divine positive law, or by the comparison of natural law, as the reception of Eternal Law, with positive law, as received from the human legislator. These points will be more fully discussed later. V. Section III, below, and footnotes 91, 94, 95, 96.

5. As a matter of fact, the problem proposed is too complicated for treatment in a single article. It deserves a whole question, following question 91, in which the non-univocity of law would be considered with regard to each pair of distinctions among the kinds of law, and then the positive analysis of the analogy would be undertaken. Here I shall deal primarily with one part of the problem: the non-univocity of natural and positive human law. Unless indicated to be otherwise, all Thomistic references are to the *Summa Theologica.*

6. V. p. I, q. 79, aa. 12 and 13; and p. I-II, q. 94, a. 1. Note the relation of *synderesis* to the work of prudence: p. II-II, q. 47, a. 6, reply to obj. 3. To say that natural law deals with the end is not to deny that it concerns the means. Just as in the theoretic order, conclusions are implicitly contained in their premises, so in the practical order, the prescription of an end to be sought implicitly contains the prescription of all the means necessary to achieve it. "Seek the good" tells us, first of all and explicitly, that the good is our end and to be sought; but it also tells us by implication that we must perform the acts and use the means which will bring us to this end. When I say that the first principles of the practical reason (i. e., the natural law, strictly speaking) do not deal with means, I am simply referring to the fact that the means are not in any way specified by the principle except that they be means to the right end. Furthermore, when I say that the principles of natural law are judgments about the end, I mean that they are practical, not theoretic, judgments, albeit speculatively-practical in mode of intellection. The proposition "The good is what all men seek" is a purely theoretic statement in metaphysics. In contrast, "Seek the good" is a practical principle, which is prescriptive even though it directs conduct from afar. V. footnotes 27 and 28 below.

Cf. Maritain's discussion of the relation between *cognoscere* and *dirigere* on the level of speculatively-practical judgments and on the level of prudence, in *Science and Wisdom*, New York, 1940: pp. 222-4. St. Thomas, it should be noted, speaks of "the end which is appointed by natural reason" (p. II-II, q. 47, a. 6, reply to obj. 3), though in a stricter manner of speech he would say that the end is appointed by natural desire and known by natural reason.

7. This fourfold division of types of practical judgment can be fitted into the usual threefold division of practical thinking into (a) the speculatively-practical, which deals with necessary truths about the end and about the means universally defined; (b) the practically-practical, which deals with contingent truths about particularized means; and (c) the purely practical or prudential, which deals with immediate singulars. Both principles and precepts (the latter being necessary conclusions from self-evident premises) belong to the speculatively-practical; rules of all sorts, of the various arts as well as of social conduct, such as positive laws, belong to the practically-practical; and decisions (or decrees, commands, etc.) belong to the prudential, i. e., to the work of prudence properly, if the rules being applied are moral rules or civil laws; to the work of artistic prudence, if the rules being applied are technical, i. e., rules of art.

Cf. footnote 29 below, wherein the distinction between theoretic and practical truth is discussed. Speculatively-practical judgments are theoretic in their mode of truth, even though they are practical in object and end. Only practically-practical and prudential judgments are practical in mode of truth, as well as in object and end.

8. V. p. I-II, q. 96, a. 1, reply to objections 1 and 2.

9. As the acts of the will in choice, consent, and use, are acts with regard to singular means, acts to be done or not done *hic et nunc*, so the acts of the reason which move the will in these acts must also be with regard to the singular; such are counsel and command. V. p. I-II, q. 14, aa. 2, 3, 4; q. 17, aa. 1 and 3. Furthermore, the chief act of prudence, which properly considered concerns the singular (v. footnote 7 above; also Maritain, *Art and Scholasticism*: New York, 1930, pp. 15, 16, 17, 19, 49, Notes 27, 28), is the act of com-

mand (v. p. II-II, q. 47, a. 8). Furthermore, prudence, whose chief act is command, is the virtue whereby good deeds are chosen (v. p. I-II, q. 57, a. 5), and such a virtue is needed, in addition to the other intellectual virtues, because the judgment here concerns contingent singulars (v. *ibid.*, reply to obj. 3). Hence St. Thomas does not say that a law is a command, but that "a command denotes an application of a law to matters regulated by the law" (p. I-II, q. 90, a. 2, reply to obj. 1). V. also p. I-II, q. 96, a. 1, reply to obj. 1, where it is said: "Other matters are legal, not through being laws, but through being applications of general laws to particular cases, such as decrees." Cf. p. I-II, q. 92, a. 2, where it is said that "a law is a dictate of reason commanding something." The context here indicates that what is meant is not that the law itself is properly a command, but that the acts it *regulates* are acts commanded or prohibited. In short, regulation is divided against command as the general is divided against the singular; hence, rules of law, i. e., propositions which are regulative, are not commands.

The problem here raised, about whether a rule of law is a command, requires an elaborate inquiry into the notion of command which cannot be here undertaken. If it be understood that *imperium* is an act of the reason and not of the will, if it be understood that no practical judgment can become effective as a direction of conduct unless it pass from the order of intention into the order of execution through the issuance of command, then it will make no difference to the present discussion whether the word "command" be used strictly for the last act of reason prior to execution, or loosely for any practical judgment which, combining the *dirigere* with the *cognoscere*, is effectively practical only through participation in *imperium*. As I read the text of p. I-II, q. 17, a. 1, in the light of such other relevant passages as p. II-II, q. 47, a. 8, and p. I-II, q. 57, a. 6, I find evidence for thinking that the strict notion of command restricts its sphere to the singular means to be used. Every type of practical judgment is, of course, subordinate to command, which is the chief act of the practical reason as exercising *effective direction* over conduct. But not every type of practical judgment is equally proximate to command in this mode of subordination: the singular judgment (the *decision* which

precedes *choice* of the singular means) is the most proximate and, therefore, participates most directly in the notion of command; rules of positive law, being general, are more remote; and the principles or conclusions of natural law are most remote, because they concern the end or the means as universally considered. Yet just as every practical judgment is a direction as well as a knowledge, even though speculatively-practical judgments, practically-practical judgments, and prudential judgments must be ordered in terms of their proximity to the acts they direct, so every practical judgment must participate in command, though again the participation may be remote or more or less proximate. Now it should be noted that a law is not defined as a command of reason, but as an ordination of reason. Reason's ordinations are its practical judgments, judgments which are at once knowledge and direction. Furthermore, ordination is said to be an element of command, along with intimation and motion. This, it seems to me, means that nothing could be commanded which had not first been ordained or judged as something to be done. Hence, there may be many types of practical judgment or ordination, distinguished according to remoteness from the singular, but there is only one type of command. Whatever is judged to be a good end or a good means has some relation to the singular acts which can be commanded. It makes a difference, therefore, whether one says that propositions of law (be they rules, precepts, or principles) *are* commands or that they *participate* in commands. To say that they *are* commands obliterates all distinctions among them as different types of judgments or ordinations, differing both in their aspect as *cognoscere* as well as in their aspect as *dirigere*. To say that they all participate in command, because they are practical, because they are directions as well as knowledge, enables us to preserve their distinction as judgments or ordinations, and at the same time to insist upon their subordination to command in order for them to become practically effective by issuing in executions.

The pure act of command can be abstracted from the judgments which are its content. Just as, in the speculative order, we can separate the proposition which can be affirmed or denied from the assertion of it (though, of course, the complete judgment is the asserted proposition), so, in the practical order, we can separate propositions (ordinations of practical reason) from commands. The propositions of practical reason say *what* should be done. Command simply says "Do *this*." It transforms the declarative content of a practical proposition (which is never merely knowledge but is always also direction) into the pure imperative which is motion from intention to execution. That is why, as St. Thomas tells us, "command is an act of reason, presupposing an act of will, in virtue of which the reason, by its command, moves the executive powers to their acts." Cf. p. I, q. 21, a. 2, reply to obj. 2, where St. Thomas says of the command "whereby our actions are governed according to the law," that "it resides in the will."

That there can be no act of command apart from an intellectual act of judgment is proved by the fact that there are three acts of the intellect and only three, whether the intellectual activity is practical or speculative. Now command, as an act of the practical intellect, is not an act of conception or of reasoning. Hence it must be an act of judgment or, more strictly, an aspect thereof.

10. V. p. I-II, q. 90, a. 1, reply to obj. 2, where it is said "universal propositions of the practical intellect that are directed to actions have the nature of law." The word "universal" here must be understood to mean only the general (which can be contingent) as opposed to the singular, not the universal strictly (which must be necessary). Cf. p. I-II, q. 96, a. 1, reply to obj. 2, where the generality of legal rules is indicated. It may be asked whether rules of law are the work of prudence. Strictly speaking, the answer is No (v. footnote 9 above). But the notion of prudence can be extended to cover judgments about all contingent matters relative to action (v. p. I-II, q. 57, a. 5, reply to obj. 3); and so, by extension of meaning, we can speak of juris-prudence, or the prudence whereby rules of law are formulated, for these are about contingent matters. V. p. II-II, q. 57, a. 1, reply to obj. 2, where it is said that a law is "a kind of rule of prudence." But it is absolutely impossible to regard the principles or precepts (i. e., the necessary conclusions) of the practical reason as the work of prudence. What is said about the relation of *synderesis* to prudence (v. p. II-II, q. 47, a. 6, reply

to obj. 3) applies, as well, to the conclusions drawn from the principles held by *synderesis*.

While I do not think there can be any question about whether command is ever of anything except the singular act, it may be said that prudence is concerned with the means in general as well as with the singular means *hic et nunc*. But certainly it cannot be said that prudence is indifferently or equally concerned with both, or that it is primarily concerned with the means in general rather than the singular means. The very fact that command is the chief act of prudence signifies that the judgment of prudence is *primarily* about the singular means, and only *secondarily* about the means in general. When, therefore, we speak of making laws as a work of prudence, we must remember that this is an extension of the scope of prudence from its primary field. But whereas every type of practical judgment can be said to participate in command as the ultimate act of reason in the practical order, it cannot be said that every type of practical judgment is a work of prudence. Decisions or singular judgments are prudential primarily; general rules (of positive law or positive morality) are prudential secondarily; but the principles and conclusions of natural law, being speculatively-practical in their character as judgments, are entirely outside the scope of prudence. This fact by itself is sufficient to prove that the principles or conclusions of natural law and the rules of positive law are not univocally law. Those acts of the practical reason which fall within the sphere of prudence are related to the will in a manner radically different from the way in which speculatively-practical judgments are related to the will. That it is why it is proper to say that the rules of positive law are *instituted*, whereas the principles and conclusions of natural law are *discovered*. (V. footnote 64 below). Let me caution the reader not to suppose, however, that the use of the word "discovery" here—and throughout the text—in speaking of natural law, implies that the propositions of natural law are *purely theoretic* judgments. Both the propositions of natural law and of positive law are practical judgments. If all that the word "law" signifies is "practical judgment," then, of course, natural law and positive law are univocally law—both are directive of conduct, both participate in command. But as soon as one recognizes a radical difference in mode of intellection between practical judgments which are speculatively-practical (outside the sphere of prudence), on the one hand, and practical judgments which, on the other hand, are either practically-practical (within the extended scope of prudence) or properly prudential, then one is compelled to see that both sorts of judgments cannot be law in the same univocal sense. V. footnote 95 below.

11. V. p. I-II, q. 95, a. 4. Cf. *ibid.*, aa. 2 and 3.

12. p. I-II, q. 94, a. 2 makes absolutely clear that the natural law, strictly understood, consists entirely of indemonstrable propositions or first principles. Cf. p. I-II, q. 90, a. 2, reply to obj. 3; also, q. 94, a. 1, reply to obj. 2. And it is equally clear that the *ius gentium* consists of conclusions drawn from these principles, not in determinations of them. V. p. I-II, q. 95, a. 2, where the distinction in two modes of derivation from natural law is made: "by way of conclusions from premises," and "by way of determination of certain generalities;" and I-II, q. 95, a. 4, where it is said that "to the *ius gentium* belong those things that are derived from the law of nature as conclusions from premises," whereas "those things which are derived from the law of nature by way of particular determination belong to the *ius civile*." This is completely confirmed by the distinction between what are called "the moral precepts" (strictly *precepts*) and what are called "the judicial precepts" (strictly *rules*) of the Old Law; for the former are spoken of as conclusions from natural law (v. p. I-II, q. 104, a. 1; q. 99, aa. 2, 3, 4); but "Thou shalt not kill," which is a moral precept of the Old Law, is also a proposition of *ius gentium* (v. p. I-II, q. 95, aa. 2 and 4).

13. V. p. I-II, q. 94, a. 4, where it is said that the natural law is the same for all men both in its principles and its conclusions; and p. I-II, q. 94, a. 6, where it is said that "there belong to the natural law, first, most general precepts, that are known to all; and secondly, certain secondary and more detailed precepts, which are, as it were, conclusions following closely from first principles." The "most general precepts" here signifies what I have called indemonstrable first principles; the "secondary and more detailed precepts" signifies what I have called demonstrable conclusions, i. e., the precepts of *ius gentium*. Cf. p. I-II, q. 99, a. 2 and q. 100, a. 1, reply to obj. 3. Here the "moral precepts" of the Old Law, clearly identifiable with the precepts of *ius gentium* (v. footnote 12 above) are said to belong to natural law.

Yet St. Thomas is unwilling to identify the *ius gentium* with the *ius naturale*. V. p. I-II, q. 95, a. 4, reply to obj. 1, where he says "the law of nations is indeed, in some way, natural to man, in so far as he is a reasonable being, because it is derived from natural law by way of conclusions that are not very remote from their premises. Nevertheless, it is distinct from the natural law, especially from that natural law which is common to all animals." Here the objection has rightly pointed out that if both natural law and the *ius gentium* are common to all nations, then "the law of nations is not contained under positive human law, but rather under natural law." The weakness of St. Thomas's answer is due to his reliance on the distinction made by Ulpian (*Institutiones*: D, 1, 1, 2-3), whereas the objector cites the stronger point made by Gaius (*Institutiones*: 1, 1). V. p. II-II, q. 57, a. 3, wherein Ulpian is quoted as agreeing with Gaius. The problem here can be solved only in terms of the distinction between principles and conclusions, for both are discovered by the human reason, and as so discovered belong only to men and not to animals, but they are not discovered in the same way.

14. V. p. I-II, q. 95, a. 2; and q. 91, a. 3. These texts show that if *ius gentium* can be said to *belong* to natural law because derived therefrom, so can *ius civile*. In p. I-II, q. 95, a. 2, St. Thomas says, however, that conclusions (precepts of *ius gentium*) have "some force from natural law" whereas the determinations (rules of *ius civile*) "have no other force than that of human law." But this seems to be false in two ways. In the first place, the precepts of *ius gentium* have only the force of natural law, and none of the force of human law (its enforceability through sanctions, because it is politically instituted); and in the second place, the rules of *ius civile* do not have only the force of human law, but also the force of natural law from which they are derived. This is plainly indicated in P. I-II, q. 104, a. 1, where the moral precepts of the Old Law (formally identical with the precepts of *ius gentium*) are said to have only the

force of reason itself, whereas the judicial precepts (formally identical with the rules of *ius civile*) are said to "derive their binding force not from reason alone, but in virtue of their institution."

15. V. p. I-II, q. 94, a. 5, where it is said that the natural law can be changed by way of addition—the additions being determinations made by the rules of *ius civile* or by the judicial precepts of the Old Law.

16. V. p. I-II, q. 94, a. 5, reply to obj. 3.

17. V. p. I-II, q. 95, a. 2, wherein it is indicated that conclusions from natural law (e. g., one should not kill) are further determined by rules of civil law which prescribe the punishment for killing. Cf. p. I-II, q. 99, a. 3, reply to obj. 2, wherein it is clear that the determinations, made by the positive regulations of the Old Law, are determinations of the moral precepts, which belong more to natural than to positive law through being conclusions therefrom. Cf. p. I-II, q. 94, a. 4, reply to obj. 3. Furthermore, the moral precepts of the Old Law, prohibiting killing, stealing, etc., are not only indeterminate with respect to the treatment of wrongdoers, but are indeterminate also with respect to the acts prohibited. V. p. I-II, q. 100, a. 8, reply to obj. 3, where it is said that the moral precepts, which define the essence of justice, must be further determined, in order to be applicable to individual actions, such determinations taking the form of defining what sort of actions are unjust killings (i. e., homicide) or unjust takings (i. e., larceny). Not every act of killing is murder, nor every act of taking from another stealing. In short, the positive law of homicide or of larceny consists of determinations of the precepts "Thou shalt not kill" and "Thou shalt not steal"—both with respect to *describing* the acts prohibited and with respect to *fixing* the treatment of wrongdoers. The usual statement that the positive law consists of determinations only in the second respect (as in p. I-II, q. 95, a. 2) is profoundly inadequate.

When this is understood, it will be seen that the four types of practical judgment are indispensable, just as the three levels of practical thinking are (v. footnote 7 above). Practical principles cannot be applied to action without a consideration of means; hence the need for precepts, rules, and decisions. Practical precepts cannot be applied to action because they are not determinate enough with respect to the means; hence the need for rules and decisions; and rules cannot be applied to action without decisions because action is concerned with the singular *hic et nunc* whereas rules are general. In the order of execution, principles are most inadequate practically and rules least inadequate, for they are capable of being directly applied by decisions; but in the order of intention, principles and precepts are most indispensable because they consider the end and the means universally. Cf. footnote 17a below. V. p. I-II, q. 94, a. 5, reply to obj. 1, wherein it is pointed out that positive law is needed "to correct the natural law" in one way by supplying "what was wanting to the natural law." This is another way of saying that both the *ius naturale* and the *ius gentium* are inadequate practically because insufficiently determinate to be applied to action; hence the need for positive regulations, i. e., the rules of *ius civile*.

17a. Throughout this discussion, it is absolutely necessary to remember that the propositions of *ius gentium* do not exhaust all the conclusions which can be drawn from the indemonstrable principles of natural law. The *ius gentium* consists only of those conclusions which are propositions about the universal means to be employed in the sphere of social conduct, means ordained to the social common good as proximate end. But happiness is the ultimate end which the natural law directs us to seek, and there are many means which serve this end in the sphere of private conduct. The propositions which define these means universally are, therefore, also conclusions from natural law, though they are not precepts of *ius gentium* strictly conceived. All the precepts of the Decalogue, for example, are conclusions of natural law, but not all belong to the *ius gentium*. Just as the propositions of *ius gentium* are the speculatively-practical judgments which underlie the determinations made by the rules of positive law, so the other sort of conclusions from natural law are speculatively-practical judgments underlying the determinations made by the rules of positive morality. If we use the word "law" in a strict sense as always related to the acts of justice, and hence as always concerned with social or political conduct, then we should not call these other conclusions, or the rules which may be derived from them, laws. Furthermore, whereas the propositions of *ius gentium* cannot ever be applied to action by decisions without the mediation of rules of positive law (which rules supply the determination lacking in the precepts of *ius gentium*), the conclusions of natural law, which are precepts in the sphere of private morality, can sometimes be directly applied to singular acts without the mediation of positive rules. The reason for this difference is not easy to state, nor is it relevant here, for all that matters here is the distinction between two sorts of conclusions from the principles of natural law. Since this discussion is concerned with the problem of law, in the strict sense, and not with the whole sphere of practical reason, I shall always be referring to the propositions of *ius gentium* when I speak of conclusions of natural law, unless I specifically indicate my meaning to be otherwise. Cf. footnote 17 above and 20 below.

18. V. C. W. McIlwain, *The Growth of Political Thought in the West*: New York, 1932, pp. 119-131. The jurists, notably Gaius and Ulpian, tried to give a philosophical account of those "principles of law" which are not instituted as part of the municipal law of Rome, governing transactions among Roman citizens, but which Roman administrators, notably the *Praetor Peregrinus*, acknowledged in dealing with cases involving transactions between Roman citizens and subject peoples. They succeeded to the extent that they recognized these principles to be common to all nations, though instituted by none, for, so far at least, they saw that *ius gentium* must be sharply distinguished from positive law; but they failed to the extent that they did not understand the relation between *ius naturale* and *ius gentium* in terms of the rational derivation of conclusions from principles. Hence they did not understand the real difficulties about *ius gentium*—the sense in which it was a part of natural law, and thus divided against positive law, and the sense in which it was not natural law, because natural law, strictly, consists only of indemonstrable principles concerning the end, and not conclusions about means. Unfortunately, the opinions of Gaius and Ulpian, confused in themselves, and inconsistent with each other, were incorporated in the eclectic *Institutes* of Justinian, and so exercised an undue influence upon mediaeval thinking about *ius gentium*. St. Thomas could have, and probably would have, given a much

better account of *ius gentium*, had he either been ignorant or more critical of the Legislator (i.e., Justinian). V. footnote 13 above.

19. V. footnotes 16 and 18 above. The precepts of *ius gentium* are common to all nations, because they are necessary conclusions from the principles of *ius naturale*; moreover, they are indispensable to the diverse bodies of municipal law (*ius civile*) because in so far as the latter is derived from natural law, it must be derived by way of determining the conclusions from natural law (the precepts of *ius gentium*). These points are made by Grotius when, in the Prolegomenon and Bk. 1 of his *De Jure Bello et Pacis*, he talks of an *a priori* deduction and an *a posteriori* induction of natural law. He does not mean natural law at all, of course, but the precepts of *ius gentium*, which can be deduced from the natural law (which is prior), and can be induced from diverse bodies of municipal law (which are posterior). The induction proceeds by finding the common principles (i.e., universal precepts) that underlie the rules of diverse bodies of municipal law.

Cf. McIlwain, *Constitutionalism, Ancient and Modern*, Ithaca, 1940, p. 61-2, wherein he reports the threefold distinction made by Saint-Germain early in the 16th century. There is (1) "The law of reason primary" which we are calling natural law; (2) "The law of reason secondary general" which we are calling *ius gentium*; (3) "The law of reason secondary particular" which we are calling positive law. As McIlwain points out, "Saint-Germain's 'law of reason secondary general' is in fact the *ius gentium* of Gaius. St. Thomas failed to analyze the opinion of Gaius, especially the latter's insight that "all peoples who are ruled by laws and customs employ a law partly peculiar to themselves, partly common to all mankind."

20. From the natural law, which declares or "appoints" the end, two sorts of conclusions can be drawn, which define the means universally: (a) those which define the means in the sphere of private conduct (i.e., all the virtues regarded as productive of happiness); and (b) those which define the means in the sphere of public conduct (i.e., the acts of justice serving the common good). Now, the precepts of *ius gentium* are conclusions of the latter sort; they underlie the rules of positive law, which determine means to the same end,

as conclusions of the first sort underlie the rules of positive morality (i.e., rules for becoming virtuous). Hence not all conclusions from the natural law are precepts of *ius gentium*, but only those which define means to the common good. As from the notion of happiness, we can deduce the virtues as productive means (v. my discussion of this in *A Dialectic of Morals*: c. 6), so from the notion of the common good as an end, we can deduce the precepts of *ius gentium* as to the social means. In both cases, knowledge of nature (of man or of society) provides the minor premise. V. p. I-II, q. 51, a. 1, where the principles of natural law are called "the nurseries of virtue." This they are by way of conclusions of the first sort.

St. Thomas appears to distinguish two sorts of propositions belonging to *ius gentium*: those which define means to happiness in terms of the nature of man, and those which define means to the social common good in terms of the nature of human society. V. p. II-II, q. 57, a. 3. But, strictly speaking, only the latter are precepts of *ius gentium*; the former are conclusions of natural law in the sphere of private morality, not political ordination. Furthermore, the fact that certain of the means, such as the division of property, the wearing of clothes, or the enslavement of men, are judged to be universally desirable in the light of man's fallen nature, and the consequences thereof for human society in the world as contrasted with Eden, does not alter the status of the precepts prescribing these means. They are necessary conclusions even though the fact upon which they are founded is not a necessary fact, i. e., not something in the absolute nature of man. Every precept of *ius gentium* considers the historic social condition of man and, in the light thereof, defines a means which is desirable in every society as serving the common good. That the institution of slavery may be a wrong conclusion from the natural law is not the question here. The only point here is that the negative precept "Thou shalt not kill" and the positive precept "Institute divisions of property" are the same as precepts of *ius gentium* in so far as both define means indispensable to the social welfare of any human society; they differ only in that the former has reasons other than those of social utility, whereas the latter is entirely founded upon service of the

common good. Furthermore, both sorts of precepts require determination by rules of positive law: the positive law of homicide, in the one case, and the positive law of property, in the other case. The institutions of private property are different in different communities living under different economic systems. Cf. p. II-II, q. 66, a. 2, reply to obj. 1, where St. Thomas must be speaking of particular modes of division of property—which are instituted by positive law; he is not there speaking of the precept of *ius gentium* which prescribes that there be *some* division of property in *any* society for the sake of the common good. V. also p. I-II, q. 94, a. 5, reply to obj. 3. In short, the practical judgment about property (or any similar thing) is either universal (applicable to all societies), or determinate (applicable to this society): in the one case, it is a conclusion of natural law and a precept of *ius gentium*; in the other, it is a rule of positive law. Precepts of *ius gentium* are always conclusions, never determinations.

In a recent address, "The Natural Law and Human Rights," Maritain distinguished between two sorts of conclusions from the first principles of practical reason: (1) those which follow "in a *necessary* manner and *from the simple fact that man is man*"; and (2) those which follow "in a *necessary* manner, but this time supposing certain conditions of fact, as for instance, the state of civil society or the relationship between peoples." The second sort of conclusions are the precepts of *ius gentium*, prescribing universal means to the social common good; the first sort of conclusions are the precepts of private morality, prescribing universal means to natural happiness. Both depend on the nature of man, but only the second depend on that aspect of man's nature which is social, and upon the nature of human society as a means to human happiness, and hence as an intermediate end to be sought.

21. Certainly, the natural law which is common to all creatures as passively in them by way of participation in Eternal Law is not identical with the natural law that man actively possesses by the work of reason and freely applies to action or violates. Though the natural law is in man in both ways, it is not univocally *human* in both cases. V. p. I-II, q. 91, aa. 1 and 2.

22. V. p. I-II, q. 91, aa. 1 and 4; also q.

99, aa. 3 and 4, and q. 104, a. 1. I shall return later to a consideration of the precise mode of analogy which obtains between Eternal Law and Divine positive law. V. Section III below, footnotes 95 and 96. Here suffice it to point out how radically different is the "promulgation" of law in these two cases: by creation and by revelation.

23. V. p. I-II, q. 99, a. 5, where it is said that duty or obligation is twofold: "One according to the rule of reason; the other according to the rule of a law which prescribes that duty." This distinction between legal and moral obligation corresponds to the distinction between moral and political, or legal, authority, according as the former is nothing but the voice of reason, whereas the latter is reason supported by the power to impose sanctions. V. Maritain, *Scholasticism and Politics*: New York, 1940, pp. 92-93; cf. Fr. Farrell, The Roots of Obligation, *The Thomist*: 1939, vol. 1, n. 1, pp. 14-30. We can, therefore, distinguish between intrinsic and extrinsic authority according as the authority is moral or political (i.e., legal), according as it is or is not conjoined with the power to enforce extrinsic sanctions.

Now it is clear that the authority of *ius gentium* is entirely moral or intrinsic, whereas the authority of *ius civile* is political or extrinsic. Hence if by "positive law" we mean the expression of political authority; if we mean that which depends (causally) on the will of the legislator (v. p. II-II, q. 57, a. 2, obj. 2 and reply thereto); and that which has coercive power (v. p. I-II, q. 96, a. 5; and also q. 90, a. 3, reply to obj. 3, wherein advice is distinguished from law; cf. q. 108, a. 4); then only the *ius civile* is positive law, and whether or not *ius gentium* can be called human law, it can never be called positive law. This is further confirmed by the fact that the rules of *ius civile* are just only in relation to political constitutions, whereas the precepts of *ius gentium*, being common to all nations, are prior to the constitutions of particular states. Confusion results from using the phrase "human law" as if it were equivalent to "positive law." In p. I-II, q. 95, a. 4, St. Thomas divides the positive law into the *ius gentium* and the *ius civile*; but here the first objection, maintaining that the *ius gentium* is not positive law, is certainly right, and St. Thomas's answer does not suffice. The

reason is simple: that which is a necessary conclusion from the principles of natural law cannot be a positive enactment, having its origins in human legislation, and its force due to such enactment. Cf. p. II-II, q. 57, aa. 2 and 3. V. also Yves Simon, *The Nature and Functions of Authority*: Milwaukee, 1940, Note 10, wherein the relationship of *ius civile* and *ius gentium* to the notions of authority and of prudence shows that both types of law cannot be positive, in the same strict sense, despite the fact that Professor Simon, following St. Thomas, calls them both positive law.

24. V. p. I-II, q. 94, a. 5; q. 97, a. 4, reply to obj. 3; q. 100, a. 8. These texts indicate that dispensations from the precepts of *ius gentium* (considered in themselves and apart from the determining rules of positive law) are warranted only by considerations of national well-being, in circumstances when an act, otherwise intrinsically just, would redound to the harm of the commonwealth. This is illustrated by such cases as restoring goods held in trust to the enemies of one's own country at war with it; it can also be illustrated by dispensation from "Thou shalt not kill" in the case of soldiers engaged in a just war.

25. The ambiguity of the phrase "common good" is exhibited in the discussion of the end of law, in p. I-II, q. 90, a. 2, where St. Thomas distinguishes between happiness and the well-being of the body politic. In discussing the utility of positive law, St. Thomas speaks of the end it serves, not as happiness, but as the commonwealth (p. I-II, q. 95, a. 3). This meaning of "the common good" as the end of positive law is confirmed in p. I-II, q. 96, a. 1. For a complete analysis of the meanings of "common good," especially with reference to the Eternal good, temporal happiness, and the social welfare, v. Farrell and Adler, The Theory of Democracy, Part II, *The Thomist*, 1941, vol. 3, n. 4; and also Part III, *The Thomist*, 1942, vol. 4, n. 1.

26. V. footnotes 14 and 17 above. As conclusions, they result from deductive reasoning. As premises, they provide the rational grounds for positive determinations. Means must be universally defined before they can be determinately particularized.

27. V. *A Dialectic of Morals*: Notre Dame, 1941, pp. 53-4, for the distinction between natural law as a mere *description* of behavior, and natural moral law as a *prescription* of

conduct, which can be violated. Now it belongs to the essence of law to be violable, for law is direction, and there is no need of direction when what occurs cannot happen otherwise. Hence, the injunction to seek the good, real or apparent, is no law at all, because men cannot do otherwise than seek whatever they seek under the *aspect* of the good.

The fact that the natural moral law must be understood as a prescription indicates that it is not a purely theoretic, but a practical judgment, albeit speculatively-practical. It indicates, furthermore, that although the principles of natural law are not, *as such*, commands, they cannot be divorced from commands, for every practical judgment, which is essentially directive as well as cognitive, becomes effective only through subordination to, and participation in, command. What is here said of the principles of natural law applies also to the conclusions of natural law and the propositions of positive law. They are all essentially *prescriptions*, though we speak of some as *precepts* and others as *rules*. Cf. footnote 6 above.

28. V. p. I-II, q. 94, a. 2, where the purely theoretic statement "that good is what all things seek after," is distinguished from the practical statement "that good is to be done and evil is to be avoided," which is at once the first principle of the practical reason and the natural law. Cf. footnote 27 above.

29. In so far as practical truth is necessarily true, it is by conformity to *natural* desire and in so far forth as it does not differ from theoretic truth, which is by conformity to the *nature* of things. But practical truth which is only contingently true is by conformity to right desire, i. e., the *elicit* desire of the sensitive or intellectual appetite, rectified by accord with reason; such truth differs radically from theoretic truth. V. p. I-II, q. 57, a. 5, reply to obj. 3. Hence the truth of the principles of natural law and the precepts of *ius gentium* is theoretic in mode, though these propositions are practical in terms of object and end; whereas the truth of the rules of *ius civile* is practical in mode, as well as in object and end.

When, in the text, I speak of "practical truths" I do not always mean judgments which are practical in their mode of truth, but I do always mean judgments which are practical in object and end. Of such judgments of the practical reason, only those which are *contingently* true (*rules* and *decisions*) have a practical mode of truth (by conformity with *right, elicit* desire); those which are *necessarily* true (*principles* and *precepts*) have a theoretic mode of truth (by conformity with nature, i.e., with *natural* desire).

30. V. p. I-II, q. 91, a. 4, wherein the natural law is said to direct men to an end proportionate to their natural powers, and· p. I-II, q. 91, a. 5. wherein St. Thomas distinguishes between an earthly and a heavenly good.

31. V. *A Dialectic of Morals*: c. 6.

32. V. I-II, q. 94, a. 2, reply to obj. 1, where it is said of the several principles of *ius naturale*, that they all "have the character of one natural law, inasmuch as they flow from one first principle." The word "flow" here cannot signify deductive derivation, for then the many principles would be as conclusions drawn from the one first principle as a premise; and this would be contrary to St. Thomas's insistence on the point that all the principles of natural law, considered as one or as many, are indemonstrable (v. p. I-II, q. 94, a. 2, *per contra*). Hence, the word "flow" must signify an analytical derivation, whereby a complex unity is expressed explicitly as an ordered many. This being so, the multiple principles of the natural law are not related to the single principle of the natural law as secondary precepts to a primary precept. In contrast, all of the precepts of *ius gentium* can be called "secondary principles" of natural law in so far as they are conclusions from the first principles. Those who make a distinction between what they call secondary and tertiary principles of natural law must be distinguishing between two grades of precepts among the propositions of *ius gentium*—those which follow proximately from the first principles, and those which follow remotely. The former, though they are more detailed than the first principles, fall within the grasp of even an uneducated man, says St. Thomas; whereas the latter are not so evident to everyone, but only to the wise. V. p. I-II, q. 100, a. 11. Cf. q. 94, a. 4.

33. "According to the order of natural inclinations is the order of the principles of natural law." (p. I-II, q. 94, a. 2). V. also p. I-II, q. 10, a. 1, reply to obj. 3, and q. 10, a. 2, reply to obj. 3; and cf. *A Dialectic of Morals*, pp. 83-85, and pp. 93-97.

34. The single principle is analytically equivalent to the whole set of several principles, but not to any one principle in this set. Cf. footnote 32 above, where the derivation of the many principles from the one is compared with the analysis of a whole into its parts. Now the happiness of each man is a whole, of which the common good is a part, though each man as a citizen is a part of the community as a whole. V. The Theory of Democracy, Part II, *The Thomist, loc. cit.,* for criticism of the error of identifying the common good (the well-being of the community) with happiness. It is not true to say that the good of one man—*if this be happiness, whether temporal or eternal*—is ordained to the common good (understood as the social welfare), on the ground that the part is ordered to the whole. Strictly speaking, it is the other way around: the common good is a partial good, and is ordered, as a part must be, to the whole of goods, which is individual happiness. The *whole good* is the last end, not the *good of a whole,* i. e., the good of a society.

35. V. The Theory of Democracy, Part II, *The Thomist, loc. cit.* Henceforth in this essay, I shall always use the phrase "common good," in the second sense, to signify the good of a community (i. e., the social welfare, the common weal); and I shall always use "happiness" instead of "common good" in the first sense.

36. This principle of the natural law is the principle of natural justice. It expresses the nature of justice in so far as it appoints the social end of human acts, and in so far as it calls for a fair apportionment of goods and burdens. Thus the first two clauses constitute the principle of general justice, directing the acts of every virtue to the good of others; and the last clause "render to each his own" is the principle of special justice. V. p. II-II, q. 58, aa. 5, 6, 7, 11; cf. p. I-II, q. 100, a. 12. A positive law is just only by conformity to this principle: that is, by directing acts to the common good as an end, and by equalizing goods and burdens fairly. V. p. I-II, q. 96, a. 4. "Positive law is ordained for the civil community, implying mutual duties of man and his fellows; and men are ordained to one another by outward acts, whereby men live together. This life in common of man with man pertains to justice, whose proper function

consists in directing the human community. Wherefore human law makes precepts only about acts of justice, and if it commands acts of other virtues, this is only in so far as they assume the nature of justice" (p. I-II, q. 100, a. 2). It should be observed, furthermore, that it is indifferent whether we say that a law has the nature of a law only through being derived from natural law, or whether we say that it is a law only in so far as it is just through confirming to the principle of justice (v. p. I-II, q. 95, a. 2). This indicates that that principle of natural law which underlies law is identical with the principle of natural justice.

What is here said about the relation of natural law to the principle of natural justice should not lead anyone to suppose that law and justice are being confused. Law, in any of its senses, is an act of the reason; whereas the acts of justice are acts of the will. But although the acts of justice, and the virtue of justice itself, are subjected in the will, the principle of justice is a practical truth which the reason enunciates. It is in this sense that "seek the common good" or its analytical equivalent "Do good to others, harm no one, and render to each his own," is at once *the* principle of justice and *one* of the principles of natural law.

37. V. footnote 20 above. For a fuller discussion of the relation of government and law to the virtues as means to happiness, v. *A Dialectic of Morals,* cc. 6 and 7.

38. V. Preamble to the Treatise on Habit (p. I-II, q. 49).

39. V. Preamble to the Treatise on Law (p. I-II, q. 90). In view of the Treatise itself, the statement in the Preamble is obviously inadequate in that it mentions only God as an extrinsic cause of good acts. St. Thomas's arguments for the necessity of human laws (and primarily positive laws), over and above Eternal Law and natural law (v. p. I-II, q. 91, a. 3; q. 95, a. 1), indicates that men, in their political capacity, also constitute an extrinsic cause of good acts in other men— both by way of help and by way of direction. The incompleteness of the Preamble reveals that the Treatise, as primarily theological, is mainly concerned with Divine positive law which, like human positive law, is needed over and above Eternal and natural

Bibliography

law (v. p. I-II, q. 91, a. 4; q. 104, a. 1). Cf. footnote 2 above.

40. This is a problem for the theologian, but I suggest that the answer is No, for the same reason that natural law and positive law are not univocally law. I shall return to this point subsequently. V. Section III below, footnotes 95 and 96. I must add here, however, that the Old Law is positive law only in its ceremonial and judicial precepts, not in its moral precepts (v. p. I-II, q. 99, aa. 2, 3, 4; q. 104, a. 1); and that the New Law is not law at all in so far as it is identical with Grace (v. p. I-II, q. 106, aa. 1 and 2; q. 108, a. 1) or in so far as it consists of counsels rather than precepts, i.e., *rules*, strictly speaking, (v. p. I-II, q. 108, a. 4); it is law only in its ceremonial precepts (v. p. I-II, q. 106, a. 1; q. 108, aa. 1 and 2).

41. Both the natural law and Grace are intrinsic principles in their mode of operation, though extrinsic in their source. "There are two ways in which a thing may be instilled into man. First, through being part of his nature, and thus the natural law is instilled into man. Secondly, a thing is instilled into man as being, as it were, added on to his nature as a gift of grace. In this way the New Law is instilled into man, not only indicating to him what he should do, but also helping him to accomplish it" (p. I-II, q. 106, a. 1, reply to obj. 2). In sharp contrast, Divine positive law and human positive law are extrinsic principles, both in their mode of operation and in their source. And grace is more of an extrinsic principle than natural law because it is added to nature. Clearly, then, in the full sense of what is meant by extrinsic principle (both as to source and in mode of operation), only positive law and human help are extrinsic.

42. In the speculative order, there are two modes of learning: by discovery and by instruction. Strictly speaking, instruction is nothing but aided discovery, and "discovery" names unaided learning of the truth. This must be so because the teacher, as an extrinsic cause, is always a secondary or cooperative cause of learning in the student; the primary cause, the activity of the student's own intellect in learning the truth, must be operative when it is extrinsically aided, as well as when it is not. But in the practical order, there is, in addition to discovery and

instruction (aided discovery), something we must call "pure instruction"—a process of learning in which the extrinsic cause is the sole cause. Thus, the promulgation of positive laws is pure instruction, whereas the principles of natural law and the precepts of *ius gentium* can be learned by any man through discovery, aided or unaided. In the context of our discussion, therefore, I shall use the words "discovery" and "instruction" as absolutely opposed to one another, "discovery" signifying both aided and unaided learning in which the intrinsic causes are primary, and "instruction" signifying *pure instruction*, i.e., learning in which extrinsic causes are primary.

43. V. p. I-II, q. 58, a. 1.

44. The human positive law is a cause of virtue only to the extent that it requires external acts to be good; it does not require that these acts be done with the right intention, without which virtuous habit does not exist. V. p. I-II, q. 92, a. 2, reply to obj. 4; q. 95, a. 1; q. 92, a. 1. This does not mean, however, that positive law aims only at the goodness of external acts; its intention is to form virtue, but by its very nature it cannot be an effective cause of this result. V. p. I-II, q. 96, a. 3, reply to obj. 2. This distinction between the external act which can be good or bad as an act and the interior cause of good and bad acts is possible only in the case of justice, with the external acts of which, but not the virtue itself, positive law is effectively concerned. V. p. II-II, q. 57, a. 1. Furthermore, positive law does not require all acts of virtue or forbid all acts of vice, but only acts of justice, i.e., only acts in relation to the common good. V. p. I-II, q. 96, aa. 2 and 3; q. 100, a. 2. In contrast, the natural law prescribes all acts of virtue, i.e., acts which lead to the formation of every virtue; the prescription here is not of the acts themselves, but of their ends (the virtues as means to happiness). V. p. I-II, q. 94, a. 3. In sharper contrast, the Divine law, in its moral precepts, directs interior as well as exterior acts. V. p. I-II, q. 91, a. 4, where it is said that "man is not competent to judge of interior movements, that are hidden, but only of exterior acts which appear. . . . Consequently human law could not sufficiently curb and direct interior acts; and it was necessary, for this purpose, that a

Divine law should supervene." Cf. p. I-II, q. 99, a. 6, which deals with the temporal sanctions of Divine law; q. 100, a. 2, in which it is said that "The Divine law proposes precepts about the acts of all the virtues," though in some cases it obliges and sanctions, whereas in others it merely admonishes by counsel; and q. 100, a. 9, which distinguishes between human and Divine law with regard to the way in which they are related to the mode of virtue.

45. V. *A Dialectic of Morals:* cc. 6 and 7. If the positive law could not be obeyed both by the man of unformed character and by the man of formed character, it could not work as an extrinsic cause in the formation of character. V. p. I-II, q. 92, a. 1, reply to obj. 2; q. 92, a. 2, reply to obj. 4. Furthermore, if the positive law, through the threat of punishment, did not coerce vicious men to act for the common good, it would not protect the peace and order of the community. V. p. I-II, q. 95, a. 1. If the possession of virtue had to precede obedience to positive laws, sanctions would not be necessary either to form good character in the young or to restrain vicious men. In contrast, the natural law can be obeyed only by a man who possesses the moral virtues as well as prudence. This is obvious in itself, but it is also shown by the fact that the possession of prudence is indispensable for obedience to the natural law, and prudence cannot be possessed apart from the moral virtues.

46. V. p. I-II, q. 91, a. 2, reply to obj. 2, where it is said that "the first direction of our acts to their end must needs be in virtue of the natural law." Cf. p. I-II, q. 94, a. 2; and q. 95, a. 2, where the natural law is identified with the first principle of practical reason, which must, of course, be about the end. In contrast, it is clear that the positive law does not appoint the end, but is directed to an end appointed by the natural law. V. p. I-II, q. 90, a. 2. (On the use of the word "appoint" in this connection, see p. II-II, q. 47, a. 6, reply to obj. 3; and cf. footnote 6 above.) It is for this reason that the goodness of positive laws consists, in part at least, in their utility or expediency as regulating means in the service of the common weal. V. p. I-II, q. 95, a. 3, where the necessity and utility of positive law is said to mean "that law should further the

common weal." Cf. p. I-II, q. 96, a. 6 and q. 97, a. 1. These things being so, the pragmatist or utilitarian is right in his conception of the goodness of positive laws as dependent on their utility or expediency, so long, of course, as he rightly understands the end being served as the common good. V. p. I-II, q. 96, a. 4, where it is said that one of the ways in which a positive law can be unjust is in respect to its end. Cf. E. Lewis, "Natural Law and Expediency in Mediaeval Political Theory," *Ethics,* vol. 50, n. 2, pp. 144-163. The pragmatist, however, usually fails to recognize the other two ways in which a law can be unjust; in respect to its source, and in respect to its intrinsic unfairness, though it is true that both of these types of injustice work against the common good. Cf. Bentham, *The Principles of Morals and Legislation;* J. S. Mill, *Utilitarianism:* c. 5; and Garlan, *Legal Realism and Justice.*

47. V. footnote 17 above. V. p. I-II, q. 91, a. 3; q. 94, a. 4; and q. 94, a. 5, reply to obj. 1, where it is said that "the written law is given for the correction of the natural law because it supplies what was wanting in the natural law," i.e., sufficient determination for application to action. This point is confirmed in St. Thomas's discussion of the Old Law: v. p. I-II, q. 99, a. 3, reply to obj. 2; q. 99, a. 4, reply to objections 2 and 3; and q. 100, a. 8, reply to obj. 3.

48. V. p. I-II, q. 90, a. 2; q. 91, a. 4.

49. V. footnotes 25, 34 and 35 above.

50. V. p. I-II, q. 95, aa. 2 and 4, which taken together show that the precepts of *ius gentium,* such as "one must not kill" or "one must not steal," define universal means to the common good, which are then further determined by the rules of positive law (v. p. I-II, q. 96, a. 1; q. 97, aa. 1 and 2). This is confirmed in St. Thomas's discussion of the moral precepts of the Old Law, for these, in so far as they concern the relation of man to man, are formally identical with the precepts of *ius gentium* as conclusions from natural law. V. p. I-II, q. 100, aa. 2, 4, 5.

51. V. footnote 20 above.

52. The proposition mentioned is: "Do good to others, harm no one, and render to each his own." This can also be stated simply as: "Serve the common good." Stated either way, this is that part of the natural law which is

identical with the principle of natural justice. V. footnotes 34 and 36 above. Pragmatists who fail to see that laws can be unjust, not only through disserving the common good, but also through intrinsic unfairness, neglect the clause "render to each his own," and hence do not realize that acts of special justice are a part of general justice, and serve the common good. V. footnote 46 above.

53. V. p. I-II, q. 96, a. 3, reply to obj. 2. Cf. p. I-II, q. 91, a. 4.

54. V. p. I-II, q. 61, a. 5; q. 96, a. 3.

55. V. p. I-II, q. 94, a. 3. Cf. footnote 44 above.

56. V. I-II, q. 96, aa. 2 and 3. Cf. footnote 44 above.

57. V. p. I-II, q. 90, a. 3, reply to obj. 2; q. 92, a. 1, reply to obj. 2; q. 95, a. 1, and here esp. reply to obj. 1; q. 96, aa. 4 and 5.

58. V. footnotes 23 and 45 above.

59. Here two further points must be mentioned. First, the Old Law exercises the same sort of coercive force that belongs properly to human positive law (v. p. I-II, q. 99, a. 6) and is thus contrasted both with the natural law (v. p. I-II, q. 104, a. 1), and with the New Law, which works through love rather than through fear (v. p. I-II, q. 107, aa. 1 and 4; and q. 91, a. 5). Second, the coercive force of positive law is imposed upon every member of the community, upon its legislators and administrators as well as upon those who hold no ruling office. (For violations of the criminal law, the President of the United States can be impeached and, once out of office, tried by a court of law.) St. Thomas wrongly says that "the sovereign is exempt from the law as to its coercive power" if he supposes, as he appears to, that individual men who occupy ruling offices of any sort are sovereigns (v. p. I-II, q. 96, a. 5, reply to obj. 3). In the temporal order, the only sovereign power is the community itself; the vicegerent represents the sovereign, but as a man he is not sovereign. V. p. I-II, q. 90, a. 3. Hence, not only is the natural law above all men as binding them in conscience, but so is the positive law, both in its directive and in its coercive force. Wherever this is not the case, wherever rulers are above the coercive force of positive law, the rule of men exists, not the rule of laws. This point is essential to the distinction between Royal

(or non-constitutional) and Constitutional government. V. The Theory of Democracy, Part I, *The Thomist*: 1941, vol. 3, n. 3, pp. 418-422.

60. V. footnote 42 above. Practical instruction through the promulgation of rules of positive law is *pure instruction*, i.e., not the sort of instruction which, in the speculative order, is nothing but aided discovery. Such instruction can be accomplished either by word, as in the case of written law, or by deed, as in the case of custom, or unwritten positive law. V. p. I-II, q. 97, a. 3.

61. The natural law, both in its principles and its conclusions (i.e., the precepts of *ius gentium*) can be known by all men through discovery, by some without the aid of others, by others only through aid (i.e., instruction in the sense of aided discovery). V. p. I-II, q. 94, a. 4. Cf. p. I-II, q. 100, aa. 1, 2, 11, wherein the wise man is described as teaching the conclusions of natural law. In other words, in so far as the practical reason deals with necessary matters (principles and conclusions), learning proceeds in the same manner as in the speculative sphere: induction of principles, deduction of conclusions; but in so far as the practical reason deals with contingent matters, learning proceeds in a manner peculiar to the practical sphere: by *pure instruction* through promulgation of what has been instituted. Cf. footnote 29 above. The practical truth that is the same for all, though not known in the same way by all, consists in the principles of *ius naturale* and the precepts of *ius gentium*; the practical truth which is neither the same for all nor known in the same way by all consists in the rules of *ius civile*.

62. V. p. I-II, q. 17, a. 6; p. II-II, q. 1, a. 4 and reply to obj. 4 of a. 5. Cf. p. II-II, q. 57, a. 2, reply to obj. 2, wherein the point of the objection is admitted, namely, "that a thing is called *positive* when it proceeds from the human will."

63. On the fact that positive rules are not unerring, v. p. I-II, q. 91, a. 3, reply to obj. 3; q. 96, a. 1, reply to obj. 3; q. 96, a. 6, reply to obj. 3. On the diversity of positive laws, v. p. I-II, q. 95, a. 2, reply to obj. 3. On the mutability of positive law, v. p. I-II, q. 97, aa. 1 and 2. On the point that the positive law determines what was, prior to its institution, a matter of indifference, v. p.

I-II, q. 92, a. 2; q. 96, a. 1, reply to obj. 1; p. II-II, q. 57, a. 2; q. 60, a. 5, and here esp. reply to obj. 1. With respect to the indifference of positive regulations, prior to their enactment, traditional analysis is incomplete. It seems to say that it is absolutely indifferent whether this or that positive rule be instituted with respect to a given matter. This is not the case, for if it were, there could be no intrinsic justice in positive rules, but only justice with respect to the end being served by their institution. But there is intrinsic justice in some positive rules in so far as they are determinations of the precepts of *ius gentium*. Positive rules can be divided into two groups: first, those which are just *formally* as well as *finally* (i.e., *intrinsically* as well as *extrinsically*) through being determinations of natural law (through particularizing the universal means defined by its conclusions); second, those which are just only finally through instituting means which cannot be defined universally by way of conclusion from natural law. Herein lies the traditional distinction between *mala per se* and *mala prohibita*. In both cases, however, positive rules contain an element of indifference: the first sort of rules determine what was previously indifferent, i.e., the mode by which the universal means can be particularized. Thus, the positive law of homicide and of larceny particularizes the precepts of *ius gentium* (one must not kill; one must not steal) both as to the treatment of offenders and as to the description of the crimes (*mala per se*). V. footnote 17 above. The code of traffic regulations, in contrast, devises means which are entirely relevant to a contingent situation; its ordinances, concerning *mala prohibita*, are not determinations of universal means which can be concluded from the natural law. Therefore, it must be said that positive rules are binding in terms of practical reason (either through having extrinsic justice, or both intrinsic and extrinsic justice) as well as in terms of their institution by political authorities, whereby they make legally obligatory matters which were previously indifferent. The element of indifference in every case is identical with the possibility of a greater determinacy in regulation than can be achieved by natural law and by *ius gentium*. V. p. II-II, q. 57, a. 2; and q. 60, a. 5. Cf. footnote 46 above which

shows the bearing of this point on the pragmatic or utilitarian doctrine. The adequate analysis of the justice of positive laws is indicated in p. I-II, q. 96, a. 4; but the traditional discussion of the determination of what is otherwise indifferent fails to take account of the distinction between the fair and the lawful, which follows from the distinction between special and general justice. V. footnote 36 above. The pragmatist is right about positive law only in his insistence upon the truth that the determination of what is otherwise indifferent can be just or unjust only extrinsically—by its utility for the common weal. This can be judged in a particular society only by reference to historic facts, which may be so complicated as to require the research of social scientists.

64. V. p. I-II, q. 97, a. 3, reply to obj. 1, in which it is said that both the natural and the Divine law proceed from the Divine will; and *ibid.*, q. 90, a. 1, reply to obj. 3, in which the relation of will to reason is discussed. But the Divine positive law does not proceed from the Divine will in the same way as the natural law, for one is by institution and the other by creation. Furthermore, the human positive law proceeds from the human will by institution, as the Divine positive law proceeds from the Divine will. V. p. II-II, q. 57, a. 2, obj. 2 and reply.

The traditional controversy concerning whether law is a work of reason or of will is insoluble so long as the word "law" is used ambiguously to signify natural law and positive law without distinction, and so long as the word "proceeds" remains unanalyzed. What does it mean to say that law proceeds from the will if, at the same time, it must be said that law is a work of reason? The answer turns on a distinction between the faculties according as one is the elicit faculty in which the act is subjected, and the other is the moving faculty upon whose operation the act causally depends. If we apply this distinction, we see that a law, being a judgment or ordination participating in command, must be an act of reason, for the will is a blind faculty, and neither judges nor commands, though it chooses and uses. But as a faculty of desire, tending toward the good which is apprehended and judged, the will not only is moved by the reason, but also moves the reason in two ways: always as to exercise, and sometimes as to specification. Now it is the latter sort of rational act which can be said to be willful, because of its double causal dependence on the motion of the will. Thus, an act of opinion, in contrast to an act of knowledge, is a willful act of the reason: reason is the elicit faculty in the formation of an opinion, because an opinion is a judgment, and only reason can judge; but will is the moving or causal faculty in the acceptance of *this* opinion rather than *that,* because in the sphere of such judgments (which do not bind the intellect to assent by their intrinsic necessity), the act of assent to a given proposition is caused by the will. As we have already seen, in footnote 9 above, a complete judgment consists in an asserted proposition. Hence a purely rational judgment (an act of knowledge) is one in which both the formation of the proposition and the assent to it falls within the power and causality of reason (except, of course, for the voluntary aspect of reason's exercise); whereas, in clear contrast, a judgment which is not purely rational (an act of opinion) is one in which the formation of the proposition is an act of reason, but the assent to *this* proposition rather than *some other equally possible* is not within reason's causality, but requires the determining motion of the will. Such a judgment can, therefore, be said to be a work of reason (with respect to formulation of the proposition to be asserted), and also to proceed from the will (in so far as the assent which completes the judgment requires the will's causal efficacy).

With this clarification of such phrases as "work of reason" and "proceeds from the will," we can now consider the distinction between natural and positive law in terms of reason and will. The fact that natural law is like an act of knowledge in respect to the relation of reason to will, whereas positive law is like an act of opinion, should not lead anyone to suppose that either type of law is here being treated as if it were a purely theoretic, rather than a practical, judgment. The comparison is valid because the distinction between speculatively-practical judgments and practically-practical, or prudential, judgments parallels the distinction between knowledge and opinion in the theoretic order

of judgments, with respect to mode of intellection.

The judgments of natural law (principles or conclusions) are purely rational acts, the practical analogue of the theoretic judgments we call knowledge. The will is not needed for assent to these propositions. The judgments of positive law are not purely rational acts; they are the practical analogue of the theoretic judgments we call opinion. This means that the formulation of the proposition which declares what should be done is entirely a work of reason (i.e., reason is the elicit faculty of this act); but the acceptance of *this* proposition rather than *some other which is equally possible* in the same connection requires the will to move the intellect in its act of assent and, ultimately, in its act of command. Cf. footnote 9 above. If this were not true about a rule of positive law, such rules could not consist in determinations of matters otherwise indifferent; they would have to deal with necessary rather than contingent matters, and it would make no difference to their justice and legality whether they were made by duly authorized persons. The reason of any man may be competent to teach the precepts of natural law, but positive rules can be instituted and promulgated only by a sovereign will through its official representatives. V. p. I-II, q. 90, a. 3; q. 96, a. 4. This explains, moreover, the meaning of the word "instituted" in relation to the meaning of "positive." Strictly speaking, the phrase "positive institutions" is redundant; for whatever is politically *instituted* is something *posited* in the sense that it "proceeds" from the causal efficacy of the will as a moving power, even though it is a "work" of reason as to formulation. Hence, only rules of positive law can be said to be instituted; and their institution must be referred to the *causality* of the will, as their formulation must be referred to the *activity* of reason. Herein lies the truth of the statement that "a thing is called *positive* when it proceeds from the human will"—made in p. II-II, q. 57, a. 2, reply to obj. 2, which St. Thomas does not deny in answering the objection on a quite different point. Herein also lies the meaning of St. Thomas's own statement that "all law proceeds from the reason and will of the lawgiver; the Divine and natural laws from the reasonable will of God; the human law from the will of man, regulated by reason" (p. I-II, q. 97, a. 3). St. Thomas could not have foreseen the Suarezian interpretation to which these words lend themselves; but a Thomistic understanding of reason and will prevents these passages from being misread. Because we are living in a world in which the Suarezian errors have such great popularity and currency, it might be advisable for us to avoid even the language of St. Thomas in expressing his thought. Let us never say that a rule of positive law proceeds from the will, even if we add "as regulated by reason." Let us rather say that a rule of positive law is *instituted by the will*, but that, as instituted, it is always an *act of reason*, both as a judgment or ordination and as participating in command. In short, for the phrase "proceeds from the will, regulated by reason," let us substitute "a willful judgment of reason" or, at greater length, "an act of reason, moved to specification by the will."

The precision of analysis, and the clarification of language, which I have here tried to establish, is so important that I must ask the reader to be guided by what has here been said when he interprets any passage of my essay that deals with law in relation to reason and will. Cf. footnote 97 below.

65. The natural law is not just by conformity to anything except the nature of justice itself. V. footnote 36 above. In contrast, the positive law is just only by conformity to the natural law, both as to end and as to means. In fact, a positive law which is not just through such conformity is a law in name only. V. p. I-II, q. 96, a. 4; q. 92, a. 1, reply to obj. 4; q. 93, a. 3, reply to obj. 2; q. 95, a. 2. Thus, the natural law and the positive law are sharply distinguished with respect to justice, the one being an absolute expression of justice, the other an expression of justice only relatively to what is demanded by the natural law as useful in these contingent circumstances. Hence it follows that all men are obliged by the natural law, whereas only the members of a given community can be obliged, or coerced, by its positive laws." V. p. I-II, q. 96, a. 5, where it is said that the subjects of one state are not bound by the laws of another.

66. V. p. I-II, q. 95, a. 4; q. 104, a. 3.

reply to obj. 2; q. 97, a. 3, reply to obj. 3; q. 105, a. 1.

67. V. p. I-II, q. 95, a. 2, reply to obj. 3.

68. The mutability of positive law is perfectly obvious. V. p. I-II, q. 97, aa. 1, 2, 3. But what is sometimes overlooked is the precise meaning of "change" when it is said that positive laws can be changed. What is meant is that one positive rule can be entirely abolished, and replaced by another. Just as a positive law comes into being by enactment, so it can cease to be through repeal. Now in this precise sense of "change," the natural law is absolutely immutable; it changes neither in its principles nor in its conclusions (the precepts of *ius gentium*), for what cannot be enacted, cannot be repealed. The texts which are often quoted to the contrary (p. I-II, q. 94, aa. 5 and 6), if carefully read, will show that this is so. Therein it is said that the natural law never changes in its principles, nor can these be abolished from the heart of man. But it seems to be said that the natural law changes with respect to its conclusions, in certain rare cases. If this last point be examined, it will be seen that what is being said is not that these secondary precepts are changed, but that in certain rare cases they can be dispensed from. But so can positive laws be dispensed from, and we do not regard such dispensation as repeal. Hence neither is dispensation from the conclusions of natural law repeal. V. p. I-II, q. 94, a. 4; and cf. q. 96, a. 6, and q. 97, a. 4, reply to obj. 3; also q. 100, a. 8. V. footnote 24 above. These things being so, it is clear that, when the notion of change is univocally applied, the natural law is absolutely immutable, whereas mutability follows from the essence of positive law. Certainly it cannot be said that the natural law in itself is changed by the additions of positive law to provide the determinations in which it is, of itself, deficient. This would be like saying that the structure of a house is changed by the addition of furnishings.

69. V. p. I-II, q. 97, a. 3, esp. reply to obj. 1.

70. V. p. I-II, q. 94, a. 6. Here I say "natural law, *strictly* speaking" to signify only the first principles; for, as the text points out, when the natural law, loosely speaking, is taken as including the conclusions which are the precepts of *ius gentium*,

the natural law can be abolished from the hearts of men, with regard to these "secondary precepts . . . either by evil persuasions . . . or by vicious customs and corrupt habits." Cf. *ibid.*, reply to obj. 1.

71. Rules of positive law can be abolished. V. footnote 68 above. The conditions under which such rules *should* be abolished (i.e., repealed) are indicated in p. I-II, q. 97, aa. 1 and 2.

72. V. p. II-II, q. 60, a. 5. Cf. p. I-II, q. 97, a. 4; q. 96, a. 6; and q. 100, a. 8.

73. V. footnotes 24 and 68 above. The relevant texts here, as already indicated, are p. I-II, q. 94, a. 4; q. 96, a. 4, reply to obj. 3; and q. 100, a. 8. These are rightly interpreted only when it is understood that dispensation from the precepts of *ius gentium* is possible only in the sphere of international affairs; the conclusions of natural law are as indispensable as the principles, within the life of a single community. This is clearly shown in the reasoning of p. I-II, q. 100, a. 8.

74. I have shown the following properties to belong to positive law: (1) that it exercises coercive force; (2) that it is communicable only through extrinsic promulgation, i.e., pure instruction; (3) that it depends on the *causality* of the will as well as upon the *activity* of the reason; (4) that it obliges only those who fall within the power of the community in which it is instituted; (5) that it is variable from community to community; (6) that it is just only relative to the constitution of a given community; (7) that it is mutable, by the repeal of old laws and by the enactment of new ones, within the history of a given community; (8) that it is dispensable within the affairs of a single community. These eight properties flow from the essence of positive law as conventionally instituted about matters otherwise indifferent. None of them can be affirmed of natural law, strictly understood, or even as broadly understood to include the precepts of *ius gentium.* Since things differing in their properties must differ in essence, it is demonstrably clear that natural law and positive law differ in essence, and hence that the word "law" cannot be used univocally in these two cases. Cf. footnote 95 below.

75. The practical propositions of an art are rules of production, as laws, and moral rules, are rules of action. But the essential

difference between action and production, between the spheres of prudence and of art, requires us to observe that rules of art cannot be called "laws" univocally with political or moral regulations. V. p. I-II, q. 97, a. 2, reply to obj. 1, which indicates, furthermore, that rules of art, like the precepts of natural law, are not positively instituted. Such traditional phrases as "the law of contradiction" are compact of ambiguity; for, in the first place, as signifying a metaphysical principle, the phrase names a theoretical truth, and neither a law nor a rule; and, in the second place, as signifying a logical principle, the phrase names a rule of art, but not a law.

76. The causality is formal in the case of law, and efficient in the case of medicine. There is, in a sense, therefore, a little more of intrinsic denomination in speaking of natural law as law than in speaking of medicine as healthy.

77. Maritain, *Degrés du Savoir:* Appendix 4.

78. V. footnote 21 above.

79. Participation in Eternal Law is proportionately analogous to participation in human positive law; but theoretic knowledge of natures is not analogous with practical rules. V. footnotes 21 and 75 above.

80. V. p. I-II, q. 96, a. 5, and see the comment on the reply to obj. 3 in footnote 59 above.

81. V. p. I-II, q. 93, a. 4.

82. V. footnote 40 above. The relevant texts are in p. I-II, q. 106, aa. 1 and 2; q. 108, aa. 1, 2, 4.

83. V. footnote 40 above. The relevant texts are in p. I-II, q. 99, a. 2, reply to obj. 1; a. 3, reply to obj. 2; a. 4. Cf. q. 100, aa. 1, 2, 11; and q. 104, a. 1. The whole point can be seen in the single fact that "Thou shalt not kill" is at once a moral precept of the Old Law and also a precept of *ius gentium*. If the latter belongs to the natural law by way of conclusion, as I have shown, and cannot be regarded as positive law because lacking its properties (v. footnote 74 above), then the precepts of the Decalogue or any other moral precepts of the Old Law cannot be regarded as positive law—law by Divine institution—even though they are part of Divine law because revealed by God for the direction of men.

84. V. p. I-II, q. 99, aa. 3 and 4; also qq. 101-105, esp. q. 104, a. 1. Note the dis-

tinction between the Decalogue, as given by God Himself, and the code of judicial and ceremonial rules which was given through Moses, and hence is called the Mosaic Law (v. p. I-II, q. 100, a. 3).

85. As in speculative matters, there is a distinction between those truths which belong to reason purely, those which belong to both faith and to reason, and those which belong to faith alone (v. p. I, q. 1; cf. *Summa Contra Gentiles,* b. I, cc. 3-8), so in practical matters one can distinguish those principles and precepts which man can know without Revelation (the natural law), though these may also be revealed by God (the moral precepts of the Old Law); those rules which are entirely of human institution (human positive law); and those which are entirely of Divine institution (Divine positive law). V. p. I-II, q. 99, a. 2, reply to obj. 2; q. 100, a. 1; and q. 91, a. 4. These texts indicate that the reason why truths discoverable by reason are also revealed is the same in both speculative and practical matters; they also indicate that the need for truths which exceed reason's grasp to be received through faith (relative to a supernatural end) is the same in both cases.

86. The distinguishing accidents of Divine positive law (i.e., the Old Law) are (1) that it is inerrant (v. p. I-II, q. 91, a. 4); (2) that it directs man in his interior acts (*ibid.*); (3) that it is for the Jewish people · alone (v. p. I-II, q. 98, aa. 4 and 5); that it came into existence in entirety at one time (v. p. I-II, q. 98, a. 6); (6) that it was entirely repealed at one time (v. p. I-II, q. 103; q. 104, a. 3); and (7) that its sanctions are effective by the Divine will without exterior administration (v. p. I-II, q. 99, a. 6, reply to objections 2 and 3; q. 100, a. 9).

87. V. p. I-II, q. 91, a. 4, esp. reply to obj. 1.

88. V. p. I-II, q. 107, aa. 1, 2, 3. Cf. q. 98, a. 4; and q. 91, a. 5.

89. V. p. I-II, q. 106, aa. 1 and 2; q. 108, aa. 1, 2, 4. All that remains as positive law in a strict sense, when the Divine Law is considered as directing men to their supernatural end, is the code of ceremonial precepts in the New Law.

90. V. p. I, q. 14, a. 8, a. 13, reply to obj. 3; a. 16, reply to obj. 2; q. 15, aa. 2 and

3; q. 16, aa. 1, 3, 6; q. 17, a. 1. Cf. *De Veritate:* q. 1.

91. V. footnotes 21, 75 and 79 above. This explains a number of things: (1) how Eternal Law is causally related to human positive law through natural law as a mean term in the causal nexus; just as the truth of things connects the Divine truth and human truth causally; nor is this inconsistent with the fact that Eternal Law and human positive law are analogous proportionally (v. footnote 77 above); (2) how Eternal Law and Eternal Truth are the same, for the Eternal Law is a sovereign type existing in God (v. p. I-II, q. 93, a. 1) and the Eternal Truth may be either an Exemplar or a Type (v. p. I, q. 15, a. 3); and (3) how, in consequence, the truth in things and their passive participation in Eternal Law are the same, both being identical with their natures, exemplifying the Eternal Exemplars and known by the Eternal Types. This last point explains the play on the meaning of the word "law" when the scientist speaks of his theoretic formulations as "laws of nature."

92. V. p. I-II, q. 90, a. 4.

93. V. p. I-II, q. 90, a. 3.

94. The analogy of proportionality between Eternal Law and human positive law requires us to understand "made by him who has the care of the community" to apply in the one case to God as sustaining the created universe, and in the other to a public official who exercises vicegerency for the sovereign community as a whole; and to understand "common good" to signify the natural end of each species of creature, in the one case, and the well-being of a human community (a means to temporal happiness), in the other. This indicates that it is impossible to comprehend both Eternal Law and human positive law in a single definition, if its terms be univocally interpreted.

95. Things which are "analogous by attribution" can be comprehended in the same definition even less than things which are "analogous by proportionality." V. footnote 94 above. A definition, strictly formulated, can only express the signification of a univocal concept, as, for example, the concept of positive law. Despite the differences between human and Divine positive law (v. footnote 86 above), these differences being accidental, human and Divine positive law can be com-

prehended in a single definition, for both have the essence and the properties of positive law. "Positive" can be said univocally of both. It may be said that Divine positive law and human positive law are dissimilar in source (God and man) and in end (eternal beatitude and temporal happiness) and that there is a proportionality here between the eternal and supernatural and the natural and temporal. Nevertheless, they are not analogous as kinds of law, as is clearly the case with Eternal Law and Divine positive law, which not only have different ends but are operative in different ways; so, too, in the case of Eternal Law and human positive law, which have comparable ends, but operate in different ways.

To say that natural and positive law cannot be comprehended in a single definition because they are not signified by a univocal concept of law, does not mean that there is nothing common to the two types of law. On the contrary, strict equivocation would result if there were no common element of meaning in the two impositions of the name "law."

Because natural law is a formal, not an efficient, cause of positive law, they have certain formal characteristics in common: of each it can be said that it is an effective direction of conduct; that it is a practical and not a theoretic judgment; that it is a practical judgment or ordination which becomes effective through participating in command. But effective direction of conduct can either be more remote or more proximate to action; a practical judgment can either be speculatively-practical (a purely rational act) or practically-practical (a willfully rational act); and though every practical judgment must participate command in order to be effective, the declarative content of the ordination, which command makes imperative, may either be like knowledge of necessary matters or like opinion about contingencies.

Though St. Thomas may often use the word "law" to name what is *common* to the first principles of practical reason and to positive legal enactments, *he does not define anything except positive law.* Crucial texts in the Treatise on Law reveal that when St. Thomas does offer a definition of law, he has only positive law in mind. V. footnote 96 below.

96. That law is in its very essence positive is affirmed by St. Thomas in the following passages: in p. I-II, q. 100, a. 9, where he says that "a precept of law has compulsory power" and "compels through fear of punishment"; and in p. I-II, q. 95, a. 5, where he says that "the notion of law contains two things: first, that it is a rule of human acts; secondly, that it has coercive power." Nor can it be said that these passages speak only of positive law and hence that the point applies only to positive law, because both refer the reader to p. I-II, q. 90, aa. 1, 2, 3, wherein law itself is defined. Special reference is made to p. I-II, q. 90, a. 3, reply to obj. 2, where it is said that "a private person cannot lead another to virtue efficaciously for he can only advise, and if his advice be not taken, it has no coercive power, such as the law should have. . . . But this coercive power is vested in the whole people or in some public personage to whom it belongs to inflict penalties." Hence it is clear that what is being defined in q. 90 is positive law, Divine or human, and that law, univocally understood, is essentially positive. Otherwise, it would be impossible to say that coercive force belongs to the essence of law, and that law can be made only by one who has both the authority and the power to punish. Certainly, natural law, both in its principles and its conclusions (i.e., *ius gentium*), is excluded from the univocal notion of law by this definition, for as humanly discovered it binds only in conscience, it is or can be known to all men equally, and if its conclusions are taught by the wise to others, this teaching is by way of counsel, not command, for the wise who teach the conclusions of natural law need not be public personages representing sovereign power. V. p. I-II, q. 100, aa. 1, 3, 11, wherein the role of the wise in teaching the conclusions of natural law is discussed. The only problem which remains concerns Eternal Law. As we have seen (v. footnotes 94 and 95 above), it is impossible for a definition to comprehend things which are only analogically the same. Hence Eternal Law is in no wise comprehended by the definition of positive law given in q. 90. It is impossible to apply any of the terms of this definition to Eternal Law without violence in interpretation; strictly speaking, Eternal Law

Essays in Thomism

is not *made,* for like Eternal Truth it is identical with God's being; and, strictly speaking, the end of Eternal Law is not the good of any *community as such.* Hence, if we conclude that, in the human sphere, positive law is law properly speaking, and natural law is law only by an extension of meaning, so, too, in the Divine sphere, we must say that Divine positive law is properly law, and Eternal Law is law only in a manner of speaking. This does not prevent Eternal Law and human law (i.e., positive law) from being analogous proportionally, for in any analogy between the Divine and the human there is an infinite dissimilarity. Eternal Law is as unlike human law (i.e., positive law as defined), as Eternal Truth or Divine knowledge is unlike truth and knowledge in the human mind.

Professor Yves Simon agrees that "The definition that St. Thomas gives of the law refers properly to the law issued by the state," that is, to positive law (*Nature and Functions of Authority,* p. 50). Furthermore, he also views "The several kinds of law as an analogical series" in which "The civil law is, *for us,* the first analogate of the whole series." But he supposes that *all* the elements in this series constitute an analogy of proper proportionality. On this point, I sharply differ from him, for the reasons already given.

97. I find it necessary, therefore, to disagree with Professor Simon's statement that "law and authority, when taken in their most typical forms, are said in contradistinction to one another. A law which is a self-evident or demonstrable rule of conduct (natural law or law of nations) realizes more completely the ideal notion of law than a law which is but a prudential determination (civil law)" (*loc. cit.* in footnote 23 above). On the contrary, St. Thomas's conception of law is essentially positive, for the way he defines it (v. footnote 94 above) shows that, far from being opposed to the expression of political authority or removed from the work of prudence, law is inseparable from such authority and is always the work of prudence. I agree with Professor Simon that "authority realizes completely the ideal notion of social prudence when it deals with more particular and concrete circumstances (decrees of executive power) than when it deals with more general and lasting situations (civil laws)"

(*ibid.*). Cf. footnote 10 above. Nevertheless, the making of laws (civil laws, positive rules), falls within the scope of prudence, though the making of decisions (executive decrees, etc.) is most properly the work of prudence. Furthermore, the very notion of jurisprudence indicates that positive law in its essence does not belong to the reason simply, but to the reason as moved to specification by the will. V. footnote 64 above. The fact that it must be made by a duly constituted authority to be law (p. I-II, q. 90, a. 3) and to be just (p. I-II, q. 96, a. 4) shows that law, as conceived by St. Thomas, is not purely rational, for who makes a rule can only matter if its institution depends upon the free will of the maker.

98. The little word "of" is the source of much ambiguity here. We speak of "rules of law" and "principles of law." In the first case, "of" signifies iden:ity, for the rules of law *are* laws; they are legal propositions. But, in the second place, the principles of law (i.e., of positive law) are not laws, for they are not rules or legal propositions; strictly speaking, they *are* propositions of *ius naturale* or *ius gentium.* Here, then, the "of" signifies that what is spoken of *belongs to* law (i.e., positive law) as a source or a foundation. If, however, we speak of "principles of natural law," then the "of" means the same thing as it does in saying "rules of positive law"—i.e., the principles *are* those propositions of the practical reason which are identical with natural law.

99. V. footnote 65 above.

100. V. p. I-II, q. 96, a. 4, where St. Thomas speaks of "legal laws," meaning positive rules which are rightly founded in the principles of justice and conform to the essence of law, which accords with the nature of man and human society. The point that is here being made can also be seen in terms of constitutionality. A political constitution, strictly speaking, is neither a law nor a body of laws, for it is the source of law-making and law-administering powers in those who hold office under the constitution, and it is the test of the justice of positive enactments in their relativity to the particular society in which they are made. Hence it is laws which have or lack constitutionality by conforming to or violating the provisions of a constitution. We cannot significantly speak of the

constitution itself as being constitutional or legal, if the legality of laws depends upon their being constitutional; though we can speak of a constitution as just or unjust by relation to principles of natural justice. Now the legality of laws depends upon their conforming to the principles of practical reason as well as to the constitution; hence these principles are, like the constitution, a source of legality, a measure of it; and for that very reason the essence of legality does not properly pertain to them. To speak of the natural law or of the constitution as legal is as improper as it would be to speak of metaphysics as physics because metaphysics provides principles which are employed in the philosophy of nature, as ultimately regulative of the conclusions which are proper to physics.

100a. In the *Rhetoric* (I, 13, 1373b2-15 and I, 15, 1374a25-35), Aristotle does appear to distinguish between the natural law, the universal law, the unwritten law, or the eternal law, on the one hand, and positive, particular, written, or mutable law, on the other; but the context in which this distinction is made, always with reference to Sophocles' *Antigone*, shows that the poets may speak of "natural law" but that Aristotle himself would prefer to speak, more strictly and carefully, of "natural justice." What is loosely rendered in English by "natural law" would always be better translated from the Greek by "common law," meaning the propositions which are common to actually diverse bodies of positive law. Cf. McIlwain, *Constitutionalism, Ancient and Modern*, pp. 39-40: if the Greeks thought of natural law at all, he writes, they meant by this "no more than that portion of a state's actual laws which *in fact* happens to be identical in all other states—what Aristotle in his *Rhetoric* called 'common law.'" Vd. also p. 56, where English *common* law is interpreted as an English *ius gentium*, having an origin comparable to the origin of Roman *ius gentium* in the edicts of the *praetor peregrinus*.

My friend Professor A. C. Pegis has pointed out to me that it may be said that the reason why Aristotle "never speaks of the natural law" is that Aristotle did not know any natural (moral) law of which to speak. Certainly he can support this remark by citing the fact that Aristotle nowhere considers the habit of *synderesis*. Yet Aristotle

does acknowledge that there is a first principle of the practical reason in so far as he asserts that the first principle in the practical order is the end of conduct. Moreover, I should insist that what Aristotle means by the principle of natural justice is identical with that proposition of natural law which can be enunciated prescriptively in such words as "Seek the common good" or "Do good to others, harm no one, and render to each his own." The whole question here, it seems to me, is not whether Aristotle's analysis is as explicitly complete with respect to these principles as that of St. Thomas; but rather whether the complete analysis can be made without ever using the word "law" for any practical judgments other than the rules of positive law. I mention the authority of Aristotle here only to suggest that it can be done. I venture to suggest further that, if the tradition of Roman jurisprudence admixed with Stoic errors had not intervened between the mind of Aristotle and the mind of St. Thomas, the theologian would have completed the work of the philosopher in the account of the practical order without ever having used the word "law" for the first principles of the practical reason—the foundations of natural morality in the spheres of both private and public conduct. St. Thomas could have improved Aristotle's analysis in every respect in which its pagan defects required Christian alteration, whether in metaphysical or moral matters, without ever departing from the Aristotelian understanding of *a law* as a positive enactment, a conventional rule, a political institution.

101. V. *Nichomachean Ethics*: 1134b18-20, where it is said: "Of political justice part is natural, part legal—natural, that which everywhere has the same force and does not exist by people's thinking this or that; legal, that which is originally indifferent, but when it has been laid down is not indifferent." (Cf. p. II-II, q. 57, aa. 2 and 3. V. also *Nichomachean Ethics*: 1134b30-1135a4 in which the legal and the conventional are identified). That Aristotle conceives laws entirely as positive rules, politically enacted, is confirmed in the *Politics*, where he discusses their coercive force (1286b31), their mutability (1268b26-1269a), their relativity to constitutions, albeit distinct therefrom (1282b10), and the limitations of general rules (1287b-

20-25). Cf. also the discussion of the just and the lawful, *in Nichomachean Ethics*: 1130b8-15, where the just is understood as including the lawful, but not conversely, which indicates that the just is according to nature, whereas the lawful is what conventions add to nature for the sake of the common good. V. footnote 36 above. There can be no question, therefore, that Aristotle identified laws with conventions (hence with positive enactments or customs), and opposes the legal to the natural. Justice can be natural or conventional, but laws cannot be natural.

102. V. *Nichomachean Ethics*: 1137a32-1138a38. It should be noted that the defectiveness of laws in particular cases is due to their generality, or, in other words, to the fact that they are not sufficiently determinate to apply justly to every possible case, in view of the unforeseen contingencies which arise in the sphere of human affairs. While rules are more determinate than precepts or principles, and therefore can be directly applied to action, as principles and precepts cannot (v. footnote 17 above), they are still not sufficiently determinate to make equitable dispensation from them unnecessary in particular cases.

103. V. *De Legibus*: b. I, cc. 12, 15, 16; b. II, cc. 4 and 5; b. III, cc. 1 and 19. Cf. McIlwain, *The Growth of Political Thought in the West*, pp. 116-130. The phrase *"lex naturalis"* is just as violent a conflict of meanings, as the Greek combination of *"physis"* and *"nomos"* would be. The word *"lex"* was employed by the Romans to signify one type of positive enactment which, along with *plebiscita, senatus consulta*, etc., constituted *ius civile* (v. Justinian, *Institutes*: 1, 2, 5, 6); it also stood for the written law, as opposed to customs (*ibid.*, 9). The trouble, therefore, is not with the phrase *"ius naturale"* for *ius* (right) is derived from *iustitia*

(justice), and both right and justice can be natural. The trouble is with the phrase *"ius civile"* which is fundamentally ambiguous—meaning, on the one hand, the whole set of positive enactments, written or customary, which are the laws of a particular realm, and also, on the other hand, that which is right or just by convention. As a result of this ambiguity, *ius naturale*, which should mean only "that which is right or just by nature," comes to mean "a set of laws." *Ius civile* should not have been identified with positive rules, written or unwritten; it should have been the Latin phrase for what Aristotle understood as *political justice*, which combines *natural justice (ius naturale)* and conventional or legal justice (i.e., *ius legale*, the justice that is in laws). And the Latin word *"lex"* should have been used as a strict equivalent of the Greek *"nomos"*—to name the sort of rule which is a law. The ambiguities of Latin are continued in both French (*droit, lois*) and German (*Recht, Gesetz*), and become most apparent in English when the one word "law" is used to translate both members of each of these sets of words. If the speech of jurists and philosophers had been restrained by precise analysis, they would not have talked themselves into a multitude of difficulties, which are not genuine problems to be solved, but confusions to be clarified. V. St. Thomas's comment on linguistic distortion in the case of such words as "medicine" or "ius," in p. II-II, q. 57, a. 1, reply to obj. 1.

104. V. McIlwain, *The Growth of Political Thought in the West*, cc. 4 and 6, esp. pp. 326ff; R. W. and A. J. Carlyle, *A History of Mediaeval Political Theory in the West*: vol. V, p. I, cc. 4, 5, 6, p. II, cc. 1 and 2; O. Gierke, *Natural Law and the Theory of Society;* and P. Vinogradoff, *Roman Law in Mediaeval Europe*.

Eleventh Essay

THE ECONOMIC PHILOSOPHY OF ST. THOMAS

1. In his commentary on "Quadragesimo Anno" entitled *Die Soziale Enzyklika*, the Rev. Oswald von Nell-Breuning, S.J., observes (p. 170): "In theological treatises the concepts of 'social justice' and 'social charity' have been as yet only slightly studied and investigated. To be sure, the concepts are neither new nor strange, even though the

Bibliography

terms have come into use quite recently. . . .
An important task confronts theological science to build up and deepen the teaching on both social justice and social charity."

2. "La Notion de Justice Sociale, d'Apres les Encycliques de Pie XI," *Dossiers de l'Action Populaire*: October 25, 1938, p. 4. This is one of the very best productions that has appeared on this subject.

3. Cf. *Atheistic Communism*: par. 52. Also, Dempsey, *The Reorganization of Social Economy*: p. 178.

4. *Mediaeval Socialism*: p. 47.

5. *De Virtute Justitiae*, Fourth Edition: p. 32.

6. *Ibid.*: p. 47.

7. *S. T.*: p. II-II, q. 66, a. 2.

8. *Politics*: b. II, c. 5.

9. *S. T.*: p. II-II, q. 66, a. 2.

10. *Op. cit.*: p. 89.

11. *Ibid.*: p. 88.

12. *S. T.*: p. I-II, q. 114, a. 1.

13. *L'Idée du Juste Salaire*: Paris, 1903, pp. 73-75.

14. *An Essay on Medieval Economic Teaching*: London, Longmans, Green, 1920, pp. 177-78.

15. *S. T.*: p. II-II, q. 77, a. 2, reply to obj. 5.

16. Cf. O'Brien, *op. cit.*: 198-202.

17. *English Economic History*: vol. II, pp. 435, 436, 437, 438.

Twelfth Essay

BEYOND THE CRISIS OF LIBERALISM

1. See P. J. Proudhon, *De la capacité politique des classes ouvrières*: Bouglé-Moysset ed., Paris, 1924, p. 93 ff; and E. Berth, *Du "Capital" aux "Réflexions sur la violence"*: Paris, 1932, p. 74 ff.

2. We have in mind an accurate concept of the proletariat as a class made up of people who enjoy personal freedom without having their freedom steadily supported by any property, and consequently are, in most cases, bound to remain permanent and hereditary wage-earners. See Goetz Briefs, *The Proletariat*: McGraw-Hill, New York, 1937.

3. Harold J. Laski, *The Rise of Liberalism*: New York, Harper, 1936, p. 6 ff, 258 ff, 269 ff.

4. *Nichomachean Ethics*: 1095 a 4.

5. L. T. Hobhouse, *Liberalism*: New York, Holt, 1911, p. 116.

6. S. Matthew, c. V, 37.

7. The act of supernatural faith is an assent of the mind freely commanded by the will; its formal motive is the authority of God and His Church. Let us remark, in this connection, first, that the freedom of which it is spoken does not imply by any means any moral right to choose between assenting and refusing to assent to the revealed truth; second, that the intervention of authority, here as well as in any other theoretical matter, is made necessary by a lack of evidence on the side of the object. When the divine mysteries become evident to the intellect (beatific vision), faith is no longer necessary or possible. Divine authority *substitutes* here below for the *evidence* which beatifies the blessed intellects. When the term of supernatural life is reached, that is, in the beatific vision, the assent to supernatural truth is no longer a matter of authority and a matter of liberty: it is exclusively a matter of objectivity.

8. See his theory of *rational belief*, in *Essais de Critique générale: 1854-64, Second Essai*.

8bis. Faith-knowledge is infinitely more precious than any rational knowledge: this higher perfection is not due to its being partly determined by the will, but to the sublimity of its object (the divine mysteries) and to the most indefectible guarantee of its certainty (the Divine Word).

9. In this connection, St. Thomas has most suggestive statements about a partial discrepancy between the law of perfection of the intellect and the law of perfection of the will. Both intellect and will are univocally and naturally determined with regard to their proper object (self-evident principles for the intellect, ultimate end abstractly taken for the will); but the intellect is not naturally determined so far as conclusions are concerned, the will is not naturally determined so far as particular goods are concerned. It is highly

[411]

significant that St. Thomas describes this absence of determination as a perfection in the case of the will, an imperfection in the case of the intellect. In a discussion about the freedom of the angelic will (*S. T.*: p. I, q. 59, a. 3, reply to obj. 2) it is objected that the will of the angel must be as determined as his intellect, and that consequently there cannot be any freedom in it. St. Thomas shows that the capacity of "se habere ad utrumlibet" is a deficiency in the intellect, because truth exists *in the intellect* of which it is the perfection. An intellect that is not determined in relation to every truth naturally knowable to it, is in a state of imperfection. Such is the case of the human intellect, such is not the case of the angelic intellect. On the contrary, the good, object of the appetite, *lies in things*; now not all things are indispensable to the perfection of a being. The more a being is elevated in the ontological hierarchy, the more it is self-sufficient, and independent of particular means in the achievement of its perfection. "Sed actus appetitivae virtutis est per hoc quod affectus inclinatur ad rem exteriorem. Non autem dependet perfectio rei ex omni re ad quam inclinatur, sed solum a superiori. Et ideo non pertinet ad imperfectionem angeli, si non habet voluntatem determinatam respectu eorum quae infra ipsum sunt; pertineret autem ad imperfectionem ejus, si indeterminate se haberet ad illud quod supra ipsum est." See also *S. T.*: p. I, q. 60, a. 2: "Hoc tamen differenter se habet ex parte intellectus et voluntatis: quia sicut dictum est (59, 2) cognitio intellectus fit secundum quod res cognitae sunt in cognoscente. Est autem ex imperfectione intellectualis naturae in homine, quod non statim ejus intellectus naturaliter habet omnia intelligibilia, sed quaedam a quibus in alia quodammodo movetur. Sed actus appetitivae virtutis est e converso secundum ordinem appetentis ad res: quarum quaedam sunt secundum se bona, et ideo secundum se appetibilia; quaedam vero habent rationem bonitatis ex ordine ad aliud, et sunt appetibilia propter aliud. Unde non est ex imperfectione appetentis, quod aliquid appetat naturaliter, ut finem, et aliquid per electionem, ut ordinatur in finem. Quia igitur natura intellectualis in angelis perfecta est, invenitur in eis sola cognitio naturalis, non autem ratiocinativa; sed invenitur in eis dilectio et naturalis et elec-

tiva." Also *S. T.*: p. I, q. 62, a. 8, reply to obj. 2.

The error of Charles Renouvier is two-fold: first, he confuses the law of perfection of the intellect with the law of perfection of the will when he assumes that the capacity of *se habere ad utrumlibet* is a perfection in the intellect as it is in the will. Second, he fails to recognize that in the will as well as in the intellect, the capacity of *se habere ad utrumlibet* cannot be primary, but is necessarily based upon a natural determination.

10. Let us remark that while liberalism, in the last hundred years or so, generally proved favorable to positivistic conceptions of the world, the positivistic movement often proved hostile to liberalism. Auguste Comte and his school fought liberalism with consistency and a characteristic bitterness.

11. We have in view truths that are within the reach of the natural possibilities of the human mind and we abstract from them very particular problems connected with supernatural truth gratuitously imparted to man by God.

11bis. In order to remove a possible misinterpretation, let us point out that we are referring here to technically elaborated metaphysics. It is not questionable that metaphysics, considered in a condition of technical perfection, is *de facto*, less intersubjectivable than positive science. Metaphysicians disagree among themselves much more than positive scientists.

On the other hand, metaphysical knowledge is capable of a non-technical form that positive science does not admit of. Most elevated metaphysical truths are accessible to ordinary people, who never were given any technical training, provided their common sense is entirely sound. With regard to this non-technical form of knowledge, it should be said that metaphysics is more intersubjectivable than positive science. On this, see Garrigou-Lagrange, *Le sens commun, la philosophie de l'être et les formules dogmatiques*, Paris, Desclée De Brouwer.

12. The most typical examples of a liberal attitude free from connections with agnosticism are found among the great Catholic liberals of the period preceding the Syllabus of Pius IX, Lamennais, Lacordaire, Montalembert. See Waldemar Gurian, *Die Politischen und Sozialen Ideen des Französichen Katholizismus*: München-Gladbach, 1929.

Bibliography

13. In order to remove any possibility of misinterpretation, I wish to make two remarks:

1. The problem of the relationship between liberalism and democracy, which would require extensive developments, is not treated in this study. Accordingly, the criticism of liberalism that we are carrying out good cannot, by any means, be interpreted as a criticism of the principles of democracy. As a matter of fact, history shows clearly that the concepts of liberalism and democracy are neither identical nor necessarily connected.

2. The broad statement that society cannot be indifferent to certain truths pertaining to the transcendental sphere does not imply any determined consequence as regards the means to be used by society in order to favor and protect the reign of truth in the minds of men. Those means are not univocally determined and must vary considerably according to historical circumstances. It is childish to assume, as so many people do, that every society which refuses to put truth and error on the same footing is bound to revive mediaeval practices.

14. Economic liberalism, also, shows the character of an optimistic naturalism. Within the economic order itself, liberalism assumes that the greatest possible amount of wealth is produced, and the fairest distribution effected, when there is no organization of the economic life as a whole, when elementary centers of economic interest are permitted to develop as they feel inclined. This obviously presupposes a pre-established harmony. Liberal economists of the classical period were accustomed to make frequent appeal to the notion of a benevolent nature or to that 'of Providence. Their postulate was that relationships of external finality prevail in human affairs without the human reason taking the trouble of unifying the innumerable lines of action that take place in economic life.

On the other hand, liberalism assumes, or at least constantly tends to assert, that politics does not answer any positive need of society. The political government is thought to be necessary only insofar as peace and the respect of contracts must be enforced by coercive procedures against dishonest persons. The state would have nothing to do except substituting its power for the spontaneity of natural honesty when honesty is lacking. It is suggested,

furthermore, that the main and possibly the only cause of dishonesty is lack of adjustment in economic relations; anything that fosters the development of an harmonious economic life is thought to be a step toward the realization of an economic society able to achieve security by itself and to do without the state-organization.

1. This conception implies a basic failure to understand what is most proper and most elevated among the functions of the state: fostering a virtuous coöperation in which men can find their ultimate temporal perfection. 2. The plan of rendering the state unnecessary by perfecting the order of economic society is common to traditional liberalism and to several socialist schools. What is proper to liberalism is the individualistic, atomistic, and falsely providentialistic idea of a spontaneous harmony assured by the autonomous working of autonomous elements. 3. It has often been said that facts have inflicted a crude denial upon the illusion of an order spontaneously resulting from a competition of forces. It seems that such facts can be divided into two groups: (a) A number of facts establish that when individuals' initiatives are given their own way, the weak are crushed by the strong. These facts belong to what may already be called the classical period of the crisis of liberalism. Associations, trade unions, etc., were found to be the proper remedy. (b) No less relevant to the criticism of liberalism are a number of facts resulting from modern developments in technology and from the creation of industrial abundance (see the publications of the technocratic school, e.g., Stuart Chase, *The Economy of Abundance*: New York, 1934; Allen Raymond, *What Is Technocracy?*: New York, 1933; Howard Scott, and Others, *Introduction to Technocracy*: New York, John Day, 1933). Whatever may be the amount of oversimplifications found in the literature dealing with abundance phenomena, it seems plain that exchange cannot, in a regime of abundance, provide for the actual distribution of wealth so regularly as it does in a regime of scarcity. Accordingly, abundance makes it necessary to multiply and to organize procedures of free distribution.

15. On this, see the admirable analysis of Georges Sorel, *Réflexions sur la violence*: 6th ed., Paris, 1925, p. 13 ff.

16. This extraordinarily felicitous expression

[413]

is from the Hungarian writer Odon von Horvath in his novel *Jeunesse sans Dieu* (French translation): Paris, 1938.

17. See *Réflexions sur la violence*: 6th ed.,

Paris, 1925, p. 32 ff., 176 ff.; E. Berth, *Du "Capital" aux "Réflexions sur la violence"*: Paris, 1932, p. 9, p. 107 ff, p. 183 (1).

18. *Réflexions sur la violence*: p. 178.

Thirteenth Essay

THE FATE OF REPRESENTATIVE GOVERNMENT

1. St. Augustine, *De Libero Arbitrio*: b. I, c. 6. St. Thomas, *S. T.*: p. I-II, q. 97, a. 1. This distinction of peoples is sometimes phrased differently and given much wider significance when peoples are spoken of as "naturally free" and "naturally slave." "Naturally" in such usage cannot refer to anything intrinsic to the nature of some men which gives others the right to exploit them; nature does not condone, much less command, injustice, and each man's personal end is supreme. Nor on these same intrinsic grounds is there justification for the domination of one people over another for the direction, and hence for the benefit, of the subject people. There is nothing in the very nature of an individual or of a people rendering them incapable of self-direction to personal or social ends; in fact the contrary is true. To say that a people is naturally incapable of such self-direction is to use "naturally" in a sense other than of intrinsic natural principles (natural law). There are, and always have been, such incapable peoples, not by reason of nature but by the operation of such factors as have been mentioned in the text as contributing to the degeneration of men and societies.

2. *S. T.*: p. I-II, q. 95, a. 4; *De Regimine Principum*: b. I, c. 1; *ibidem*: c. 2; b. II, c. 9; b. IV, c. 8; *S. T.*: p. I-II, q. 97, a. 1.

Note: The opusculum *De Regimine Principum* is also known as the *Tractatus de Rege et Regno* (e.g., in the Vivès edition of Aquinas's *Opera Omnia*).

3. As will be clear as this study progresses, the precise philosophical question here deals with the intrinsic goodness of representative government. The question answered is: is representative government solidly good government?

The question of the goodness of government is really a double one; for besides the determination of its goodness, there is also the de-termination of the grade of its goodness. The generic question of goodness is answered by showing that the government is not bad but good; the specific question of the grade of goodness can be answered only by determining whether the form of government is good, better, or best. In the present study, we are concerned only with the generic question; an investigation of the specific question can be found in the series of articles on "A Theory of Democracy," by Walter Farrell, O.P. and Mortimer J. Adler, *The Thomist*: 1941, vol. 3, n. 3.

4. Christopher Dawson, *Beyond Politics*: New York, Sheed & Ward, 1939, p. 38 ff. Walter Lippmann. *The Good Society*: New York, Little, Brown and Co., 1937, p. 241 ff., p. 268 ff.

5. In all good government there is some participation by the citizens, at least what might be called the passive participation involved in the consent of the governed. This is the fundamental participation at the root of the right to revolt against tyranny. But over and above this passive participation, there is, in some forms of good government, an active participation by which the citizen exercises some power in the choice of the officials of government. It is of this latter participation that we speak here.

6. Such summaries can be found in innumerable modern works on political theory, e.g., George D. H. Cole, *A Guide to Modern Politics*: New York, Knopf, 1934; Francis W. Coker, *Recent Political Thought*: New York, Appleton-Century, 1934, especially c. 11.

One constant criticism which is not mentioned in our discussion is that of government by average men. This criticism takes two forms: (1) a disparagement of the actual results of democracy and a recitation of its mistakes and defects; (2) a distrust of, and contempt for, the human individual. In its first

Bibliography

form the criticism simmers down to a question of fact. In its second form, such criticism certainly needs to be answered; but the issue it raises is much deeper and wider than any political issue. In this form, such criticism demands a defense of human nature itself; it is only indirectly an attack on representative government, as it is, in exactly the same way, an attack on all government. Directly, it calls into question the humanity of man. For these reasons we have considered it outside the scope of this paper.

7. Alfredo Rocco, *The Political Doctrine of Fascism*: New York, International Conciliation Bulletin, n. 223, 1926; Adolf Hitler, *Mein Kampf*: New York, Reynal and Hitchcock, 1939.

8. Dawson, *loc. cit.*: pp. 8, 12; Coker, *loc. cit.*; p. 304. Cf. A. G. Hays, *Democracy Works*: New York, Random House, 1939; and Cole, *loc cit.*

9. This distinction of ethical and political principles will be treated at length later in this article (v. pp. 295-300; 300-304). It will be sufficient for the present to note that the term "ethical principle" is reserved for principles that are directly of natural law, i.e., not only first principles but also secondary principles derived from the first *by way of conclusion*. By the term "political principles" only those principles are referred to which are, not conclusions, but *determinations* of ethical principles by human authority; whether these political principles be ultimate or derived, they are always arrived at *by way of determination*. The first political principle, as will be seen later, is always in the field of practical politics a factual instrument establishing the other institutions of government.

10. As a matter of fact the interest in this field goes far beyond mere discussion. The attempt to mold, immediately and directly, the pre-political dispositions of a people is a fundamental policy of totalitarian régimes. Cf. Hans Barth, "Reality and Ideology of the Totalitarian State," *Review of Politics*: 1939, vol. 1, n. 3. On the other hand, opponents of totalitarianism frankly admit that the crisis centers in these dispositions, e.g., Ross J. S. Hoffman, *The Will to Freedom*: New York, Sheed and Ward, 1935.

11. *S. T.*: p. I-II, q. 94, aa. 2, 4, 5; *ibid.*: q. 71, a. 6 corpus and objections.

12. *De Regimine Principum:* b. I, c. 1.

13. *S. T.*: p. I-II, q. 71, a. 6; q. 95, a. 2; p. II-II, q. 104, a. 1, reply to obj. 2.

14. *Ibid.*: a. 4; *De Regimine Principum*: b. I, cc. 1, 2; *S. T.*: p. I-II, qq. 90, 95, 96.

15. *Ibid.*: p. II-II, q. 104, a. 5.

16. *Ibid.*: p. I, q. 96, a. 4.

17. *Ibid.*: p. II-II, q. 104, a. 5. *In Libros Sententiarum*: b. III, d. 44, q. 1, a. 3; *De Regimine Principum*: b. III, c. 9.

18. *Ibid.*: b. I, c. 1.

19. *Ibid.*: b. III, c. 11. *S. T.*: p. I-II, q. 90, a. 3, reply to obj. 3; p. II-II, q. 104, a. 5.

20. *De Regimine Principum:* b. I, c. 1.

21. *Ibid.*: cc. 1, 2.

22. *Ibid.*: b. II, cc. 2, 15; b. I, c. 15.

23. *Ibid.*: b. I, cc. 14, 15; b. III, c. 3.

24. Cf. footnote 17 above.

25. *S. T.*: p. II-II, q. 104, a. 1; *De Regimine Principum*: b. II, c. 1.

26. Cf. footnote 11 above. *De Regimine Principum*: b. IV, c. 16, b. III, c. 11; b. I, c. 3.

27. *S. T.*: p. II-II, q. 50, a. 1, reply to obj. 3; p. I-II, q. 90, a. 4.

28. Cf. footnote 11 above. Also, *S. T.*: p. I-II, q. 94, a. 1, reply to obj. 4.

29. *De Regimine Principum*: b. I, c. 2; b. II, c. 9; b. IV, c. 8. *S. T.*: p. I-II, q. 97, a. 1. This variability of political principles has been consistently recognized by statesmen themselves, e.g., Alexander Hamilton: "The science of politics, however, like most other sciences, has received great improvement. The efficacy of various principles is now well understood, which were either not known at all, or imperfectly known to the ancients." *The Federalist*: Washington, D. C., National Home Library, 1937, n. 9, p. 48. Cf. Mortimer J. Adler, "Parties and the Common Good," *Review of Politics*: 1939, vol. 1, n. 3, p. 62 ff.

30. *S. T.*: p. I-II, q. 91, a. 3 corpus and reply to obj. 3; q. 95. a. 2, reply to obj. 3; a. 3; q. 96, a. 1, reply to obj. 2; a. 2; q. 97, a. 1 corpus and reply to obj. 1.

31. *Ibid.*: q. 95, a. 2.

32. The Constitution and the Supreme Court are excellent examples of ultimate and derived political principles, the Supreme Court deriving from, and established by, the Constitution, which latter is preceded by no political principles. As an example of a concrete distinction between political and ethical principles we might point to the Bill of Rights and the Con-

stitution: the latter is strictly political, the former—though framed as amendments to the Constitution—is for the most part ethical, not established but repromulgated by a political instrument.

33. In order to avert the danger of mistaking this conclusion, it must be noted that this whole discussion is on the plane of political philosophy rather than on that of practical politics. It is obvious that a group can seize power, set up a tyrannical government and in their constitution, or first political principle, expressly reject all ethical principles; in such a case, though the government call itself representative, actually it is no *de jure* government at all, nor is its constitution a political principle (v. above, pp. 300-302). On the other hand, a particular representative government may be unable to meet the threats offered by a change in the pre-political dispositions of its people and so becomes obsolete through what appears to be intrinsic weakness. Actually the forces to which it succumbs are extrinsic to the nature of representative government; and the reason *this* government is here and now weak is not because of an intrinsic defect of representative government as such, but because of the stifling of some of the essential principles by the administrators or citizens of *this* representative government. In other words, what was once representative government has ceased to be good government of any kind.

34. Adler, *loc. cit.*: p. 52.

35. *Ibid.*: p. 51. An example of democratic independence of equality of conditions is had in the case of the extremely democratic, though sharply class-conscious and class-differentiated, Swiss.

36. We use the word "social" here in the modern and extremely limited sense of the word; so, for example, it is used in such expressions as "social security," "social legislation," etc.

37. "Before all else, it is certain that the radical and ultimate cause of the evils which we deplore in modern society is the denial and rejection of a universal norm of morality as well for individual and social life as for international relations; We mean the disregard, so common nowadays, and the forgetfulness of the natural law itself, which has its founda-

tion in God, Almighty Creator and Father of all, supreme and absolute Lawgiver, all-wise and just Judge of human actions. When God is hated, every basis of morality is undermined; the voice of conscience is stilled or at any rate grows very faint, that voice which teaches even to the illiterate and to uncivilized tribes what is good and what is bad, what lawful, what forbidden, and makes men feel themselves responsible for their actions to a Supreme Judge." Pope Pius XII, Encyclical, *Summi Pontificatus*: October 20, 1939, Official Translation; A. A. S., XXXI, p. 544.

38. Quoted in the New York *Times* for Sunday, Jan. 8, 1939, p. 10 D. It is pertinent here to note that a crucial point has frequently been overlooked in modern political discussion, namely, that representative government really developed on a heritage to which claim had already been surrendered, i.e., the Christian heritage. The fundamental notions of inalienable rights, justice and equality before the law, and so on, stem from the notion of the sacred character of the individual as a person, a notion that is, as Gilson has pointed out, a distinctly Christian notion. As the Christian ethical basis disappears—as it has been disappearing for the past three hundred years—there is a gradual bankruptcy of representative government.

39. This summary treatment of the agencies of change in the pre-political disposition of a people is not to be taken as an index of their importance. These forces can operate to the extent of making the continuation of this particular government immoral and even physically impossible. Indeed the most crucial political problems of our times are, for the most part, centered in this field of change. The factual side of the question in any particular nation must be and is being dealt with by historians of the present. Interpretations and remedies are flowing in a steady stream from the pens of political commentators and philosophers. In the next few pages little more than an indication is given of the sources of these changes and the issues at stake. A thorough philosophical study of this phase of the question would be invaluable, particularly in view of the seriousness of the matter.

Bibliography

Fourteenth Essay

THE THOMISTIC CONCEPT OF EDUCATION

1. *S. T.*: p. I, q. 77, a. 1. Unless otherwise indicated, all the references which follow are from the *S. T.* of Aquinas.
2. p. II-II, q. 37, a. 2, reply to obj. 2.
3. p. I, q. 76, a. 1.
4. p. I, q. 75, a. 3.
5. p. I, q. 76, aa. 3 and 4.
6. p. I, q. 83, a. 1.
7. p. I, q. 83, a. 3.
8. p. I-II, q. 92, a. 1.
9. p. I-II, q. 81, a. 2.
10. p. III, q. 8, aa. 1 and 2.
11. p. I, q. 85, a. 2.
12. p. I, q. 50, a. 2; q. 84, a. 1.
13. p. I, q. 84, aa. 1-8.
14. p. I, q. 79, a. 3.
15. *Q. D. de Veritate*: q. 10, a. 6, reply to obj. 2.
16. p. I, q. 3, a. 4.
17. *De Intellectu et Intelligibili* (Vivès edition, opusculum xlix).
18. p. I, q. 16, a. 5, reply to obj. 3.
19. *C. G.*: b. III, c. 54.
20. *C. G.*: b. I, c. 5.
21. *Q. D. de Veritate*: q. 1, a. 2. Also. *Q. D. de Potentia*: q. 7, a. 10, reply to obj. 5.
22. *Q. D. de Veritate*: q. 11, a. 1.
23. p. I-II, q. 94, a. 2. Also, *Q. D. de Veritate*: q. 10, a. 6 and reply to obj. 6.
24. *In Metaphysicorum*: b. IV, l. 1.
25. p. I, q. 3, a. 7.
26. p. I, q. 44, a. 4.
27. *Q. D. de Veritate*: q. 11, a. 1.
28. *C. G.*: b. I, c. 1.
29. *Q. D. de Veritate*: q. 11, aa. 1-4.
30. p. I, q. 84; also, *C. G.*: b. II, c. 98.
31. p. I, q. 4, a. 1.
32. p. I-II, q. 49, a. 4.
33. p. I-II, q. 51, a. 1.
34. *Q. D. de Veritate*: q. 1, a. 12.
35. *Q. D. de Veritate*: q. 20, a. 2.
36. p. I-II, q. 57, aa. 1 and 2. Also, *C. G.*: b. III, c. 97.
37. p. I-II, q. 57, a. 1.
38. p. I-II, q. 57, a. 2.
39. p. I-II, q. 53, a. 3.
40. p. I-II, q. 57, a. 3.
41. *In Libros Sententiarum*: b. I, d. 39, q. 2, a. 1.
42. p. I-II, q. 58, aa. 4 and 5.
43. p. I-II, q. 47, a. 8.
44. p. I-II, q. 57, a. 5; q. 85, a. 3.
45. p. I-II, q. 61, a. 2.
46. *C. G.*: b. I, c. 1.
47. p. I, q. 117, a. 1. Also, *Q. D. de Veritate*: q. 11, aa. 1-4.
48. Encyclical letter on *Christian Education of Youth*: official English translation, p. 32

Fifteenth Essay

THE PERENNIAL THEME OF BEAUTY AND ART

1. St. Thomas not only regarded the beautiful as a transcendental implicitly when he discusses it in connection with the true and the good, but explicitly in many instances: "Nihil est quod non participat pulchro . . . Omnes creaturae habent aliquo modo particulatam pulchritudinem sicut et particulatam naturam, etc.," (*In de Divinis Nominibus*: c. 4, l. 5). Just as certainly is beauty, like the other transcendentals, analogical: "Pulchritudo, sanitas et hujusmodi dicuntur per respectum ad aliquid . . . alias est pulchritudo unius alia alterius" *In Psalmos Davidis*: XLIV, v. 2. The example of *sanitas* frequently used by St. Thomas to illustrate metaphysical analogy, shows that beauty is realized analogically or proportionately to the subject in which it is found: "Omnibus entibus creatis dat pulchritudinem secundum proprietatem uniuscujusque" *In de Divinis Nominibus*: c. 4, l. 5:
,2. All the texts on the beautiful in the writings of St. Thomas, as listed by Gerald B.

Phelan, are to be found in the following works:

S. T.: p. I, q. 5, a. 4, reply to objections 1 and 2; q. 39, a. 8; p. I-II, q. 11, a. 11, reply to obj. 2; q. 27, a. 1, reply to obj. 3; p. II-II, q. 145, a. 3; q. 142, aa. 2 and 4; q. 116, a. 2, reply to obj. 2.

Q. D. de Veritate: q. 22, a. 1, reply to obj. 12.

Q. D. de Potentia Dei: q. 6, a. 6, reply to obj. 5.

In Libro de Divinis Nominibus: c. 4, ll. 5, 6, 9, 10.

In librum Sententiarum: b. I, d. 31, q. 2, a. 1, reply to obj. 4; b. IV, d. 3, q. 2, a. 1.

In Psalmos Davidis: XXV, v. 5; XLIV, v. 2.

3. This highly condensed sentence reads: "Forma autem a qua dependet propria ratio rei, pertinet ad claritatem: ordo ad finem, ad consonantiam, et sic motus et quies reducuntur in causalitatem pulchri" *In de Divinis Nominibus*: c. 4, l. 6.

The praises of Divine Beauty are sung throughout this work, as the following abridgement of a paragraph which should be read in its entirety shows: . . . "Deus semper est pulcher secundum idem, et eodem modo et sic excluditur alteratio pulchritudinis. Et iterum non est in eo generatio aut corruptio pulchritudinis, neque iterum augmentum vel diminutio sicut in rebus corporalibus apparet . . . Deus non est in aliqua parte pulcher et in alia turpis sicut in rebus particularibus contingit quandoque: Neque est in aliquo tempore et in aliquo non sicut contingit in his quorum pulchritudo cadit sub tempore" . . . *In de Divinis Nominibus*: c. 4, l. 5.

This is not the place to present the metaphysical demonstration that Divine Beauty is the cause of all that exists: "Quia tot modis pulchrum (divinum) est causa omnium, inde est quod bonum et pulchrum sunt idem, etc." *Ibid.*

This demonstration would prove that beauty like being is participated: "Pulchritudo creaturae nihil est quam similitudo divinae pulchritudinis in rebus participata (*Ibid.*); Deus est species prima a qua omnia sunt speciosa" *Q. D. de Potentia Dei*: q. 6, a. 6, reply to obj. 5.

4. "Singula sunt pulchra secundum propriam rationem, id est secundum propriam formam . . . Unumquodque est pulchrum se-

cundum propriam formam . . . etc." *In de Divinis Nominibus*: c. 4, l. 5.

5. As St. Thomas states it, in terms of beauty this time: "Deus qui est esse tantum est quodammodo species omnium quae esse participant et non sunt suum esse" *Q. D. de Potentia Dei*: q. 6, a. 6, reply to obj. 5.

6. *S. T.*: p. I, q. 39, a. 8.

7. "Perfectio prima est secundum quod res in suo esse constituitur" *S. T.*: p. I, q. 6, a. 3; q. 73, a. 1 . . . "Integritas attenditur secundum perfectionem quae consistit in ipso esse rei" *In Libros Sententiarum*: b. IV, d. 26, q. 2, a. 4.

8. "Et universaliter omnes creaturae quantamcumque unionem habent, habent ex virtute pulchri" *In de Divinis Nominibus*: c. 4, l. 5.

9. "Ordo autem ad finem, ad consonantiam." *Ibid.*

10. "Forma autem a qua dependet propria ratio rei, pertinet ad claritatem." *Ibid.* "Ratio veri ex ipsa specie consurgit prout est intellecta sicuti est" *Q. D. de Veritate*: q. 22, a. 2, reply to obj. 3. Adequatio rei et intellectus dicitur: 'et in hoc formaliter ratio veri perficitur, etc." *Ibid.*: q. 1, a. 2.

11. "Pulchrum in debita proportione consistit quia sensus delectatur in rebus bene proportionatis sicut in sibi similibus nam et sensus quaedam ratio est et omnis virtus cognoscitiva" *S. T.*: p. I, q. 5, a. 4, reply to obj. 1. "Intellectus noster non est proportionatus ad cognoscendum naturali cognitione aliquid nisi per sensibile" *In Libros Sententiarum*: b. I, d. 3, q. 1, a. 2, reply to obj. 3. "Cognitio fit per assimilationem, similitudo autem respicit formam" *S. T.*: p. I, q. 5, a. 4, reply to obj. 1. "Omnis cognitio fit per assimilationem cognoscentis ad rem cognitam" *Q. D. de Veritate*: q. 1, a. 2. "Scientia in nobis est sigillatio rerum in animalibus nostris." *Ibid.*: q. 11, a. 1, reply to obj. 6.

12. How the aesthetic judgment can be intuitive and intellectual at the same time, the problem which so divides the different schools of aesthetics, is rightly solved only by Thomism, but to develop this further would require more space than can be allotted here.

13. James Joyce, *A Portrait of the Artist as a Young Man*: New York, The Modern Library. All the quotations in the text will be found between pages 239-54 of this edition.

14. "Deus immittit omnibus creaturis cum

quodam fulgore traditionem sui radii luminosi, qui est fons omnis luminis: quae quidem traditiones fulgidae divini radii secundum participationem similitudines sunt intelligendae, et istae traditiones sunt 'pulchrificae' id est facientes pulchritudinem in rebus." *In de Divinis Nominibus:* c. 4, l. 5.

15. *S. T.:* p. I-II, q. 23, a. 1 and ff.

16. "Pulchra dicuntur quae visa placent," *S. T.:* p. I, q. 5, a. 4, reply to obj. 1. "Pulchrum dicatur id cujus ipsa apprehensio placet." *S. T.:* p. I-II, q. 27, a. 1, reply to obj. 3.

17. "Pulchrum respicit vim cognoscitivam." *S. T.:* p. I, q. 5, a. 1, reply to obj. 1. "Ad rationem pulchri pertinet quod in eius aspectu seu cognitione quietetur appetitus." *S. T.:* p. I-II, q. 27, a. 1, reply to obj. 3.

18. "Nomen visum primum impositum est ad significandum autem sensus visus: sed propter dignitatem et certitudinem huius sensus est hoc nomen secundum usum loquentium ad omnem cognitionem aliorum sensuum . . . et ulterius etiam ad cognitionem intellectum" *S. T.:* p. I, q. 67, a. 1. "Illi sensus praecipue respiciunt pulchrum qui maxime cognoscitivi sunt scilicet visus et auditus rationi deservientes." *S. T.:* p. I-II, q. 27, a. 1, reply to obj. 1.

19. "Perfectio et finis cujuslibet alterius potentie continetur sub objecto appetitivae sicut proprium sub communi" *S. T.:* p. I-II, q. 11, a. 1, reply to obj. 2.

20. "In vita contemplativa quae consistit in actu rationis, per se et essentialiter invenitur pulchritudo" *S. T.:* p. II-II, q. 180, a. 2, reply to obj. 3.

21. "Omnis homo amat pulchrum." *In Psalmos Davidis:* XXV, v. 5. "Omnibus est pulchrum et bonum amabile" *S. T.:* p. II-II, q. 114, a. 2, reply to obj. 1.

22. "Pulchritudo non habet rationem appetibilis nisi in quantum induit rationem boni . . . sic enim et verum appetibile est." *In Libros Sententiarum:* b. I, d. 31, q. 2, a. 1, reply to obj. 4.

23. "Nam bonum proprie respicit appetitum: est enim bonum quod omnia appetunt; et ideo habet rationem finis: nam appetitus est quasi quidem motus ad rem." *S. T.:* p. I, q. 5, a. 4, reply to obj. 1.

24. "Appetitum terminari ad bonum et pulchrum et pacem non est terminari in diversa. Ex hoc enim ipso quod aliquid appetit bonum, appetit simul et pulchrum et pacem: pulchrum quidem inquantum est modificatum et specificatum quod in ratione boni includitur: sed bonum addit ordinem perfectivi ad alia. Unde quicumque appetit bonum appetit hoc ipso pulchrum." *Q. D. de Veritate:* q. 22, a. 1, reply to obj. 12.

25. "Pulchrum et bonum in subjecto quidem sunt idem: quia super eamdem rem fundatur, scilicet super formam: et propter hoc bonum laudatur ut pulchrum Dionysius, *De Divinis Nominibus:* c. 4, l. 5: sed ratione differunt: nam bonum respicit appetitum: est enim bonum quod omnia appetunt: et ideo habet rationem finis: nam appetitus est quasi quidem motus ad rem: Pulchra autem respicit vim cognoscitivam: Pulchra enim dicuntur quae visa placent: unde pulchrum in debita proportione consistit: quia sensus delectatur in rebus bene proportionatis sicut in sibi similibus: nam et sensus ratio quaedam est et omnis virtus cognoscitiva: et quia cognitio fit per assimilationem, similitudo autem respicit formam: pulchrum proprie pertinet ad rationem causae formalis" *S. T.:* p. I, q. 2, a. 1, reply to obj. 4.

"Pulchrum est idem bono, sola ratione differens: cum enim bonum sit quod omnia appetunt, de ratione boni est quod in eo quietetur appetitus, sed ad rationem pulchri pertinet quod in eius aspectu seu cognitione quietetur appetitus . . . Et sic patet quod pulchrum addit bonum quemdam ordinem ad vim cognoscitivam; ita quod bonum dicatur id quod simpliciter complacet appetitui; pulchrum autem dicatur, id cujus apprehensio placet." *S. T.:* p. I-II, q. 27, a. 1, reply to obj. 3.

INDEX

Index

Index

[423]

Index

Index

Leo XIII, 18, 20
  on modern usury, 259-60
  on wage justice, 251
Lewis, E., 400
Liber de Causis, 132, 133, 147
Liberalism, crisis of, 263-86, 411-14
Liberality, 239, 249
Lindworsky, J., 368
Lippmann, W., 414
Llewellyn, K., 388

Maimonides, 377
Mandonnet, P., 113, 371, 374, 375, 376, 377, 378
Manichaeans, 114, 142, 145
Manser, P. G., 20
Mansion, A., 371
Maritain, J., 7, 17, 20, 83, 84, 365, 375, 389, 395, 396, 405
Marx, K., 23
Masnovo, A., 365
Materialism, 83
Mathematicals, 115, 116
Matthew, St., 375, 378, 411
Maximus, St., 373
Mazzini, G., 281
McDougall, M. S., 388
McIlwain, V. C. W., 394, 410
Memory
  intellectual, 46, 62
Mercier, 20
Metaphysical intuition of being, 338
Mill, J. S., 271, 400
Modes of being, 92
Montalembert, 412
Monte Cassino, 8
Moody, E. A., 381
Moore, T. V., 46, 367, 368
Mosaic Law, 231
Moses, 231
Motion, 116-19, 122, 131, 139
Movement
  repose tension, 337
Movers, cf. intelligences
Multiplicity, 338
Mussolini, B., 92

Nagy, A., 372
Necessity, 27-37, 366-67
  absolute, 27
  de facto, 27, 30
  de jure, 27, 28, 30, 31
  hypothetical, 27
Neoplatonists, 8
Nicholas of Oresme, 16

Nietzsche, F., 269
Nominalism, 83
Non-being, 338
Nuyens, F. J. C. J., 368

O'Brien, G., 256, 411
Old Testament, 84
Oligiati, 20
Ontology, 83-100
Order, 339
Origin, 134, 135

Paris, University of, 9
Parmenides, 153, 157
Parts
  in the subject of habitus, 105
Pascal, 77
Passion
  as a non-permanent quality, 104
  is not a habitus, 108-9
Patterson, E. W., 388
Paulus, J., 379, 381
Peckham, J., 13
Pedagogy, 313-31
Pegis, A. C., 409
Peripatetics, 144
Personalism, 7
Pétain, H. P., 265
Peter Lombard, 371
Petrus Calo, 365
Phantasm, 50, 51, 55, 56, 58, 61
Phelan, G. B., 387, 418
Phenomenalism, 83
Physical premotion, 90
Pilate, 65
Pius IX, 412
Pius XI, 240, 305, 330
Pius XII, 416
Plato, 3, 6, 8, 52, 65, 86, 115-23, 127, 130, 132, 139, 143, 147, 148, 152, 153, 154, 156, 157, 162, 167, 168, 169, 172, 173, 179-83
Platonism, 114-48, 151-83
  Aquinas's critique of, 179-83
Platonists, 114, 116, 117, 119, 120, 121, 122, 133, 134, 141, 144, 146, 147, 148, 151-83
Plotinus, 153, 158, 171, 173
Polier, L., 251
Politics, 289-309, 414-16
Pollock, Sir Frederick, 388
Porphyry, 117, 146, 167
Pos panta, 22
Positivism
  legal, 236
Positivists, 17

[425]

Index

Index

Trading, 252-55
Transcendentals, 85, 335, 338-41, 345
Truth, 65-79, 338, 340, 344, 369
    kinds of, 66, 67
    Thomistic theory of, 66

Ugliness, 337, 338, 346
Ulpian, 392, 394
Understanding, habit of, 323
Unity, 86, 88, 339
    problem of
        in God, 151-83, 379-82
Universals, 52-60
Urban IV, 11
Usury, 239, 255-60

Vacant, A., 377
Value, 51
Vignaux, P., 379, 380, 381
Vinogradoff, Sir Paul, 388
Virtue, 104
    defined by Cicero, 105
    defined by St. Augustine, 105
    infused moral, and theological virtues as
        habitus, 109
    moral, 322, 323, 324
Vis aestimativa vel cogitativa, 46, 48-51, 57

von Horvath, O., 414
von Nell-Breuning, O., 410
von Prandtl, K., 368
von Wolff, C., 20, 58

Walker, L. J., 369
Walsh, F. A., 368
Watson, J. B., 368
Wealth
    duties of, 239, 246-49
    use of, 239, 244-46
Wébert, V. J., 368
Wertheimer, M., 47
Will, 189-90
William of Champeaux, 53
William of Moerbeke, 43, 53
William of Ockham, 15, 16, 152, 153, 154,
    156, 159, 171, 172, 368
William of St. Amour, 10
Willwoll, A., 60, 61, 368
Wisdom, 323
Wittmann, M., 376
Woodworth, R. S., 60, 368

Zeitgeist, 20
Zoeckler, 10
Zybura, J. S., 366